SCOTT'S PAPERS

SCOTT'S PAPERS

KENTUCKY COURT AND OTHER RECORDS

———

Compiled by

HATTIE MARSHALL SCOTT

Presented by

MRS. WILLIAM BRECKINRIDGE ARDERY

———

BAYLESS E. HARDIN, Editor

———

Southern Historical Press, Inc.
Greenville, South Carolina

This volume was reproduced
from a personal copy located in
the Publishers private library

Please direct all correspondence and book orders to:
SOUTHERN HISTORICAL PRESS, Inc.
PO Box 1267
Greenville, SC   29602-1267

Originally printed: Franfort, KY. 1953
Copyright 1953 by:
    The Kentucky Historical Society
ISBN #978-1-63914-045-9
Printed in the United States of America

In Memory of My Friend

HATTIE MARSHALL SCOTT

whose life was dedicated and devoted to her fellow Kentuckians, their honored past and to uncovering the authentic links which join this past to future generations.

All of the records appearing in this book together with a great amount of other priceless data was given to me by Miss Scott out of the infinite depths of her generous heart.

I believe it is both fitting and right that this portion of her labor of love be given through the Kentucky Historical Society for publication and that all proceeds from its sale should go to the Society.

April, 1953   Julia Spencer Ardery (Mrs. William B.)

FOREWORD

The records presented here were copied by Miss Hattie Scott in the 1930s—perhaps some earlier—some later. While Miss Scott was a careful and painstaking researcher, mistakes are bound to creep into a work of this sort where so many names, variously spelled, and dates are involved. Also, much of the submitted material was carbon copies, some badly faded and difficult to decipher. In editing, only the obvious errors, when noted, were corrected, because it would have been impossible to check against the original records. Accordingly, the Kentucky Historical Society cannot be responsible for mistakes occurring herein. It is hoped, though, that there are few errors, and that this volume will be a great contribution to the genealogical field.

BAYLESS E. HARDIN, Editor.

TABLE OF CONTENTS

*Alphabetically grouped, not in General Index

SCOTT'S PAPERS

BOURBON COUNTY RECORDS

The following notes showing *approximate ages* of numerous Bourbon Co. pioneers were contributed by Mrs. W. B. Ardery. These ages were shown in old Circuit Court suits and County court Order Book B as follows:

Suit—Thos. Morris' Hrs. vs. McGee (box 38-40, 1820-22)—Abijah North aged 61, Jonathan Marsh aged 50 who states his father settled near certain improvements in Bourbon Co., Patrick Iordan aged 71—in Kv. 1776 and "set out from Leestown", Archibald Bilbo, deposition taken at Perryville, Ky. (1822), William Meredith, deposition taken in Warren Co. Ky. (1820) states he was in Bourbon county with John Floyd, John Haggin deposition taken in Mercer Co. Ky. (1820).

Bourbon Order Bk. B. 1796—Isaac Ruddell aged 64/5 (Oct. 1796), Nath'l. Randolph aged 43, David Gass aged 64/5 (June 1797), Wm. Bailey, orphan of Wm., aged 17 (1797), Elizabeth Endicott orphan of Jas., aged 11 (1797), Henry Wilson Jr. aged 37 (Sept. 1797), Robt. Morrison orphan abt. 2 yrs (Dec. 1795), Lewis Reno was abt. 37, in 1779, Jno. Stockwell, orphan of Sam'l., aged 14 (1796), John Virgin aged 41(?), (Aug. 1796), Mary Smith aged 10, orphan of Peter Smith (Oct. 1796), Jas. Kelly aged 50, (Oct. 1796) Thomas Kennedy aged abt. 53, later given as 53 (1797), Wm. Bailey aged 17, orphan of William, Aquilla White aged 53 (1797), Richard Graves aged 42, (1797), John McIntire aged 34 (1797), Jas. Galloway aged 45 (1795), John Sellers (1798) states he made improvement 1776, Eneas McDaniel and son same, David Cook aged 40 (1797), Jacob Starns aged 42 (1797), Jas. Berry states from Boonesborough in 1779, Jesse Coffee aged 42 (1797), Wm. Markland aged 43 (1797), Davis Beard Sr. aged 53 (1797), Michael Stoner aged 50 (1797), Patrick Logan aged 46 (1798), Major John Miller 43/44, John inft. orphan of John Miller aged abt. 10, (1798), James Moss, infant aged 7, orphan of Triplet Moss, aged 7 (1798), Wm. Rule infant orphan of—Rule chose Thos. Rule gdn., Jas. Duncan aged 47 (1798), John Bruice aged 50, Abraham Bowman aged 49 (1798), J—? Sodowsky aged 47 (1798), Jno. Donaldson aged 28 (1798), Henry Delay aged 49 (1798), Jno. Holder aged 45 (1798), Mathew Walker states "in 1782 on return from expedition with Clark" (p. 636 Order Bk. B), Edward Bradly aged 69 (1798), John Parks, infant orphan of John (1798), Robert Johnson aged 52 (1798), Jno. Craig Sr. aged 63 (1798), John Miller 42 (1798), Jas. Kenney aged 45 (1798), David Gass deposition 1797- aged 65, "was here 1775-'76, was at spring where Alexander Breckenridge Senr. now lives," Thos. Dunn aged 55 (1798).

Suit—Duncan vs. David Bowles (box 78—filed 1799) Thos. Jones aged 54, Jas. Spurgin aged 30, Jas. Sconce aged 41, Benedict Couchman aged 47, Peter Troutman aged 30, Edward Wilson aged 51, Thomas Kennedy aged abt. 55, Wm. Martin aged abt. 25, Walter Caldwell aged 21.

District Land Trials Bk. Basement of Court House—1797—Wm. Turner abt. 44, Robt. Snodgrass 40, Thos. Jones 52, Benj. Coleman aged 44, Robert Trimble aged abt. 56. John Sunnard 40, Wm Forman 40, James Sodowsky aged 45, Thompkins Barlow aged 34.

Suit—Steele vs. Powers (box 663)—Wm. Huston, son of Joseph Huston, aged 60 in 1818.

Suit—Soloman Litton vs. Thos McClenachen and Thos. Strother—1795 (box 52)—Francis Berry deposeth on May 1779 he and a number of others were living at Isaac Ruddle's Station and he went out from thence with Jno. Haggin, Richard Davis and Complt. Soloman Litton to mark etc.—Letton removed his family to this country fall of 1779 and carried them first to Ruddle's Station and afterward removed to Martin's Station as it was nearer his improvement and Letton was taken prisoner at Martin's June 1780, deposition taken at home of George Nicholas in Mercer Co.; statement by Soloman Litton that he was taken prisoner 26 June 1780 and remained prisoner until 1784. Deposition of Benjamin Cooper taken at home of Jno. Harvie in Madison Co, Nov. 29, 1797, says he was with Soloman Litton and party that set out from Ruddles May, 1779.

Suit Miller vs. Nunn (box 39)–filed 1797–Depositions: Robt. Smith aged abt. 64, Wm. Turner abt. 44. Robt. Snodgrass abt. 40, Thos. Jones 52, Benj. Coleman 44, Robt. Trimble abt. 56, Wm Forhman abt. 40, Jas. Sandusky abt. 45, Thompkins Barlow abt. 34.

Suit–Holt vs. McMillan and Neale (box 15)–filed March. 1791–John Napier states he settled at Lexington 1780 and went with Clark following July 28th against Shawnee Indian towns.

Bourbon Co. Office of Circuit Clerk (Box 757)

Thos. Young vs. Alexander Marshall–Bill filed Nov. 1805–Deposition of Gen. Henry Lee at house of John Johnson, Washington (Ky.) Nov. 27, 1805–states in winter of 1779 or '80 deponant lived at Lexington where a number of the old improvers of the neighborhood lived amongst them Richard Masterson, Simon Kenton, and Wm Triplett, last mentioned did not arrive until '80; in 1783 he went from Lexington in company with Masterson and others to go to Limestone. In 1784 came out with said Masterson to survey his own entry etc. Deposition of Humphrey Marshall taken at house of Philip Bush, Frankfort, Ky. July 8, 1806, deposeth in March 1784 he made survey of 10500 a. in name of Thos. Marshall now claimed by complt. on N. fork Licking and branches under direction of Simon Kenton, in Mason Co. Deposition of John McIntire taken in Montgomery Co. July 22, 1805 states he became acquainted with N. fork Licking in spring of '84, he with others at that time were coming from Stroud's Station, Capt. Triplett led Co. Deposition of Major Robt. McMillen taken at tavern of Mr. Geo. Webb, Clark Co. Oct. 15, 1804. Deposition of David Owen taken in Gallatin Co. July 5, 1805 states in 1776 he in company with Richard Lee, Joseph Linsey, Willis Lee, Henry Lee, Wm Linsey, John Williams, Bartholomew Fitzgerald, Samuel Boggs and others went from Leestown to Mayslick to make improvements. Deposition of Robt. Patterson taken at Joshua Wilson's tavern, Lexington, states he landed in Ky. at mouth of Salt Creek Nov. or Dec. 1775 and proceeded with three others in order to pass lower Blue Licks to Limestone; left McClelland's (now Georgetown) Sept. 1776 with 7 or 8 in Co. for Monongahela Co. and passed lower Blue Licks, those in company were Joseph McNutt, Jas. Warnock, Isaac Grier, Jas. Templeton, Edward Mitchell, David Perry. Deposition of Capt. Robt. Craddock at house of Jno. Cochran in Danville, Nov. 2, 1805. Deposition of Capt. Wm. Bush taken Oct. 15, 1804 at Webb's Tavern, Clark Co. states he has been acquainted with Mayslick, formerly called Mays Spring, for great number of years. Deposition of Cornelius Drake, states in July 1788 he came in company with John Shotwell and others, with Simon Kenton as pilate to show them May's settlement, later Abraham Drake came with him to spring where Shotwell's still house stands, taken Aug. 16, 1806, Mayslick. Deposition of John Shotwell states he came with Cornelius Drake 1788. Deposition of Jonathan Stout states he came to Mayslick 1787. Jacob Drake states he came to Mayslick 1788, '89. Depositions of Gen. Henry Lee and David Flora taken July 25, 1808. Deposition of Jno. Williams taken in Fleming Co. Nov. 1805 states in 1783 he first traveled road from lower Blue Licks to Mayslick. Thos. Sweet in Fleming Co. Nov. 1805 states he landed in Ky. 1783. Col. Jno. Logan deposeth in Frankfort Apr. 1805, states sometime in year 1778 he set out from Logan's Station with party to explore Indian country, N.W. Ohio, this company composed as he recalls, of Jno. Kennedy, Simon Kenton, Alexander Barnet, Alexander Montgomery, Jared Menefee and himself, at Boonesborough others joined the party headed by Col. Boone, reached lower

Blue Licks and remained all night to obtain provisions for expedition, about 18 in company, crossed Ohio some distance below Limestone. Deposition of Capt. Jno. Dowden taken at Johnston's Tavern, Washington, Aug. 1806 states he landed at mouth of Limestone Apr. or May 1784 or '5 and settled at Simon Kenton's Station, he being a minor and with his father. Deposition of Thos. Ritten, aged 51 yrs. taken at home of Phillip Ebert, Washington, Oct. 1805, states about Apr. 20, 1776 he in company with Samuel Arrowsmith, Jno. Mills, Jacob Duncan came to spring now called Drennens Spring, then called Jacobs Garden and found near spring Simon Kenton, then called Simon Butler, Thos. Williams and Geo. Deakins, company built cabin and he with Arrowsmith raised corn, remained there near 3 mos., traveled little being young and not much woodsman, but frequently was along from encampment of Kenton, then Butler, to field where he raised corn. Deposition of Richardson taken in Gallatin Co. 1805 states in spring of '76 he came with Jas. Batterton, Jno. Fitzgerald, and others to improve land, to Limestone. Bartlet Fitzgerald states he was acquainted with N. fork Licking 1775, taken Dec. 1805. Deposition of Jno. Williams taken in Fleming Co. at home of Jno. Faris, states in fall of '82 he was acquainted with road from lower Blue Licks to Limestone. Deposition of Thos. Sweet taken at Flemingsburg, states he landed at Limestone 1783 and was among first settlers in Mason Co. Deposition of Gen. Samuel Wells, taken Jefferson Co. Ky. July 1805, states in 1776 arrived on N. fork Licking with his father, Wm. Triplett. William Edwards and others opposite improvement made for Samuel Wells by his company 1775, as he told him. Deposition of Jas. Power taken Lexington, Oct. 17, 1804, states as early as 1779 he was at place now called Manslick, was there with Simon Kenton Nov. 1779, Jas. Bryan and David Hughes also along. Deposition of Alexander McClelland taken Alleghany Penn. June 1807, states former deposition was taken in Mason Co. Ky. 1800, which is annexed and states he came to state with others to improve land in spring 1775, frequently traveled trace from Wm McConnell's improvement at the lick or branch of Lawrence's Creek near where town of Washington stands to lower Blue Licks. Deposition of Robt. Patterson taken Montgomery Co. Ohio June 1819, supplemental to deposition taken 1804. Deposition of John Martin, aged abt. 64 yrs., taken Washington Sept. 1805, states he came to Ky. 1775, lived here since, he and his company of fifteen men came down Ohio and landed at Maysville, formerly Limestone, and went out to hunt, returned to Limestone and proceeded down river to mouth of Licking and then up Licking in canoes to lower Blue Licks, or lower Salt Springs upon Licking, one Daniel Micky who had before been in Ky. surveying with one Thompson gave us a memorandum of their names, landed and proceeded to Hinkston's, or Ruddle's, Station and deponant planted corn, returned to Blue Licks and Limestone 1775 and 1776 several times in company with Jno. Hinkston and either Jno. Woods or Jas. Cooper and once in 1775 Indians stole some of horses and they followed them and believes on this occasion Jno. Townsend and Wm. Huskins were along. Deposition of Hayden Wells taken Montgomery Co. 1805 states in 1775 he in company with Samuel Wells, Richard Masters, Wm. Triplett and others descended Ohio and landed at Limestone for exploring and improving. Deposition of Jno. Durye, 48 yrs., taken at house of Philip Ebbert in Washington, states he had been acquainted with neighborhood of mouth of Lees Creek N. fork Licking for 16 or 17 yrs. settled at Jno. Kenton's Station. Deposition of Caleb Carman taken in Washington 1805 states he has resided at Mayslick four or five years.

BOURBON-NICHOLAS COUNTIES TOMBSTONE INSCRIPTIONS

NOT IN GENERAL INDEX

These tombstone records were obtained from the old Millersburg, Ky. graveyard. This is outside of Millersburg (Bourbon Co.) but just over the Nicholas county line. A few from Mt. Gilead, so marked.

Alexander, Jane, wife of Samuel T. James, b. Mar. 23, 1823, d. Jan. 27, 1850.

Adair, Martha, wife of Wm. Adair, b. 1793, d. Mar. 20, 1883.

Allen, Annie L., dau. of J. B. and M. Allen, b. Feb. 5, 1862, d. Dec. 19, 1863.

Allen, Pinkey, dau. of J .B. and M. Allen, b. Oct. 22, 1858, d. Dec. 28, 1859.

Allen, Jane V., b. Feb. 8, 1796, d. Jan. 29, 1858.

Allen, Granville, b. Nov. 15, 1786, d. Feb. 1, 1844.

Bailey, Nancy W., wife of Elisha, d. Jan. 26, 1842, aged 32 yrs., 1 mo. 5 das.

Barnett, Sarah, dau. of J. D. and J. M. Barnett, d. Sept. 25, 1840.

Barnett, Mary, wife of James Barnett, b. Oct. 10, 1786, d. Dec. 20, 1828.

Battson, Eleanor, wife of Reuben, d. Mar. 3, 1849, 30th year.

Brown, Abel, b. Mar. 2, 1801, d. Feb. 11, 1883.

Brown, Eliz, A., consort of Abel Brown, b. Sept. 2, 1807, d. Oct. 11, 18—

Baker, Thos., b. Jan. 2, 1829, d. Aug. 17, 1849, aged 20 yrs., 7 mos., 3 das.

Baker, Mary C., dau. of Benj. and Nancy Baker, b. Mar. 15, 1845, d. Jan. 11, 1846.

Baker, Eliz. G. W., dau. of Benj. & Nancy Baker, b. Mar. 20, 1847, d. Aug. 18, 1849.

Baker, Lorinda Ann, consort of Benj. Baker, d. July 18, 1835, in the 25th year, and on her right lie her two infant sons, Presley T. and Wm. T. Baker.

Baker, Wm. T., son of J. S. and Elizabeth Baker, b. Oct. 15, 1846, d. Oct. 20, 1846.

Batterton, James, b. Oct. 23, 1793, d. May 7, 1859. Erected by H. T. and J. M. Batterton (shaft)

Brown, John, a native of County of Cavan, Ireland, d. July 29, 1851, aged 30 years. His bereaved wife M. A. Brown erected the stone.

Branham, Mary, wife of William, d. Dec. 24, 1862, aged 91 years and 22 das. (She was formerly the wife of Michael Burroughs, Virginia)

Burroughs, Nancy Hill.

Brown, Margaret, inf. dau. of F. W. and M. Brown, b. Apr. 3, 1832, d. Apr. 10, 1832.

Boulden, G. F. and J. G., b. Mar. 1, 1833, d. Nov. 30, 1855.

Boulden, H., wife of N. Boulden, (this should be Eliz. H. Boulden, wife of N. Boulden), b. June 6, 1817, d. Mar. 18, 1859. Devoted wife and mother.

Boulden, Nathan, b. 1803, d. May 1, 1861.

Battson, Elizabeth, dau. of J. M. and Amanda Battson, b. Apr. 18, 1845, d. Aug. 21, 1850.

Barton, Thos., b. Jan. 14, 1821, d. July 8, 1852.

Barton, Joshua, d. July 8, 1852, aged 62 years.

Barton, Benj. F., son of Joshua and Louisa Barton, b. June 24, 1830, d. July 5, 1852.

Baldwin, G. W., b. July 17, 1820, d. Dec. 14, 1852.

Barnett, John William, inf. son of John D. and Jane M. Barnett, b. Mar. 6, 1837, d. Jan. 13, 1838.

Burroughs, see Branham.

Current, Margaret, wife of Thos. Current, b. Feb. 24, 1758, d. June 29, 1836. Mt. Gilead.

Current, Thos., d. June 19, 1838, in 78th yr. of his age. Mt. Gilead Cem.

Corrington, Stephen, b. Apr. 15, 1770, d. May 2, 1851.

Cunningham, Lucinda--see McKim.

Curtis, James, b. Jan. 3, 1834, d. Sept. 23, 1897.

Curtis, Cynthia, wife of James Curtis, d. Sept. 14, 1888, aged 50 yrs.

Dykes, Martha, dau. of J. & M. Dykes, d. July 25, 1856, aged 11 yrs.

Dykes, Martha, wife of John Dykes, d. Aug. 1, 1856, aged about 40 yrs.

Eades, Priscilla, wife of Thos. Eades, b. May 28, 1769, d. 6-21, 1815.

Eades, Thos., b. Dec. 25, 1761, d. Dec. 14, 1838.

Fox, Nat. b. Oct. 9, 1774, d. Feb. 5, 1851.

Fox, Margaret, died Feb. 15, 1851, aged 63 years.

Gorham, Adalie, dau. of W. H. and S. S. Gorham, b. May 6, 1854, d. Oct. 22, 1854.

Grafton, Nancy Jane, d. June 1, 1818, aged nine months. (box grave)

Grafton, Dorothea, dau. of John and Jane Grafton, (dates illeg., box grave)

Grafton, Wm. Mark, b. Feb. 13, 1815, d. Dec. 25, 1816. (box grave)

Gregory, Walter, 1848-1910.

Gregory, Elizabeth, wife of John G., b. Mar. 15, 1770, d. Feb. 7, 1858.

Gregory, John, b. Mar. 30, 1768, d. July 11, 1844.

Gregory, Amos T., d. Sept. 11, 1844.

Gregory, Henry A., b. Jan. 18, 1794, d. July 17, 1857.

Gregory, Margaret, b. Nov. 25, 1803, d. July 1, 1881.

Gregory, John S., b. Nov. 4, 1805, d. Apr. 5, 1873.

Gregory, Nancy T., dau. John and Eliz. Gregory, d. June 5, 1843.

Gregory, Mary, dau. of J. & E. Gregory, d. Dec. 26, 1889.

Gregory, Lewis W., son of J. T. and M. A. Gregory, b. Apr. 5, 1829, d. Apr. 8, 1856.

Gregory, Rachel, dau. of J. & J. K. Gregory, b. June 16, 1844, d. Nov. 5, 1851.

Hagan, Wm. K., b. Mar. 17, 1833, d. Aug. 17, 1854.

Harmon, Mary, see Summitt.

Hamilton, Mary C., wife of Wm. H., d. 4-18-1848, aged 60 yrs., 6 mos. 8 days.

Hannah, Noah S., son of J. & E. A. Hannah, b. Jan. 5, 1850, d. 3-11,1858.

Harris, Margaret--see Layson and Miller.

Haydon, Mary Eliza, dau. of E. G. & A. D. Haydon, b. May 9, 1849, d. Aug. 24, 1854.

Holliday, Eliz., wife of John H., b. 2-13-1796, d. Jan. 17, 1865.

Holliday, Nancy Jane, dau. of John and Jane Holliday, b. Nov. 22, 1832, d. Mar. 1, 1835.

Holliday, Elizabeth, dau. of John and Jane Holliday, b. Apr. 8, 1820, d. Jan. 12, 1840.

Holliday, Thos., son of John and Jane Holliday, b. Feb. 5, 1826, d. July 5, 1848.

Holliday, John L., b. June 22, 1830, d. Jan. 15, 1883.

Hopper, John, b. Mar. 14, 1806, d. June 25, 1840.

Hutchings, Kader, b. Feb. 1, 1786, d. Mar. 8, 1860, aged 74 years, 1 mo. 2 days. (shaft, "friend, father and husband")

Hutchings, Julia R., wife of D. J. Hutchings, b. Mar. 19, 1834, d. Apr. 2, 1860. (shaft)

Hutchings, William, son of D. J. and J. A. Hutchings, b. July 24, 1857, d. Oct. 8, 1861.

Hutchings, Wm. R., b. Mar. 1, 1827, d. July 11, 1851 (shaft)

Hutchings, Andrew J. A., son of Kader and Jane T. Hutchings, b. June 3, 1838, d. Nov. 13, 1840. (on shaft of Wm. R.)
Huff, Ellen A., wife of John Huff, b. July 14, 1826, d. Feb. 19, 1856.
Holliday, Fannie E., dau. of Wm. & Patsy Holliday, b. Mar. 21, 1824, d. Apr. 6, 1825.

Isgrig, Mary, wife of Daniel Isgrig, b. Aug. 26, 1782, d. Feb. 11, 1852. Mt. Gilead graveyard.
Isgrig, Daniel, b. Apr. 8, 1786, d. Feb. 11, 1871. (Mt. G.)
Isgrig, Mary, d. Apr. 8, 1848, aged 17 years, 6 mos., and 14 das. (Mt. G.)

James, Alice, dau. of S. T. and H. T. James, b. June 17, 1862, d. Feb. 10, 1866.
James, Jane Alexander, wife of Samuel T. James, b. Mar. 23, 1823, d. Jan. 27, 1850.
James, Rev. John, the devoted minister, d. Jan. 14, 1860, aged 77 years, 5 mos. and 9 days.
James, Margaret, wife of Rev. John James, d. July 6, 1871, aged 86 years (76?)
James, Hezekiah H., son of Rev. John and Margaret James, b. Nov. 22, 1827, d. Jan. 18, 1852.
Johnson, Victor, son of W. M. and M. M. Johnson, b. Jan. 14, 1853, d. Aug. 31, 1859.
Johnson, Martha M., wife of W. M. Johnson, b. Apr. 25, 1824, d. May 8, 1874.
Johnson, Jonathan, b. May 26, 1784, d. Mar. 18, 1869.
Johnson, Rachel, wife of Jonathan J., b. June 21, 1786, d. June 16, 1860.

Kenney, Alex. Robertson, d. Dec. 12, 1884, in 65th year of his age.
Kenney, Mary Eliz., dau. of A. R. and Eliz. Kenney, b. Sept. 14, 1837, d. Apr. 18, 1845.
Kenney, Mary, consort of A. R. Kenney, d. June 26, 1833, in 34th year of her age.
Kenney, John B., (by his affec. wife Sally D. Kenney) b. Feb. 25, 1828, d. Sept. 6, 1862.
Kenney, Rosannah, affec. wife. (by her husband, Wm. Kenney) b. Nov. 2, 1829, d. Aug. 24, 1852.
Kenney, ——, infant son of Wm. & Rosanna, b. Aug. 2, d. Aug. 8, 1852.
Kenney, Nannie, b. Feb. 13, 1834, d. Aug. 8, 1854.
Kenney, ——, "our little Clara", b. Apr. 23, 1857, d. Aug. 8, (1859) Wm. & Serena Kenney.
Kimbrough, Hannah, wife of J. G. Kimbrough, d. Sept. 25, 1869, aged 57 yrs.
Kimbrough, John G., d. Mar. 13, 1848, in 30th year of his life, on his return from Mexico. ("father and husband")
Kimbrough, Robert H., d. June 16, 1834, aged 48 years and 3 mos.
Kimbrough, Eliz., dau. of L. & C. Kimbrough, d. Oct. 25, 1842, in nineteenth year of her age.
Kimbrough, Martha M., dau. of L. & C. Kimbrough, d. Mar. 30, 1844, aged 3 years and 3 mos.

Latham, Anthony, b. Jan. 27, 1805, d. Apr. 13, 1839.
Layson, Jane M., wife of John M. Layson, Jr., b. Jan. 2, 1815, d. Jan. 4, 1856. Mt. Gilead graveyard.
Layson, Margaret Harris, wife of J. M. Layson, late dau. of Wm. & Marg't. Miller, b. Mar. 1, 1821, d. Dec. 31, 1851, 30 years, 10 mos.
Lenney, Barbara, wife of C. D. Lenney, b. Apr. 3, 1793, d. Aug. 2, '49.

McCall, Thos., d. June 26, 1848, in his 23rd year.
McClintock, John, father, b. Feb. 21, 1793, d. July 9, 1840 (Shaft-E)
McClintock, Nancy, mother, wife of John McClintock, b. Jan. 19, 1802, died Nov. 23, 1874. (West side of the shaft).
McClintock, Ann—see John Miller.
McClintock, Hugh, soldier of the Revolution, d. Jan. 28, 1850, aged 93 years.
McClintock, Jane, wife of Hugh McClintock, d. June 3, 1834, aged 72 years.

McClelland, James W., b. Feb. 1, 1813, d. June 29, 1852. To the memory of my mother, Carolyne Forsythe McClelland, who on the 29th day of Jan. 1853, at the age of 38 years and 8 mos. was called away—, etc.'

McClelland, Martha, d. May 7th, 1826, in the ——

McClelland, William, d. Dec. 7th, 1812, in 68th year of his age.

McClure, Mattie, dau. of J. & Elizabeth, b. Nov. 1845, d. June 1859.

McClure, America, dau. of John and Martha A. McClure, b. May 13, 1852, d. Apr. 16, 1853.

McClure, John Dorsey, son of John T., and Martha A. McClure, b. Nov. 15, 1850, d. Apr. 13, 1853.

McKim, Loutie, dau. of W. A. and Sarah McKim, b. May 21, 1851, d. 11-13-57.

McKim, Louie, son of (above), b. Nov. 25, 1849, d. July 30, 1850.

McKim, Lucinda, wife of W. A. McKim, and dau. of John and Mary Cunningham, b. Mar. 22, 1827, d. Jan. 13, 1850.

McKim, Louisa M., wife of W. A. McKim, b. Nov. 13, 1823, d. July 18, 1847.

McKim, Lucinda M., dau. of G. W. and Joann McKim, b. Feb. 28, 1852, d. Sept. 2, 1853.

McKim, Carrie S., dau. of W. A. and Sarah G. McKim, b. Feb. 21, 1853, d. June 6, 1855.

McKim, Joseph, b. Nov. 19, 1773, d. Aug. 17, 1849.

McKim, Martha, wife of Joseph McKim, b. Jan. 26, 1783, d. Oct. 16, 1838.

Marshall, David, Sr., b. Feb. 23, 1754, d. Apr. 24, 1821.

Marshall, Sarah, wife of David Marshall, Sr., b. Dec. 24, 1761, d. Dec. 16, 1838.

Miller, John C. 1826-1872.

Miller, Maggie E., dau. of J. C. and J. E. Miller, b. Nov. 3, 1864, d. Dec. 29, 1864.

Miller, Margaret Harris, dau. of Wm. & Margaret.

Miller, Eliz. M. D., dau. of William and Margaret Miller, b. Jan. 25, 1830, d. Aug. 19, 1845.

Miller, Margaret, consort of William Miller, b. Nov. 19, 1789, d. June 9, 1859.

Miller, William, d. May 8, 1847, aged 58 years.

Miller, John, (shaft) born Sept 21, 1752, d. Sept. 5, 1815. He was born in Carlisle, Pa., to Kentucky in 1775, located where Millersburg is now situated. Soon returned to Cumberland Co., Pa. and married Ann McClintock, returned with her to Ky. Beneath this monument repose the remains of both.

Miller, Ann, wife of John Miller, b. July 9, 1755, d. Dec. 19, 1825.

Miller, Elizabeth, b. Oct. 11, 1824, d. Aug. 1, 1826.

Miller, James, b. Mar. 4, 1827, d. Sept. 29, 1828.

Miller, Martin B., b. May 31, 1822, d. Aug. 18, 1827.

Miller, Joseph, Jr., son of J. W. and A. N. Miller, b. Oct. 9, 1859, d. Oct. 19, 1859.

Miller, Lela, dau. John C. and Jane Em Miller, b. Mar. 5, 1859, d. 9-5-1859.

Miller, Thos., 1862-1878.

Miller, Mary, d. Nov. 5, 1848, 59th year of her age.

Miller, Robert, d. Feb. 4, 1845, in his 63rd year.

Miller, Horatio J., b. Oct. 13, 1812, d. July 15, 1818.

Miller, John A., b. Apr. 26, 1814, d. Nov. 3, 1815.

Miller, Jane E., b. Jan. 13, 1819, d. Sept. 7, 1820.

Miller, John R., b. Feb. 10, 1804, d. Jan. 10, 1811.

Miller, John, b. Nov. 13, 1783, d. Oct. 20, 1827. "father, husband, etc."

Miller, Preston W., b. Apr. 3, 1827, d. July 11, 1833.

Miller, Casandra, b. May 2, 1790, d. Sept. 1, 1833.

Moore, ——, (slab broken) tribute from Pa. Wm. F. & H. S. Moore.

Monson, Edy, wife of Thos. Monson, d. July 28, 1835, in 34th year.

Moore, Abram, d. Dec. 9, 1852, aged 30 years.
Moore, Virginia T., wife of N. S. Moore, b. 7-23-1824, d. June 11, 1848.

Nelson, James, b. Sept. 5, 1817, d. Jan. 21, 1848.

Outten, Rebecca, wife of Isaac Outten, d. Oct. 16, 1846, in 30th year.

Paris, John W., d. Feb. 5, 1858, aged 20 yrs. 11 mos., 20 days.
Paris, Richard S., b. July 7, 1810, d. Aug. 23, 1868.
Padgitt, Elizabeth, d. Aug. 6, 1842, aged 16 yrs., 6 mos., & 7 days.
Patten, Betsy, wife of John Patten, b. Feb. 21, 1799, d. Oct. 30, 1853.
Patten, Susannah Mc————, dau. of John and Betsy Patten, d. Feb. 4, 1845, aged 26 years, 8 mos. and 6 days.
Patten, John, b. Nov. 14, 1801, d. Sept. 27, 1848.
Poe, Sarah E., wife of A. F. Poe, b. Sept. 11, 1826, d. Apr. 18, 1848.
Pollock, John S., son of James and Margaret Pollock, b. Apr. 27, 1840, d. July 3, 1858.
Pollock, Margaret D. Steele, wife of James Pollock, b. May 21, 1816, d. Nov. 8, 1895.
Pollock, James, b. Nov. 9, 1814, d. Oct. 25, 1854.
Pollock, Hannah, b. Nov. 2, 1783, d. Sept. 7, 1834, consort of James Pollock.
Pollock, Walton, d. Nov. 21, 1841, aged 13 years, 8 mos., 21 days.
Pollock, Mary E., dau. Robt. and Amanda Pollock, b. Nov. 18, 1844, d. Aug. 5, 1849.
Pollock, Amanda, dau of Robt. and A. A. Pollock, b. Dec. 4, 1848, d. 8-15-1852.
Pollock, Amanda Ann, wife of Robt. Pollock, Jr., d. July 24, 1849
Pollock, Ann, dau. of James and Margaret Pollock, d. ————— 1843, aged 6 years, 3 mos. 21 days.
Purnell, Betty A., b. Apr. 17, 1847, d. Oct. 29, 1856.
Purnell, Mary Agness, dau. of W. T. and G. M. Purnell, b. Feb. 23, 1852, d. July 10, 1853.

Ratliffe, Nancy J., wife of W. D., b. Nov. 17, 1830, d. Mar. 8, 1852, dau. of Wm. & Anna Talbott.
Redmon, Samuel T., son of W. P. and N. H. Redmon, —————
Rogers, Drusilla, wife of Samuel G. Rogers, b. Dec. 1834, d. Sept. 2nd, 1857.
Rule, Sarah, wife of John Rule, b. Jan. 16, 1774, d. July 15, 1819.
Rule, John, b. Jan. 23, 1764, d. Apr. 30, 1813.

See, Mary, wife of George, b. Mar. 1, 1790, d. Sept. 9, 1865
See, George, b. July 16, 1783, d. May 12, 1843.
Shanks, Nancy, wife of David Shanks, Jr., d. Mar. 4, 1858, aged 24 yrs. 4 mos., 22 days.
Stitt, Hugh, d. 9-27, 1829, in 64th year of his age.
Stitt, Mary, wife of Hugh, b. 2-16-1773, d. Mar. 15, 1857, for 56 yrs. a Meth.
Summitt, Elijah, b. Nov. 6, 1795, d. Jan. 27, 1864.
Summitt, Oscar E., son of E. and Nancy Summitt, b. Feb. 18, 1830, d. Apr. 12, 1851.
Summitt, Aby Louisa, dau. of E. & N. Summitt, b. Dec. 7, 1834, d. Jan. 27, 1873
Summitt, Nancy P., wife of Elijah Summitt, 1806-1872.
Summitt, Mary Harmon, dau. of B. and Nancy Summitt, b. Apr. 29, 1838, d. Aug. 23, 1852.
Summitt, Jonathan G., son of B. & N. Summitt, b. June 22, 1834, d. Feb. 27, 1857.

Talbutt, Marcus, son of M. & S. Talbutt, b. Oct. 13, 1844, d. Mar. 10, aged 4 years, 4 mos., 25 days.
Talbot, Wm., d. July 19, 1840, aged 56 years, 2 mos., 19 days.

Talbot, Anna, wife of W. M. Talbot, d. July 2, 1852, aged 59 yrs. 2 mos. 20 days.

Talbott, Wm. H., d. July 3, 1852, aged 30 years, 9 mos., 11 days.

Talbott, Eliz. N., dau. of Presley J., and M. E. Talbott, b. June 30, 1830, d. Jan. 19, 1833.

Talbott, Presley J., b. Sept. 11, 1809, d. Nov. 5, 1831.

Talbott, Eliz. J., dau. of Wm. & Anna Talbot, b. Nov. 18, 1826, d. Sept. 10, 1827.

Talbot, Mary J., dau. of Wm. & Anna Talbot, b. Mar. 13, 1820, d. Oct. 21, 1820.

Talbot, Eliza J., dau. of Wm. & Anna Talbot, b. Apr. 6, 1815, d. Jan. 22, 1816.

Talbot, Rosaline M., dau. of Wm. & Anna, b. Aug. 6, 1812, d. 8-31-1812.

Talbot, Jane, wife of Aris J. Talbot, dau. of H. G. and M. Clay, b. Nov. 1, 1816, d. Feb. 24, 1852.

Talbot, Jane Clay, dau. of A. J. and Jane Talbot, d. Feb. 20, 1852, aged 30 days.

Taylor, Matthew, d. Apr. 12, 1849, aged 60 years.

Taylor, James V., son of J. L. and N. H. Taylor, b. 6-29, 1853, d. 1-17, 1865.

Thompson, Sara Luella, dau. of D. & E. J. Thompson, b. Nov. 5, 1851, d. June 18, 1853.

Thompson, Ann, b. Oct. 9, 1777, d. Dec. 14, 1827.

Thompson, Henry, Sr., ruling elder in Associate Reform Church, 24 years, b. 1740, d. June 26, 1827.

Thompson, Mary, wife of Henry T., Sr., b. 1742, d. Dec. 14, 1827.

Thompson, Jane, b. Apr. 15, 1776, d. Dec. 13, 1789.

Thompson, Martha H., dau. of W. H. & M. J. Thompson, b. June 14, 1852, d. 6-26-55.

Thompson, Henry, d. Feb. 16, 1852, aged 69 years, 3 mos., 8 days. Ruling elder in Associate Reform Church for 30 years.

Thompson, Mary, wife of H. T. Thompson, d. Feb. 15, 1860, aged 65 years, 10 mos.

Thompson, Joseph, b. Jan. 21, 1774, d. Jan. 1800.

Thornberry, Susan M., dau. of J. F. and M. Thornberry, b. Feb. 9, 1850, d. July 31, 1856.

Trigg, Lavinia, wife of Horace A. Trigg, b. May 29, 1818, d. Sept. 7, 1856, also her two infant babes.

Trigg, Anna A., wife of A. C. Trigg, b. Mar. 3, 1791, d. July 1, 1850.

Trigg, Allen C., 1789-1868.

Trigg, Joseph S. S., 1828-1873.

Trigg, Rachel M., b. Aug. 10, 1808, d. Aug. 26, 1852.

Trigg, Robert Battson, son of A. C. and Ann Trigg, b. 9-30-1826, d. June 21, 1835.

Varnon, Acquilla, son of D. & S. Varnon, d. 10-12-1830, 18th year.

Varnon, Napoleon, son of D. & S. Varnon, d. Sept. 6, 1840, aged 15 years 5 mos., and 5 days.

Varnon, Benjamin, d. Sept. 18, 1847, in 66th year.

Varnon, Mary T., d. Nov. 19, 1848, in 31st year.

Varnon, Newton W., b. Oct. 7, 1827, d. Aug. 3, 1855.

Varnon, Sarah, wife of Benjamin Varnon, b. Feb. 7, 1791, d. Dec. 31, 1856.

Victor, Mollie C., dau. of G. M. and S. M. Victor, b. Jan. 15, 1859, d. Mar. 1, 1864.

Victor, Louellen, dau. of G. M. and S. M. Victor, b. May 12, 1853, d. Sept. 27, 1859.

Victor, Elizabeth, d. Mar. 3, 1843, aged 47 years—(a mother)

Victor, George M., b. Sept. 14, 1826, d. Jan. 6, 1866.

Victor, John, Sr., b. Sept. 13, 1790, d. Apr. 19, 1868.

Victor, Elizabeth, b. May 25, 1794, d. Apr. 19, 1866.

Victor, Mima B., dau. of G. M. and S. M. Victor, b. Jan. 17, 1856, d. Sept. 28, 1858.

Watson, Eliz., dau. of Jas. H. & Letitia Watson, b. July 13, 1853, d. Mar. 11, '55

Wiley, Chas. W., son of Wm. & Maria Wiley, d. June 7, 1848, aged 16 mos.

Willett, Electra Francina Wilder, wife of Aquilla Willett, b. June 19, 1817, d. Sept. 2, 1839.
Willett, Aquilla, d. Sept. 29, 1843, aged 55 years.
Willett, Louisa Snow, wife of Aquilla Willett.
Williams, William G., b. in Jefferson County, Va., Jan. 1807, d. Jan. 30, 1857.
Woods, John, d. Apr. 23, 1853, in the 90th year of his age.
Wright, Morgan, Jr., b. Dec. 29, 1824, d. Apr. 25, 1825.
Wright, Sarah J., b. May 29, 1837, d. Aug. 19, 1846
Wright, Martha, wife of Thos. Wright, b. Oct. 30, 1799, d. July 3, 1853.
Wright, Thos., b. Apr. 15, 1801, d. Apr. 15, 1853.

(Formed from Madison and Clark Couuties 1808)

WILL BK. A

Burton, Constant (Constance)–will–11/7/1808–Dau. Milly, dau. Sus. Wolf, son Charley, Jenny Clinkenbeard, dau. Sarah Jane. Wts: John, Joshia and Francis Bush. July 1808.

Massie, Harris–Of Madison Co. Ky.; to bro. Thos. Massie and son, Harris Massie land in Station Camp; to Thos. Massie rest of property. Exrs. Wm. and Sam'l. Bush, 'till Harris Massie comes of age. 3/18/1808–Wts: Isaac Mize, Wm and Joshua Mize, May 1808

Note: Deed Bk A, p. 393–Thomas Massie of St. Charles Co. Territory of Mo. appts, Israel Massie of same county atty. to attend to interest of his son, Harris Massie under age of 21 yrs. late of Mo. 7/15/1815.

Ray, Benj.–Will–Dau. Susan Crawford, all, dau. Eliz. Townsend, 5 shillings, sons John and Wm, dau. Lettice Ellison, sons, Moses and Aaron, dau. Keziah Furves, dau. Anna Kindel, son Jesse, dau. Polly Waters, son Jennings, dau. Roda Bennett, each 5 shillings. Exrs: Valentine Crawford, and Wm Crawford, Wts: Bennett and Aarn McMonyte. 6/21/1819

Quick, Tunis–Nuncupative Will–Died 6/3/1809–called Jno. H. Barnes to bedside–left all to wife. July 1809, Wm Cooper Wts.

Mize, Isaac–Nuncupative Will–Wm. Mize testifies 2 or 3 weeks before my father's death he said my mother to have land etc, and at her death between two youngest sons, Isaac and John Mize. Wm Cooper says 11 days before the death of Isaac Mize etc. Oct. 1809

Noland, Lodston (Ledston?)–Inv. 6/21/1811

McCarty, John, Inv. 8/18/1811

Pearson, Jeremiah 5/29/1813–Jno. Williams Admr. "trip to Richmond" etc.

Coyle, Thos. Inv. 5/2/1814

Fitzzetce? Tarence, Inv. "Fitzgarel" and wife Elizabeth–May 1814.

Park, Jonathan–Will–Wife Caty all for benefit of ch. 1/11/1814–Wts: Jas. White, Ebenezer Park, Armstead Owens etc. July 1814

Park, Nathan–Inv. 4/25/1814

Bowman, Joseph–Inv. 10/14/1814

Baker, Thos.–Will–son-in-law Wm Bell; son Jacob, hrs. of Joseph Baker, Humphrey Baker, Wm Baker, hrs. of Thos. Baker Jr. decd., to several daus: Betsy Nix, Polly Bell, Sally Hubbard, dau. Katy Baker. Thos. Baker died 9/29/1814 at house of Wm. Bell.

Heathman (Hethman) Jas.–Inv. Jan. 1816

Sharp, Adam–Inv. Apr. 1816–Phebe Sharp–widow's dower.

McKinley, Patrick—Will—friend Barnett McMonnigh all in trust and to pay Matilda Murphy, dau. of Jno. Murphy of Tenn. and Nancy Murphy of Lexington, Ky; acc. vs. Aaron Forman and board to him to be pd., to ch. of Barnett McMonnigh rest equally. 6/18/1816 Oct. 1816

Sparks, Isaac—Inv. 5/24/1815

Pairsel, Benj.—Inv. Jan. 1815

Jacobs, Henry—Will—To sister Alesha Jacobs, sister Margaret Hightower, rest to estate 2/1815 —Oct. 1815

Waters, Baley—Inv. July 1817

Ferrill, Peter—Inv. 8/12/1817

Hendricks, Jas.—Will—"Of Madison Co."—wife Nancy 1/3, ch: son, James excepted—Mary West wife of Richard West owned by me as my natural dau. as by law she can not come in for my estate unless by me directed to be hr; wife to keep and school all my young ch., to Andrew Hendricks and Mary West their shares and rest as they come of age; my ch: Mary West, Andrew Hendricks, Allen, John, William, Nancy, Sarah, Mariah— gave Mary West and Andrew Hendricks $100 when they left me. Exrs: Wm Kerley, Josiah Phelps. 6/19/1811—Wts: Wm., Ann and Jno. Kerley. 8/5/1817

Eaton, Sam'l.—Inv. 12/18/1818

White, John Jr.—Will—Wife Esther all 'till youngest ch. come of age and all equally, the ch. of my 1st wife viz: Nancy Martin, Aquilla White, Lydda White and Jno. White, $1.00 out of estate of present wife and her ch. 4/11/1818—Oct. 1818

Clark, Wm—Will—To son, David (Bible etc.) to son, Thos. Clark, to Leah Clark my gr. dau., son Henry Clark, Sarah Parker Clark, Leah York Clark $1.00 each, wife Sarah Clark, all (stock, etc.) she and Isaah Wilcoxin Exrs. 7/29/1818—May 1819

Ray, B.—Inv. 8/13/1817

Maybry, Amelia—Inv. of estate by her gdn. Joel White—recd. of Joel Mabry Exr. of estate of father. 8/25/1816—(Note: see Clark Co.)

Crawford, Wm—Inv. 3/8/1820—Valentine Crawford Admr. and Sus. Crawford widow.

Daughtrette (Daugherty?), John—Will—Wife Nancy Daughtrette, dau. Mary Ann Horsly and husband Wm. Horsely, dau. Rachel Darnold and husband Thos. Darnold, son-in-law Wm. Meadows, dau. Elizabeth Mark and husband Robert Mark, sons, Moses and Wm. sons Isaac, Thos. Joel, dau. Sally Fisher, all equally, sons Isaac and Wm. Exrs. 3/14/1820— May 1820

Pitcher, Morgan—Inv. 6/6.1820—Henrietta Pitcher Admrx.

Holloway, John Sr.—Will—Dau. Temozin Russell, son Gregory, son John, dau. Sarah Jackson, dau. Rachel Jennings, grandson Jas. Mcton Wood, granddau. Mary Morton North. rest sold and div. between 2 sons and 3 daus, Sons Exrs. 5/8/1820—Wts: Zere and Richard Oldham Feb. 1821

Webber, Augustine—Inv. 3/9/1821

Gresham, Jno.—Will—"My Lydia Gresham" all, to eldest son Wm. 2nd son, John H., eldest dau. Nancy Roberon (?) (Roberson?), rest to 9 ch. viz: James, Fountain, Thompson, Elijah, Polly and Nancy Gresham, niece (not named) 7/17/1821—Aug. 1821

White, Jas.—Inv. 9/12/1821

Sharp, Col. Aarn—Sale—much bought by Ann Sharp and Jno. Snowden

Campbell, Thos.—Inv. A. D. Campbell Admr. (Andrew C.)

McCarthy, Jas—Will—9/4/1819—Wife Nancy then to ch. viz: Sally Jackson, Elizabeth Brookshear, Ezekiel McCarthy, Patsy Matherly, Sinnea McCarthy, Anne Tyre. Seba Moryason, Irea McCarthy, Matilda McCarthy, Jemimiah(?) McCarthy and their ch. Lennea McCarthy, Ire McCarthy and Jemima McCarthy. Dec. 1823

Cullum, Susannah—Will—"Old and near death"—slave Chas. which Col. Francis Jackson has pre-emancipated by paying etc.; to Abba Waters my gr. dau., property left me by decd. husband, Francis Cullam. 4/25/1823—Dec. 1823

White, Jas—"Extensive Estate"—1823(?)

Bennett, Jno.—Inv. 7/3/1823

Brown, Edm.—Inv. 1/25/1823

Brown, Edward "Of Madison Co."—Will—To dau. Ruth, to ch. of son John, son Joshua, son Caleb, ch. of dau. Ann. dau. Jane, dau. Sarah. son Nicholas, dau. Margaret. dau. Mary, son Hugh, rest of estate to wife Sarah she to live in house I live in until March 1st then to move to land I bought of Moses Price in Estill Co., sons and son-in-law Jas. Sappington Exrs. 2/2/1822—9/1823

Cox, Jas.—Inv. 11/15/1823—at sale Lucy Cox bought much.

Wiseman Abner—Inv. 3/11/1824—at sale Wm. and Isabel Wiseman bought most, others Thos. and Abner

Noland, Pleasant—Inv. 4/19/1824

Cooper, Richard—Inv. Jan. 1824

Bennett, Jno.—7/31/1823—Estate

Wilson, Isaac—Inv. 1/10/1824

Campbell, Daniel—Will—Wife Winny all and Exrx. 12/16/1823—Mar. 1824

Cooper, Richard—Sale—12/20/1823—Purchasers—Polly Cooper, Josiah Cooper etc.

Fowler, Joseph—Will—To son, John, dau. Jemima. dau. Druscilla, dau. Patience. dau. Winny Mintz. son Jeremiah (land) until youngest ch. of age—want real estate divided among ch. of last wife. Nov. 1824

Daugherty, Moses—Inv. 9/24/1824

Coyle, Thos.—Sett. of Estate 3/14/1824

Smith, Martin—Estate—9/20/1824

Barnett, Jeremiah—Estate Dec. 1824

Holmes, Wm.—Inv. 12/6/1824

Barnes, Brunsley (Brinsley)—Moses Barnes Admr. 11/17/1824

Lutes, Chas. Inv. 11/27/1824—Jno. Lutes Admr.

McKinzie, John—Estate 2/1825—Aaron McKinzie and "Widow" bought.

Lacks, Timothy—Inv. 10/1824

Sharp, Aaron—Inv. June 1825

Wagers, Francis—Sale Bill—12/5/1825—"Patient Wages" bought at sale.

McMahan, Jas. Sr.—Will—12/25/1818—To dau. Sarah Todd, son Wm., son, Moses, son John, sons Samuel James, Joseph. Exrs. Moses and John McMahan. Aug. 1826

Noland, Smallwood B.—Inv. 7/20/26

Branat, Edw.—Inv. Dec. 1827—at sale Gen'l. E. Combs bought much, also Col. H. Beatty

Straughen, Sophia—Will—To dau. Sally Woodruff, rents that fall due from sons Joseph and Jacob, want Joseph to buy plantation, cloth for cloak for Sally, gr. dau. Polly Woodruff, her sister Sophia Woodruff, gr. dau. Sally Woodruff. 5/18/1826—Nov. 1826

Wilcoxson, Samuel—Inv. Mar. 1827—Sam'l. Plummer bought much at sale.

Owens, Armstead—Will—Wife Elizabeth all, then to 4 daus. Polly Weagle, Nancy Reynolds, Jeremiah Owens, Malinda Owens, Exrs. Wife and Joseph Scrivener, 11/23/1823—9/17/1927

Wilson, Sampson—Will—Wife Mourning Wilson 400 acres to raise ch. Exrs. Wife, Eli B. Wilson, Isaac Thornberry, 8/9/1827—9/17/1827—Wts: Wm. Skinner, Tarlton Fielder

Wilson, Isaac—Sale Bill—9/1/1827

Meddous (Meadows) Isreel—Will—That Sydney S. Meddous, son of Jacob B. Meddous, have cow also Perry A. Meddous son of Jacob, land in Estil adjoining said Jacob and land of John Horn be devised to said Sydney S. Meddous and Perry A. Meddous, land to John Horn, wife Barbary land then to John Horn, land Wm. Edens lives on to grandson Jas. W. Cole, wife rest, colt to Sally Horn and one to Eliz. Horn. 9/20/1827—Codicil—gr. dau. Tabitha Meddous. Feb. 1828.

Abell, Jno.—Inv. 11/21/1828—Sett. Bk. B.

Bishop, Geo.—Inv. 1/22/1829—To Millison Bishop—John Bishop. Miller Bishop and William Bishop bought at sale,

Park, Jno.—Inv. 3/3/1828

WILL BK. B.

Abney, Jno.—Will—Wife, Martha 1/3 rest to my ch: Berry, Jane Tucker, Nelly (Milly?), John William, Joshua, Polly, to Dosha Wiseman—her inf. hrs. 'till of age to wit: Martha J. Wiseman, Jacob and Abner Wiseman, Joshua Abney to hold monies for Doshea's hrs. May 1838

Arvine, Jamison Sr.—Will—Wife Nancy, dau. Polly Arvine, son Joseph Arvine, son Thos. (land; Garrard Allumbough trustee), two sons Nathan and Davis—his dau. Nancy T. Arvine (child of Davis' 1st wife). hrs. of son John in trust for his ch., son, James, Jesse, dau. Sally King, hrs. if son Jamison, only what I advanced him in his lifetime, sons Nath'l. and Joseph Exrs. 6/18/1841—Wts: Jno. Arvine, E. W. Bowman etc. Oct. 1841

Akers, Jno.—Sale Bill

Brinegar, Rachel—Will—Son John Brinegar to take care of my four gr. ch. living with me: Louisa Brinegar, Mary Ann Brinegar, Wm Milton, Emeline Carney. Exr. David Hagins, the ch. to remain with Patrick Masterson to raise and support them. 5/6/1832—May 21/1832

Barnett, Jeremiah—Will—Wife Elizabeth and her ch., son Burgain, son Hiram, rest of my ch. viz: Sally and Nancy, Polly Jackson and Eliz. Barnett same as two sons. 8/20/1824—June 1832

Barnett, Eliz.—Inv. 11/19/1832

Broadus, Beverly—Reuben Monday and wife Frances Exrs., land I bought of Jeptha W. Crawford, to Edward N. Broaddus, inf. son of Whitfield Broaddus decd. (left in trust by his gr. father), Edw. J. to have and Benj. D. to have etc., Elijah W. to have, Mary Jane to have—each of my four ch. aforesaid to have when 21, all three of my boys to remain with their mother until 21. 4/2/1824—Aug. 1835

Blackwell, James—Will—Wife Nancy and her ch. Delila and Joel W. Blackwell all, to raise my two infs. Exrs: Joel White, Robt. Clark. 9/24/1829—Feb. 1837

Best, Jas. Sr.—Noncupative will—Wife Susan all. 8/15/1836

Burgin, John—Will—Wife, Elizabeth all for life and if any left then to John Hall, son of Jeff Hall, or to Nancy Hall—4/7/1837—Aug. 1837

Berryman, Amy—Will—Son John, land he lives on, dau. Winny Berryman—3/29/1841—Oct. 1841

Campbell, Thos. Sett. Estate

Crawford, Wm—Sett. Estate

Crawford, J. D. and M., gdn.

Combs, Eph.—Inv.

Cobbs, Jesse—Will—Son-in-law John Stofer and son Jesse Cobb Exrs., wife Edy, son Richard, my 8 oldest ch.—property among 6 oldest, John and James to have land formerly owned by Richard Oldham, land my son Henry lives on, my 8 oldest ch: Anna Merrills hrs., Deborough White, Milly Wilson, Betsy Baldwin's hrs., Polly Stofer, Henry, Jno and Sam'l Cobb.

Covington, Chas. Sett. Estate

Dunaway, Isaac—Inv.

Estis, Elisha—Will(?)—not abstracted

Grubbs, Jas. Inv. 8/31/1826—Sett. gdn. hrs.—Thos. Grubbs gdn. of hrs.—to Lucy Irvine, Nancy and Martha Grubbs—

Henderson, Daniel—Will—Wife, Sarah Henderson, all my sons and daus.—certain advancements made sons, John and James, dau. Margret Green, late Margaret Henderson, son Newman, son Silas, dau. Sarah Henderson, dau. Mary Henderson, son, Wesley Henderson, son Daniel, if ch. come of age before I die—al lsons: Sam'l., Jno. James, Newman, Silas, Wesly, Daniel (lands)—9/27/1826—11-19-1832

Harris, Thos.—Inv.

Horn, Nathan—Inv.

Huntsman, Jno.—Inv.

Harris, Daniel—Will—not abstracted.

Johnston, Hudson—Will—not abstracted.

Kincaid, Jas.—Inv.

Kelly, Andrew—Inv.

King, Major—Will—Wife Celia, son, Sam'l. (farm), to take care of his mother, dau. Lucy. dau. Amelia, 3 sons, Sam'l. Wm. and Skyler, dau. Thankful Vepox(?), sons, Nathan, Skyler, Wm. and Jacob King, Peter McIntosh and Jno. W. McIntosh; Mary Jane, Fanny's oldest child (slave?) to stay with my wife, have given other ch. 3/19/1836—Sept. 1837—Elihu Park Wts

Kelly, Sam'l.—Inv.

Lutes, Henry—Inv.

Lackey, Jas.—Inv.

Linden (Lyndon), Wm.—Noncupative will at house of his bro. James Lyndon, Dec. 14, 1835, leaves all to sister Ann Linden—12/17/1835—May 1836

Linden, James—Inv.

McKinney, Jno.—Inv.

McCreery, Jas.—Will—9-20-1832—To wife, Mary, land in Union Co. where Thos. Sudduth now lives, to son Robert for use of dau. Margaret Sudduth, son Edm. Robert McCreery Exr. have given dau. land in Union Co., son-in-law, Thomas Sudduth. Wts: Jas. Cox, Schuyler (?) King. 1-20-1834

Moreland, Wm.—Will—3/23/1836—Elijah Moreland has recd. also Enoch Moreland, Anna King to have same as my wife, land between two youngest ch. at wife's death—Sally Moreland and George Washington Moreland. June 1836

Moore, Jno. W.—Inv.

Moore, Jas. R.—Sett. Estate

Malory, Jno.—Inv.

Noland, Jesse—Inv.

Noland, Rebecca—Will—Not abstracted

Oldham, Absolem—Will—Bro. Jno. R. Oldham Exr., bro. Hezekiah to sell my half of 1000 acres on Drowning Creek, land James lives on to be sold for my wife Dolly and her ch., negroes in my possession belong to my father, land belonging to my son Deen Swift. Feb. 1831-Feb. 1831 Caleb Oldham Wts.

Oldham, John Sr.—Will—Wife, Amy Oldham, farm, dau. Polly Grubbs, dau. Betsy Fisher, dau. Sarah Moberly. dau. Nancy Grubbs, son Abner Oldham, my son Absolem, grandson John Oldham son of son Absolem when 21, Absolem's family, son Hezekiah, son Caleb, son John R. land in Madison Co., parts going to son Absolem and dau. Polly Grubbs to be used to educate their ch., dau. Betsy Fisher. sons Abner and John Exrs. 8/2/1831-Feb. 1832

Oldham, Richard—Inv.

Oldham, Amy (Amis, Annis)—Inv. 3/31/1840

Pierson, Joseph—Inv.

Proctor, Joseph—Will—Wife Polly all—2/28/1826—Codicil—To Elizabeth Noland dau. of Joseph Noland and his dau. Mary Jane Noland, rest to Joseph Noland and his hrs. 12/16/1844

Park, Tunes—Inv.

Rucker, Jas.—Inv.

Riddell, Aquilla—Will—Wife, Sally Riddell, farm. daus. Elender Stevens and Sally Riddell, dau. Elizabeth Henry, farm she lives on I deeded to Moses Henry, Exrs: Robt. Clark and Ansel Daniel to value land, son Adam, my gr. dau. Patsy Riddell and same to Eliza Jane Riddell, Sally's dau., son Adam trustee for dau. Elender Stevens and her ch. 12/15/1835—Mar. 1836
(Note: Sally Riddell (wife) formerly Riddell, dau. of Adam and Jane Riddell, died 1854, 95 yrs.)

Richardson, Jno, Sr.—Will—not abstracted.

Smallwood, Nathan—Inv.

Sheffield, Geo.—Inv.

Scott, Jas,—Inv.

Sparks—?his gdn.

Vaughn, Gab'l.–Will–Wife, Nancy Ann Vaughn, all, 10-26-1840–Dec. 1840

Woodlan, Wm–Div.

West, Richard–Inv. and Sett.

Witt, Elisha Sr.–Will–"Infirm", wife Phebe and dau. Nancy, home place, begin with fence between Elisha and Silas Witt, son Elisha, gd. son Milton Witt, son Silas Witt, son Elisha Witt the land willed to wife and dau. at their deaths, rest sold and 1/2 to David Witt and 1/2 to Elisha and Silas, son Chas. Witt to be apprenticed, gd. son, Washington Holeman, 11/18/1835–Dec. 1835–Wts: Chas. Witt, Elizabeth Holeman.

Order Bk. A–p. 162–Alexander, Willis, inf. of Rebecca Alexander aged 13 last Dec. to be bound to Jos. McMahan Apr. 1809; also p. 165, Walter bound.

Order Bk. A, Burgher, Nich. gdn. to Manson Burgher, inf. of Nich. Burgher Nov. 20, 1809 Stephen Trigg Sec. Also Polly Burgher inf. of Nich. Burger, he to pay her estate due her when 21 (p. 214), also Nancy (p. 216).

Order Bk. A, p. 289, 291–Bowman, Andrew, aged 3 yrs. last July 13 and Wm. inf. of Hez. Bowman–bound out–Oct. 1810 to Andrew Lackey

Order Bk. A. Farmer, Eve–Inf. gdn. 1/16/1809

Order Bk. A, p. 242 Oxshear, Mary, inf. of Nancy Auxier (?) aged 9. Dec. 1809–bound to Stephen Collins, Feb. 19, 1810

Order Bk. A, p 429–Poor, John–inf. of Peggy King, late Peggy Poore, aged 12 yrs. last Jan. to be bound to Peter Evans Sr. 10/19/1812

Order Bk, A. p. 483–Sea, Martin–Oct. 1813–Inf. orphan of Geo. Sea, 18 yrs. the 25th of last Sept. bound to Douglas Wyatt

Order Bk. A, p 276–Young Zachy.–inf. orphan of Polly Young, aged 2 yrs. 5 mos.–1810–bound to Andrew Alexander

Plummer, Samuel Sr.–Deed Bk. E. p 232–9/22/1832–Deed to Samuel Plummer Jr., both of Estill Co. Ky., my right of 25 yrs. possession etc.

ALPHABETIZED NAMES NOT IN GENERAL INDEX

Allen, James of Augusta Co., Va., Oct. 18, 1790. (3-96)

Ashby, Benj. & Jane, Apr. 10, 1790. (3-139)

Allison, John (will), sister Martha, . . . brother Thom . . . bro (7-28) Andrew . . . wife and children equ . . . June 15, 1791 . . . Mar. 1795.

Alexander, Wm. & Robert . . . nephew Ro . . . ander . . . bro. James Alexander . . . (7-37) will of John Alexander, nephews R . . . and Wm. Alexander, exrs. June 12, 1793. Oct. 1793. (7-38 and 39)

Anderson, Robt. of Bedford Co., Va, appts. atty. May 14, 1793, land in Green co. Ky., (7-126)

Arnett . . . see Phil. Thomas, decd. 1792.

Bloxson, Rich. and wife Ann of Campbell county, Oct. 2, 1788. (3-184)

Brown, Jno. (6-339) & Sarah (6-509)

Bartlett, Henry (will) (7-1) bro. John Crane B ——— es (slaves?) . . . other Harry Bartlett and mother Sa . . . rest of my estate my brother John . . . after decease of my said father and m . . . John Crane Bartlett and my 5 sisters . . . Phoebe, Polly, Sally and Franky Bartlett, before they marry or come of lawful age . . . bro. Thos. Bartlett, exrs. July 25, 1792. Dec. 1794.

Boston, Joseph (6-109)

Byers, Joseph, (will) (7-40) my sister Margaret . . . of Thos. Bodley, Sr., by bro. Ja . . .s's children . . .and bro. Samuel Byers, Aug. 4, 1793 . . .

Barton, Stephen (6-144)

Bowman, Abraham of Fayette county, May 30, 1793, and Jacob Bowman, of Lawrence Co., S. C. heirs at law of Joseph Bowman, decd., and John Bowman of Mercer county, Ky., heir and legal reps. of John Bowman, decd., 1 part and Isaac Hite of Frederick Co., Va., part of 2000 acres granted to John Bowman, Isaac Hite, Abraham Bowman, and Joseph Bowman, Oct. 10, 1780. etc . . . (7-320)

Brown, Sarah, (will) 1792. (6-509)

Bibb, Ann (see Phil. Thomas)

Burton, Robt. of N. C. Aug. 13, 1787. (3-271)

Craig, Benj. & Ann, 1792. (3-39)

Crockett, Joseph and Eliz., July 1792. (3-123) also wts. Fred. Moss.

Calloway, Flanders and Jemimah . . . 1792. (3-182)

Craig, Elijah and Frances, 1790. (3-153)

Craig, Lewis and wife Eliz. (see Phil. Thomas)

Couchman, Benj. & Mary . . . Apr. 1790. (3-179)

Cade, Chas. & Cath. Jan. 1789. (3-266).

Carr, Walter & Eliz. Aug. 1790. (3-285)

Camper, Henry (will) (7-13) son William, son Reuben, son Henry . . . dau. . . . wife . . .
(mostly missing) (see Kamper) . . . at wife's death, my six children, viz. John, William
. . . Nancy, Letty and Alcey . . . (Wm., exr.) Nov. 2, 1792. Jan. 1793.

Compton, Joseph (will) my children to wit: John, Elizabeth, Jenneh Eli . . . lly, Jenne . . .
bonds in New Jersey, in hands of Thos. Cook. Apr. 13, 1793. (7-21)

Clark, John, Will, Oct. 1792. (7-43) Wife and my 4 children, friend David Blanchard, Oct.
19th, . . . Jan. 1794.

Coleman, Daniel, ... my land in Mason county, Oct. 9, 1792, apts. Col. Henry Lee,
atty. (7-93)

Cobb, John of Ga. Feb. 2, 1793. (7-102)

Campbell, Wm. & Tabitha, sell land in Logan county set apart for soldiers etc . . . (7-335)
666 2/3 acres. 7-179)

Campbell, Jno. (6-187)

Dunaway, Benj. and wife Sarah, July 1792. (3-22)

Duvall, William (will) (7-45)—wife Mary, land I got from Thos. Ellis, my 3 sons Thomp . . .
Rich., Mitchell and Thos. Duvall, exrs. Sept. 5, 1792 . . . Dec. 1793.

Davis, Joseph (6-171)

Dunn, Michael (6-340)

Ellis, Aggie (see O'Neal, Sus.)

Ellis, William (will) . . . son John . . . dau. Susannah Clark and her husband . . . son John
Ellis . . . dau. Phoebe, son William, son Thomas, son William (when 21), dau. Betsey
El . . ., (when 18), son Charles Ellis, dau. Polly Ellis, (when 18), son Hezekiah Ellis,
(when 21), 4 younger children, Nancy, Walter, Charles and Polly Ellis . . . son Walter
(when 21), 3 younger sons under 15 . . . wife Aggie Ellis (suit in court vs. John Cobb).
My 7 eldest children . . . my bro. Ja . . . and wife Aggie and 2 sons . . . (Wm. Ellis,
Jr. and Timothy Parrish, etc. wts.) many pages, and probated, Oct. 1793. (7-56 . . .)

Fisher, Thos. (6-294)

Faulkner, Jno. (6-332)

French, James and wife (Keziah?) Cuzza of Madison Co., Va. (Ky), 1792 (3-26)

Foley, Richard (will), (7-23) wife Margaret, son Elijah . . . son in . . . (much missing here)
son Wm. Foley, under age, son Richard Foley, under age, son David Foley, (under age)
son John Foley (under age), dau. Mary Foley and Ann Foley, dau. Margaret (under age),
wife Margaret and son Elijah, and son-in-law John H . . . exrs. Probated Jan. 1795.

Farrar, Joseph Royal and wife Jane, July 25, 1793, Mar. 1794. John Watts, wts. (7-371) division 6-115

Gordon, Geo., and wife Sally Winn, to Peter and Thos. January, (3-10) Dec. 1, 1792.

Gray, David and wife Ruth, 1792 (3-124)

Gilman, Jno. (6-352)

Gray, Wm. (6-502)

Gray, David, (Inventory 7-5), will-20 wife . . . 3 youngest daus. . . . and Fanny, and my wife, . . . son John . . . Patrick . . . land on which I now live, son Samuel . . . dau. . . . son David . . . wife Ruth . . .ne, 26, 1791. July 1793.

Gatewood, Andrew . . . Jan. 25, 179 . . . May 1794. (47-53)

Halley, Wm. of County of Loudon, Va., Oct. 24, 1792, and wife Catherine . . . and Mary Crump . . . John Halley, Jr. and Rich. Halley. (3-5)

Hite, Isaac and Harriet, Sept. 22, 1788. (3-342). deed.

Howard, John and wife Mary to Benj. Howard, (7-229) 1680 acres, Aug. 1793.

Henderson, John, decd., Nancy Clark Henderson, infant heir, etc. (7-337) . . . 1794.

Hazelrigg, Wm., Sr., of Fayette and Joshua Hazelrigg, part of survey of 750 acres, to Jas. Hazelrigg's corner, (Wm. Hazelrigg, Jr., Graham and James Hazelrigg, wts.) Oct. 1792. (7-   )

Hazelrigg, Wm., Jr. (7-427) James Hazelrigg, Oct. 1792.

Higgins, Aaron, heirs, 1793. (7-443)

Helms, Achilles, part of Leonard Helm's preemption. (7-453)

Johnson, J. W. (6-119)

Johnson, S. (7-30)

Jameson, Geo. & Mary, to John Mayfield, 179–. Jan. 12, (3-244)

Johnson, Thos., of Frederick Co., Md., 1790. (3-283)

Johnson, Samuel, decd. Nov. 4, 1795, dau. Margaret Johnson, . . .ldren as follows 3 sons J . . . Johnson, Benjamin D. Johnson, and . . . ohnson, son Samuel and son James W. . . . Oct. 17, 1795 . . . (7-30)

Jett, Stephen appoints Reuben Searcy atty. to recover property etc. in Ga., 1784 . . . money due me from Col. Jos. Pannell and others in Ga. May. 1793. (7-132)

James, Geo. of Culpeper Co., Va., and Jonathan Swift of Alexandria, Fairfax Co., May 28, 1792. 3080 acres, pat. April 16, 1789, from Gov. Randolph, etc. much (7-190)

Jones, ——(6-98)

Jo . . . Geo. (6-115)

Kersner, Casper of Hanover co., Va., Aug. 15, 1787. (3-183) also spelled Karsner.

Keen, Francis apts. friend . . . miah Hutcheson of Loudon Co., atty. to collect rents due me, etc. . . . 1790. (3-205)

Kamper, Henry (will) at wife's death . . . my 6 children, viz. John, William, . . . Nancy, Letty and Alcey. (Wm., exr.), Nov. 2, 1792, Jan. 1793. (see Camper, evidently not the same persons)

Killgore, Chas. (see Love)

Love, Wm. of Woodford county, appoints Daniel McClure of Jefferson Co. to recover from Wm. Clark of Cumberland Co. . . . as exr. of Chas. Killgore's will, all remains due, Nov. 10, 1789. (3-227)

McConnell, Alexander and wife Hannah, acquit James McConnell, land June 1789. (3   )

McConnell, Wm. and wife Eliz., deed, Apr. 1789. (3-215)

McConnell, James, appts. Wm. Morton of Cumberland Co., Pa., atty. to receive money due me, to sell lands in Cumberland county etc. as legacy from my father. Apr. 9, 1790.

McConnell, Jas., heirs . . . and Mary McConnell, heirs and reps. of Wm. McConnell, decd., of age 21, and Elizabeth . . . Wm. McConnell, Francis McConnell, . . .et McConnell, infants and reps. of James McConnell, decd., by Mary McConnell, and John McConnell, guardians, aptd. by the court, and Moses Daugherty . . . said Mary McConnell, John McConnell, and Mary McConnell for themselves, and said Mary and John in behalf of said infants . . . 200 acres, part of late Francis McConnell's preemption. (Eliz., James, Wm., etc., infants,) . . . 1790. (8-101)
(Francis McC. killed in Battle of Guilford court house was bro. of James, Wm., etc.)

McConnell, James and Esther his wife, of Woodford, to Casper Carsner. (7-111)

McConnell, William (will) . . . (6-499) wife Elizabeth, 2 children James . . . James and Martha . . . son James . . . sister, Elizabeth McC . . . 100 acres . . . sister Mary Steve . . . Sept. 26, . . . 1793 . . . (Andrew Steele, wts.) . . . many deeds for heirs.

McCan . . . , Neal . . . will . . . blank . . . (6-113)

McCord, John apts. friend Wm. Gist, atty., to collect from Baltimore, Md., etc. . . . county of York . . . etc. . . . Feb. 1790. (3-238)

McMillan, Samuel and wife Esther . . . 1790. (3-258)

McDowell, Samuel and wife Mary of Mercer county, 1789. land patented Nov. 1779 to him. (3-260)

McKinney, John, aged 32 years, late private in militia of Augusta Co., Va., previous to the Revolution was disabled in the battle of . . . Pleasant by 2 balls, etc. . . . he is continued on the list of pensioners, Richmond, Va., Oct. 2, 1789. Beverly Randolph, Aug. 1790. (3-283)

McKinney, Alexander, (will) . . . dau. E . . . 2 daus. Esther . . . Elizabeth, land in Augusta . . . Va., my children to wit: John, . . . ander, Esther, David, Elizabeth, and Robert. sons John and Robt., exrs. May . . . 1793 . . . Aug. 179– . . . (7-16)

McDonald, Angus, of Frederick Co., Va., apts. bro. John McDonald, atty. Dec. 21, 1793. (7-307)

McCorkle, Joseph apts. Andrew Mitchell of Iredell Co. N. C., atty. to settle etc., pay for services due me in late war with Great Britain . . . due me as rep. of Richard Scott, for 10 mos. services under Gen'l. Sumter, Mar. 6, 1793 . . . (7-187)

McCreary, . . . (will), son William (6-17).

McMurtry, Joseph (will) (6-103) wife Isabella . . . family . . . Isabella, John, Wm., Samuel, David, Levi, Nancy, etc. . . .

Madison, Thos. and wife Susanna, of Botetourt Co., Va., to John Martin of Fayette Co. (Vol. 3, page 1) Oct. 24, 1791. Gabriel and Benj. Madison, wts.

Meredith, Samuel, Jr. and wife Eliz., 1792. (3-135) many deeds.

Meredith, Samuel, Sr., and John Breckinridge, his atty., of Amherst Co., Va., land to Meredith, 1779. (3-157)

Mallory, Uriel, of County of Orange, Aug. 21, 1785, to Peter Gatewood, of Lincoln county, 1785. (3-231)

Meredith, Samuel of Amherst county, Va. apts. son Samuel Meredith, Jr., atty, Mar. 1790. (3-283)

Meredith, Samuel, Sr., of Albemarle county, Va. apts John Breckinridge, atty., Mar. 19, 1790. (3-352)

Mitchell, . . . deed . . . Jan. 1795. (7-25)

Masterson, Hugh, (7-43) will . . . blank, probated 1794. (6-510)

Moody, James, to Alex. McClain, 1794. (7-293)

Mallory, Roger and wife Sally for love and affec. to Wm. Robinson, 1793. (7-295)

Morton, John, of Prince Edward Co., Va., July 19, 1793, to Wm. Graves of Mercer co., 391 3/4 acres, July 19, (7-381)

Masterson, . . . wife Elizabeth . . . John . . . Moses Masterson, (6-510)

Mann, Wm. (6-518)

Moss, Frederick–Nuncp. will, Mar. 1795, young son and wife, Feb. 2nd, (Joseph Crockett, wts.) 1795. (7-12)

Nichols, Geo., (6-137)

Overton, Richard, George Overton, Batle Cockey Lacy, Ann B. Overton, Mary Overton, (Sally Overton), Clough Overton and Dabney Carr Overton of Rockingham Co., North Carolina, apts. bro. J. Overton, atty. Sept. 18, 1792. (7-391)

O'Neal, Susanna, June 1792 to dau. Aggie Ellis, Mar. 1, 1792. (3-134)

Pickett, Frances (6-148)

Poindexter, Lucy, Francis, etc, see Phil. Thomas. 1792.

Par . . . , Robt. (6-133)

Patterson, Esther, (will) (7-33) well beloved nie . . . (M)ary Craig, wife of John Craig, all cash I have in the state of . . . to her . . . ter Martha Craig . . . to her son James Craig . . . niece Esther Patterson dau. of Wm. Patterson of Lincoln County, Carolina, all in N. C. or Pa. . . . John and my niece Mary Craig his wife . . . gust, 179– May 1794. signed Esther Patterson.)

Patterson, Francis (6-46)

Parrish, Timothy, see Wm. Ellis.

Procter, . . . wife Mary, son sons George and Benj. Procter, 150 acres, . . . and wife Elizabeth . . . to inherit where Geo. Hume lives till–his decease . . . 179–(1?), (6-348) 179– 1791?

Patterson, Francis, will, July 1800, (6-47), dau. Mary Ewing, June 1801.

Price, Bird, will (6-113) blank . . . wife Martha . . . Sept. court. 179–

Richardson, Thos. (6-311)

Russell, . . . (6-19)

Russell, Wm., Sr., wts. Robert Russell and wife Deborah, 1788, of Shenandoah Co., Va., Oct. 9, 1788. (3-149)

Rowe, Ed. (6-177)

Robinson, Alex. and Margaret of Mercer co., 1789, (3-157). deed.

Ring, Wm. (6-916)

Randall, . . . (6-100)

Shepherd, Geo. and wife Mary Ann, to Jacob Keizer, Dec. 11, 1792. (3-12)

Simpson, Samuel and wife Catherine of Fayette, Nov. 11, 1792 (314) . . . of Co. of Washington, exrs. of Ja . . . of Ky., Joseph Simpson of Clark Co., James Simpson in his lifetime in Co. of Botetourt . . . Aug. 13, 1793. (3-15)

Steele, Andrew, and wife Jane . . . Dec. 1791, (3-117)

Steele, Andrew (will) Book 1, . . .

Shelby, John of Sullivan Co., N. C., apts. son John Shelby, Jr., atty. to transact business, etc. for me–lands in Ky., etc. ec. 1789. (3-231)

Sha . . . , Geo. (6-5)

Singleton, Joseph, apts. . . . Wilkinson and Peyton Short, attys. of county of Mercer, to recover, etc. all due me as heir at law of Capt. John Singleton, etc. . . . May 1790. (3-252)

Shelby, Moses and Evan, Jan. 6, 1790, (3-288), 700 acres being part of military right, to John and Wm. Young,

Shaw, Nat'l.--6-7)

Simpson, Gilbert, . . . (will) (7-   ) son Thos. Simpson, son Samuel Simpson, dau. Jemima Byrn . . . dau. Ann Masteron . . . youngest child Tamas (Tanias?) Simpson . . . , son John Simpson, after wife's death, . . . nd Gilbert Simpson, to my dau. Hannah . . . Thos. Simpson . . . John and Gilbert Simpson all my stock to be equally divided . . . —uary 27, 1794 . . . May 1794.

Smith, Samuel . . . wife . . . son John Smit— tract land . . . son Wil . . . sons Martin—— James Smith . . . dau. Na———— th dau. Milly . . . all my children . . . (Geo., Joseph and Darbey Smith, exrs.). Probated May 1794. (7-6)

Simpson, James (7-19) wife Jane, children, Agnes, Alexander, Elizabeth and R . . . advice of N . . . Simpson, and James Johnson, Dec. 12, 1792 . . . July 1793. (Gilbert Simpson, Sr., Samuel Simpson, wts.)

Smith, Wm. . . . July 37, 1793 . . . Oct. 1793. (7-53)

Scott, Margaret to Wm. Scott. (7-405)

Scott, Margaret of Fayette and John Nichols of Mason, late will of Andrew Scott, decd., and James Scott of Fayette. Dec. 1, 1792.

Smith, Mary (6-107)

Saunders, Caty, widow of Hugh Saunders, Nov. 13, 1793. (7-488)

Suggett, James (6-154) . . . Book 1.

Scire?, Andrew (6-158)

Spuer, Rich (6-330)

Todd, Levi and Jane. (3-18)

Thomas, Philémon and wife Polly, Lewis Craig and wife Elizabeth, and David Arnett, Ann Bibb, Sally Graves, James Arnett, Wm. Arnett, Henrietta Brown, Lucy Poindexter, Francis Poindexter, Nancy Richardson, John Arnett, Lastly Arnett, Samuel Arnett and Zacharia Arnett, Jan. 13, 1792.

Thomas, Michael (6-92)

Torbitt, James and Robt. of Woodford county, apts. John Stewart of Sullivan, North Carolina atty. to represent estate in Bedford Co., Pa., of our father John Torbit. June 8, 1790. (3-178)

Turnpart, . . . (6-343)

Todd, Robt., Sr., and wife Ann, Feb. 4, 1790, to Hannah Todd, Sr., 770 acres grant to said Robert. (3-204)

Taylor, Jonathan of Fayette, apts. son Wm. Taylor of Botetourt Co., Va. atty., et . . . 179– 0?, (3-404)

Taylor, Walter late of Md., 1790 (3-406)

Taylor, Reuben and Rebecca of Orange Co., Va., May 30, 1792. (7-317)

Todd, Rev. John, legatees late of Lou . . . are entitled to 1 moiety of military survey of 2000 acres made for Alex. Spotswood Dandridge 11 Ju . . . Fayette, adj. military survey of Samuel Meredith, etc. . . . Nov. 29, 1792. etc. (7-340)

Tandy, Wm. (6-505)

Wallis, Joseph (6-323)

Watts, Wm. and wife Eliz., 1792. (3-24)

Ward, John, late of Greenbrier now Fayette, apts. son Benj. Ward, atty., Jos. Ward, wts. June 27, 1790. (3-275)

Watts, John, Jr., from Joseph Rogers, Jr., (Jr. crossed out then put in in another place.) 8-102. . . . 1796.

Ward, Wm., deceased . . . (7-32) deed? 573

Walker, Merry of Culpeper Co., Va., Mar. 25, 1793, to James Twyman of Woodford Co., (7-121) entry 162, 518, acres on Big Sandy.

Ware, Isaac and wife Clary . . . 1794. (7-290)

Worley, Caleb (6-326)

Young, Wm. . . . (7-61-66) son Minor Young, dau. Judah Marta . . . to James . . . rtain husband of Judah Martain, 210 acres . . . adj. John Young, Sr., James Young, F. and Thos. Morton, son Richard Young, under age, my brother John Young . . . wife Milly Young . . . dau. Lett . . . now in possession of her youngest son Harry . . . son John (under age), bro. John . . . my wife . . . given son Douglas Young . . . to my youngest children John . . .ng, Patsy Young and Douglas Y . . . (many pages) May 15, 1793 . . . Oct. 1793.

Young, Wm., Sr., and wife Milly, deed May 1793. (7-147)

GALLATIN COUNTY ESTATES

(County formed from Franklin and Shelby 1798)

WILL BOOKS A and B

Ayres, Thos. Bk. A, p. 204–Wife, Mary Ayres and her ch. equally; grandch., ch. of son, Thos. Ayres, decd.; two sons, Dan'l. C. and Lewis Ayres bal. land. 11/23/1811–Wts: Jno. Scott, Sally Jones–11/13/1812

Braston (Briston?), Nicholas, Bk. A, p. 130–To Jas. Spraull Sr. all in Port Wm. Mill etc.; Exr. Jno. V. Conover. 3/22/1807

Bledsoe, Rice, Bk. A, p. 190–Admrs. Bond. 9/11/1811

Bledsoe, Joseph, Bk. A, p. 210–Wife Nancy 80 acres and no claim to other land; sons John and Moses; "as ch. come of age"; son Aaron; Bob and Gilbert (slaves?) to be hired out; bro. Isaac Bledsoe and Mordecai Jackson Exrs. Wts: Abraham Bledsoe. 7/27/1812–9/1812

Bruce, Jas., Bond–Bk. A, p. 20

Bariger, Jno. Inv. Bk. A, p. 276

Blanton, Jas. Bk. A. p. 280–Wife, Jane; ch. to be educated; son, Thompson, when 21; daus. each when 18 or marry. Exrs: Wife, friend, Wm Blanton, John Scott. 9/18/1814–Feb. 1815

Bledsoe, Zachary–Bk. A, p. 288–To wife, Ann to support herself and child until he is capable of supporting himself. Exrs. J. Orr and Moses Bledsoe. 2/9/1815–Mar. 1815

Bennet, Joshua–Bk. A, p. 316–Wife, Catherine, our ch. land I own in Nelson Co. if she go there to live. 5/19/1815–11/13/1815

Bailey, Davis, decd. Bk. A, p. 330

Baker, Joshua–Bk. A, p. 347–To Stephen John North, a still; rest to wife and family, when ch. of age all equally; to Sophia and Polina Baker, Pamila Baker, Jesse Baker, Doscia and Greenup Baker, Wm. and Malinda Baker, Shelby and Letitia Baker. Exrx. wife, Mary, Exrs., Wm Morgan and Jonathan Kemper. 3/23/1816–Wts: Alvin Minor, Jesse Baker, Jesse Alnut etc. 5/13/1816

Boling, Geo. Admr. bond–Bk. A, p. 356–Inv. p. 393

Bledsoe, Wm.–Bk. A, p. 460–Wife; all ch. equally, son George, rest to Gabriel and all my ch. Exrs. Duncan Campbell etc. 2/26/1817–10/13/1817

Bledsoe, Aaron and Daniel–Bk. A, p. 471–Gdn. Bond–sec. for Sanders etc. 10/11/1819

Calnet (Calvet?) Philip–Bk. A–Admrs. Bond–Inv. p. 4–1/14/1800

Crawford, Jno. Bk. A, p. 44, 61, 91–Sarah Crawford Admrs. 11/24/1806 (Sarah Masterson and Richd. Masterson, Admrs. of Richard Masterson, decd.–signed Sarah Crawford)

Campbell, Arch'd.—Bk. A, p. 86

Cayton (Caton), Jacob—Bk. A, p. 139—To son, Wm Cayton, son Corullas, (Cornelas?), dau. Elizabeth Lane, dau. Nancy Odle each equally, wife Margaret and after death ch. equally viz: Philip Clayton, Margaret Odlen (Edlen?), Catherine Burks, Bethary Washington and Margaret Huffman, Exrs. wife and son, Philip—6/17/1813—Wts: Bulton Lane, Joseph Goodwin, Preston Hampton. Aug. 1808
(Philip Caton m. Peggy McLaughlin 1810.)

Cline, John—Bk. A, p. 243—Gdn. of Jacob Kiser, inf. of Fred. Kiser. 8/9/1813

Cobb, Saml. Bk. A, p. 248—To Elizabeth Spellman, Martha and Elizabeth Brown Spellman infs. of Thos. Spelsman? decd. 9/13/1813

Daniel, Thos. decd. Bk A. p. 394—12/9/1816—Note—Wife was Mary Sneed, dau. of Benj. Sneed.

Davies, Jno. Bk. A, p. 387—Wife, Sally until oldest ch. comes of age, their education etc. Wife Exrx. 11/2/1814—11/11/1816—Wts.: Jno. Scott.

Bioley, Jacob—Bk. A,—Inv.—6/14/1819

Butler, Wm O.—Bk A, p. 496—Gdn. bond—gdn. of Nath'l. McGuire—1/10/1820

Edmiston, Philip—Bk. A, p. 40—Wife, Sus., son, Robt rest and to be schooled 'till 14. Exrs: Capt. Robt. Sale and Wm Blanton. 2/27/1805—3-1805—Wts: Moses Ray, Moses Jackson, Jas. Furnish

Ennis, Ezekiel—Bk A, p. 301-332 Inv.

Eaton, Wm.—Bk. A, p. 464—Inv.—9/1/1807

Gaunt, Sarah—Bk. A, p. 6—My husband Reuben Gaunt allowed me to dispose of property as I see fit; lend him slaves my father Sam'l. Rolins gave me—slaves at sa leof Reuben Sullinger's estate.—then to will my ch. 12/9/1800—Apr. 1805. Wts., Sally Sullinger.

Gray, Drakeford—Bk. A, p. 29—Inv. 9/1804—Jemima and Jesse Gray, Admrs.

Gardner, Jno.—Bk. A, p. 79—Wife, Nancy, all my ch. 4/29/1806—Aug. 1806. Wts.: Robt King etc.

Guin, Jno. decd. Bk. A, p. 147—Admrs. Bond—Thos. Guin Admr. 12/12/1808

Guin, Robt. Bk. A, p. 149—Admrs. Bond—Thos. Guin Admr. 12/12/1808

Guin, Wm—Bk. A, p. 151—Admr's Bond—Thos. Guin Admr. 12/12/1808

Gullion, Thos. decd. Bk. A, p. 183—Jer'h. Gullion Admr.

Gardner, Jno. Hrs. Bk. A, p. 187—Robt. King gdn. to Anna, Wm, Hiram and Jno. Gardner infants. 9/10/1810

Gambrel, Paris, decd. Bk. A, p. 361—Wm. Kendall Admr. 5/13/1816

Gullion, Jer'h. decd. Bk. A, p. 378–9/3/1816–Bell Gullion, Admr. p. 489, div. 8/19/1819–
Hrs: Thos. Gullion decd.; Jer'h. Gullion; Rachel Gullion; Jno. Kelly; drawn by Allen
May for Geo. Gullion; drawn by Jno. Brown for Wm. Gullion; drawn by Jer'h. Gullion
who bought two lots from bro-in-law Caverns; Wm. Cavorns; Wm. Gullion; wid. Bell
Gullion dower; John Kelly's part.

Harris, Vincent, Bk. A, p. 76–Inv.

Hoagland, Cornelius, Bk. A, p. 135, Inv. p. 506– Hrs: Moses T. Hoagland, Wm. White;
Martin Hoagland, John Hoagland; Okey Hoagland, Geo. W. Hoagland, Samuel F. Kentz;
Cornelius Hoagland; Emile Hoagland; John H. Morris. 5/10/1818

Hait, Margt. Bk. A. p. 262–6/13/1814–Admrx. of John Hait, decd.

Hammond, Jno. Bk. A, p. 293, Inv. p. 320, Nancy Hammond and others Admrs. 5/8/1815

Hamilton, Allen, A. Bk. A, p. 303-317–Inv. Lucy Hamilton & others Admrs. 9/11/1815

Hardin, Chas. Bk. A, p. 305, gdn. of Philip Wise, inft. of Henry Wise, decd. 9/11/1815

Holladay, Joseph, Bk. A, p. 384–Will–471 etc. Wife Sally, son, Joseph land in Covington;
'till youngest child is of age and all equally; wife pregnant; ch. to wit: Rachel Ann,
Joseph and Sally. Exrs., wife and David Lillan (?) 8/28/1816. Wts: Bernard and Edw.
Spencer, David Norton. Nov./11/1816–p. 486–Sally Holladay gdn. for Rachel Ann,
Joseph, Sarah and Mary Holladay inf. orphans of Joseph decd.–9/13/1819

Hayden, Wm., decd. Bk. A, p. 497–Gersham Lee, Sr., Benj. and Bland B. Hayden, Admrs.
1/10/1820

Johnson, Jno. Bk A, p. 219, Inv.

Johnson, Dan'l. Bk. A, p. 232–Inv.

Jennings, Jonathan–decd. Bk. A, Inv. p. 359; div. Alvin Minor; Sam'l. Jennings; Peyton Jennings; John Jennings, Nancy Jennings; widow's dower. Jan. 1817

Jackson, Wm., decd. Bk. A, p. 508–Admrs. bond, 6/4/1819

Jackson, Mordecai, Bk. A, p. 341–Bond as gdn. of Thos. Jefferson, Polly and Elizabeth Bledsoe, orphans of Joseph Bledsoe, decd. 2/12/1816

Jennings, Jonathan, decd. Bk. A, Alvin Minor gdn. of John and Nancy Jennings infs. 5/13/1816

Jones, Martin, Bk. A, p. 479–11/21/1818–Will–Wife, Feby J.; to Fanny Wilson, rest sold and
to my surviving ch. Wts: Joseph and Thos. W. Jones, 5/14/1819

Johnson, John, Bk. A, p. 499–10/23/1819–Will–Wife, Reb. J. (land), Jacob Ball Exr.; rest
between my parents, bros. and sisters. Wts: Jas. D. Ball etc. 1/10/1820

Jackson, Wm. decd. Bk. A, p. 505–6/14/1819–Jno. Scott others gdns. to Barny, Martha and
——–Jackson, orphans

King, Wm–Bk. A, Inv. p. 52, Eliz. King, widow, dower. p. 134–1/18/1808

Lowe, Jas. R. Bk. A, p. 185—gdn. of Mary Lowe, Nancy. Esme, Rachel and Sarah Lowe. inf. orphans of Ralph Lowe, decd. (Netty Lowe and others gdn.) 8/13/1810

McNair, Christina (Anna) Bk. A, p. 7.—Will—"Of Port Wm."; dau. Margt. then between ch., Robt Plummer their gdn. 6/15/1801-2-1803—p. 155—dau.—Margt. Hawkins—Jno. F. (T?) Hawkins gdn. of hrs. of Margt. Hawkins.

Masterson, Rich. Bk. A, p. 77, decd., Sarah Masterson and Thos. Peniston admrs. Aug. 1806—p. 93—Div.—Wesley Masterson, inft. hr. p. 215, 11/10/1812

Mattox, Jas. decd. Bk. A, p. 81—David Mattox, Jos. Jones and Sherwood Mattox others. 9/22/1806

Mayfield, Geo. Bk. A, p. 234—Will—Wife, Hannah, rest to ch. Exrs. Francis Fresh, Ziber Holt. 11/5/1810—9/26/1812—Gdn. app. for Fred Mayfield. inf. of George. 1/13/1817

McGibney, John—Bk. A, p. 375-6—Inv.

McCleland, Joseph H. Bk. A, p. 448—Will—"Of Port Wm."; wife Mary Mills McCleland; father, Daniel McCleland of Shelby Co., tenant of land of my mother, five mi. from Shelbyville; I the only child of decd. mother, leave said land at father's death to my only child, Andrew Henry McCleland when 21, my uncle Andrew Homes of Shelby; I own land in Pa. Wm Winslow gdn. for my child, Andrew Henry McCleland and Henry Winslow Extr. 1817—Wts. Jas. R. Lane others. 7/14/1817

Mayfield, Fred, inf. orphan of Geo. Mayfield—Bk. A, p. 402—1/13/1817

McGuire, Nath'l. inf. orphan, with Wm. O. Butler gdn. 1/10/1820

McDowell, Wm. and Robt. gdns. of Vinah Stafford, inf. of Henry Stafford, decd. July 1817.

Montgomery, Robt. Bk. A, p. 477—7/12/1819—Admr. of Wm. Whitecotton, decd. (Robt. Montgomery m. Patsy Whitecotton)

Neely, Sam'l. Bk. A, p. 220—1/11/1813—Will—Wife, Mary, all she pleases, Wts: Robt. and Osborn King and Jno. Thomas. 2/8/1813

Owen, David, Bk. A, p. 245—9/13/1813—gdn. of Jno. Johnson, inf. orphan of Dan'l. Johnson

Overton, Moses, decd, Bk. A, p. 295—Mildred Overton Admrx. 9/11/1815—Inv. p. 312

Pauley, Edw. decd. Bk. A, p. 466—Admrs. Frances L. Pauley and others, Inv. p. 492—10/11/1819. Jas. Parks, gdn. of Hiram and Jos. Pauley, infs. of Edward. 1/10/1820

Plummer, Robt. Bk. A, p. 419—Will—Wife, Mary; four ch. now living; Wm. Plummer, Robt. Jas. Blair Plummer, Jno. Dudley Plummer and Mary Whitecotton Plummer, wife pregnant, wife gdn. of all ch. I now have or may have by her, she and John VanPelt Exrs. 2/8/1817—3/10/1817

Rilley, Mathis, Inv. Bk. A, p. 158

Rainey, Jno. Inv. Bk. A, p. 236

Russell, Geo. Bk. A, p. 286—"Of Fayette Co. Ky.—Will—About to descend Ohio and Miss. Rivers to New Orleans, sister, Sarah Stewart Boote, wife of Capt. Wm R. Boote of U.S.A. all; Extr.—Mark Pringle of Baltimore, in case of my death will to be probated Gallatin Co., copy recorded in Maryland, Wts. Robt. Plummer. P. Butler etc. 3/13/1815

Sneed, Benj. Bk. A, p. 2-5, 3/21/1800—Admrs. Thos. Daniel and Wm. Blanton.

Sneed, Sam'l. Coleman—Bk. A, p. 444—Wife Polly to support my family, all ch. equally when of age, Wife Exrx. 4/4/1817

Smith, Jonathan, decd. Bk. A, p. 435—Sarah Smith and Jno. Vanpelt, Admrs. 12/11/1814

Smith, Geo.—Bk. A, p. 11, Will—Wife, Elizabeth; son. Jas., son. Francis, dau. Elizabeth Chinn, dau. Kitty Boswell, dau. Nancy Smith 400 acres Montgomery Co. Ky. out of 1500 tract, dau. Sally Robinor(?) 200 acres adjoining Nancy; grandson Geo. Chinn 200 acres adjoining dau. Sally Robinan(?), (Roleman)?; dau. Lucy Ellis 200 acres in Gallatin—plantation on which I live wife, Elizabeth rest for life then equally, Exrs. sons, Jas. and Francis. Wts: Wm C Boswell Wm. Ellis 10/31/1801—June 1802

Stafford, Henry—Bk. A, p. 15-8/5/1803—Will—Wife Mary; dau. Catherine when 18; two daus. Cinthea and Vieneah land on Floyds fork in Shelby Co. Ky. Exrs: Jno Campbell and John Violet. Sept. 1803—p. 115—Jno. Violet gdn. to Cinthea and Lavinia Stafford infs. of Henry Stafford, decd.

Sanders, Jno. Bk. A, p. 21—Will—son, Sam'l. when of age; wife—1/2/1804—1/23/1804

Spillman, Wm.—Bk. A, p. 166—Will—Son, Thomas, already given him, dau. Sarah Brinton, dau. Nancy Hensley; wife Mary to raise my ch. to wit: Chas. James, Michael, Wesley, Pheby, Zach'h., Fielding, Ezekiel, Martha Frank Spillman and Elizabeth Brown Spillman, last named ten children now with us; estate due me from Thos. Brown, wife's father; Jesse Cannell Sr. Presley Gray, David Owen, Thos. Joseph and Michael Spillman, Exrs. 3/14/1810—5/14/1810

Smith, Jonathan, Bk. A, p. 192, Inv. 9/26/1811

Sanders, John—Hrs. Bk. A, p. 192—Nath'l. Sanders, Jas. Smith gdns. of Sam'l. Sanders, orphan of John Sanders decd. Nov. 1811

Sanders, Chas. Bk. A, p. 207—decd. Inv. 6/8/1812

Sanders, Nath'l.—Bk. A, p.—Sam'l. Sanders as gdn. of Gideon Sanders inf. orphan of Nath'l. Sanders decd. 2/13/1815; p. 391 Isiah Smith and Sam'l. Sanders gdns. of Barzella Sanders and Nath'l., inf. orphans of Nath'l. decd. 11/11/1816

Scott, Wm.—Bk. A, pps. 297, 336—Inv.

Smith, Giles, decd. Bk. A, p. 392—11/11/1816

Sale, Robt. decd. Bk. A, p. 442—Bond—Wm. Sale, Andrew Ross, Daniel C. Ayres, Robt. Bram(?) Jos. Curd. 1/10/1814

Spencer, John—Bk. A, p. 478—Inv. 1/28/1819—Jos. D. Spencer and others at sale.

Sanders, Nath'l. Jr. decd. Bk. A, p. 470—Sam'l. Sanders gdn. of Lemuel Sanders inf. orphan of Nath'l. Sanders Jr. decd. Bondsman, Valentine Sanders. 1/11/1819

Taylor, Abraham. decd. Bk. A, p. 299—Inv. etc.

Tombleston, Isaac—Bk. A, pps. 339, 353—Inv. etc.

Tandy, John Sr. Bk. A, p. 406—Wife, Polly, one third, rest to lawful hrs. Exrs. "my loving and trusty wife, Louise Moses Tandy" and Roger M. Tandy. probated 1/13/1817—p. 401 —bondsmen: Moses Tandy, Roger M. Tandy, Joshua Wayland, Wm. Tandy, Thos. Hanks, Mark Tandy, Wesley Tandy and Lewis Easterly.

Vanpelt, John—Bk. A, p. 224—Inv.12/13/1813—John Vanpelt admr. and gdn. for Marg't. inf. orphan of John decd. 10/11/1819—at sale much purchased by Hannah Vanpelt and Saml. Vanpelt

Whitehead, Richard—Bk. A, pps. 48, 97, bond etc. John Whitehead gdn. of Geo. Whitehead, orphan of Richard 12/22/1806—Div. of slaves p. 164—We John Davis, Jno. Whitehead, Nathan Hair, Henry Ramey, Wyatt Jones, Wm. Richard and Geo. Whitehead legatees, three legatees under age of 20 viz: Wm., Richard and Geo. Whitehead. 1/20/1810

Williams, Wm.—Bk. A, p. 109—Inv. 3/23/1807

Wise, Henry. Bk. A, p. 173—Inv. p. 181 dower—widow Elizabeth Wise—Nov. 1810–2/7/1811 —p 186—We Eliz. Wise, Daniel Wise, Smith King and Daniel Barbee bondsmen—9/10/ 1810—Elizabeth and Daniel Wise as gdns. of Elizabeth Wise, Henry Wise, James and David Wise, Philip and Isaac Wise, Nancy and Phebe Wise and Milly Wise, inf. orphans of Henry Wise decd.

Williamson, Joseph—Bk. A, p. 197—Sett. 11/7/1811–1/11/1814, Daniel Farley Exr. p. 119— will—Frees all slaves; nephew, Joseph Williamson son of Jno. Williamson land I live on; owes Elizabeth King from 5/15/1807; to bro. John's sons money due from Geo. Helms and Josiah Baker of Montgomery Co. Va., Exrs. Daniel Farly and David Bottom. 11/3/ 1807—Wts: Geo. Strother, Daniel Maddox, Thos. Potter. Nov. 1807

Whitehead, Wm. Bk. A, p. 476-509—Will—wife and bro. Richard Exrs; estate equal when ch. come of age. 3/1/1819–6/14/1819—Wts: Wm. Tandy, Jno. Whitehead, Thos. Hanks

Whitecotton, Wm.—Bk. A, p. 477—Inv. 7/12/1819

Winscott, David—Bk. A, p. 502—Inv. 2/12/1820

Hoagland, Cornelius—Bk. A, p. 506—Div.—Moses T. Hoagland, Wm. White, Martha Hoagland, John Hoagland, Okey Hoagland, Geo. W. Hoagland, Samuel F. Kentz, Cornelia Hoagland, Emili Hoagland, and John H. Morris. 5/10/1818

Abbett, Jonathan—Bk. B, p. 282—Inv.

Arkitt, Joseph—Bk. B, p. 299—Admr.

Allen, Henrietta S. Bk. B, p. 275—To sons and Exrs. Wm. H. Allen, Samuel S. Allen; to dau. Charlotte S. Allen and Henrietta S. Allen. 9/1/1821—Oct. 1821

Bledsoe, Wm. Bk. B, p. 102—George Bledsoe, inf. orphan of Wm. Bledsoe; dower to Winey Bledsoe p. 126

Brown, Jno. Bk. B, p. 150—gdn. bond of Wm. Gullion

Bledsoe, Joseph, Bk. B, p. 180—Mordecai Jackson Exr. Mar. 1819

Bargo, Jno. Bk. B, p. 195—Andrew Bargo Admr.

Bargo, Lydia, Bk. B, p. 198–Andrew Bargo Admr.

Bernard, Joshua M. Bk. B. p. 211–Wife Phil, all, slaves to be freed. 3/17/1818–Wts: Will Winslow, Thos. Woolridge. 10/9/1820–probated. Richmond, Va. 7/10/1820

Barrett, Daniel–Bk. B, p. 215–Inv. Ruthy Barret and Richard Henry Admrs. 11/13/1820, also p. 244

Bledsoe, Zacha–Bk. B, p. 218–Wife Anne to support self and child–"our child until he is capable of caring for himself". Exrs. John Bledsoe, Moses Bledsoe. 2/9/1815–Mar. 1815

Barnes, Francis Sr. Bk. B, p. 270–Wife Jane all then ch.–son, Leonard 3/4 and 1/4 to all other ch. 2/14/1815–6/11/1821

Blanc(?) Gilvain–Bk. B, p. 272–Inv. 7/9/1821

Brite, Jesse–Bk. B, p. 281–Admrs. bond–Hopkins Brite, Dennis and Levi Brite. 11/13/1821

Butler, Percival–Bk. B, p. 298–Admrs. bond–Wm. O. Butler, Richard P. Butler, Thos. L. Butler, 11/13/1821

Bledsoe, Wm., Bk. B, p. 360–decd. (Inv?)–9/7/1822

Bargo, John Bk. B, p. 195–decd.–(Inv.?) 3/13/1820

Bond, Jas. Bk. B, p. 416–Eleanor Bond inf. orphan–Gdn. 6/9/1823

Butler, Percival–Bk. B, p. 374–Will–"Of Fayette Co. Va." (later Ky.); wife–have flattering hope she will do impartial justice to all our ch; to her only son; if wife marry again equal div. with all the ch. I have by her or may have by her. 8/15/1790–9/7/1792–Codicil–Sons, Thos. L. utler and Wm. O. Butler and Daniel Barbee and Sam'l. Todd, Attorney, Exrs. Oct. 1822

Beazly, Joseph–Bk. B, p. 376–Inv. Hiram Beazly Admr. 10/14/1822

Bailey, Thos. Bk. B, Admrs.–Jno. and Stephen Bailey. 1/13/1823

Bodley, Thos. Bk. B, p. 386–Inv(?)–3/10/1823

Caterson, Jas. Sr. Bk. B, p. 196–Jas. Caterson, Admr. 3/11/1820

Clifton, Henry, Bk. B, p. 241–Mary Clifton Admrx. 2/12/1821–gdn. to Wm. F., Mary Ann, Emily F. and Magdalen Clifton, inf. hrs. of Henry decd.

Craig, Levi–Bk. B, p. 256–Inv(?) 3/14/1821

Cannel, Francis–Bk. B. p. 256–Cynthia inf. dau. gdn. Jesse Cannel. 3/11/1822

Cooper, Sam'l.–Bk. B, p. 406–We Esther Cooper, (?) Lindsay Cooper, Jas. Taylor and Liza Hatt(?) Zelia Hatt Admrs. and gdns. of Malissa, Milton, Artemesia and Minerva Cooper inf. orphans 9/8/1823–p. 408–also Lucy Cooper, p. 408

Dayley, Owen, Bk. B, p. 124–Inv. 5/11/1818–Ann Daily, late Ann Tomlinson (p. 169) widow of Isaac Tomlinson, decd, May 1819

Ellis, Henry, Bk. B. p. 324—Inv. Jas. A. Ellis etc. admrs. 3/11/1822

Green, Jno. Bk. B. p. 89—Will—Wife Ann to raise my ch., lot in town of Ghent. 2/23/1817—12/8/1817

Goodwin, Daniel—Bk. B. p. 165—9/11/1805—Will—"Of Franklin Co. Ky.," son, John, dau. Alice Dean, son-inlaw Wm. Savoree (Laveree?), son Daniel, dau. Elizabeth Goodwin, son Jno e(?), son Davie, son-in-law Jas. M. Green—not finished or signed—on p. 167—a new will:—son, Thos. part of survey of 888 acres, son-in-law Wm. Laveree, son, Daniel, dau. Elizabeth, son, John, sons Sam'l., David, son-in-law Jas. McGuire, dau. Polly Pogue. Exrs. David(?), Daniel and son-in-law Jas. McGuire, June 1818

Gray, Drakeford—Bk. B, p. 276—decd.—Estate Nov. 1821

Giltner, Bernard—Bk. B. p. 276—Will—To Caty Giltner widow of son, Abram decd. ¼ part of land in Bourbon Co., mentions land in Indiana, son, Francis land in Bourbon, son, John and hrs. of dau. Mollie Couchman decd. to Frances, Michael and John Giltner. Son Frances etc. Exrs. 10/12/1821—11/13/1821

Gray, Jno. D. Bk. B. p. 383—Inv.—1/13/1823

Goddard, Jno. Bk. B. p. 390—Admrs.—Sam'l. Vanpelt, Sarah Goddard. 3-1823

Gambriel, Paris—Bk. B. p. 409—Inv. and Sales, 5/17/1816—Dec. 1822

Harrison, David—Bk. B. p. 99—Inv. Wm. Harrison Admr. Jan. 1818

Hardin, Chas. Bk. B.—gdn. of Philip Wise, May 1819

Hoagland, Cornelius—Bk. B. p. 164—div.

Haydon, Wm. Sr. Bk. B. p. 197—Inv. Nancy Haydon's dower (note: She was Ann Ballard—see Spotts. Co. Va.)

Haydon, Joshua—Bk. B. p. 200—Inv.

Hampton, Jas. Bk. B. p. 269—Will—Son, Samuel, son Henry, son, Preston, dau. Theodocia Bramim(?) wife one third, Exrs. Wm. and Jas. Hampton, son Preston. 5/2/1821—6/11/1821

Hawkins, Perry—Bk. B. p. 363—Will—Wife Mary land contracted for with John T. Hawkins, ch. Maria Antoinette, Thomas, Theodocia—my wife and her father Thos. Tibbatts of Lexington gdns. of ch. Exrs: Garland Bullock, Richard P. Butler. 5/9/1822—Wts. Thos. J. Tibbotts—9/9/1822

Innis, Ezekiel—Bk. B. p. 151—Wm. Innec, Winifred, Rachel, Francis, Ezekiel and Mary inf. orphans of Ezekiel decd. Daniel Trout gdn. 7/13/1818

Jennings, Jonathan—Bk. B. p. 141—Sett. as gdn. to Robt. Emerson late orphan of Philip Edmondson(?) decd. 3/28/181—

Jackson, W.—Bk. B, p. 238—Inv.

Jennings, Samuel (Son of Jonathan Jennings)—Bk. B. p. 175—Will—1/11/1819. To bro. John, sister Nancy Jennings, to Eliza Ann Minor, to Ann Jennings, dau. of Peyton, to bro. Payton Jennings, bro. John Jennings and Wm. Q. Minor son of Oliver Minor have interest in lands whereon my father resided and possessed at his death. Exr. Wm. Blanton. 4/13/1818—Jan. 1819

Kean, Benj. Bk. B, p. 173—Will—To Malinda West, watch to Benj. Tully named for me, to bro. Chas. L. Keen, to Clement W. Wheeler, to Luke Keen sons of bro. 11/11/1818—Wts: Ann Keen, Malinda West, Jan. 1819.

Kent, Sam'l. T. Bk. B, p. 280—Inv. 10/13/1821

Lee, Gresham—Bk. B.—Inv. 6/11/1821

Lewis, Craddock—Bk. B, p. 356—Inv. gdn.—Clarissa Lewis for Patsy, Judy, John Stevens Lewis and Arissa Lewis inf. orphans of Craddock Lewis decd. 9/9/1823

McMillen, Joseph—Bk. B, p. 202—Estate

Mitchell, Wm. Bk. B, p. 272—Wm. Mitchell Admr. p. 321 Inv. 7/9/1821

Martin, Thos. Bk. B, p. 274—Inv. 9/16/1821

McDaniel, John—Bk. B, p. 317—Inv, Polly McDaniel—div. 2/11/1822

McNair, Christine—Bk. B, p. 375—Estate Oct. 1822

Montgomery, Robt. Bk. B, p. 404—Inv. 6/9/1823—p 416—Jno. Montgomery gdn. of Francis Montgomery orphan of Robert and gdn. of Jane Montgomery orphan of Robert.

McCormack, Robt. Bk. B, p. 413—Sarah and Jno. McCormack admrs. and gdns. of orphan, Louise McCormack. 10/13/1823

Plummer, Robt. Bk. B, p. 1—Mary Plummer Admr. March 1817

Phillips, Jeremiah—Bk. B. p 120—Estate

Pauley, Edm. Bk B. p 239—Estate

Ross, Coleman—Bk B. p 305—Will—To Sally Ross wife of David Ross my bro; rest to bro. Daniel Ross to divide among his ch. 12/7/1821—1/14/1822

Robinson, Wm.—Bk. B. p. 313—Inv.(?) 1/14/1822

Pauley, Edward—Hrs. Bk, B, pps. 338, 389—Nancy. Abigail and Edward Pauley inf. hrs. of Edward decd. 5/13/1822

Roberts, Wm.—Bk. B, p. 349—Inv.

Stafford, Rowland—Bk. B, p. 115—Estate 5/11/1818

Spencer, Jno. Bk. B, p. 176—Estate 1/11/1819

Sanders, Wm.—Bk. B, p. 179—gdn. bond

Sale, Robt. Bk. B, p. 182—Estate 2/10/1814—p 185—Div. 3/7/1819—Hrs. all of age, widow, Jane Sale, Robt. Bond, Jas. H. Sale, Lucy Hamilton, John Sale, F. H. Sale

Spillman, Wm.—Bk. B, p. 224—Estate

Scruggs, Jno. Bk. B, p. 231—Estate sett. p. 369

Spilman, Mary—Bk. B, p. 314—Will—Two daus. living with me, Martha Frank Spillman, Elizabeth Brown Spilman, estate of my father Thos. Brown of Fredericksburg, Va., son, Thos. Spilman, all my sons now living: Thos. Chas. James, Zacha, Fielding W., Ezekiel Spilman and Robert Brinton and my dau. his wife Sally, dau. Nancy and husband Thos. Hensly. 8/13/1821–1/14/1823

Spilman, Wm.—Bk. B, p. 224—Sett.

Severn, David—Bk. B. p. 398—Inv.

Tandy. Jno. Sr. Bk. B, p. 91—Roger M. Tandy gdn. of Elizabeth, Judy and Lucy Tandy orphans of John decd. 12/8/1817

Trout, Daniel—Bk. B, p. 151—gdn. see Innis

Tomlinson, Isaac—Bk. B, p. 169—Will—Ann Daily late Ann Tomlinson, dower, she formerly widow March 1819—p. 300 Henry Brenton gdn. of Robt. and Geo. Tomlinson, orphans of Isaac, Jan. 1822

Tandy, Wm.— Bk. B, p. 203—gdn. to Eleanor Gullion, dau. of Thos. Gullion.

John Tandy—Bk. B, p. 265

Webber, Philip—Bk. B, p. 92—Inv. 12/8/1817—David Gibson Admr.—Dower to Polly Webber, p. 158–2/27/1818

Waller, Mary—Bk. B, p. 147—Will—To grandson, Thos. B. Scantland son of Wm. Scantland, granddau. Nancy Waller Scantland. dau. of Wm. grandson, Wm. Hardy Scantland, son of Wm. my son, Eben C. Waller and Joseph Hardy Exrs. 8/18/1815—Oct. 1818

Wilson, Jno. Bk. B, p. 152—Inv.

Winscot, David—Bk. B, p. 188

Webster(Welester?) Bk. B, p. 204—My bro. Andrew Welester(Welster) Exr. 9/14/1820—11/12/1820 on p. 210—Robt. Webster decd. We Andrew Welester(?) and Robt. Sanders and Isaac Webster bondsmen.

Whitecotton, Wm. Bk. B, p. 225—Inv.

Whitehead, Jno. Bk. B, p. 236—gdns. sett.

Wyant, Jacob—Bk. B, p. 242—Estate

Whitecotton, Wm. A. Bk. B, p. 267—Inv.

Whitehead, Wm.—Bk. B, p. 271—Inv.

Wade, Jerh. Bk. B, p. 378—Will—Wife and Wm. Kendall Exrs., my four ch: Sam'l., Mary, Elizabeth and Sarah Wade, two sons, Horatio B. and Pleasant Wade land in town of Licksville, North Carolina on Dan River recorded in town of Rockingham, my son Sam'l. to have schooling—9/18/1822–12/9/1822

GREEN COUNTY DEEDS AND COURT ORDERS

(Formed from Lincoln and Nelson 1792)

Allen, Nathaniel of Mason county, gives to Robert Allen of Green county, power of attorney, July 27, 1795. (deed A-67)

Allen, David heirs—division from 1821 to 1825, (Vol. 3 of Inventories) to Wm. B. Allen, James Allen, Fannie Allen, Eliza Allen (alias Harry), Martha T. Allen. p. 303, etc.

Allen, David, appointed guardian to Samuel L. Allen, Wm. P. Allen, James B. Allen, Robert R. Allen, Rebecca Allen, Sarah and Polly Allen, inf. heirs of Elizabeth Allen, decd., late Elizabeth Price. (Order 6, page 312, Dec. 22, 1817.)

Bradford, David and wife Elizabeth (attorney at law of Washington Co., Pa.) deed to Richard Yates of Ohio county Ky., Nov. 17, 1792.—(deed 1, page 38) 1,500 acres on L. Barren.

Brown, Daniel, deposition in book 1, page 76—given Nov. 25, 1795, said he was in June 1776, passing from Harrodsburg to Cumberland with Wm. Stewart, Walter Briscoe, John Clark, John Peters, John Robinson, and Arch. McNeal, and others.

Bass, Thos., decd.—guardian appointed for Archy, Peter and Theresa, inf. heirs. Sept. 24, 1821. (Order 7, page 82)

Bale, Jacob, decd.—Sophia Bale, appointed gdn. to Solomon, Wm., and Susan Bale, inf. heirs, June 20, 1825. (Order 7, page 408)

Brockman, Samuel heirs—Jan. 5, 1835: Derret Brockman of Todd county, Ky., John Brockman, Washington Brockman, Joel Durham and wife Lucetta (late Brockman); John Caffee and wife Sarah (Brockman); Joseph Smith and wife Martha (Brockman), John W. Colvin and wife Nancy (Brockman); Gatewood Quisenberry and wife Jane (Brockman); Robt. Harding and wife Paulina (Brockman); Frances Moore (late Brockman); John Harding and wife Rebecca (late Brockman) all of Green county; Thos. Kemble and wife Elizabeth of Warren county, Eastin Ship and wife Nelly (Brockman); Tandy Brockman of Shelby county, Indiana, legal heirs of Samuel Brockman, decd. deed to Joseph Richerson of Green county. (deed 16, page 63).

Brockman, John heirs—Sept. 9, 1842—Hamilton, James, Lucy, Ann, Mary, Tandy, John and Elenor, infs. Joel C. Durham, their gdn. (Order 5, page 298)

Bass, Sally, inf. dau. of Henry Bass, aged 13 years, July 11th next bound to Eliz. Bass till she is 16 (Order 6, page 353) June 22, 1818.

Clifton, Baldwin and wife Sarah of Mason county, June 27, 1808, deed 106 a. in Green county. (5-365) Many Clifton deeds in Green, Mason, Nelson Cos.

Clendenin, John and wife Mary, May 9, 1809, of Green, deed to Wm. Royal of same, 103 acres on Pittmans creek. (5-434)

Clendenin, John buys Sept. 8, 1799 of Wm. Brockman, (2-107)

Chisholm, John and Susannah heirs: Richard, John, Nancy, Elizabeth, Demetrius, Dyonisius, and Mary Chisholm, ch. of John and Susannah, get deed to 300 acres from B. Chisholm, Aug. 10, 1835. (16, page 166, deeds.)

Cook, Eliz., admr. of Thos. T. Cook, decd. appointed gdn. to Henry Cook, Thos. Cook, Eliz. Cook, they over 14 chose her; and also to Giles Cook, under 14. (Order 6, page 52), Dec. 26, 1814.

Dyer, William and wife Nancy of Green county, deed to Henry Harding of Shenandoah county, Va. 154 acres in Shenandoah, on Dry Run, July 12, 1796. (1-84)

Durrett, John appointed gdn. to Mary Ann Durrett, inf. orphan of Elizabeth Durrett, decd. wife of Achilles Durrett (Order 6, page 98)

Draffen, Robert of Albemarle county, Va., agreement with Wm. Buckner of Green county, Feb. 17, 1794. (1-21, deed)

Drinkhard, Wm. R. and wife Molly C., Mar. 10, 1796, of Charles City County, Va., deed to George Marable of Halifax Co., Va., being a military tract. (Deed 1, page 105) (see Lincoln county for Drinkhard names.)

Dudley, Harvey, decd. Mar. 16, 1795; Wm. Dudley, exr. of Harvey Dudley, decd. of Stratton Parish, County of King and Queen, Va., deeds to Arch'd. Kennedy, part of mil. tract, 1000 acres, Patent No. 314, Jan. 6, 1788. (deed 1, page 51) Harvey Dudley died about Feb. 17, 1788, and willed to nephew Henry Fleet Dudley, son of Wm. & Ann Dudley, also 1000 acres in Ky., niece Ann Pinchback Dudley, dau. of Wm. & Ann, 1000 acres in Ky., to bro. Wm. Dudley, 2000 acres in Ky. Mil. Wt. for 4,000 acres (Mordecai Cook, Jr., Henry Fleet Dudley, Baylor and Wm. Fleet, wts.)

Duvall, Claiborne Sr., of Green county, appoints son Claiborne Duvall, Jr., atty. May 14, 1808. (Alex'r. Duvall, wts.) (deed 5, page 323.)

Duvall, Claiborne, formerly of Hanover county, Va., deed, Oct. 26, 1805. (deed 4, page 211)

Duvall, Philip, Sr., of Buckingham County, Va., appoints as attorney, Samuel Henry Duvall of Franklin, Williamson Co., Tenn. Mar. 7, 1829. (deed 12?–14?)

Draffen, Robt., of Albemarle Co., Va. deeds to Wm. Buckner, of Green county, 373 acres of 2000 acres tract on Pitmans cr., Feb. 17, 1794. (deed 1, page 21)

Dyer, Wm. and wife Nancy of Green county, appoint Thos. Muck of Shenandoah county, Va., attorney to sell land in Shenandoah county, bequeathed by Wm. Hart in his last will and test. to aforesaid Nancy Dyer, Mar. 9, 1796. (1-59)

Elmore, Wm. and wife Esther, deed, Dec. 20, 1805. (4-267)

Embry, George K., inf. son of John Embry, bound out Sept. 22, 1817 (Order 6, page 286)

Forbis——— Maria, Patsy and Eliza, infs. of Robert Forbis, decd. Jas. Mitchell appointed their gdn., Apr. 27, 1818. (Order 6, page 340)

Freeman, Elisha and wife Eliz. of Lincoln county, Ky., July 21, 1795, deed to Samuel Shy of Mercer, 480 A. in Green, part of John Holliday's preempt. (1-73)

Gum, Jacob, Jr. and wife Rhoda, Mar. 2, 1798, deed to Sam'l. Burks. (A-217, deed.) (see Hardin county for this family). Jacob Gum left will in Green county.

Graham, John, aged 14, bound out Mar. 18, 1822, till 21 (Order 7, page 121)

Gray, Jesse and wife Mary, appoint Joseph Meredith atty. to sell 115 acres in Russell county, Va., on Kenchridge. July 8, 1794. (A-22)

Gray, James of Green, appoints James Duffee of New York, attorney to dispose of 10,000 acres in Mason county, which I (J.G.) bought of Simon Kenton. Feb. 9, 1796. (A-59)

Grayham, Polly, aged 7, on Mon. 7th, last, inf. of Susan Grayham, apprenticed to Solomon Speers till she is 16. (Order 6, 335) Apr. 27, 1818.

Grayham, John, aged 12, Sept. 23, next, apprenticed to Solomon Speer, till 21. (Apr. 27, 1818. Order 6, page 335)

Grayham, Anderson, bound out to John Barbee, till he is 21, which will be Dec. 2, 1829. (Order 6, page 456)

Grayham, John bound to David Shofner till he is 21, which will be Sept. 23, 1827. Nov. 23, 1819 orders. (6-456)

Grayham, Turner, about 13 years of age, bound to Wm. Skaggs, Sr., Jan. 24, 1820. (Order 6, page 473).

Harding, John, (will 3, page 197) says my Bro. Payne Harding, $500, sisters of my decd. wife, Jemima Wright, Eliz. Wright and Sally Harding wife of James Harding, $100.00 each to Henry McDonald $300.00. to bro. Aaron Harding; rest to bro. to distribute to needy, etc. as follows: ch. of my decd. bro. Samuel Harding; ch. of my decd. sister Rebecca Preyear (now spelled Puryear) who m. Hezekiah Preyear; the ch. of my decd. sister Rhuany Reed who m. Nathaniel Reed and the ch. of my decd. sister Sally Carlisle who m. John Carlisle; to bro. Aaron land in Franklin county, Indiana— I to be buried burying ground of old Pitman meeting house, near Campbellsville in Taylor county, by side of my wife and child. Dated Nov. 7, 1854— Nov. 20, 1854.
(This John Harding was son of Thos. Harding and his wife who was a Payne. John was a Rev. soldier. Aaron Harding aforesaid was born 1805—buried Georgetown, Ky. cemetery 1875.

Hurt, Wm. and wife Sarah of Green county, deed Aug. 15, 1797 to Wm. Bennett. (1-156)

Harding, Stephen and wife Elizabeth of Green, deed to Samuel Lewis of Christian county, 100 acres 1/2 of my settlement right granted by Gen. Assembly Act of 1795, then Logan county, but now of Warren, and lying in a grove called "Blackberry Pond". May 20 1800. (2-167) another deed shows the above is "Davis".

Hart, David and wife Margaret of Green, deed Aug. 21, 1806. (5-97)

Harding, Abraham and wife Sarah, deed, Dec. 30, 1808. deed to James Hill, 130 acres, bound by Stephen and Ab. Harding, it being a tract intended to be given to Mary Ball by her father Abraham Harding. (Wts. Stephen Harding, and Reuben Ball.) (5-439)
Same above to son in law James Dawson, for love and affection Mar. 24, 1810. (6-78)

Hutcheson, David, Sr., and wife Hannah, June 29, 1811, Hutty B. Hutcheson and wife Elizabeth, deed to Mitchell. (Samuel Hutcheson, wts.) (6-268)

Helms, Leonard of Green, gets by deed from John Crawford and wife Mary of Amherst county, Va. Oct. 9, 1802. (3-195)

Hay, Indenture between Polly Hay, widow, of 1st part, and we, Robt. Hay, John Hardin and wife Nancy, Dimeck Hay and wife Peggy, Wm. Moore and wife Caty, Sally Hay and Polly Hay, Jr. that whereas we, Robt. Hay, Jr., (and above) sold to Polly Hay, widow, 100 acres on Sinking cr. Sept. 6, 1817. (8-264)

Hardin, Robt., June 20, 1825, bound to Wm. Turner, to learn farming, till he arrives at age of 21, which will be about Apr. 1st, 1830. (deed 11, page 441)

Hubbard, Joseph, heirs (14-242) June 10, 1831, John Barrett appointed by the court to take charge of Jonathan Cowherd and his estate . . . Dianna Walden, widow and devisee of Joseph Hubbard, decd., and Carter Hubbard, Wm. Bailey and wife Sally(?), Polly Hubbard, Dandridge Poor and wife Amelia, Elizabeth Hubbard and Walker Hubbard, all of Green county.

Helm, Leonard, Sr., deeds to L. Helm, Jr., Feb. 14, 1837. (17-26)

Humphreys, Alex. and wife Mary of County of Augusta, Va. to James Craven of Rockingham Co., Va. 4,000 acres in Nelson county, part of tract patented to Alex. St. Clair, in 1788. (A-64)

Hogan, James appointed gdn. to James Hogan, inf. heir to John Hogan, decd. Sept. 25, 1815. (Order 6, page 118)

Hash, Sally, admr. of Jas. Hash, decd. Alex. Scott, Jr. her husband and Alex. Scott, Sr., her sec. (Order 6, page 353)

Hopkins, Washington, inf. orphans of Mattie Hopkins, decd. age 11 years, bound out. Apr. 24, 1820. (Order 6, page 489)

Hooper, Jeremiah deed to Jas. Spilman, 7-22-1793. (1-4)

Harding, John appoints bro. Abraham Harding attorney to dispose of land in Washington County, Va., on West Fork of Monongalia river, being partnership tract between myself and Wm. Roberson, Mar. 21, 1797. (deed 1, page 123)

Gill, James, aged 14, bound till aged 21. Nov. 18, 1822, Order 7, page 177.

Gill, Walter, aged 13, bound,

Gill, Eleanor, aged 10, bound, November 18, 1822. p. 178.

Johnson, John and wife Margaret, of Fyatt county, Tyrone Township, Pa., deed to Benj. Lodge of Huntington Township, Westmoreland County, Pa. Mar. 18, 1788. (1-7)

Johnson, John appoints Robert and James Allen, attys. Apr. 11, 1794 (A-23)

Jones, Daniel bound out till 21, which will be July 11, 1822. Apr. 26, 1819. (Order 6, page 421)

Lynn, Ben and wife Hannah, of Green, deed to Thos. Howard of Nelson county, Nov. 11, 1794. (1-44)

Lile, Wesley aged 9, Jan. 22, 1819, inf. of Peter and Sally Lisle to be bound out. (Order 6, page 427)

McCaffree, Owen of Green and Simeon McCaffree of Lincoln, deed Mar. 11, 1794, 100 acres in Green. (A-33)

McCaffree, Owen of Green to John Patrick of Mercer, Oct. 13, 1795, 146–3/4 acres in Green Co. (1-68)

Moore, John, July 24, 1815, appointed gdn. to his children: Robert, James, Joseph, Andrew, Samuel and Peggy Steele Moore, inf. heirs of Margaret Moore, late Margaret Steele, decd. (Order 6, page 104)

Myers, Jacob of Lincoln Co., deeds May 22, 1792 to Elisha Freeman, 480 acres on Pitmans cr. (1- page 3)

Montgomery, James and Alex., of Richmond, Va., Oct. 8, 1793, deed to John Craig, military lands (pat. Aug. 19, 1785, (page 18, deed 1) and to Toliver Craig, page 19.

May, Wm. and wife Mary of Nelson Co. May 29, 1795, to Nat'l. Owens. (1-54) (If this Wm. May is the son of John May who was killed by the Indians early, he is buried in the Frankfort Cemetery by side of his sister Polly May Eppes.)

Matthews, Wm. and wife Jemima, deed May 12, 1812. (6-310, deed)

Matthews, John, son and heir of Archer Mathews, deceased of Greenbrier County, Va., Oct. 29, 1800, deed to Samuel Moore of same, 2500 acres surveyed for Arch. Mathews, decd. in Kentucky on Sinking creek. (Deed 6, page 312)

Mathis, Wm. Sr., decd., Sept. 26, 1814, wife Jemima. all ch. equal. (will page 110, "1804.")

Patrick, John of Green county, deed 1800. (D-526)

Pettus, Rhoda came into court and appointed admrx. of estate of Thos. Pettus, decd. Daniel White, Thos. Elmore, etc. her securities. Oct. 24, 1814. Order 6, page 34.

Pringle, James, Cloe, and Henry bound out to Henry Shofner till each is 21. Jan. 24, 1820.
Said James Pringle was born Nov. 5, 1804.
Said Henry Pringle was born May 20, 1815.
Said Cloe Pringle was born Nov. 5, 1808. (another page says 1818)
(Order 6, page 466)

Powell, Thos., decd., Nov. 24, 1817, Court Order, 6– page 299

Philips, Thos., decd.–Frances C. Dickerson appointed gdn. for inf. heirs of Thos. Phillips, viz: James and Nancy Phillips. Thos. Gains was appointed gdn. of Susanna Phillips. Oct. 6, 1818. (Order 6-377)

Pelham, John, will be 21 years old July 26, 1825, and bound to Sandidge, July 26, 1819 Order 6, page 436)

Poor, Nathaniel's widow got her dower. (Order 6, page 412) 1814. widow, Ann appointed gdn. to Edward, Agnes, Nat'l., Martin, Robt. and Silas P.

Price, Joseph bound out–will be 21 on Jan. 1, 1829. (Apr. 1821– (7-50)

Price, John, over 14, bound out Apr. 20, 1824.

Price, Calloway, aged 5 years, July 22, 1821, bound out till 21.

Price, Nancy, aged 7, Aug. 28, last, 1821, bound out till she is 16.

Price, Moses C. will be 21 on Jan. 22, 1837.
All bound out at Mar. 18, 1822 court, (Order 6, 7, page 40, 318, 117.)

Phillips, Thos., heirs. gdn. was appointed for James, Nancy and Martha Phillips, July 24, 1821. (Order 7-82)

Pemberton, Bennet of Green Co., deed 1828. (12-427) (see Franklin and Woodford Cos. for him, or same name.)

Penn, Richeson of Botetourt county, Va. appoints brother Edmund Penn of Green county, attorney to collect from the admr. of Aaron Dewitt, decd., Nov. 4, 1828, borrowed money. (12-496)

Puryear, Samuel and wife Levinia, deed to Aaron Harding, June 29, 1832. (15-22)

Patterson, Chas., Sr., heirs: Chas. Patterson, Jr., appointed gdn. to Elizabeth, David, Henry, Matilda and Wm. Patterson, inf. ch. Nov. 21, 1837. (5-39)

Powell, Burr bought land from the Hite heirs. 1799 (2-194)

Powell, Thos., decd. Nov. 24, 1817, Order 6, page 299.

Quisenberry, Moses, decd., gdn. appointed to his heirs: Nancy, Polly, Gatewood and Moses, Dec. 24, 1822. (Order book 7, page 100) Extensive Quisenberry data in Warren county, and some in Bourbon and Clark where they lived before going to West Kentucky. p. 132, June 1822.

Quisenberry, Mary, decd., Moses Q. appointed admr., July 25, 1814. (Order 6, page 22)

Richerson, Joseph, Nov. 5, 1796, of Caroline Co., Va., to Matthias Weant of Green county, 100 acres on Roberson's cr. (Thos. Cook and Isaac Wilham, wts. (1-258)

Richerson, Joseph of county of Caroline, Va., Mar. 11, 1795, deed to Jas. Miller and sons of Port Royal of same county, for 274 pounds a tract in Green county, 10,000 acres, patented to said Jos. R. (1-56)

Richerson, Joseph of Green county June 6, 1797, deeds to Notley Duvall of Mason county, 200 acres in Green. (1-152)

Richerson, Joseph of Caroline Co., Va., Nov. 10, 1795, deeds to Thos. Richerson of Fayette county, a tract in Green, (1-71)

Richerson, Thos. of Green county: "to all whom it may concern— I moving from Caroline county, Va.—leaving business unsettled, appoint my brother, Giles Richerson of Caroline County, Va. to act for me as attorney. June 20, 1797. (1-145)
Also many other Richardson deeds.

Rice, Rev. David, decd., (Order 6, page 193) July 22, 1816. James A. Rice and Benj. Rice, exrs.

Roberts, Wm. of Shelby county to Chas. Creel of Woodford county, Ky., Sept. 20, 1796, 275 acres in Green Co. (1-219)

Richeson, Thos., June 20, 1807, to Baldwin Clifton, John Chandler, Stephen Hardin, Richard Ship, and James Calvin, trustees of Baptist church of Pittmans cr. 1 1/2 acres (John Richeson, wts.) (5-177)

Richeson, Joseph and wife Polly, Apr. 28, 1809, deed to Lawrence Campbell, 212 acres on Pittmans Cr. (5-437)

Rice, Geo. W. of Jessamine county, Oct. 17, 1820. (9-527)

Rice, Jasper of Jessamine county. Sept. 17, 1832. (15-175)

Renick, Henry to Arthur Hopkins, Mar. 11, 1794 (1-24)

Roberts, Wm. of Shelby to Ezra Morrison of Lincoln, Oct. 12, 1793, 255 acres in Green. (1-27)

Skaggs, Thos., appointed gdn. to William, Sarah, Jane, Margaret, John and Jemima Ward, inf. orphans of John Ward decd., Oct. 28, 1818 (Order 6, page 375)

Skaggs, Henry, Stephen and James buy land 450 acres from James Skaggs, patented to him in 1784. (Jan. 15, 1793. (1-5)

Skaggs, Thos. and wife Nancy, Jan. 2, 1818, deed (8-148)

Samples, John and wife Fanny, (m. Fanny White Dec. 24, 1798. p. 28 of m. register)

Scott, James and wife Eleanor. . .

Sympson, Eliz., decd., Order 6, page 152—Jan. 22, 1816.

Sympson, Henry, decd., Inv. Aug. 1806. (A-113)

Spilman, James and Lydia, Feb. 27, 1795, deed to Warren and Barbee of Danville, 842 acres in Campbell county, formerly Fayette. (1-26)

Sidebottom, Chas. (1-42 deed) Oct. 14, 1794, says he did not say that Michael Hall swore to a lie, and that his father, John Hall had trained him to lie, etc.

Shively, John and Susannah of Washington county, deed to Robt. Jay of Green, 100 acres, Mar. 8, 1796 (1-75)

Schooler, Milly, formerly Milly Quisenberry, widow of Moses Quisenberry, decd., dower, Jan. 1823. p. 167 Invs.

Skaggs, Moses buys from Draffen about 1794. (1-45)

Saunders, Samuel and wife Anne, May 12, 1795, deed to Joseph Saunders, 200 acres. (1-49)

St. Clair, Alex. of Augusta County, Va. deed, Aug. 3, 1807 (5-215)

Spear, Thos. and wife Sally deed to Samuel Spear, Oct. 16, 1810. Solomon and Jas. Spear, wts. (5-108)

Skaggs, James, Sr., decd., division to his 3 sons who are already decd., then to the heirs of his three sons: Stephen Skaggs' heirs, 219 acres; James Skaggs' heirs, 120 acres; Henry Skaggs' heirs, 170 acres. Nov. 1, 1816. (560 acres. Wm. Skaggs, present. (deed 8 page 157)

Sublett, Valentine, son of Branch Sublett, decd., bound, Sept. 16, 1833, 'till 21, Sept. 4, 1831 (Order 7, 153)

Sublett, Branch bound Nov. 11, 1822 'till 21 Feb. 10, 1834, p. 174.

Sympson, Wm. gave tax list, Oct. 18, 1824. (7-343 Order)

Spears, Jacob appointed gdn. to Caroline, Wm., Zarel, Mary and John Spears, infs. of John Spears, decd., July 1824, (Order 7, page 33)

Sympson, Alex. and Nancy, m. 1837, deed to Henry Simpson, being part of tract on which Joseph Carter lived. (17-114)

Sympson, Wm., decd, Henry Sympson, admr. Order 5.

Taylor, Hubbard and wife Ann? of Orange county, deed to Thos. Graves of Louisa, July 20, 1786, land in the Western Country, Nelson County, on Cumberland Fork. Orange county, Va. court July 27, 1786 Green county, Ky., Oct. 14, 1794.

Thurman, John of Green county, Nov. 13, 1793, to John Emerson, (1-6) (One John T. was in Lincoln early.)

Taylor, Zacharia, decd., heirs, June 28, 1805, Samuel Peters agent and atty. for Absolom Atkinson and wife Nancy, George Taylor and wife; Uriah Taylor and his wife; Mouman? Taylor and his wife, heirs of Zach. Taylor deed to David New, 1004 acres on Robinsons cr. in Green Co. (4-297)

Taylor, Sally to son Wm. Taylor, atty. to receive of James Martin, admr. of Jas. Roberson, decd., money due me—Gibson county, Ind. Feb. 24, 1816 (7-227)

Taylor, James and Reuben T. Taylor, Robt. Todd and wife Mary A. (late Taylor and dau. of Edmund T., decd., Thos. S. Hind and Daniel Mayo, gdn. to Martha S. Taylor, inf. heirs of Ed. Taylor, decd., John McKinney and Mary T. McKinney, gdns. for Monroe H. McKinney and Wm. Buckner of Green. (Oct. 4, 1828) (12-454).

Taylor, Samuel and wife Sally, to Wm. Mathews, Wm. Willis, Nathaniel Latimore, Samuel Bern, Wm. McMurray, 1/9 each; 1/3 to be divided among ch. of Mathews Taylor, decd. —Susanna Harding and Barbara Greenwell, decd., namely: Sarah E. Taylor, 1/9, Wm. Mathice, Stephen, Mary, Sary, Elenor and Eliz. Harding to have 1/9 part, also Pennick Harding, Elinor Grinwell, and Richard Grinwell, Jr., balance or 1/9 part. Sept. 10, 1819. (page 46, of will book "1816-1838."

Taylor, Mathew m. Prudence Harding, Feb. 1800. (p. 49)

Vance, Alex. and wife Jain, Mar. 14, 1793, to John Hall (1-1) (1st deed in the county.)

Vance, Alex. and wife Jane deed Mar. 14, 1793 to John Hall, 100 acres, part of 714 acres patented Mar 15, 1790 and again to Wm. Vance. (1, p. 2 and 1)

Vowles, Henry and wife Mary of Stafford county, Va., Sept. 10 1793 deed to Wm. McClanahan, Jr. of Culpeper Co., Va. land pat'd. Dec. 3, 1787 to said H. Vowles, heir to Walter Vowles for part of military. Wt. No. 163, of 1783, for 2686 and 2/3 acres, Va. Cont'l. Line. (Jacob, Benj. Martin and Jesse Coons, wts. (1-40)

Ward, John, heirs.

GREEN COUNTY MARRIAGE BONDS

GROOMS NOT IN GENERAL INDEX

Marriage bonds—supposed to be all from beginning of the county, 1793, thro 1810. Many of these are not recorded in the marriage Register. Many are recorded in the Register, but complete dates are not given owing to careless keeping by the ministers. In many instances the spelling is varied, and inaccurate.

Names in parentheses are bondsman; parents are given when so stated. Notes of parents inclosed unless otherwise stated.

Abbett, Wm. and Rebecca Hall, May 23, 1808. (Thos. Hall, bondsman)
Abbott, Wm.—Patsy Wilson, Oct. 4, 1798, dau. Spencer Wilson, note.
Abner, Joshua—Pattie Phelps, May 6, 1795. (Wm. Phelps).
Abney, John—Betsy Gill, May 1, 1800, dau. Wm. Gill.
Allen, Ben—Polly Ross, dau. Delilah Ross, Jan. 22, 1799. (Jas. Ross)
Allen, David—Betsy Price, dau. Wm. Price, Sept. 17, 1793.
Allen, James—Ann Barrett, May 7, 1806.
Alston, Jinkins—Ann Emerson, June 12, 1806. ("her consent," Silas Burks)
    (This is also spelled "Astin" on same bond, and may be Austin.)
Anderson, Reuben—Rachel H. Mills, (consent of parents in office) (full date not gotten) 1810.
Andrews, John—Rebecca Wells, dau. Philip Wells, Feb. 13, 1805.
Andrews, Thos.—Rutha Jones, Aug. 22, 1807. (Samuel Jones).
Astin—see Alston, above.
Atkinson, Thos. W.—Betsy Carlile, Nov. 5, 1810. (John Carlile).
Austin, Jinkins—see "Alston."

Bailes, Westley—Rebecca Bass, Mar 25, 1809. (Peter Bass).
Ball, Benj.—Peggy Mourning, April 26, 1805. dau. Roger Mourning, (John Mourning).
Bandy, Elihue—Elizabeth Thompson, Apr. 28, 1809. (Wm. Thompson).
Barbee, Joshua—Elizabeth Hobson, Sept. 21, 1805.
Barnett, Will—Nancy Richason, Feb. 5, 1798, dau. Thos. Richeson, Feb. 4, 1798. (Thos. Richeson's note is in such very fine penmanship.)
Barrett, Robt.—Margaret S. Brownlee, Aug 29, 1809.
Barringer, Joshua—Elizabeth Bates, Sept. 20, 1809. (Note from herself)
Bartlett, Solomon—Rosey McMurtry, (no dates), (with 1795 packet) John Summers gives consent. (Wm. Summers).
Barton, John (Burton?)—Nancy Price, dau. Wm. Price, Sept. 17, 1793.
Bashfield, Henry—Elizabeth Rumbaugh, Apr. 6, 1799. (Jas. Allen) (This looks like Harsfield in one place).
Bass, Josiah—Anny Moody, Mar. 27, 1799. Thos. Bass says that Anny Moody lives with him and has no parents in Kentucky and is 21 years of age.
Bass, Nathan—Roema Leonard, Dec. 22, 1796, dau. Wm. & Sarah Leonard.
Bass, Tyre—Rebecca Roberson, Jan. 24, 1804. (Note from herself.)
Bass, Norrel—Polly Stearman. Nov. 28, 1809.
Bass, Wm.—Judith Herndon, July 25, 1808. (Wm. Herndon).
Bass, John—Polly Edwards, Jan. 24, 1808.
Belcher, Isham—Betsy McDaniel, Sept. 14, 1808, consent of John McDaniel. (Betsy McDaniel wts. to his note.)
Bell, John—Elizabeth Watt, dau. Samuel Watt, Aug. 21, 1798.
Benefield, John—Sally Rice, Jan. 23, 1805 (Randolph Rice—"father's consent".)

Bennet, Samuel–Sarah W. Short, Oct. 22, 1810. (Joshua Short).

Benning, James–Maria Tandy, Feb. 27, 1809. (Smith Tandy).

Biggs, Simeon–Leannah Atkins, Feb. 27, 1806. Consent of Jesse & Elizabeth Atkins.

Bins, Armstrong–Elizabeth Davis, Oct. 17, 1807. Dau. of Goolsby and Jemimy Davis (Goldsby Davis).

Black, John–Mary Pointer, dau. Wm. Pointer, Apr. 18, 1798. (Dan'l. Upton)

Blakeman, Aaron–Nancy Lacefield, Mar. 25, 1799, dau. Wm. Laswell, note. He spells it "Lace-field" in the body of note, and "Bleakman", and his own signature in same penmanship is "Lasswell". (Benj. McQueen).

Blakeman, Adam–Patty Wilcox, Dec. 14, 1807. She says in a note that she is "thirty odd" years of age.

Bleakman, Adam–Catrine McKinney, Mar. 22, 1797. (Catron McKinney).

Bloyd, Ely–Polly Graham, Apr. 26, 1806. Son of Wm. Bloyd & Keziah, and dau. of Peter Graham. (Tabby Bloyd–Wm. Graham).

Bloyd, Tubby–Nancy Goldsby, May 27, 1805. (Will Bloyd–father)

Bloyd, Levi–Barbara Winn, Jan. 24, 1810. consent of Joseph Pearson,? (illegible and faded) (Thos. Winn)

Bond, Wm. Thos.–Martha Tolbert Walker, dau. Wm. W., Dec. 19, 1795.

Bonner, Moses–Nancy Smith, Apr. 1, 1807. (John Smith)

Bottom, Abner–Betsey Chandler, Nov. 28, 1808. (Horatio Shandler?)

Bowles, Pleasant–Susanna Wright, Dec. 24, 1805. (Richard A. Buckner)

Brownfield, Theron–Susannah Murry, dau. Jas. M., (Wm. Murry). (The clerk says "Brumfield", but groom as before).

Brownlee, Chas.–Betsy Allen, Sept. 6, 1809. dau. of Margaret Allen.

Brownlee, Alex–Jane Thornton, June 24, 1807. (John & Robt. Barret).

Brunk, Jesse–Neoma Jones, June 13, 1808. (Wm. Jones).

Brunt, Thos. O Fanney Bates, July 12, 1808. (Thos. Bates).

Brunts, Thos.–Eliz. Clark, Dec. 27, 1796. Note from herself, and John & Rebecca Brunt, wts.

Brunts, Samuel–Elizabeth Marshall, Oct. 29, 1804.

Brumfield, Theron–see Brownfield.

Buckner, James–Levina West, Nov. 5, 1804. Son of Wm. & Anna Buckner; dau. Joseph and Nancy West.

Buckner, Richard Aylett–Elizabeth L. Buckner, Oct. 7, 1805. (Alex. Irvine)

Buckner, Thornton–Matilda Buckner, Mar. 3, 1806. Consent of Will Buckner (Horace Buckner, John and A. B. Buckner).

Bull, Eli–Hetty Mills, June 3, 1799. (Joshua Phipps).

Bunch, Rodden–Jane Harris, June 20, 1805. Eliza Harris says " all are of age".

Bunnell, Peter–Susanna Erwin, June 19, 1810, consent of Wm. Erwin, Jas. & Robt. Erwin, wts.

Burk, Silas–Betsy Graves, July 24, 1798, dau. Mary Graves and Benj. Graves.

Burns, Wm.–Dorothy Link, Mar. 13, 1797. (note from herself).

Burton–see Barton, John

Butler, Wm.–Polly McCafferty, Apr. 6, 1795. Owen McCafferty, her guardian gives consent.

Butler, Isaac–Nancy Millikin, Mar. 11, 1797, consent of Jas. Millikin, (John Butler).

Butler, Jas.–Polly Forbis, Mar. 27, 1804. (Jas. Forbis).

Butler, Wm.–Polly Black, Sept 16, 1808. Patrick Black says she is of age.

Butterfield, Elijah–Mary Ann Tucker, Feb. 13, 1808. Dau. of John Miles who gives consent in note.

Byons, Jesse–Rhoda Bloyd, Jan. 23, 1809. dau. John Bloyd, (Levi Bloyd, and John Bloyet, Jr., wts.)

Cabanis, Wm.–Polly Harper, dau. Samuel?, Apr. 2, 1807. The name is not legible, it could be *Jams* (James?).

Cabell, Samuel–Sarah Mann, dau. Moses and Fanny Mann. May 18, 1810. (Joseph Cabell).

Caldwell, David–Lucy Cabaniss,– 19th, 1799, dau. John Cabiness (Marshall Despain)

Caldwell, Wm.–Nancy Trabue, Sept. 20, 1808. (she of age).

Caldwell, David–Patsy Wilcoxson, Feb. 20, 1810. (Wm. Wilcoxson).

Campble, John–Polly Gray, Oct. 9, 1804. Jesse Gray.

Campbell, James–Rachel Spears, June 23, 1809. (Samuel Spears says she is of age.)

Candler, Zacharia–(see after Cruse).

Canon, Bird–Lucy Jarvis, Jan. 3, 1807. (Eliphalet Jarvis).

Cannon, John–Elizabeth Jarves, Mar. 1, 1799. (Jabez Jarves) She writes note that she is twenty. (Henry & Moses Skaggs).

Carlisle, Richard–Rhoda Candler, Aug. 4, 1798. Thos. B. Pelham in a note says Rhoda is his sister, and is 21.

Carnahan, Wm. Thompson–Fanny Quigley, Aug. 27, 1795. (Andrew Kelly).

Carter, Thos.–Judith Bass, Feb. 22, 1810. (Thos. Bass).

Cartwright, Joseph–Mary White, Apr. 19, 1799. dau. John White, note.

Casteel, Joseph–Sarah Black, May 2, 1804. (Patrick Black).

Cavin, (Cavean) John–Polly Chism, Sept. 10, 1796, dau. Rich. C., (Benj. Chism).

Cates, John–Nancy Crouch, dau. John C., Jan. 19, 1808.

Chandler, David–Margaret Phelps, Nov. 14, 1793, dau. Wm. Phelps.

Chaney, Elisha–Polly Dutton, Dec. 2, 1807. "by consent". (Obediah Chaney)

Chapman, Neal–Sally Pointer, Jan. 21, 1800. (Wm. Pointer)

Chisham, Gabriel–Jane Dean, Sept. 5, 1807. Augustine Smith says she is of age. (John Smith, Richard Yeates).

Chism, John–Esther Lynn, Sept. 27, 1798. consent of Benj. Lynn. (Marshall Despain)

Chaudoin, John M.–Sally Chaudoin, Jan. 11, 1808, dau. Andrew C., (David and John Chaudoin)

Cheak, Nicholas–Susannah Summers, May 20, 1805. Consent of Elijah Summers, her father.

Cirbow, Samuel–Saley Riley, Aug. 13, 1795 (note from herself.)

Clark, Moses–Nancy Bartlett, Feb. 23, 1793. Note from herself.

Clement, "Clemmons" Andrew–Sarah Skaggs, June 14, 1793, dau. Sarah and Richard S.

Clifton, Burdet–Susannah Sublett, Jan. 26, 1807. (Valentine Sublett).

Coffe, Anonias–Jane Hineman, Aug. 28, 1809. (of age)

Cole, Jesse–Sally Chinn, Nov. 24, 1806. dau. Ana Chinn.

Cole, Wm.–Martha Bass, dau. Joseph Bass, Jan. 18, 1806.

Collier, Aaron– . . (no bride!) Jan. 29, 1800. (Wm. Hurst).

Combs, Samuel–Jane Hash, Oct. 15, 1804. (Jas. Hash).

Compton, Samuel–Martha McCorkle, Oct. 17, 1810, dau. Martha McCorkle, consent. (Anthony Bicket).

Copage, Ellexander–Sarah Malone, dau. John and Nancy Malone, who say she is in her 18th year. Dec. 16, 1808. (Simeon Malone).

Corn, Andrew–Jane Cooper, Sept. 7, 1796, dau. Samuel Cooper (Patey?) Cooper, wts.

Cowherd, Simeon–Sally Smith, Oct. 27, 1806. (Jas. Smith)

Cox, Gambrel–Franky Bartlett, Jan. 30, 1798, dau. Jas. Bartlett. (Henry Cox).

Creel, Cager (Micajah?)–Milly Burbridge, (dau. Thos. & Esther Burbridge. Dec. 8 1800. See Adair wills.)

Crowder, Philip–Rachel Sanders, June 25, 1796, dau. Henry Sanders. (Michael Reed).

Crowder, Philip–Sally Chandler, dau. John C., July 16, 1797 (Darkey and Horatio Chandler.)

Cruse, John–Elizabeth Perry, Oct. 28, 1805. dau. Wm. Hallbrooks, consent.

Candler, Zacharia Moman (Morrison?)–Rhoda Pelham, Apr. 9, 1793, dau. Francis and Nancy Pelham. (Hijah Pelham).

Damron, Geo.–Polly Mourning, Feb. 23, 1809, Roger Mourning.

Dale, Isaac–Margaret Gum, Oct. 7, 1808. Jacob Gum says she is of age.

Damron Willis–Sarah McClain, Mar. 14, 1800, dau. Chas. McClain. Son of Geo. D. decd. Robt. Thomas, gdn. of *Wm.?* Damron.

Davis Norton–Sarah Williamson, May 7, 1799, note from herself. (Chas Gum, Jacob Williamson)

Davis, Edward–Sarah Courtney, Dec. 1, 1790.

Davis, James–Anny Wollard, May 19, 1800.

Davis, Ezekiel–Aby Stout, July 25, 1810. (Wm. Woodard).

Davis, Jarrot–Susannah Pepper, Nov. 28, 1797. (John Pepper).

Davis, Chas.–Sarah Cummins, June – 1797. dau. Thos. and Susannah Cummins, (Davis Skaggs).

Dawson, James–Hannah Hardin, Jan. 30, 1804. (Aaron Hardin).

Despain, Jno. D.–Sharlott Daniel, 6-28-1801

Desarn, Edmund–Mary Saltsman, Oct. 24, 1808, dau. Wm. Salsman.

Despain, Marshal–Rachel Lynn, dau. Benj. Lynn, Jan. 8, 1799.

Despain, Solomon–Nancy Bell, dau. Zehaniah Bell, July 4, 1807.

Despain, Solomon–Levicey Grayham, Sept. 25, 1805, dau. Sary Grayham. (Solomon Despain)

Dickson–see Dixon.

Dillingham, Peter–Becky McCoffree, July 15, 1800.

Dixon, John–Sarah Crane, May 16, 1797, dau. Wm. Crane. (David Dickson)

Dobbs, Will–Betsey Riley, Oct. 18, 1809. (John Riley).

Dobson, Joseph, Jr.–Mary Davis, Apr. 2, 1804. (Joseph Dobson, Sr.)

Donan, John–Susannah Despain, May 17, 1806. (Peter Despain).

Douglas, Nathaniel–Ann Gilmore, Oct. 8, 1798, dau. Jas. Gilmore.

Douglas, Hugh–Milda Hurt, dau. Wm. Hurt, Jan. 25, 1796. (Nathan Hurt)

Downing, Wm.–Susannah Rice, June 7, 1808, dau. David Rice.

Duckworth, Wm.–Nancy Waters, Dec. 19, 1798, Pleasant Waters, (Jas. Waters) wrote note as guardian of Nancy W.

Duckworth, Isaac–Polly Cantrel, Sept. 1, 1806. Sister of Thos. Cantrel; son of Wm. Duckworth.

Dudley, James–Leely Ratliff, July 18, 1808. Thornton Dudley consents.

Duncan, Andrew–Betsy Goff, May 27, 1808 (Wm. Goff).

Durham, Wm.–Polly Shreve, June 11, 1810, dau. Wm. Shreve. (Thos. Haile)

Durrett, Benj.–Sally Hubbard, Dec. 24, 1810. (John Durrett).

Dutton, Aaron–Margaret Powel, Mar. 5, 1804. dau. Thos. Powel.

Dyer, Chas.–Polly Campble, (of age), July 17, 1798. Wm. Dyer says son is not of age, gives consent.

Easten–see Eastess.

Eastess, John–Jane Bell, Feb 6, 1806. (Geo. Goble)this may be Easten.

Eaton, Wm.–Frances Baley, Sept. 10, 1806. (Thos. Baley). Joseph Denton gives consent for Wm. Eaton to marry.

Elkins, Nathaniel–Elizabeth Hart, dau. David Hart, June 25, 1798.

Elkins, Wm.–Becka Perry, Jan. 28, 1809. (Abel Elkins). Elizabeth Perry gives consent for her dau. Rebecca Perry to marry Wm. Elkins. (Abel & David) On back of the bond is written: –"to be changed to Abel Elkins"–proven by Abel Elkins that Rhael Elkins is willing for the license.

Enyart, Silas–(see Inyard).

Elliott, Alexander–Polly Stotts, Oct. 28, 1800.

Embry, Wm.–Keziah B. Cook, Jan. 20, 1810. (Wm. B. Cook).

Emerson, . . . –Nancy Emerson, dau. of John Emerson, Apr. 23, 1807. (Frances and Renety H. Emerson).

Estes–see Eastess

Esten–see Eastess

Etherton, Wm.–Polly Elkins, Jan. 9, 1810, son of Wm. Etherton, (Abel & Wm. Elkins) dau. of Rachel Elkins.

Ewing, David–Hannah Todd, Dec. 9, 1809.

Ferguson, see Furguson.

Findley, John S.–Jenny Walker, Jan. 8, 1800, dau. Jas. Walker.

Finley, Reuben–Elizabeth Chism, May 19, 1795, dau. Richard Chism, (Benj. Chism).

Fisher, John–Sally Latham, Sept. 22, 1799, dau. Jonathan Lathom.

Fletcher, James–Nancy Hash, dau. Thos. Hash, Nov. 6, 1809. (Philip Hash).

Forrest, Jekiel–Mary McCanliss, Aug. 17, 1807, dau. Mary McCanless.

Fossett, Robt.–Fanny Chandler, dau. John Chandler, Sept. 30, 1806.

Frazer, John–Susannah Frazer, Oct. 26, 1799.

Furgason, Will–Patsy McMahan, Jan. 9, 1799. Note from herself.

Gaddie, James–Betsy Hash, Oct. 9, 1798, dau. Thos. Hash. (Michael Simpson)

Gaddie, George–Susannah Keen, Sept. 20, 1809 (Gaddy)

Gaddie, George–Margaret Clendenan, Dec. 3, 1807. (Geo. Clendenan)

Galloway, James–Ruth McCarly, dau. of Abraham and Wineford McCarlay, Dec. 11, 1797. (McCarley), (Thos. McEarley). Note book says "McCourly"

Gibbons, Isaac–Eliza Buckner, Dec. 22, 1807. (Rich. A. Buckner)

Gibson, James–Katherine Beats, July 1, 1796, consent of James Beats.

Gibson, Wm.–Sally McClure, Mar. 16, 1805, dau. John McClure (John Overstreet).

Gimlin, Daniel–Ann Hasten (?) ,Apr. 5, 1799

Gimlin, Samuel–Betsy Moore, Mar. 8, 1808. (Thos. Moore)

Goble, John–Elizabeth Blakeman, of age, June 15, 1810.

Goff, Elijah–Unity Rogers, July 8, 1804. (Edward Rogers).

Goff, Leonard–Betsy Skaggs, Oct. 10, 1809.

Gordon, Noah–Nancy Bartlett–Nov. 19, 1799, dau. John Bartlett. (Solomon Bartlett).

Graham, Johnson–Cassy Stone, Dec. 18, 1797, dau. Elizabeth Stone, (John Elmer, and Jas. Clement).

Grayham, Wm.–Leah Boyd, Feb. 23, 1807 (Peter Graham).

Grayham, John–Margaret Cummins, Nov. 30, 1808. of age. (Jos. Vance)

Grayham, Freeborn–Sally Grayham, July 19, 1810, dau. Peter Grayham (Wm. Grayham).

Graves, Francis–Drucilla Cowherd, Nov. 20, 1806, dau. James C., (Yelverton Cowherd).

Gray, Rowdon–Jinny C. Moore, Jan. 13, 1807, dau. of Mar ? Tramore.

Green, John–Rachel McKy (McKee), dau. Wm. McKy, Nov. 20, 1796. (McKee?)–note: Book says "Becky").

Greenstreet, John–Mary Gibson, June 19, 1798, dau. John Gibson. (Jas. Gib.)

Greenstreet, Peter–Mary Bell, Aug. 1, 1800 (Zephaniah Bell).

Griggs, Thos.–Margaret Bodkins, Feb. 1, 1799, dau. Wm. Bodkins, (John Griggs, Squire Griggs)

Griggs, Squire–Mary Ann Bates, Dec. 1, 1795. She says she is of age, and has neither father nor mother "in this place".

Grinnell, Joseph–Barbary Taylor, July 24, 1809, dau. Samuel Taylor.

Grundy, Felix–Nancy Rodgers, spinster, Apr. 27, 1797, dau. John Rodgers, (John Reed, Polly E. Rodgers, and Samuel Grundy.)

Guinn, Arthur–Mary Dobson, June 14, 1808, consent of "widow" Mary Dobson.

Gumm, Chas.–Elizabeth Rhea, July 22, 1800 (Wm. Rhea).

Gum, Jehue (John?)–Mary Jones, July 25, 1804. (Wm. Jones).

Gum, Elijah–Lucy Bruner, Feb. 25, 1807.

Gum, Jacob–Margaret McComus, Mar. 25, 1793.

Hadley, John–Priscy Guthry, Nov. 28, 1800. (Stephen Guthry)

Haile, Thos.–Caty Sandifur, Mar. 31, 1806, dau. Jas. Sandefur. (Peter Newell, Jas. Durham.)

Hail, Durham–Peggy Sympson, Apr. 13, 1810, dau. Wm. Sympson.

Hagan, John–Agnes Sally, Sept. 27, 1809. (note inside says "my dau. Agnes West, and signed Nancy West.)

Hall, Wm.–Mary McDannel, dau. John McDonald, Mar. 15, 1809.

Hall, John–Dolly Abbot, June 3, 1807, step-dau. of Bryant Trent, (Wm. Abbott).

Handy, Jesse–Elizabeth Hall, June 23, 1797. (Thos. Hall)

Harrod–see Herod

Hardin, John–Nancy Hayes, July 20, 1796, dau. Robt. Hays, (Samuel Hardin)

Hardin, Samuel–Lucy Whitlock, Aug. 20, 1796. She says in note she is 21. (John Harding).

Harding, Abel–Elizabeth B. Calvin, Feb. 3, 1807, dau. Henderson James Calvin (Samuel Hardin).

Harsfield, Henry–Eliz. Rumbaugh, Apr. 6, 1799 (see Bashfield?)

Harlan, John–Fanny Hufman, Feb. 25, 1799, dau. Ambrose Hufman. (Aaron Harland). (Robt. & John Hambleton.)

Harris, Rich.–Rebecca Nevill, Nov. 20, 1798, dau. Wm. & Winniford Nevill.

Hash, Philip–Sally Nance, Jan. 10, 1809, dau. Zacharia Nance, and son of Thos. Hash

Hash, James–Polly Martin, Sept. 25, 1809. (Hartwell Martin)

Hash, James–Sally Martin, Oct. 20, 1807, (Hartwell Martin).

Harris, Wm.–Nancy Highsmith, dau. Thos. H., Sept. 23, 1797. (Samuel Faulkner).

Hawk, Frederick–Sally Wright, Jan. 20, 1809, dau. Thos. Wright (Sampson W Hawkes)

George–Joanna Dobson, Feb. 25, 1806. Joseph Dobson.

Hay, Dimack–Sarah Chandler, Feb. 18, 1807, dau. Isaac Chandler; son of Robt. Hay.

Hay, Robert– . . . (The bond is blank for bride, but Register says Nancy Moore), Mar. 20, 1806. (John Hardin, bondsman).

Hazle, Jedson–Nancy Graham, 1806 (Full date not gotten), (Jeremiah Graham)

Hazel, Richard–Sarah Jones, Jan. 28, 1807.

Hazle, Peter–Betsy Rightmier, Mar. 7, 1808. (Caleb Hazel).

Heather, (Heither, Huther?), Thos.–Mary Warren, Aug. 10, 1808. Consent of father and mother James and Barbary Warren who spell his name "Heather".

Helms, Wm.–Caty Gibson, dau. John and Mary who say she is 21, June 9, 1806.

Helton, Thos.–Betsy Pepper, Sept. 30, 1805.

Henry, Benj.–Martha Jones, Mar. 2, 1809.

Henry, Daniel–Nancy Cayce, May 13, 1807. (Jas. Horton).

Herndon, Cadder–Betsy Bennet, June 30, 1809. (Wm. Bennet).

Herndon, Thos.–Nancy Keen, May 28, 1810, "consent of parents in the office." (Geo. Gaddy).

Herndon, Nathaniel–Betsy Gaddy, May 17, 1806. Consent of Geo. Gaddy.

Herod, John–Nancy Peace, May 31, 1798, dau. Simon Peace, (Harrard)

Herod, Jas.–Nancy Burks, – 16, 1799, dau. John Burks, (Silas Burks)

Hodgens, Isaac–Phebe Trabue, Dec. 26, 1804, dau. Elizabeth Trabue. (Robt. Trabue).

Hodgens, Isaac– . . . Dec. 28, 1807. (Bride's name not shown.)

Holbrook, Jeremiah–see Holdbrook.

Holdbrook, Jeremiah–Elizabeth Scott, Oct. 6, 1804. dau. Alex. Scott, son of Geo. H. Holbrook.

Hogeland, James–Margaret Campbell, Feb. 10, 1800. (Chas. Campbell)

Holland, Will–Patsy Belcher, Jan. 12, 1799, dau. John Belcher. (Berry Belcher, Silas Burks)

Holland, Benj.–Peggy Forbes, Jan. 26, 1804.

Holland, Wm.–Betsy Prince, Aug. 8, 1807.

Hopkins, Robt.–Elizabeth Stone, Dec. 27, 1798, dau. Wm. & Dicy Stone.

Hopkins, John–Martha Moore, of age, Feb. 13, 1807.

Hord, Richard–Nancy Chisham, sister of B. Chisham who says she is of age, and looks to him as she has no parents. Dec. 26, 1808. (Henry Moore).

Hovins, Wm.–Sarah Hardin, Aug. 3, 1795, dau. Stephen Harding, (John C. Hardin).

Hudgen, Wm.–Susan Tucker, Aug. 27, 1810, dau. Wm. Tucker.

Hughs, Thos.–Susannah Moore, Oct. 22, 1810. (Henry Moore)

Hudson, Pleasant–Margaret Vance, Dec. 17, 1810, dau. Wm. Vance, (Rich. Vance).

Hudson, Henry–Jane Vance, Jan. 23, 1810, "consent of parents in the office." (Will Vance).

Hudson, Fanny–Alex. Vance, Oct. 23, 1810. (John Peter Hudson.)

Humphrey, . . . –mar. Nancy Carlisle, dau. of Stephen Harding who gave consent, Sept. 15, 1807.

Hunt, Simeon–Betsy Rivers, Oct. 16, 1797, dau. John Rivers.

Hutcheson, Thos.–Catherine Phillips, June 21, 1809. (Wm. Phillips)

Hutcheson, David, Jr.–Anne Rhea, dau. Wm. R., Aug. 6, 1805.

Hutcheson, Hutty B.–Elizabeth H. Lee, dau. Joshua Lee, Mar. 20, 1810, (Thos. Hutcheson).

Hutcheson, Joseph–Nancy Mason, 10-11-1794 (book).

Inyard, (Enyart) Silas–Martha Duckworth, Nov. 1, 1806, dau. Wm. D. (spelled both ways on same bond)

Irvine, John–Mary Bell, dau. Zepeniah Bell, Aug. 2, 1793. ("Joseph" in Register)

Jack, Robt.–Nancy Flemin, Sept. 5, 1804.

Jackson, Will P.–Jenny Sally (Salle?) Nov. 9, 1810. (John Sally)

Jarboe, John–Elender Crouch, Sept. 13, 1808.

Jarvis, John–Patey Bloyd, June 15, 1809. (Eliphalet Jarvis) "parents in office consent."

Johnson, John–Hannah Lastley, Aug. 21, 1798, note from herself.

Johnson, John–Peggy Moore, June 11, 1806.

Johnson, Isham–Sally Warren, Feb. 11, 1805. Wm. Warren, "father's consent"

Johnson, Isiah–Sarah Hilbert, dau. Wm. Hilbun, Feb. 21, 1810, consent of G––? (Gesse?) Johnson.

Joliff, Richard–Rebecca Hover, Feb. 27, 1810. (Felix Hover).

Jones, Will–Sarah Holland, Aug. 20, 1799, dau. Wm. Holland. (Wm. and Barchy Holland) John Stahl.

Jones, Wm.–Nancy Studdart, Nov. 9, 1795, dau. of "Samuel x Studart"

Jones, Enoch–Sally Ratliff, dau. W. R., Aug. 22, 1809.

Jones, Morgan–Nancy Lewis, July 10, 1809, dau. Jeremiah Lewis.

Jones, Robt.–Franky Henry, of age, Oct. 3, 1809. (Robt. Henry)

Kelly, Andrew–Betsy Clinch Donan, Aug. 27, 1795, dau. Amy Donnan. (Will T. Carnahan).

Kemble, Thos.–Elizabeth Brockman, Mar. 21, 1810, "consent of girl's parents in the office." Samuel Brockman.

Kersey, John–Elizabeth Bale (Ball?), 1808 (complete date not gotten). Wm. Hawks.

Kinney, John–Ann Jeffreys, dau. John J., Dec. 8, 1809.

Kirkpatrick, Amos–Sarah Ellis, Nov. 27, 1798, dau. Ephraim Eles, note son of Robt. Kirkpatrick, note.

Knifley, Philip–Sarah Mourning, dau. Rodger Mourning, Mar. 10, 1799. (John Mourning, and Thos. Vandiver.)

Lacefield, see Blakeman

Landers, John–Lucy Rivers, dau. John Rivers, Feb. 3, 1806.

Latimore, Jacob–Jane Poore, Feb. 15, 1809, note from herself. (John & Jas. Poore, wts.)

Lawson, Moses–Anny Thomas, June 5, 1798, dau. Henry Thomas note Sary Thomas, wts. (Aaron Robbins)

Laxton, James–Zelpha Meredith, Jan. 3, 1799, dau. Wm. L. M.

Laxton, Thos.–Hannah Elkin, Dec. 7, 1799, dau. Jesse Elkin.

Layman, Reudian (?)–Eliz. Husland, Feb. 14, 1800, dau. Abraham Hiestand, note.

Leamon, Daniel–Agnes Black, Aug. 6, 1806. (Patrick Black).

Leamon (see Lemon)

Lee, Thos.–Patsy Bartlett, Nov. 14, 1807. son of Abigail Crafward (?) who gives consent. (Joshua Bartlett, bondsman)

Lee, Chas.–Elizabeth Warren, Aug. 8, 1810. (Isaiah Johnson).

Legg, Samuel–Mary Blunt, Feb. 17, 1810, "consent of father in the office." (Levi Blunt, bondsman).

Lemon, Jacob–Mary Smith, Jan. 4, 1804. (Thos. Smith).

Lemon (see Leamon) Many of these are in Nelson county, Ky.

Lewis, Abraham–Peggy Gibbons, July 31, 1799, dau. Morgan Gibbons.

Lile, Wm.–Sally Slinker, Sept. 18, 1797, dau. "Fadre Linker"–in his note he spells daus. name "Slinker", but his own "Linker". (Jas. Lile).

Lile, Peter–Sally Sexton, Aug. 5, 1807. (Lexton?) Geo. Seaton.

Lile–see Lisle & Lyall

Linville, Moses–Peggy Lee, dau. Wm. Lee, Jan. 6, 1809.

Lisle, Daniel–Dolly Miller, Aug. –, 1804. (Thos. Miller).

Lobb, Reuben–Sally Whitmon, July 3, 1807.

Long, James–Sarah Wooldridge, May 2, 1797, dau. Richard W., (Will Pope, John W. Pope, and Wm. Pope).

Lucas, Robt.–Sally Marshall, Feb. 18, 1808. (John B. Marshall)

Lynn, Joseph Thomas–Dicey Skaggs, Jan. 18, 1810. (Balus Harrison)

Lyon, John–Nancy H. Dawson, dau. Wm. Dawson, Aug. 29, 1810.

McCann, Neal–Delitha Duggins, dau. of Wm. & Mary, of Green county, May 6, 1807.

McCarty, William–Margaret Belcher, dau. John B., Mar. 4, 1796. (Elijah McC.)

McConnell, Francis–Margaret Love, dau. John Love, Sept. 14, 1804.

McCorkle, Samuel–Jane Black, July 22, 1806. (Patrick Black).

McCorkle, John, Jr.–Ann Speer, dau. Samuel Speer, June 13, 1805. (John McCorkle, Sr.)

McDaniel, James–Nancy Wardrope, dau. Edward Wardrope, Feb. 9, 1810 (Wm. Wardrope).

McDonald, Niel–Sally Woodard, Apr. 27, 1799, dau. of Wm. & Sally W.

McGill, James–Jane Hardin, of age, Oct. 15, 1804. (Alex. Carson).

McGlothin, Thos. T.–Nancy, Hunter, dau. Titus H., 1810. (Hardin W. Chenning)

McMahan, John–Anne Martin, Dec. 18, 1797, dau. Betty Wright, note; (Martin McMahan).

McMurtry, James–Hatty Bloyd, dau. Wm. Bloyd, July 6, 1805. (Tubby Bloyd, son of Wm. McMurtry.

Mahon, Wm.–Elizabeth Brumfield, July 13, 1804, dau. of Samuel Latmer, note; Lydda Latmer, wts.

Mann, Joseph–Betsy Hill, Dec. 21, 1799, dau. of Jas. & Mary Hill (Moses Man)

Mann, Wm.–Nancy Wilcoxin, Apr. 4, 1808; dau. William Wilcockson, note (Geo. Wilcockson).

Martin, Wm.–Sally Shofner, Oct. 17, 1807. (David Shofner).

Marshall, Joseph–Franky Richeson, dau. Thos. R., Jan. 26, 1807. (John R.)

Marshall, Samuel–Margaret Bartlett, June 6, 1804, dau. Priscilla B.

Mason, John–Hannah Hutcheson, dau. David H., Mar. 15, 1797 (Matthew Hutcheson)

Mathis, Will–Hepsy Philpot, Nov. 11, 1799, dau. Mary Filpot, note.

Maxwell, Thos.–Clarkey Williamson, Feb. 3, 1809, consent of Thos. W. (Darkey?–Dorcus?)

Mayes, John–Elizabeth Griggs, dau. Catherine McKinea who is her guardian. (John Grigs). Mar. 21, 1797.

Mays, Matthew–Polly Galloway, Mar. 29, 1796, Robt. and Mattie Galloway give consent in note. (John Galloway–Boston Damwood.)

Medlock, Wm.–Patience Randolph, dau. Joseph, May 3, 1809.

Mears–see Meers (now spelled Mears, and many spelled in that way)

Meers, John–Susannah Preeces, Jan. 24, 1808. (David Preeces–also spelled Preices)

Meers, James–Rutha Parrish, Feb. 11, 1805. Thos. Meers. Nathaniel Carr, step-father of Rutha, gives consent.

Melican, Julius–Caterena Heart, dau. David(x)Hart, note. June 1, 1798. (Geo. x Hover).

Miller, Jacob–Polly Antle, Sept. 22, 1799, dau. Henry Antle.

Miller, John–Dicey Stapp, dau. Thos. Stapp, June 5, 1798. (Wm. Worley, and Benj. Stapp, wts.)

Miller, Wm.–Mary Wooldridge, Dec. 8, 1800. (Richard Wooldridge).

Miller, John–Dorcus Lile, dau. Elizabeth Lile, June 10, 1807.

Minor, Larkin–Ann Gimblin, Apr. 27, 1807.

Mitchell, Adam–Nancy Marshall, dau. Thos. M., Aug. 14, 1799 (Robt. F. Marshall)

Mitchell, John–Juda Mills, dau. Topiah Bass, Jan. 25, 1798. (Josiah?)

Mitchell, Chas.–Hetty Mills, Feb. 10, 1800, grand dau. of Hetty Phipps, and Joshua Phipps, who write note of consent.

Mitchell, Robt.–Lucy Bass, dau. Josiah Bass, Jan. 13, 1806. (John and Robt. F. Mitchell)

Money, Wm.–Lydia Pries, May 1, 1809, son of James Money, consent. David Priest, and Hepsibah Money)

Montgomery, Allen–Rutha Vaughn, Oct. 11, 1809. (Henry Vaughn.)

Montgomery, Simpson–Sally Skaggs, May 29, 1795. (Samuel Burks)

Moore, Will–Patsy Lane, May 30, 1799, she says she is 21. (Robt. Allen)

Moore, Archibald–Martha Sympson, Oct. 3, 1807. (John Clendenen)

Moore, Henry–Sally Shipp, Nov. 12, 1810. (Ambrose Ship.)

Moore, Robt.–Patsy Smith, Mar. 7, 1806. (Isaac Smith).

Moore, John–Polly Tate, Sept. 26, 1808. (Isaac Tate).

Morris, Thos.–Fanny Payton, Apr. 1, 1794. (note from herself).

Morris, Philip–Polly Link, Sept. 16, 1800.

Munford, Thos.–Elizabeth Winlock, dau. Wm. Winlock, Sr., Jan. 26, 1808. (George Winlock).

Munford, Richard–Elizabeth Carter, dau. Robt. Carter, Dec. 8, 1810.

Murray, Eli C.–Ann M. Gooch, dau. Thos. and Tabitha Gooch, Mar. 28, 1808.

Nance, James–Zebah Money, Dec. 22, 1810 (Wm. Money), dau. James Money, note. Hephzibah Money, James Money, Jr., wts.

Naylor, James–(Wm. Bennet) married Sarah Selby, dau. James Selby, Feb. 5, 1798. (Joshua Selby) (note: book says "1797")

New, John–Nancy Hill, Feb. 7, 1800, dau. James Hill (David New)

Nowling, Patrick–Nancy Jones, May 19, 1800.

Owens, Wm.–Betsy Ambet, Nov. 4, 1807, (Wm. Pointer).

Owens, Nathaniel–Nancy Grayham, dau. Wm. Grayham, Dec. 8, 1795.

Payton–see Peyton.

Parrott, Richard–Jane Cumpton (Compton?) Dec. 12, 1804. son of Rhodham Parrott, note of consent, and dau. of Meredith C. (Robt. C.)

Patterson, Samuel–Polly Cardon, Sept. 24, 1810. "consent of parents in the office." (Samuel White, bondsman).

Peace, Simeon–Polly Akin, Jan. 15, 1810, dau. James Akin.

Pels, (Polo?) Joseph–Polly Warren, Dec. 4, 1799, dau. of Wm. Warren. (Hugh and Rhody Warren, wts.)

·Pemberton, Wm.–Viney Skaggs, Feb. 10, 1800. consent of Geo. Pemberton.

Pepper, James–Lyddia Vaughn, June 10, 1799, dau. Thos. Vaughn, (Henry & Michael Sympson.)

Pepper, Robt.–Genny Vaughn, Dec. 12, 1795, dau. of Thos. & Ruth Vaughn, (John Vaughn, Robt. Young.)

Pepper, Robt.–Nancy Pepper,   1808 (full date not gotten). The body of bond says "Nancy Pepper", but the note says "Nancy Carel", and consent of John Pepper, and Starling Carel. Witnesses: Starling Carel, Pations Carel, John Pepper.

Peace–see Preece. . . .

Pearce–see Preece and Pirce.

Perry, John–Urgnvicy? Lowry, Aug. 3, 1808.

Perry, Ebenezer–Precilla Priece, Oct. – 1804. (John Precis)

(This name seems to be spelled "Preces" most often, and also Perry. "Preeces")

Peyton, Daniel–Betsy Burks, Nov. 8, 1796, dau. John Burks, note.

Phelps, Nicholas–Mary Bigerstaff, Mar. 16, 1793. She says in note that she is of age. (Wm. Phelps).

Phillips, Solomon–Delilah Davis, Feb. 26, 1804.

Phillips, Lot–Patsy Emerson, Aug. 31, 1809. (Wm. Phillips).

Phillips, Francis–Margaret Dudgeon, Aug. 17, 1809, dau. Mary Dudgeon.

Phillips, Samuel–Sabret Lee, dau. Joshua Lee, June 14, 1809. (Elizabeth Lee, Joshua B. Lee, Jr., wts.)

Philpot, Joseph – Milly Lynn, Apr. 18, 1797, dau. Benj. Lynn.

Pile, Wm.–Lurena Atkison, Apr. 15, 1806. (Absolem Atkison).

Philpot, Joseph–Ann Dobson, –––– no date (note from herself.)

Pirce, Wm.–Mary Wright–dau. Joseph W., July 6, 1799.

Pirce, Geo.–Jane Holdsbrook, Feb. 25, 1805. (Geo. Holbrook).

Pointer, George–Delphia (x) Burton, Aug. 24, 1798. her note is signed "Burch" and she says she is over 21. Clerk says "Burton".

Pointer, Wm.–Micky Abbot, Sept. 6, 1796, (Joel Yeates) Micky in a note says she is 21, and dates it Aug. 6, 1796. (Wm. Abbett)

Poor, Abraham–Sally Berry, Jan. 4, 1810, (Michael Campbell)

Polly, Wm.–Jemima Kelsy, June 12, 1799, dau. Robt. K., (He signs "Kelso" . . (Samuel Kelso, wts.)

Pols ?– Polo?–see Pels.

Prater, Archibald–Hannah Campbell, Aug. 31, 1809. (Debby Prater).

Preces, Daniel–Elizabeth Jones, of age,   1809 (full date not gotten) (Wm. Jones).

Preece, John–Fanny Davis, Nov. 26, 1804. (Jonas Preece)

Preece, Joseph–Nancy Skaggs, dau. Wm. Skaggs, Mar. 16, 1806.
this may be "Peace, or Pearce" (Nathaniel Pearce, Wm. Russel) consent of Precela Peece to Joseph's marriage. (Simon Peece) (see Peace)

Price, Will–Polly Graves, Feb. 8, 1800, dau. Benj. Graves, (Silas and N. Burks.)

Price, Gideon Hurt–Rachel Wright,   1810 (full date not gotten) (Wm. H. Price).

Pride, Wm.–Ruthy Howel, Mar. 2, 1807, dau. Francis Howel.

Prier, Thos.–Polly Hicks, Aug. 18, 1808. (This is also spelled Preer, and it is the same that is now "Puryear." It is spelled many ways in the Green county records.

Pringle, James–Sarah Vance, Apr. 8, 1805. (Joseph Vance), dau. of David Vance.

Puryear . . . see Puyar, Prier, Puyear, Preer, and many other ways as possible.

Puyar, Samuel–Levinah Harding, dau. Abraham Harding, Jan. 17, 1806. also "Puyear" (Aaron Harding).

Queary, Wm.–Susannah Skaggs, Nov. 2, 1799, dau. John Skaggs, (Chas. Skaggs, Levy and Robt. Grevat.)

Rafferty, Thos.–Elizabeth Cowherd, Apr. 10, 1809, dau. Jonathan Cowherd (Wm. Rafferty).

Rashford, Robt.–Kate Shofner, Nov. 5, 1808. (Henry Shofner).

Reaves, John–Caty Perrey, dau. Eliz. Perry,   1805. (Reves).

Reeves, James–Jane Durham–June 3, 1797, she says she is of age.

Reeves, James–Rewhamy Price, Dec. 16, 1796. Wm. Sary (Lasy?) Leonard give consent ("Lenard".) (John Lyons).

Reeves (see Reaves.)

Rhea, Robert–Eliza Rhea, dau. Elizabeth Rhea who says she is over 21; Dec. 25, 1798. (Thos., James and Wm. Rhea, bondsman) Thos. and James, wts. to mother's signature, and perhaps bros. of Eliza, Wm. Rhea, perhaps father of Robert.

Rice, Solomon–Sarah Stotts, Oct. 31, 1796, (He signs his name "Royce", but clerk says "Rice".

Rice, David–Sarah Hardin, dau. Abraham Hardin, note, Mar. 26, 1806. (Samuel Puyear). (Aaron Hardin).

Richeson, Thos.–Permealy Campbell, dau. L. Campbell, Sept. 19, 1806. (John Richeson).

Richeson, Joseph–Betsy Wilson, dau. Isaac, Jan. 2, 1804.

Ridgeway, Henry–Leanah Davis, Nov. 18, 1808. (Lhea? x Davis, her mark–the first letter is illegible.) looks more like "I" or "J".

Riggs, Thos.–Leah Hunt, Mar. 24, 1808, son of "Tim O Riggs" who gives consent, and dau. of Ambrose Hunt. (Coalman & Orvil Hunt.)

Rivers, Wm.–Rebecca Hunt, dau. Ambrose Hunt, Oct. 24, 1797, (Simeon Hunt)

Roberts, Elisha–Patsy Gill, Feb. 6, 1800.

Robertson, Francis–Mary Skaggs, Oct. 11, 1806, dau. Henry Skaggs.

Robinson, Joseph–Polly Rice, dau. Randolph Rice, June 7, 1806. (Thos. Preyear)

Rogers, James–Polly Douglass, Apr. 5, 1809. (Chas. Douglass).

Roran, ? (Rorase?) John–Elizabeth Wilson, Apr. 21, 1806. (Wm. Wilson)

Royce, Solomon–see Rice.

Rutherford, John–Prudence Taylor, (of age,) Oct. 1, 1804.

Rutledge, Isaac–Ann Armstrong, Dec. 18, 1797 (note from herself,) (Jeremiah Selby)

Sadler, John–Hannah Cathin, Aug. 12, 1800, she of age, also spelled "Gathin" on same bond.

Sadler, John–Franky Chisham, dau. Ann Chisam, Jan. 16, 1805. (Gabriel Chisham). see Bourbon Co. for Sadler.

Saddler, John–Nelly Powell, Sept. 15, 1797. (note from herself), (Will Wagnon)

Salsman, John–Docia Brunt, son of Wm. Salsman, June 23, 1806.

Salley (Salle?), Allen–Agnes West, May 13, 1807. consent of her mother Agnes West who says she is over 18. (She married again)

Samples, John–Fanny White, Dec. 19, 1798, note from herself.

Sanders, Samuel–Nancy Wilton, Feb. 23, 1793, Joseph Dobson in a note gives consent– relationship not stated.

Saxton, (Sexton) George–Sally Burks, May 18, 1798, dau. Isham Burks.

Scott, Wm.–Sarah Bartlett, Nov. 24, 1806.

Selby, Jeremiah–Ann Levans, Dec. 18, 1797, niece of Thos. Selby, note. (John Selby–Isaac Rutledge)

Ship, Thos.–Ruth Saunders, dau. Henry Saunders, Dec. 18, 1797.

Ship, John–Nelly Sanderson, Jan. 26, 1798, dau. Elisha S., (Henry Sanderson).

Ship, John–Elizabeth Durham, Apr. 18, 1798, dau. Samuel Durham.

Shively, Jacob–Sophia Davis, Sept. 17, 1799, dau. Rezin Davis, (John Hardin, Robt. Wick- liffe).

Shofner, David–Polly Gaddy, of age, July 8, 1809.

Short, Wm.–Polly Buchannan Campbell, dau. James Campbell, Mar. 24, 1806. (Archibald Campbell, Samuel Lindsey.)

Short, Joseph–Elizabeth McCarrel, Feb. 8, 1805 (of age)

Sidebottom, Chas.–Susannah Rowntree, Sept. 15, 1796. She in good penmanship says she is 21. (Hays Murphy, test).

Skaggs, Chas.–Sarah Grevat. Feb. 3, 1798, their own agreement, by note.

Skaggs, Abednego–Catherine Hoback, Aug. 1, 1793, note from herself (Andrew Hoback).

Skaggs, Henry–Sally (Tabey?) Laisfield, May 20, 1797, dau. of Wm. & Faney Laisfield, (Lacefield?)

Skaggs, Jacob–Lear Butcher, May 27, 1808, note not signed says both are 21. (David Skaggs, bondsman).

Skaggs, James–Fanny Bealer, Feb. 26, 1808, Fanny in a note says she is a free agent.

Skaggs, James– – – – – (no bride given) Feb. 24, 1806. (Henry Skaggs).

Skaggs, James–Anna McColgan, Jan. 31, 1795, dau. of Edward McColgan, who says she is 21. (Jas. & Wm. McColgan).

Skaggs, Jeremiah–Nancy Adair,.Nov. 13, 1806, dau. "Major Adeare".

Skaggs, Wm.–Betsy Wills, Sept. 21, 1809, note from Philip Wills, and witnessed by Philip Wills, Jr.

Slinker, Henry–Susannah Biggs, Dec. 18, 1804. dau. Stephen Biggs, (Frances Biggs).

Slinker, John–Nancy Slinker, Sept. 2, 1807. (Henry Slinker).

Slinker, Christopher–Pheby Slinker, Mar. 3, 1808 (Frederick Slinker)

Sloan Alexr–Eaby Jones, dau. Wm. Jones, Oct. 9, 1798. (Jas. McElroy)

Smith, Jonathan–Fanny Burks, Oct. 9, 1793, dau. Samuel Burks. (Isham Burks.)

Smith, Jacob–Milly Pemberton, July 19, 1796, dau. George Pemberton, (Isaac Williams) (Wm. Smith and Robt. Pendexter).

Smith, William–Barbara McFarren, June 19, 1807. (John Lemmon)

Smith, John W.–Charity Thompson, Sept. 7, 1808. dau. Mary Thompson, (Hartwell Martin).

Smith, Chas.–Mary Pemberton, Jan. 26, 1808

Smith, Chas.–Mary Pemberton, Jan. 26, 1808. Mary Pemberton in note says she was born July 25, 1786. (Jabez Jarvis, and Geo. Spears).

Smith, Samuel–Nancy Lile, Feb. 20, 1805, dau. Eliz. Lile (Peter *Lyall*)

Smith, Jacob–Jennet Pepper, May 23, 1805. (Henry Vaughn).

Smith, Chas.–Olive Jones, June 13, 1804.

Smith, John–Miley Smith, dau. John Smith, Dec. 10, 1804.

Smith, David–Hannah Lrygby? (illegible), July 1, 1806.

Smith, Isaac–Patty Weatherford, Jan. 3, 1809. (Wm. Moore).

Smith, Augustine–Patsy Smith, Feb. 22, 1810, dau. Thos. Smith, son of Jon Smith, consent. (Stokley Smith, test.)

Smith, Samuel–Betsy Bailey,   1810. Consent of Robert Bailey. (full date not gotten)

Snead, John–Micky Graham, Sept. 8, 1798, dau. Edward Grayham, (Peter Grayham).

Sneed, Wm.–Kiziah Graham, Dec. 24, 1798, dau. Peter Graham, note. (Johnson Graham, Jas. Goldsby).

Spears, Wm.–Jane Moore, dau. John Moore, Sept. 1, 1809. (Geo. Spears)

Sproul, Elexandrew–Mary Meers, dau. Moses Meers, Jan. 2, 1809. (Thos. Meers).

Stacy, Mashae–Charlotte Curtis, Jan. 10, 1809, "(Wm. Jones says he believes the parents of said Curtis are dead.)"

Stearman, Wm.–Ann S. Rafferty, Feb. 15, 1806.

Stephenson, Robt.–Ginney Ba*tes*, dau. James Ba*its*, Oct. 14, 1795.

Stone, Alexander–Ruthy Lee, Oct. 16, 1798. dau. Joshua Lee, note (Fiealds?) (Elijah McCarty).

Sublett, Fiealds–Eleanor Bralden, Sept. 21, 1809, of age, (Branch Sublett)

Sullivan, Wm.–Barbary Owley, son of Mary Sullivan, Dec. 22, 1807.

Summers, Wm.–Nancy Laremore, Aug. 16, 1808. (Richard Laremore).

Sutton, John–Rachel Rosox, Feb. 17, 1809. (Rorak, Rorax).

Tandy, Smyth–Susanna Williams, June 6, 1809. She says she is of age and has no parents or guardian in Kentucky. . . . She is his 2nd wife, for his children married about this time. The marriage was evidently not a happy one . . . see his will.

Tanner, Joel–Mary Tibbs, Apr. 9, 1810, dau. Diskin Tibbs, Apr. 9, (this in bunch of 1810, but not dated as to year).

Tansy, Nathan–Eliza Blakeman, Jan. 19, 1799, dau. Moses Blakeman, (Aaron and Sharlotte Bla*ak*man)

Tansey, Joshua–Mary Hamilton, dau. Ninian B. Hamilton, Sept. 12, 1798.

Tebbs–see Tibbs.

Thompson, Hennary–Mary Ray, Mar. 3, 1798, (Thos. Ray, and Wm. Ray).

Thompson, Ratliff–Margaret Acton, Feb. 15, 1797, dau. Wm. Aston (Acton?) (Daniel Skaggs). (note: book says Caty Compton.)

Tibbs, Wm.–Polly Brunts, Oct. 30, 1804.

Tibbs, Daniel–Lydia Edrington, dau. James E., Apr. 17, 1810.

Tiffy, Chas.–Sally Ooley, May 31, 1810, father in office gives consent (John *Ow*ley)

Todd, Robt.–Jane Yeates, dau. Richard Yeates, Nov. 20, 1796.

Todd, Wm.–Sally Compton, Jan. 27, 1800, dau. M. D. Compton.

Treaner, Isaac–Elizabeth Hicklin, Feb. 16, 1796, dau. Thos. Hicklin and wife, consent.

Trent, Bryant–Rutha Abbot, dau. Alex. Vance, note; June 14, 1793.

Truax, Isaac–Bidy Braves, Dec. 6, 1799, dau. Joseph Bavers.

True, John–Kizza Coile, dau. Michael Coyle, June 16, 1806.

Tucker, Nathaniel–Caty Hoover, dau. Jacob Hoover, July 11, 1809. (Moses Webb).

Turnbough, Jacob–Dorcas Robertson, Aug. 5, 1796, she says she is 21 (Thos. Carlile)

Turpin, Elisha–Mary Bayless, dau. Benj. Bayless, Feb. 14, 1800.

Upton, Daniel–Mary Black, dau. Robt. Black, Mar. 12, 1799, (Patrick Black, Edward Upton).

Vance, Alex.–Fanny Hudson, Oct. 23, 1810, (John Peter Hudson).

Vance, Joseph–Jinny Edgar, Nov. 23, 1808. she says she is over 21 (John Graham).

Vaughn, Thos.–Margaret McComas, Dec. 2, 1804. (Wm. McComas) this is sometimes spelled McComus.)

Vaun, John–Saly King, dau. Baker King, Dec. 4, 1797. (Vaughn?)

Vaughn, Henry–Jane Bell, June 29, 1805. Isaac Bell says she is 21.

Votaw, Henry–Eby Link, dau. Dolly Link, Dec. 13, 1796. (Wm. Kikendall, Geo. Gess. Philip Weese).

Votaw, John–Jane Incks, ("Inks") dau. Catherine Jump, Apr. 9, 1793.

Wagman, Wm.–Mary Holebrook, Dec. 29, 1796. dau. George Holbrook.

Wagstaff, John–Nancy Mitchell, over 21, Apr. 23, 1810 (Robt. Young & Robt. Bottom)

Walker, Alex.–Jinney Tilford, Dec. 26, 1799. (Robt. Tilford).

Walker, John–Elizabeth Smith, Dec. 20, 1894 (Samuel Smith)

Walker, John–Betsy Belcher, Oct. 15, 1808. (Berry Belcher).

Walker, Richard James–Betsy Moore, Oct. 19, 1798, dau. Robt. Moore, (John & Richard Moore).

Walker, James–Nancy Bass, Dec. 27, 1796, dau. Josiah Bass, consent, David & Betsy Allen, test.

Walker, Willis–Nelly Isbell, Mar. 30, 1807.

Walker, John J.? (Q)?–Elizabeth Harper, dau. James Harper, Nov. 15, 1810.

Ward, John–Annie Mathews, Sept. 26, 1807.

Warren, Will–Betsy Elkin, Aug. 8, 1799, dau. Jesse Elkins, (Hugh Warren)

Warren, Jas.–Theny Dollarhide, May 10, 1808, dau. Francis D. and wife Winny Dollarhide.

Warren, Hardin–Lydia Johnson, April 12, 1808. (Isham Johnson).

Watkins, John–Rachel Hopkins, dau. Henry H., Nov. 3, 1804. (Andrew & David Watkins.

Watkins, Joseph– – – – – Atkinson, Apr. 4, 1809. (Thos. W. Atkinson)

Watt, Joseph–Peggy Murry, Dec. 28, 1807. Thos. Vaughn says she has no parents or guardian in Kentucky.

Webb, Merry–Martha Jones, Apr. 16, 1800 (Wm. Jones).

Webb, Moses–Polly Welton, May 8, 1805. "She has no guardian."

Wells, Wm.–Agnes Rhea, April 17, 1799, dau. Wm. Rhea. His note is dated May 7, 1799.

Wheeler, Chesley–Frances Wright, Jan. 12, 1800, dau. Joseph W.

White, John–Isabel Black, Feb. 6, 1798, dau. Robt. Black, (John Black, Daniel Upton)

White, Samuel–Elizabeth Berry. Mar. 24, 1806. (Andrew White). Andrew and John Wright say she is of age.

White, James–Hanna Spears, July 10, 1804. She says she is about 21.

White, Samuel–Jane R. Duke.   1808 (full date not gotten) (A. M. Wakefield).

White, James–Nancy Harding, Feb. 22, 1810. Robt. Clark says she is of age. (Andrew White).

White, Will–Alcey Montgomery, Sept. 29, 1810. She is of age says Allen Montgomery.

White, Robt.–Esther McNabb, July 16, 1806. (Wm. McNabb)

Whitly, Reuben–Elizabeth Eads, Jan. 7, 1806. dau. of Wm. and Rebecca Eads, who say she is 15 years of age. (Jas. Hill)

Whitman, Richard–Martha Jones, Oct. 3, 1804. (Wm. Jones).

Willcox, Jacob–Nancy Hall, July 23, 1799, dau. Thos. Hall.

Wilcox, Zerah–Lydia Hazle, May 7, 1808. (Caleb Hazle).

Wilcoxson, George–Rachel Hall, dau. Thos. Hall, Apr. 4, 1808.

Wilcoxson, Ephraim–Elinor Martin, Aug. 15, 1810, dau. John D. Martin (Alex. Martin).

Willard, Samuel–Mary Laxton Dec. 7, 1799, consent of Thos. Laxton.

Williams, Daniel–Jane Murry, Sept. 30, 1799 (Henry Murray).

Williams, Isaac–Becky McNight, May 7, 1796, dau. Robt. & Jane McKnight, (Robt. Allen)

Williams, Wm.–Nancy Littlejohn, May 22, 1809. Note from herself.

Williams, Samuel–Jemimah Berry, July 7, 1808. (Joseph Berry)

Williamson, John S.–Rebecca White, Dec. 7, 1809. (Samuel White.)

Williamson, Thos.–Betsy Jud, May 2, 1809. (Thos. Maxwell)

Williamson, John–Nelly Johnson, July 16, 1805. (John Johnson).

Wilson, James–Peggy Damewood, dau. Boston Damwood, Oct. 24, 1796.

Wilson.   (Wm. Wilson).

Wilson, Randal–Peggy Muley, Feb. 15, 1800. She writes she is 21. Spencer Wilson says his son Randal W. is 21.

Wilson, Edward–Mirian Edington, of age–April 7, 1809.

Wise, Elijah–Nelly Brown, Sept. 30, 1800, over 21.

Wollard, Will–Rosanah Price, Sept. 10, 1798, dau. Wm. & Ann Pirce, note.

Woolard, Wm.–Polly Stout, Oct. 11, 1810. (Ezekiel Davis)

Wooldridge, James–Nancy Pemberton, Feb. 5, 1799, dau. George P. (Wm. Pemberton).

Woolridge, Richard–(no bride), Oct. 28, 1800 (J. Hash)

Wooley, Peter, Sr.–Priscilla Bartlett, Jan. 2, 1806. Peter Wooley, Jr. Note from Precilla; Nathan Bartlett, wts.

Wordsworth, Thos.–Nancy Skaggs, May 31, 1806. "oldest dau. of Solomon & Rhoda Skaggs, note. (James, Anna and David Skaggs, wts.)

Wright, John–Lyddy Harding, dau. John Harding, June 27, 1800 (Samuel Harding). (sometimes "Hardin")

Wright, Wm.–Elizabeth Brunt, Dec. 2, 1800.

Wright, John–Margaret Strader, Oct. 4, 1809. (Louis Strader).

Wright, Sampson–Lucinda Chandler, dau. John C. Jan. 16, 1808. (Horatio Chandler, Thos. Scott).

Wright, Richard–Anny Jackson–June 7, 1810. note from Anny Jackson . . . (self or parent?) (Wm. Jackson)

Wyatt, John–Lucy Richerson, Sept. 9, 1799, dau. of Joseph Richeson, Joseph Richeson, Jr.

Yearls, Wyatt–Winney Helms, Dec. 29, 1808, dau. Leonard Helms and Caty Helms, who say she is 17 and give consent.

Young, Robt.–Anne McFarlin, Mar. 4, 1796, dau. of Robt. McFarland, who erases "Anne" and puts "Catharine" . . . (Alex. McFarland)

Younger, Chas.–Lucy Walker, Feb. 27, 1807. Note from her father, richire Walker (Michire?, Richard?, Richerd?)

TESTATOR NOT IN GENERAL INDEX

Abstracts of Will Books "A", "B", and that part of "C" through the letter "K" which is not published in "Kentucky Court and Other Records." This also includes the inventories as well as will abstracts.

Adams, Charles, Inv. (A-71) Feb. 1807.

Adams, John—sales (B-

Adams, William, Inv. (B-190)

Anderson, John, Inv. (A-17)

Anderson, Margaret, Inv. (C-93)

Anderson, William, Inv. (C-124)

Angel, John, Inv. (A-109)

Artle, Sophia E. (will— A-203) 100 acres on which Samuel Rollins did live, 2 sons Valentine and Daniel Artle, dau. Sophia McCune, and all her children. Samuel McCune to have no privileges; to gd. dau. Sally McCune, gd. daus. Sally, Betsy and Polly McCune. Chas. Miles and Chas. Lair, exrs. Apr. 20, 1813—July 1813.

Ballard, C.—sales (B-258)

Barnett, Rich., Inv. (B-297)

Barber, Thos., Inv. (C-324)

Barber, Edward, Inv. (C-325)

Bartlett, John, Inv. (C-211)

Baxter, John—Inv. (B-87)

Bean, Wm., Inv. (C-290)

Beard, Wm., Inv. (C-337)

Bell, Joseph, Inv. A-314

Bird, John—Inv. C-137

Boyd, Thos., Inv. (A-376)

Boyd, Irvin, Inv. (B-29)

Boyd, R., Inv. (B-344)

Boyers, J. Inv. (C-1, 2)

Broadwell, S., Inv. (B-184)

Broadwell, Wm., Inv. (C-161)

Brooks, Jacob, Inv. (C-334)

Brown, Samuel, Inv. (A-270)

Brown, Alex., Inv. (C-296)

Brownfield, Nancy, Inv. (A-177)

Bryan, Jesse, Inv. C-206)

Buzzard, John, Inv. (B-325)

Campbell, Lindsey, Inv. (A-219)

Carnagy, J., Inv. (A-168)

Carlisle, Alex. H. (will—C-466) all to wife Nancy and children, at her discretion. Feb. 12, 1835 . . . ————. John Carlisle, Robt. A. and Jas. W. Collins, wts. Codicil (probated Sept. 1836) says "wife and youngest daus.—Armildy, single.

Carrick, John, Inv. (A-71)

Carothers, Thos., Inv. (B-273)

Catherwood, Chas., Inv. (B-128)

Catherwood, Samuel, Inv. (B-78), Nov. 1821.

Casey, A., Inv. (B-351)

Carlisle, A. H. (C-424)

Chambers, Martha, Inv., (B-509)

Chambers, James, Inv. (A-262)

Chambers, Josias, Inv. (C-345)

Chinn, David D., Inv. (B-367)

Chinn, Betsey, (C-276)

Chinn, Elijah (—will—C-431) my wife Elizabeth, 1/3; son George Chinn, 50 acres he lives on—dau. Betsey Smith, son Wm. Chinn, son Rawleigh S. Chinn, dau. Lucy Chinn (furniture etc, that she has) dau. Sarah Johnson, dau. Catherine Hardwick, son Charles Chinn, dau. Nancy Murdock, son Elijah Chinn; son Jas. S. Chinn, 2 grand sons Francis Chinn and John Hardwick. Dated — — — — 1835, probated April 1836.

Chipley, J. Inv. (B-83)

Clark, Thos., Inv. (B-13)

Claypole, J. Inv. (A-158)

Clayton, Jas., Inv. (A-31)

Clements, B., Inv. (B-30)

Clifford, Edward, Inv. (C-68)

Clow, Elizabeth, (C-123)

Clow, Susanna, (C-339)

Cluff, John— Inv. (A-36)

Coleman, F., Inv. (A-163)

Coleman, H., Inv. (B-383)

Coleman, Dela F., Inv. (B-197)

Coleman, E., Inv. (B-443)

Coleman, Jeff—sales (B-292)

Coleman, Richard (Inv., C-23)

Coleman, N. B., Inv. (C-77)

Coon, J., Inv. (C-26)

Coonrod, Henry, Inv. (A-38)

Conrod, Jacob, Inv. (C-140)

Colville, James, Inv. (A-145)

Coppage, Chas., sales (A-349)

Coppage, J., Inv. (B-4)

Courtney, James, Inv. (C-342)

Courtney, Robert (C-381—will) my wife Mary Courtney, exrx., my children: Alfred, Nancy, Jesse and Robert Embra Courtney, Franklin, William and James Henry Courtney (lands). Dated June 16, 1835, probated July 1835. (James, and Sanders Courtney, wts.)

Cox, C. M., sales, (A-401)

Coon, George (B-51), will) wife Sarah Coon, 40 acres; my ch.: dau. Betsey Chambers, wife of Samuel C., 3 sons: John, Isaac and David, have given—rest to all my children equally. Son John Coon and son-in-law Sam'l. Chambers, exrs. 1-10-1820 Jan. 1821.

Craig, Hannah—will (B-254) my gd. dau. Hannah Davis, late Hannah M. Craig, to sons Robert and Wm. Craig. July 27, 1820-Feb. 1826.

Critchlow, James—will (A-269) "old and infirm," my younger son John Critchlow, exr. to Eliz. Plunkett, bed, etc. Apr. 18, 1812-Feb. 1815.

Crosthwait, P., Inv. B-222

Crutcher, James, Inv. (C-360)

Cummins, Wm., sales . . . B-261)

Cummins, John B., Inv. (C-455)
Custer, Eliz., Inv. (C-46)

David, Jacob—will (B-303) lands to my 5 children: Catherine, William, Mary, Sarah and
    Thomas—land where son William now lives—house and lot in town of Washington, Mason
    county; my wife Mary—sons David and Simeon; son Wm., and son in law Henry Spears,
    exrs. June 19, 1827—Aug. 1827.
Daubenspike, Philip, Inv. (B-36) (Doubenspike?)
Davis, H., Inv. (B-2)
Debuler, J. C., (C-454)
Denny, T. (Inv. A-302)
Dickerson, John, Inv. (B-498)
Dills, John, Inv. (B-259)
Doan, Hezekiah, Inv. (A-138)
Doane, N. Inv. (B-207)
Douglass, Wm. Inv. (B-504)
Duncan, Wm. (C-283)
Duncan, F., Inv. (B-456)
Dun, Joseph, Inv. (A-58)
Dun, Samuel, Inv. (A-67)
Dunn, Edmond, Inv. (B-10)
Dunn, James, sale, (B-166)
Dunn, Benijah, C-359
Dunn, Archibald, C-369
Dryden, F., Inv. (A-46)
Dyson, George, (C-53)

Eads, Jonathan—will, (A-60), friend James Eads, Sr., and Carter Hutcheson, exrs. wife 1/3—
    all my ch. equal, Mar. 6, 1806— Apr. 1806.
Eads, John—will (C-437) my wife Helen (land) and rest to ch. equally; to be raised and
    educated—till dau. Susan shall marry . . . "all my children"—Apr. 24, 1836— May 1836.
Eckler, Samuel, Inv. (A-384)
Edgar, H., Inv. (A-188)
Edwards, Jonathan, Inv. (C-466)
Endecott, W. — Inv. (A-226)

Fightmaster, James (Jos.?) Inv. B-103.
Fooks, Wm., Inv. (B-252)
Fooks, Jesse, Inv. (C-142)
Forest, G., Inv. (B-313)
Florence, Wm. Inv. (C-313)
Fowler, Chas. —(C. 138)
Frazier, George—will (A-35) my son George Frazier, my wife Mary Frazier, "any of my
    children"—rest equal to Elizabeth Casey, Rebecca Jaquess, Joel and James Frazier, John
    Frazier, Polly Ferguson, and George Frazier, my children and their heirs. Sons Joel and
    James, exrs. Sept. 17, 1801—Dec. 1801.
Fraizer, James, (C-439)
Furnace, S. (Inv. A-10)
Fuy, Jacob, Inv. (A-) Jan. 1806. (Fry?, Fuye, Frye?)

Galbreath,— see Gilbreath.

Galbreath, John—Inv. (A-347)

Galloway, W., Inv. (A-175)

Garrett, Mary—will—(A-3) my dear children: Eli Garrett, Thomas and Morris Garrett (land); dau. Phoebe Rice; son Thos., son Morris, dau. Rebecca Lare (Lair?). Aug. 14, 1796-Sept. 1796.

Garton, J.—Inv. A-191

Gilbreath, Evan, Inv. (A-24)

Gillians, C. (Inv. A-147)

George, Gabriel, Inv. (B-275)

George, Parerick (Patrick?), Inv. (A-259)

Givens, J., Inv. (B-17)

Goodman, Samuel, Inv. (B-215)

Gossett Abraham, (will) C-384—9-12-1811—my wife Mary Fightmaster, all; my infant children—my son John has already received his part; each of the other children to have the same—2 sons William and Darius Gossett; (have received their parts)—my ch.: John, William, Darius, America, Elizabeth, Nelson, Louisa, Abraham, Lindsey and Mary Gossett—no division to be made for 20 years—son Wm. has 28 acres which he paid for—my ten children—sons John and Wm., exrs. Aug. 21, 1835—Sept. 15, 1835.

Glinn, B. R., (C-202)

Graham, (Garnett (index) (Jaret) Inv. (A-9) (Jarett (in body)

Gregg, Matthew (B-386)

Green, T.—Inv. (A-100)

Griffith, Samuel—Inv. (B-284-350)

Gruwell, John—(C-45) (Grenell?)

Gruwell, J. (C-3, 14)

Gruwell?) Isaac, decd., Katherine G., admx. C-4) Grenell?)

Hale, Robert (Inv. A-42)

Hall, Joshua, (C-422)

Hamilton, George (Inv. A-113)

Hannon, James, Inv. (A-151)

Hall, W., Inv. (A-226)

Harding, L. Z., Inv. (B-16)

Harding, Wm. E., (B-83)

Haydon, Abner (will—C-414) (wife Milly)—dated Marion County, Mo., but says "of Harrison county, Kentucky"—son Garnett, dau. Lucy Mitchell, (land in Indiana) dau. Rachel Madison, son Thos. Haydon, dau. Sarah Levi, dau. Milly Chandler, dau. Joanna Miller (her husband Dudley Miller) my wife Milly—son Jeremiah Haydon; son Abner—wife and son Garnett, exrs. June 30, 1833—Madison county, Mo., March 1834.

Hall, Daniel, (B-221)

Hall, Henry, Jr., Inv. (B-246)

Hall, Julia, Inv., (B-389)

Hendershot, J., (A-41, Inv.)

Hendershot, Wilkinson, of Indiana, Nuncp. will—(B-192) all to heirs—4 half brothers and 2 half sisters, now of Indiana. Joel C. Frazier, wts. He said this on Apr. 19, and proved Apr. 24, 1824.

Henry, John, sales (A-397)

Henry, W. T., (B-157)

Henson, G., (Inv. A-147)

Herrin, J. (Inv. A-257)

Henson, S., (B-200)

Hicks, N., Inv. (A-25)

Hinkson, Samuel (C-386)

Hitch, Walter, Inv. (B-276)

Holt, Thos., Inv. (B-448)

Howell, Wm., Sr., (C-351)

Hodges, Benjamin (will–C-429) wife Susannah, dau. Sophia, son John O. Hodges, (100 acres); son Duvall, 2 daus.–rest–to Patsy Vanderen, April 1831–April 1836.

Hopkins, Thos., Rebecca Hopkins, widow, Inv. (A-149) Oct. 1811.

Huffstudler, John, Inv. (B-42)

Humble, Noah, Inv. (B-71, C-291)

Hunt, Wm. B., (C-205)

Hutcherson, E.–Inv. A-52

Hutchison, Benj., (C-71)

Ingles, Katharine, nuncp. will (B-480) Mar. 20, 1830, aged 18 years, "low in body"–F. W. Sterne and Bryan Ingels, wts. made request, Apr. 3, 1830 . . . probated Jan. 1831.

Jackson, Jonathan, Inv. (B-241)

Jackson, L., Inv. (B-414)

Jameson, George (A-27) will–Oct. 11, 1799–wife Eleanor, 100 acres on Eagle creek, James and Andrew Jameson, 300 acres; deed by exrs. to Thos. Beard, land on Eagle creek– title to 100 acres to George James, Sr. and title to 100 acres to George James, Jr.–my 1st wife's children–my present wife's children–my lame daughter called "Nancy" . . . Prob. Jan. 1800.

Jaques, Isaac (nuncp. will) A-176–at his own house in Harrison Co., last illness, July 3, 1812–told Jeremiah Veatch and John Cartmill that wife was to have what she chose– wife and child. Recorded Aug. 10, 1812.

Jenkins, John, Inv. (C-397)

Johnson, E., sales, (A-240?)

Johnson, Wm., Inv. (B-188)

Jones, John D., Inv. (C-232)

Jones, Margaret, sales, (C-311)

Juett, Am (Ann?) (C-418-425)

Kearns, Ursula (B-501 will) son Monterville (5 acres) Nov. 15, 1830-June 1831 (Samuel Smiser, wts.)

Keith, Adam, Inv. (B-267)

Kelso, Chas., (C-29, Inv.)

Keenon, Matilda, Inv., (B-508) Joel R. Lyle, her guardian, Jan. 1, 1829

Kenney, Moses, (C-91)

Kendrick, L., Inv. (B-66)

King, J., Inv., (B-34)

King, Robert (will, B-165), my wife Jane, all, her lifetime–Joshua Osburn (a bed), also Clarissa Henry (a bed), Polly Henry (cow), rest from sale equal to all of my chil- dren. Mar. 10, 1823–July 1823. (Jesse King, etc., wts.)

Kirpman, John, Inv. (B-314) Oct. 1827.

Killem, Nancy (will, (C-304), son-in-law Thos. Moffett—my grand children, heirs of Angeloe and Polly Adams, decd., dau. Eliz. Moffett, dau. Nancy Moffett, gd. dau. Nancy Long; gd. son Wm. Moffett—Thos. Moffett, exr. Dec. 24, 1831—Aug. 1834.

Langly, Abraham and Margaret Langley, heirs of Isaac Langley, decd. Daniel Isgrig, guardian. May 4, 1801. (A-34)
Laughland, James (Inv. A-26)
Laughlin, Robt., Inv. (A-271, 273) Jane Laughlin at sale. Feb. 1815.
Laughlin, John, Inv. (B-219)
Lamme, Jonathan, (Inv. B-454, Mar. 1830.
Layton, John, Inv. B-414.
Leach, Hezekiah, Inv. B-372 Apr. 1828.
Lemmon, Jacob, Inv. A-24.
Lewis, Samuel, sales—B-362—Samuel, Peter, Griffin, Wm. and Thos. Lewis and Lewis Reno bought at the sale.
Lilly, Joshua, Inv. A-217, Nov. 1813.
Lindsey, David, Inv. (A-254) Jan. 16, 1817.
Lindsey, James, Inv. (B-342)
Logan, Samuel, decd., Inv. (A-223), Dec. 1813.
Lyle, Joel R., Inv. (B-508)

McClain, Arthur (B-394) will—Mar. 29, 1824—"old"—son Joseph, exr. dau. Jane Dunn, son Samuel, dau. Mary McClain, son Jonathan, dau. Susan McClain, my wife Sarah Mc-Clain—my 6 children. Nov. 1828.
McLean, Jonathan, Inv. (B-274)
McClure, Sarah, Inv. B-158.
McLean, Samuel, Inv. A-383.
McDaniel, Francis, Inv., B-460, July 1830.
McKee, Wm., Inv. A-77, Aug. 1807.
McMahan, James, Inv. (B-98)
McMillon, John, Inv. (B-28)
McNees, Alex., Inv. (B-61)
McMurtry, Thos. B., Inv. (B-462)
Marble, Peter F., Inv. (B-11) Nov. 1818.
Marsh, Samuel, Inv. (A-232) July 1814.
Martin, R., Inv. (A-349)
Martin, Joseph Inv. (B-76) Oct. 12, 1821.
Martin, John, (B-106)
Mason, J. Inv. (A-337)
Matkins, Joseph, Inv. (B-44)
Martin, M. sales, (B-231)
Moore, Keziah, Inv. (B-12) Oct. 1818.
Moore, Moses, Inv. (B-152)
Musselman, David, Inv. (B-18) Feb. 1819.
Martin, Wm., B-506, Inv.
Miller, Thos., Inv. (B-373.)
Morris, Gavin, (B-317) "widow, Mrs. Morris"—Sept. 1827.
Morrison, David, Inv. (B-277) July 4, 1826. (died July 2, 1825, aged 41)
Morrison, Gavin (?) Thompson Wigglesworth, admr. of Gavin Morrison, decd. (Morris?, or other Morrison, see above) Nov. 10, 1831. (B-508)

Nesbitt, Jere, Inv. B-216

Nesbitt, Sarah, Inv. B-213, Oct. 8, 1824.

Nesbitt, Robert (will B-139) dau. Eliza Jane, son James William, wife Sarah, Nov. 30, 1822, Dec. 1822.

Norman, C., Inv. (A-213)

Owen, Zacharia, (Inv. B-111) Oct. 1822

Page, Elijah, Inv. (A-148) Mar. 1811.

Parks, Benj., Inv. (B-480) Jan. 1831. (also page 235)

Parnick, George Inv. (A-259)

Paton, Joseph, Inv. (A-383)

Parker, see below

Pavey, Sarah, Inv. (A-293)

Perrin, Wm. C., Inv. (A-378)

Perrin, L. J., Inv. (B-13)

Peek, Gasper, Inv. (A-396)

Phillips, Elijah, (will B-467) to my "father," Sophia Griggs, and Elizabeth Bridges, $1.00 each, rest between my two bros. Wm. and Thos. Phillips, exr. Feb. 6, 1830–Oct. 1830.

Pickens, James, Inv. (A-251)

Pickett, George, Inv. (B-53)

‑Parker, Wm. J. (S?), (A-144, will) "now at the house of Chas. Smith, Sr."–to Mrs. Patsy Smith, negro to be sent to Bourbon county by Mr. Elijah Smith to Nathan Smith, the rest to the children of my sister Jenny Jenkins, now living–Nathan Smith, exr. June 27, 1810–Oct. 1810. (Wts: Chas. Smith, Jr., Benj. and Joseph Kendrick).

Pock, John V., Inv. B-302.

Pritchett, Wm., Inv. (B-246)

Ralston, D., Inv. (A-111)

Rankin, Simeon, Inv. (A-282)

Rankin, David (will–A-3) "very sick"–son William (200 acres); wife Hannah Rankin, son Thos. Rankin, daus. Jenny Blackburn, Sarah Roberts, Hannah Morrison, Mary Rawlings, and son David Rankin–dau. Letty Hays, (sons David and Wm., exrs.) Sept. 22, 1795-Oct. 1795. (Thos. and Isaac x Rankins, wts.)

Rankin, David, Jr., Inv., (A-49) July 1804. Jas. Blackburn, etc. commissioners. (Order B, page 61, "widow, and 7 legatees," Feb. 4, 1808.)

Richey, Stewart, Inv. (A-74)

Riley, Wm., (B-8) Inv.

Robb, James, Inv. (A-340) Caty Robb bought much at the sale.

Robinson, John, Inv. (B-245)

Rolland, John, Inv. (A-276) Oct. 1814.

Ross, James, Inv. (A-66) Oct. 1806.

Ross, Alex., Inv. (A-89) Dec. 1807, represented by Margaret and James Ross.

Rutter, Alex., (B-108) "aged and infirm"–son Alex. Rutter, (farm); son John W. Rutter, dau. Agnes Isgrig, and Mary Williamson Clarke, to former son-in-law David Clark, 50c; July 24, 1821-Aug. 1823.

Safford, Wm. Inv. (B-175)

Scofield, John, Inv. (A-159) Nov. 1811.

Scott, Robert (will, A-224) "In case I should never return"; Edward Coleman, exr. Aug. 21, 1813. Oct. 1813.

Scott, John, Inv. (B-300) June 8, 1827.

Scroggin, Levi P., (Inv. B-140) also in Bourbon county, many pp. Oct. 18, 1822.

Scott, Jas., Inv. (B-62)

Sellers, Henry, Inv. (B-46)

Sellers, John Inv. (B-49)

Shaw, D. Inv. (A-26)

Shropshire, Walet, Inv. (B-425)

Shropshire, Wm., Inv. (B-234)

Shumate, John, Inv. (B-130)

Shumate, Spencer, Inv. (B-33)

Smith, John, Inv. (B-81) Nov. 1807.

Smith, Chas. W., Inv. (B-108)

Smith, Temple, Inv. (B-5)

Smith, George, Inv. (B-23)

Sneed, Richard, Inv. (A-159) Nov. 11, 1811.

Snell, Newton, Inv. (B-353) Feb. 1828.

Snodgrass, Samuel, Inv. (A-42) Jan. 1803.

Slade, Ezekiel (B-82) will—wife Sarah, 1/3 of land, sons: Ezekiel, James, Samuel, and Wm. Slade; son John, Lameck Slade, Andrew Slade and dau. Nancy Slade. Dec. 1807— (A-82)

Safford, H.—Inv. (B-50) A-50

Stephenson, Joseph, Inv. (A-47)

Shields, David, (Inv. A-91) Peggy Shields, admr., Apr. 1808.

Snodgrass, Joseph, (B-400) Inv.

Sparks, Wm., Inv. (B-214)

Sparks, C. Inv. (B-392)

Spindle,) Edmund, Inv. (A-231,) Jan. 1814.
Spindall)

Simmons, Mark, Inv. (A-357) Peter Simmons, admr. Aug. 1816.

Steadycorn, Simon, (will, A-110), son Samuel Steadycorn living in Baltimore, Md., to George Thos. Meling son of my wife Rachel Steadycorn, of Alexandria, Va., wife Rachel, exrx. Nov. 27, 1808-Dec. 1808.

Stevenson, Joseph, Inv. (A-132) Aug. 1804.

Stevenson, Thos., Inv. (A-162) May 11, 1812.

Stevenson, Wm., Inv. (A-172) May 1812.

Story, Ase, (Inv. A-395) Jan. 1818.

Swanson, John, Inv. (A-186) 1813, Mar.

Swinford, Elisha, Inv. (A-201) July 1813.

Sydnor, Wm., Inv. (B-512)

Tate, Abner, Inv. (B-146)

Taylor, Samuel, Inv. (A-393) Dec. 1817.

Thompson, Wm., Inv. (A-12) Aug. 1796.

Thompson, R. Inv. (A-155)

Thompson, Samuel, (B-186) Jan. 1824, Inv.

Thompson, John, Inv. (B-231)

Thornley, Epaphroditus, (A-40) Aug. 1802—heirs of p. 186, Reuben Thornley, infant heirs. 1812.

Tittle, James, Inv. (A-44)

Tittle, Peter, Inv. (A-11) Aug. 1797, John Tittle, admr.
Tizdale, Richard, Inv. (A-297) Nov. 4, 1816.
Toadvine, Wm., Inv. (B-48)
Toadvine, Purnell, Inv. (B-502) July 28, 1831.
Trimble, James, Inv. (B-211)
Tucker, Wm., Inv. (A-297)
Turner, George, Inv. (A-419) Oct. 1818.
Turner, Elizabeth, Inv. (B-3)

Vance, John, Inv. (A-34) July 1801.
Vanderen, Bernard, Inv. (A-29) May 1800.
Vanderen, Godfrey, (B-406)
Van Hook, Martin, Inv. (B-502)
Veatch, Jeremiah, (B-403, Inv.) Feb. 1829.
Venard, Absolem, (A-231, Inv.) May 1814.
Venard, Thos., (A-231, Inv.) May 1814.

Wall, John (Inv.–A-257)
Ward, Wm., (Inv. A-263)
Walton, Thos., Inv. A-291, May 1815.
Warfield, Henry, (Inv. B-495)
Watson, James, Inv. (B-91) Apr. 1822.
Wells, Wm., Inv. (A-336)
Wells, John, Inv. (A-127)
Wells, Herbert, Inv. (B-182)
Whitset, Joseph, Inv. (A-250)
Williams, David, Inv. (B-27) July 1819.
Wilson, Margaret, Inv. (B-381)
Woods, Archibald, decd., Hannah Woods, admr. (A-299) Aug. 1815.
Worrel, James, Inv. (A-368) Sarah Worle, admr. May 12, 1817.

Yager, James, Inv. (B-73) Oct. 29, 1821.
Yarnall, Samuel, Inv. (B-278)

Zumwalt, Christian, Inv. (B-194) July 1824.

SCOTT COUNTY DEEDS

(Burned and recopied into court books—much missing, some errors)

Nancy Wilson, Riddle B. Wilson, Betsy Wilson, James Wilson, Wm. Wilson and wife Polly all of Owen Co. Ky. to Edward Pence of Scott, part of tract on which John Wilson resided at death which was divided between widow and hrs. Widow, Nancy Wilson—among those signing was May Wilson—3/21/1832. Deeds L p. 7.

Polly Ewing wife of Joseph Ewing, late Polly Miller, Joseph H. Miller, Wm. Ritchie and wife Betsy (Polly in body of deed but Betsy in signing) Geo. G. Miller, first named of Scott, Wm. Ritchie and wife of Fountaine Co. Ind. deed 4/6 parts of tract in Scott. May 1832—Deed L.

Deed was executed by John Sutton, Thos. C. Sutton—land of which John Sutton decd. lived and died siezed—"deed lost"—that good title may be vested in Alfred O. Sutton, Sarah T. Woolfolk, Ann Mary Sutton———hrs. of John Sutton decd. late of Louisville, Ky., Thos. C. Sutton, Joel Crenshaw and Temperance Lightburn of Scott and Geo. Jones of Oldham purchased from Wm. Sutton of Morganfield, Union Co. Ky. and wife Mary B. Sutton·his one sixth interest in tract. 2/23/1832. Deeds L p. 24.

Joseph S. Watkins, Thos. P. Watkins, Jas. Lyons, H. H. Lyons his wife, Jno. Watkins, David Shields and Mary his wife, deed land in Scott Co. to Caleb Hanna—in signing the name Judith Watkins appears instead of John Watkins, Deed Joseph Watkins Hrs. to Caleb Hanna by. R. Wickliffe, agent. 3/3/1832. Deeds L p. 34.

Samuel Hamilton of Harrison Co. to Jno. Snell of Scott, deeds int. in estate of Charles Hamilton being 1/8 pt. where Chas. Hamilton resided at time of death located in Scott. 6/1/1832—Deed L p. 50.

Wm. Morris and wife Mary of Edgar Co. Ill. deed Henry H. Prewitt tract in Scott— 6/28/1832.

Richard Cave and wife Nancy, late Nancy Brent, Fanny Williams, a widow, late Brent, Eliza Neal dau. of Mary———decd. who was formerly Mary Brent, Minor Neale husband of Eliza Neale, Priscilla Brent, Jno. L. Fisher and Molly (Mary) late Bealert?, and dau. of Mary Bealert? Lewis Collins and wife Alice, late Brent, Charnack Self and wife Betsy, late Brent, being all hrs. at law of (Wm.) Brent, some of whom reside in state of M———Ky., convey interest as hrs. of said Wm. Brent—Signed: Priscilla Brent, Charnock Self, Betsy Self, Jno. L. Fisher, Mary Fisher, Richard Cave, Nancy Cave by Agent, Co. Boone, State of Mo. and Wm. Kelly, Atty., Lewis Collins by agent Minor Neale, Alice Collins, Minor Neale and wife Eliza Neale. Deeds L p. 72.

Geo. Harlan of Warren Co. Ohio—power-of-atty. to Jacob Ewless to recover int. in estate of Ester Harlan, late Ester Ewless, as one of ch. of Jacob Ewless decd. of Scott. 8/23/1830—Deeds L p. 77.

Thos. Nutter and wife Rachel, late Rachel Martin, Jno. Kennedy and Cassandra his wife, late Martin, of Scott Co. Ky. and Montgomery Co. Ind. deed David Nutter of Scott int. in tract in Scott on which Joseph Martin lived at death which tract now undivided except for widow who has her dower which is their interest in said tract. 10/11/1832—Deeds L p. 211.

Benj. P. Watkins, Joseph Watkins, Thos. Watkins, David Shields and wife Polly, Jno. Watkins and wife Judith, Jas. Lyon and Henningham H. Lyon wife, by atty. deed Jacob Kendrick—9/28/1832—Deeds L. p. 223.

Nancy Dehaven, Jacob Miller and Nancy Miller, Bayley Payne and Sally Payne, Rebecca James, Valentine Stucker and Lydia, John Murray and Peggy, Samuel Murray and Eliza, Harriett Dehaven, Jno. Bellsland and Mahala, Joseph Algain and Tabitha and Sam'l. Dehaven of Scott Co. Ky. and Fountain Co. Ind. deed Daniel Polk—In signing the name "Blestand," Algain spelled Alkin and in recording Alquin. Deed Bk. L, p. 232—9/20/1831.

Sally Allenthorp, Addison Samuel and wife Nancy Samuel, Jno. Power and wife Rachel Power and Martha Allenthorp of Scott deed Cassandra White a tract in Scott. Deeds L, 3/23/1833.

Jas. Barlow Hrs.—Came before me Lewis A. Lamy, Parish-Judge of "Anachitta," State of La., Fountain Barlow and wife Elizabeth Barlow, wife of Elly K. Ross and represented by her husband ———, Barlow, wife of Josiah Davenport and represented by her husband, Lucretia Barlow wife of Ashley Hewitt and represented by her husband, Martha A. Barlow wife of Andrew A. K(nox?) and represented by her husband and following heirs of Lucretia Barlow decd. wife of the late Thomas C. Lewis decd. to wit: Thomas C. Lewis in his person ——S. Lewis in same, Pulchard(?) Lewis wife of Wm O. Knox represented by her husband, Eliza Lewis wife of Jeptha Hughes and represented by her husband, Geo. W.——— represented by his Tutor Fountain Barlow and Jas. F.? Lewis represented by his Tutor, John S.? L———, legal hrs. of James Barlow of the Parish of Anachitta, decd. who apptd. Alpheus F. Shephard of Scott Co., Ky. Atty. to sell land in Ky. which belongs to them as hrs. of Jas. Barlow decd. or to which they may be entitled in right of their ancestor———Barlow as hrs. of the late Wm. Barlow and Henry Barlow formerly of said state now————and to settle with admr. of said estates and any—due estate of James Barlow from estates of Wm. and Henry Barlow who were bros. of said James. Hrs. signed—Jno. S. Lewis, Jas. F. Lewis, John S. Lewis, Wm O. Knox, Pulchard Knox, Andrew A. M. Knox, Martha A. M. Knox, Jeptha Hughes, Eliza Hughes, Ashley Hewitt, Lucretia (Leneretta?) Hewett, I. Davenport, Polly Davinport, Elizabeth K(——), Elizabeth Ross, Thos. C. Lewis, F. Barlow by Atty. J. S. Lewis, Geo. W. Lewis by Tutor. Deed Bk. L, p. 301—3/19/1833—In same book deed to Jno. C. Talbott, March, 1833.

Thos. Osburn and wife Susan, Ephriam Osbourne, Lee B. Osbourne, E. R. Osbourne, Adley Osbourne and Cordelia wife, Moses Mothershead and Celia wife and Nancy Osbourn of Scott, except Ephriam of ——— deed Stephen Lucas tract in Scott—Deeds L, March 1833.

Thos. Beacher (Beatcher) and wife of Grayson Co., Jas. Carrell of Hopkins Co, Lawson Carroll of Woodford Co. Wm. Carrol of Hopkins Co., Joseph Carroll of Grayson Co. Davy (Day?) Scott Carroll of Grayson Co, all of state of Ky. deed Daniel Cooper tract in Scott— 5/28/1833—Deeds L.

Larkin Craig and wife Franky. Asa P. Ficklin and wife Nancy and Wm. Ficklin and wife Mary of Mo. to Thompson H. Ficklin of Washington Co. Mo. partys of 1st pt. being hrs. of John H. Ficklin, decd. late of Scott Co. all interest in his estate—recd. Calloway Co. Mo. Deeds L.

Susan W. Hutchenson of Fauquier Co. Va. to Wm. Mosby of Scott, consideration $1.00 all interest in tract in Ky. allotted as dower to Susan in the lands of James Y. Hutchenson decd. which allotment was made by Scott County Court. Deeds L—p. 358—5/13/1833.

Theodrick Boulware and wife Susanna W., Horace Shelby and wife Sarah of Calloway Co. Mo. appt. Valentine Rogers of Scott and Thomas C. Kelly of Franklin Attys.—pertaining to the estate of Jas. Y. Kelly decd. late of Scott—Deeds abt. 1833.

John Shortridge of Scott to Wm. Shortridge of same all interest in tract willed us jointly by father located in Scott—Deeds H, p. 366–1/26/1825.

Mary Shortridge for love and affection to son John interest in estate of Daniel Lewis decd. of Fairfax Co. Va. or elsewhere in Va.—Lewis having died without ch. and being my(——?) Wts? Joseph S. Norris, Steven Richie—Deeds H, p. 368–1/21/1825–p. 371– Mary Shortridge deeds slave from estate of Daniel Lewis to her dau. Sarah Neale—1/27/1825.

Reuben Rose and wife Margaret deed Wm. Jenkins, Elizabeth (Eliza) Jenkins and Ezra Offutt—that Henry Jenkins in lifetime executed deed by which he conveyed to James D. Offutt who has since deptd. life—Margaret the wife of Henry H. Jenkins and her ch. viz: William, Eliza, Absolum, Sarah and Henry latter of whom deptd. life—whereas said Margaret has intermarried with Reuben Rose and suits brought in Cir. Ct. by Wm. and Absolam against Reuben and Margaret and sd. Eliza and Sarah Ann and said James Offutt (decd.?) compromised etc. Deeds M. p. 390–Sept. 1834.

SCOTT COUNTY ESTATES

TESTATOR NOT IN GENERAL INDEX

(Scott formed from Woodford County 1792)

The Court House burned Aug. 9, 1837 and records partially destroyed (note spaces where instrument burned) and remainder copied. The following do not include wills published in vol. I Kentucky Court and Other Records.

Armstrong, Sampson–decd. Bk. A. p. 15

Applegate, John, gdn. bond–Bk A, p. 62

Applegate, Richard–Will–Bk. A, p. 103–published K.C.O.R. v. I

Allen, John, decd.–Will Bk. A, p. 106

Adams, Hope, decd.–Will Bk. A, p. 111

Adams, Nathan–Will Bk. A. p. 210–To son Nathan, dau. Sarah Adams, daus. Mary Adams, Betsy Tull, Ellgood Adams, son Nathan, daus, Mary and Nancy–Dec. 18, 1803–Aug. 1804–Wts: Jno. Garth, Robt. Griffith, Nina Ratcliff

Allenthorp, Benj. (see Thorp)–Will Bk. A, p. 293–To bro. Wm., sisters Martha and Ann, bro. George, my father.––––Exr. Jan. 5, 1806–Mar. 1806

Allen, Robt.–Will Bk. B, p. 116–Sons, Samuel, Robt. Jr., (land Franklin Co.), daus, Polly Lemon, Elizabeth and Sarah Allen, wife Jane, son Elijah, wife and sons, Malione and Robt. Exrs. Wts;––––Bird––––Sullivan, 4/16/1813–1/1814

Acuff, Christopher–Will Bk. B, p. 88, 118–Sale bond and sett. (see Bk. C, p. 172)

Abbott, Robt. gdn. bond–Will Bk. B. p. 118

Abbott, Henry–Will Bk. B, p. 192–Sett.

Acuff, C. C. Will Bk. B. p. 375–Gdn. bond

Allan, Polly–Will Bk. B, p. 391–dower

Abbott, Wm.–Will Bk. B. 377–recopied in Bk. D. p 221–Wife Frances, daus. Frances Abbott and Charlotte Abbott, Phoebe Pritchard, son Joseph Abbott. Francis Henry child of Benj. Abbott decd. son, gd. child Lucien Clifford Abbott, son Wm. Abbott land in Va. Exrs. Wm. and Joseph Abbott and Jas. Prichard. 4/8/1813–11/1813–Wts: Alex. Bradford, Wm. Thraelkeld

Alexander, Wm.–Will Bk. C, p. 72–Sale, (see also D. 391)

Acuff, Christopher–Will Bk. C, p. 172–Sett.

Anderson, David(Daniel?)–Estate app. Will Bk. C, p. 236

Armstrong, Wm.–Will Book C, p. 280–Admrs. bond

Adkins, Jesse–Will Bk. C, p. 234–Sale (see D, p. 28–Will)

Allen, Sam'l. H.–Will Bk. C, p. 380–Estate app. p. 381–sale

Acuff, C. C.–Will Bk. C, p. 508–widow–(see D, p. 321)

Burbridge, Thomas–Will Bk. A, p. 1–Will published K.C.O.R. v. 1

Burdet, Frederick–decd.–Will Bk. A, p. 5–Inv. 11/25/1795–p. 46–Polly Burdette orp. chose gdn. sett. with gdn.–B. p 48

Berryman, John–Will Bk. A, p. 74–Published K.C.O.R. v. 1

Brooks, Jane–Will Bk. A, p. 123

Brooks, Thos. decd. Will Bk. A, p. 154

Beaty, Wm. Senr. Will Bk. A, p. 173–Published K.C.O.R. v. 1

Bradley, Robt. decd. Will Bk. A, p. 212–Sett.

Boswell, Geo. E. "G." decd. Will Bk. A, p. 252, also Bk. B, p. 27

Berry, Sam'l. N. decd. Will Bk. A, p. 306

Barlow, Wm. decd. Will Bk. A. p. 367–1807–Bk. B, p. 2 and 68-unm. left all to bros. and sisters

Beaty, John—Will Bk. A, p. 405

Burt, Moses—Will Bk. A, p. 407

Beaty, John—decd. Will Bk. A, p. 441, 437—same div. p. 440—Wid. Nancy, to Benj. Robinson and wife Polly, to Sally Beaty 11/24/1808—Bk. B. p. 1—widow receives dower (spelled Bently in one place)

Browning, James—Will Bk. B, p. 29.—Wife Jane. Sept 1804 Sept. 1809—Wts: Wm. Glass Sr. and Jr., and Phebe Glass

Belles, Henry—Will Bk. B, p 35—Published K.C.O.R. v. 1

Burdette, Polly—Will Bk. B, p 49—Sett. with gdn.

Brooks, James—Will Bk. B, p. 38—Com. bond

Browning, Jane—Will Bk. B. p. 51—Niece Susan Humphries, Margaret Coppage, husband James Browning. Wts; Jno. Brock, Jane Nelson, John Cook 1/4/1810—Feb. 1810.

Bradley, Robt. Will Bk. B. p. 66—Wife Hannah, sons, Phillip and——(Stephen?) Bradley, dau. Lucy Valentine, Daniel Johnson and Willis Bradley, grandch, Malinda Massie, Theodorick Massie and Robt. Massie, son-in-law Wm. Massie land Montgomery Co. belonging to my bro. John Bradley, Exrs. Robt. Gaines, David Thomson, Wts: Benj. and Richard Quinn—May 1810 probated.

Brent, Harriett—Will Bk. B, p. 67—gdn. bond.

Bird, Robt. Will Bk. B, p. 95—Ord. bond.

Bailey, John, Will Bk. B, p 103—Sale Bill.

Bird, Lee—Will Bk. B, p 29—Admrs. bond.

Beaty, Geo. Will Bk. B, p. 186—Admrs. bond.

Blackburn, John—Will Bk. B, p. 189—Inv.

Branham, Taverner—Will Bk. B, p. 218—Admrs. bond.

Branham, Richard—Will Bk. B, p. 108—Wife, Hannah, ch: Wm.——Taverner, James and George, "5 div." Exrs. sons, Harlin, Tavener, Jas. George. Wts; Thos. Ficklin, Gabriel Long, Sam'l. Shepherd—7/20/1814—Sept. 1814.

Barnhill, Daniel—Will Bk B, p. 251—Admrs. bond.

Barlow, Henry—Will Bk. B, p. 329 Admrs. bond.

Brown, Joel—Will Bk. B, p. 372—Inv.

Benson, Chas. Will Bk. B, p. 384—Admrs. bond.

Barlow, Wm.—Will Bk. B, p. 68—Sett.

Bradford, Henry—Will Bk. C, p. 5

Burgess, Wm.—Will Bk. C, p. 13

Bowles, Jno. B. Will Bk. C, p. 81

Branham, T. H. Will Bk. C, p. 70

Bibb, Jas.—Will Bk. C, p. 280.

Brooking, Jno. Will Bk. C, p. 290

Branham, Tavner (Tavener)—Will Bk. C, p. 304

Branham, Cassandra—Will Bk. C, p. 311

Betty, Jas.—Will Bk. C, p. 378—"Of Scott Co."—land in Ind. equally amongst Wm. A. Beaty ——my gd. ch.——"Millers run"——gd. dau. Sary Anne——; equally, among John A. ——ch. that is—my gd. ch: James—— to Jas. B. Miller——gd. son——bal. to John A. Miller's ch. that is my gd. ch. Jas. B. Miller and Sarah excepted. Exrs. Jas. B. Miller and Jas. Emison. 4-7-1822—7-1-1822 (much missing).

Baldwin, Donaldson (Daniel)—Will Bk. C, p. 412—"I, Daniel Baldwin Sr. of Scott Co."—— my sons and daus. prior to this date "I——confirm to them"——to my——Daniel Baldwin, son Thomas——, sons, John, Moses and Joseph Baldwin, dau. Deborah Stewart ——Mary Oxley and Elizabeth Roley(?)——my son Jeremy, Exrs: Sons John and Jeremy. 3-21-1817—Oct. 1822

Craig, Wm. Will Bk. A, p. 155 etc. decd.

Campbell, Allan, Will Bk. A, p. 193—gdn. bond.

Campbell, John—Will Bk. A, p. 197—Hrs. Jane Campbell, Jas., Polly and Jno. Campbell, orphans under age (Lindsay Campbell Sett. 1806) Allen Campbell orphan (see Order Bk. A for orphans)

Campbell, Wm.—Will Bk. A, p. 205—Wife Elizabeth, two sons John and William, three daus. Mary, Lucy and Levinia, Molly Mulberry choice of beds, 8/30/1803—Sons Exrs. Wts: Toliver Craig, Wm. Mullberry—Aug. 1804.

Carrick, Wm. Will Bk. A, p. 260—decd.

Carrick, Walter, Will Bk. A, p. 266—decd.

Culbertson, Samuel—Will Bk. A, p. 325—Wife Martha, two sons, Joseph and Alexander, son, Robert (under 19), daus. Hetty, Eliza and Patsy Culbertson, 7/8/1806—Nov. 1806—Wts: Isaac Long, Jas. Lindsay, John Calhoon Sr.

Cullbertson, Martha ("Patsy")—Will Bk. A p. 343—(Dau. of above Sam'l. and Martha?) Sister Esther Lindsay, sister Nancy Adams, bro. Robert, sister Prudence, sisters Jane Adams and Polly Culbertson, three sisters Esther, Nancy and Prudence. Exrs. John Adams, Jas. Lindsay 1/23/1807—Feb. 1807—Wts Jas. and Wm. Stephenson.

Coppedge (Coppage), Isaac—Will Bk. A, p. 354—Son Chas., son Rodden, dau. Lucy Kearns and her ch., dau. Nancy Coppage, dau. Gracy Philes, son Rodin and Fielding Bradford Exrs. 2/11/1807—Mar. 1807. (Note: Rhodin Coppage m. Nancy Collins dau.-in-law of Wm. Cave 6/12/1702 in Woodford Co.; and in early records daughter-in-law often meant step-daughter).

Collins, Thos. Will Bk. A, p. 389—Estate, Jan. 1808

Clarvo, Henry—Will Bk. A, p. 402—Catholic—Wife———dau. Mary (Polly) under 21 yrs., son John under 21; my father's will left my son John property, rest of my ch., my five ch. counting one my wife is pregnant with. Exrs. bro-in-law Wm.———Thos. C. Jenkins (much missing from this will) 4/26/1808—May 1808

Craig, Elijah—Will Bk. A, p. 410—Son Simeon, son John D., my ch. Joel, John, Lucy and Mary. Exrs. John Hawkins, Isiah Pitts, son John D. 5/13/1808—June 1808

Clynton (Clayton, Clinton?) Archibald—Will Bk. A, p. 424—Wife Rachel Clayton, son Isaac Clayton, son John, hrs. of son Archd. son Moses Clinton(?), son Jacob Clinton exr. 1808-Sept. 1808—Wts: Marine Duvall, Sam'l. Lowry, Sam'l. Greenup

Craig, Wm.—Will Bk. A, p. 429—decd—Sett. in Bk. B. p 71

Combs, Elizabeth and Susan. Will Bk. A, p 435—Inf. ch. of Jas. Combs, legatees of Ellender Merryman—abt. 1808.

Cannon, Laura W.—Will Bk. B, p. 390—Gdn. bond, Nov. 1808.

Campbell, Porter, Will Bk. B, p 124—Admrs. bond.

Cannon, Newton, Will Bk. B, p. 245—Admrs. bond.

Crowder, Sam'l.—Will Bk. B, p. 5—Admrs. bond.

Cobb, Sam'l.—Will Bk. B, p. 34—Sett.

Cobb, Wm.—Will B, p. 26—gdn. bond.

Coppage, John—Will Bk. B, p. 50—Admrs. bond

Coppage, Isaac—Will Bk B. p. 72—Sett.

Craig, Martin, Will Bk. B, p. 185—gdn. bond.

Craig, Peter, Will Bk. B. p. 337—gdn. bond.

Cave, John—Will Bk. B, p. 57—Son Wm. Henry Herndon (relationship not given), son Henry, son Richard, dau. Nancy Kelly and her hus. Wm. Kelly, dau. Rebecca Hayden, gd. dau. Polly Burdett, Exrs. Wm. and Henry Cave. 5/26/1809—Wts: Jno. Thomson, Jno, and Elijah Snell. Mar. 1810 (Note: Rebecca Cave m. F. Burdette in Woodford Co. 1790, Richard Cave m. Sally Wood in Woodford Co. 1792)

Carroll, Enoch–Will Bk. B, p. 191–Mentions wife and ch. no names given. 6/24/1815-Aug. 1815

Craigmiles, Jno. Will Bk. B, p. 197–Wife Anna and sons Cyrus and James, Exr. Jno. Thompson. 1815

Carlisle, Howard–Will Bk. B, p. 385–Sett.

Combs, Robt. Will Bk. C, p. 313–(see D, p. 347 etc.)

Cason, Wm.–Will Bk. C, p. 342

Carroll, Dempsey–Will Bk. C, p. 390

Coplinger, Sarah–Will Bk. C, p. 420

Clarke, Cary L.–Will Bk. C, p. 6

Campbell, Elizabeth–Will Bk. C, p. 7

Chew, Sarah–Will Bk. C, p. 9–gdn. bond

Campbell, Alex. Hrs.–Will Bk. C, p. 10

Clarke, Cary L. (Craig?)–Will Bk. C, p. 19–Wife Eliza, house at forks of two roads leading from Georgetown to Cincinnati–Jefferson St.–bought of Jonah Pitts–her and our ch. –––as my ch. come of age or marry, W. W. Warren, Elijah Craig, John Stevenson Exrs. 5-26-1819–wits: Wm. West, Jas. W. Grant–––West–Aug. 1819.

Conyers. David–Will Bk. C, p. 160–Gdn. bond

Chalk, Jas, decd.–Will Bk. C, p. 258

Collins, Thos.–Will Bk. C, p. 260

Chalk, Jas.–Will Bk. C, p. 250–"Decd. widow of Greenwick in St. of N.Y."; to Miss Fanny Hewitt, maiden in Mason Co. my(?) house which is the Baptist Meeting House at New C–––in Township of Newbury in Co. of Orange, N. Y. etc.–––now resident of Green–––N. Y. 8-25-1807–Wts: Jno. and Sarah Hewitt, Jan. 1818–Fanny Chalk Exr.–see Order Bk. B, 380–inf. hrs.

Dehaven, Samuel–Will Bk. A, p. 41–Inv.

Dupee, Abram and Elizabeth–Will Bk. A, p. 78–Bond

Davis, Solomon, decd. Will Bk. A, p. 150–Sus. Davis gdn. bond p. 119

Dean, Geo. Will Bk. A, p. 324–Inv.

Duvall, Henry H. Will Bk. A, p. 329–Published K.C.O.R. v. I

Drake, James–Will Bk. A, p. 438–Will–Wife Winny, dau. Polly Foster, dau. Elizabeth (Van)––landingham son Thos. land adjoining Thos. Drake; three ch: Elizabeth Vanlandingham, Thos. Drake and Polly Foster, Exrs: Jas. Johnson, Thos. Drake, Lewis Valendingham and Isaac Foster. 10/4/1808-Dec. 1808 (much missing); Wts: Jas. Johnson, Jas. Suggett and Phebe White

Davis, Joseph–Will Bk. B, p. 158–Estate app.

Deane, Joseph–Will Bk. B, p. 30–Estate app.

Denning, Fielding, Bk, p. 154–Admrs. bond.

Denny, Sally, Bk. B. p. 125 Gdn. bond

Denny, Adam (or Aaron?)–Will Bk. B, p. 160–Will–gr. ch.–––Whitehead–––Edmund Townsend 1/8 part of two tracts in State of Ohio–other gd. ch: James Hammon, Lewis Hammond and Fanny Hammond now Fanny Evans; sis. Fanny Alexander, son Lewis Denny, dau. Rutha Denny, son Fielding Denny. Wts: John Calvert and Wm. Threalkell–4/19/1813-Feb. 1815.

Davis, Wm.–Will Bk. B, p. 223–Gdn. bond.

Drake, Thos.–Will Bk. B, p. 252–Admrs. bond.

Doyle, Alexander, Will Bk. B, p. 274–Admr. bond.

Dehaven, Sanford–Will Bk. B, p. 342–Gdn. bond.

Duncan, Jas. Will Bk. B, p. 425–Sett.

Dinwiddie, Thos. Will Bk. B, p. 400—Estate app.
Davis, S.—Will Bk. C, p. 168
Davis, Jos.—Will Bk. C, p. 181
Drake, Thos.—Will Bk. C, p. 233
Dehoney, Willis—Will Bk. C, p. 239
Drake, Tho.—Will Bk. C, p. 244
Dorsey, Reason, Will Bk. C, p. 303

Edwards. Uriah. decd. Will Bk. A, p—Wm. Rebecca and Henry H. Edwards, orphans of Uriah Edwards—Wts: Joseph Reding, Robt. Johnston, date 7/24/1797 (struck out?)
Elder, John—Bk. A, p. 50—Property now in possession of son Robt. Elder Exr. Margaret Alexander Sept. 19, 1796—Wts: Jno. Elder and Jas. Twymon—2/26/1798
Emison, Jas.—Will Bk. A, p. 273—Estate
Eve, Wm. decd. Will Bk. A, p. 286—3/24/1806—Geo. Eve. Milton, Lawrence and Clarissa Eve, orphans of Wm. Eve, decd.
Ewing, Samuel—Will Bk. A, p. 418—Will—Son, Joseph, wife Eleanor Exrs., plantation in Pa., dau. Martha Murray, six sons viz: John, Joseph, Wm. Robt. James and Samuel. 7/24/1808-Aug. 1808 Wts: Robt and James Ewing—see also Bk. E, 219
Eve, John decd. Will Bk. A, p. 445.
Evans, Caleb—Will Bk. B, p. 387—Admr. bond.
Estill. Thos. Will Bk. B, p. 350—Admr. Bk C, p 186—Widow Rachel.
Eve, Geo.—Will Bk. C, p. 10—see Woodford Co. for marriage
Estill, Rachael—Will Bk. C, p. 158—"Advanced in age", dear ch: dau. Anna Hughes——— son——to my ——4thly—Wm Estill——son, Thos.—other ch. sons, Stephen and Thos. Exrs. 6-7-1820—Aug, 1820 (almost all missing)
Eve, John—Will Bk. C, p. 173
Estill, Thos, decd. Will Bk. C, p. 186
Ewing, Samuel—Will Bk. C, p. 219
Eve, Wm.—Will Bk. C, p. 234

Flournoy, Elizabeth—Will Bk. A, p. 46—Published K.C.O.R. v.I
Fauntleroy, John—Decd. Will Bk. A, p. 79—Div.—Mrs. Hunter (widow), Mrs. Warren, John Fauntleroy, Wm Fauntleroy, Signed: Capt. John Hawkins———Virginia, 9/21/1799 Scott Co. Court Jan. 1800
Fauquier (Forker) Robt.—Will Bk. A, p. 139-40—Will—Exrs. Hugh Emison, John Watkins, Lewis Hieatt, dau. ——. my granddau. Mary Emison, grandson Jas. Barclay, grandsons, Robt. Barkley and Matthew Barclay Jr., granddau. Ann Barclay, dau. Agnes Scott, grand-dau., Rosanah Atcheson, dau. Jane McCumsey, dau. Elizabeth Clinton, grandson Robt. McDougal, gr. dau. Mary McDougal, granddaus., Sarah and Anne McDougal, son James Forker, gr. ch. dau. Mary Nickson now in Kingdom of Ireland, gr. sons John and Robt. McCompsey. "/23/1802—Sept. 1802 Signed Robt "Farquer".
Fee, Robt. deed. Will Bk. B, p. 20—Div. p. 110 Mary Fee 3/17/1801
Freeland, Frisby, Jr.—Will Bk. A, p. 244—"Of Calvery Co., Md.", wife Sarah $1,100 I recd. from her right of dower to lands belonging to her former husband exclusive of her legal portion, 11/16/1803—3/25/1805—Signed by Sarah "Frisby" (should be "Freeland"— evidently a mistake in copy) Wts: Francis H. Freeland and Wm. L. Chew.
Fields, Wm.—Will Bk. A, p. 441—12/19/1801—Jas. Fields Admr.
Fort, John—Will Bk. B, p. 82—Sett. with Admr.
Fields, Reason, Will Bk. B, p. 207—Admr. bond
Fields, Reason—Will Bk. C, p. 183—Gdn. bond

Foster, Thos. Will Bk. C, p. 191

Fitzpatrick, Peter–Will Bk. C, pps. 245, 288

Frazier, Wm.–Will Bk. C, p. 253–

Fitzpatrick, Peter–Will Bk. C, p. 299–"Old and infirm"——Mrs. Taylor——Congregation of St. Francis in Scott–a member—friend Joseph—8-30-1816–Dec. 1817–Wts; Thos. Twyman and Leonard——Dec. 1817 (almost all missing)

Finley, Wm. M.–Will Bk. C, p. 336

Ferguson, Jas.–Will Bk. C, p. 419 also p. 368–Will–(one p. missing)–to son John Read—— dau. Eunice Ferguson and her ch. if any etc.——ch. John Read Ferguson, Rodes Thom- son ——, Thomson—— Eunice Thomson Ferguson, Wm. Thomson Ferguson, Thos. Fer- guson, Jas. Ferguson and Jas. Ferguson when of age or marry after wife's (death?); wife Lydia, Wts: Jno. R. Ferguson. 7-1-1812–probated——

Ferguson, Larkin–Will Bk. C, p. 376—— son, John—— said dau. — my —— James Fer- guson Exr. 5-30-1821–7-1822 (almost all missing)

Grant, Israel–Will Bk. A, p. 12 & 29 (Order Bk. says Jesse Grant changed his name to "Israel") Will–Wife, Susannah, son James, two sons Wm. and Jossy (Jesse? or Joshua?), daus. Sally and Rebecca (ch. under 21), Exrs: Geo. B. Boswell, David and Jonathan Bryant, John Mosby and John Hawkins. 10/7/1796–Oct. 1796–Wts: Jas. Bryan, Jas. Lemon and Phillip J. Roots. (Note–One Jesse Grant made antique sideboard now in Duncan Tavern Shrine and Museum, Paris, Ky.)

Green, Chas. Will Bk. A, p. 40–Will–Saml. Brooking Exr.—— 27/1794 —— for Jno. K. (S?) Green, Betsy Green, reps. of Polly Green decd, Chas. gdn.–Div. 1807

Gray, Geo.–Will Bk. A, p. 94–Div. p. 114–To widow, to Wm. Gray, to Joseph Gray, to Jno. Gray, to Smauel Gray, to Jas. Gray. 9/29/1801–Admr. bond Bk. B p. 75.

Galloway–George–Will Bk. A, p. 17–p. 75–Admr. bond.

Gregg, Israel–decd., Will Bk. A, p. 116.

Graham, John–dec'd. Will Bk. A, p. 127–Fanny Graham etc. Exrs. 5/24/1802.

Green, "Spencer", Stephen–Will Bk. A, p. 57–Will–Wife Ruth, dau. Nancy, sons, Jas. and John and if either die land to eldest who have no land by this will, son Joshua, all sons to be taught Bible, rest between sons that have no land at their mother's death. Exrs: Wm. Green and wife. Wts: Joseph and Martha King 6/29/1798–12/1798 (Note: much missing from will.)

Gregg, Israel–Decd.–Will Bk. A, p. 116–Inv.

Gardner, Wm.–Will Bk. A, p. 151–Will–Wife Mary, ch. to wit: Anne, John, James, William, Jensey, Mason and Thos. Gardner, dau. Sally Goodram, "my seven ch." Exrs: John Brad- ley, Benj. Quinn. 1/12/1803–Feb.——

Gray, Wm. dec'd.–Will Bk. A, p. 156–.

Graham, Chas. decd. Will Bk. A, p. 190.

Greensby (Grunsby?) Nimrod–Will Bk. A, p 217, 227–Milly Grinsbey widow, Dec. 1804.– Peggy Greensby and Wm. Greensby orphans under 21–1805

Gibson, Jno. Decd. Will Bk. A, p 401

Grant, Susannah–Will Bk. A, p. 292–(widow of Israel)–Will–Dau. Sally Jackson, son James Grant, dau. Rebecca Grant, sons, Wm. and Israel, Susannah, Sammuel, Jeremiah also, Exrs; Wm. and Jas. Grant and Jno. Moseby. 3/29/1806–Mar. 1806–Wts: Joseph Green, Kit- turah and Elizabeth Grant.

Grant, Israel, sett. gdn. B, p. 97, p. 98 Wm. Grant admr.

Gregg, Israel, decd.–Will Bk. A, p. 334–Div.–Widow Charlotte, orphans Betsy, Joseph, John. Jan. 3, 1807

Green, Joseph–Will Bk. A, p. 75–Inv. (Note: See Mercer Co. Ky. records for hrs.)

Griggs (Gregg?) Amos–Will Bk. A, p. 183–Sett. with Exr.

Griffith, Paris–Will Bk. B, p. 120–Will–Dau. Betsy, wife Sally, sons, Wm. and Thos. 7/20/1814 –Wts: Thos. and Jno. Butler, Daniel Gano–6/20/1814

Galloway, Samuel–Will Bk. B, p. 129–Ch: Aron (or Ann?), Sally Lynn, Jane, Betsay, Ruth Henderson, Rebecca, Exrs: Jas. Linn, Lee Bird, Wm. Dickey. Wts: F. Bradford–Jan. 1815.

Griffith, Jesse–Will Bk. B. p. 215–Sett. with Exr.

Gano, R. M. Will Bk. B, p. 223–Admr. bond

Gano. Cornelius–Will Bk. B, p. 35–Gdn's. bond; same for John Gano (p. 383) and Eliza Gano (p. 404)

Gayle, Thos. H.–Will Bk. B, p. 392–Gdn's. bond.

Goddard, Michael–Will Bk. C, p. 90–

Gano, R. M.–Will Bk. C, p. 116 etc.

Golden, Thos.–Will Bk. C, p. 148

Gano. Jno. A.–Will Bk. C, p. 149–gdn. bond

Graves, Stephen–Will Bk. C, p. 201

Gatewood, Merit–Will Bk. C, p. 239

Gano, Cornelius V.–Will Bk. C, p. 242

Gale, Wm.–Will Bk. C, p. 254 and 293–ch., wife and unmarried ch. —— to wit Caty, Betsy, Susannah —— among them, —— to wit: Wm. Josiah, Temple E. and Robt. and their hrs. —— of Christopher Dehaven 71 1/4 acres; hrs. of Col. Robt. Johnston decd.; my four sons; two sons, Wm. and Robt. M. Gale, all my ch. except son Younger —— Gale —— Nancy Gale, son Younger Gale, Exrs. sons Wm. and Temple E. Gale, Nov. 1817–Wts: Henry, Danl. S. Perry. John Angleton–Dec. 1817 (nearly all missing).

Herndon, Lewis–Will Bk. A, p. 7–"Of Woodford Co." (before Scott was formed from Woodford); wife Frances, all ch. except dau. Isabell Brown, Exrs: sons, James and Henry Elly 9/17/1789–7/26/1796–Wts: Thos. Ficklin, Thos. Dinwiddie, Colby Shipp–In Orders A, p. 145 John S. Herndon inf. orphan of Louis Herndon decd. 6 yrs. old 11/27/1799 bound out 1/27/1800

Harwood, Elizabeth–Will Bk. A, Estate

Henry, Robt. decd. Bk. A.–refers to data giving hrs: Wm. Jewel (Jewet?), John Henry and Jouett Irvine

Hampton, Wm.–Bk. A, p. 109–Gdns. bond; Nelly Hampton sett. with gdn. (p. 184), 1815– William, Henry. Richard, Anthony, (Phoebe Plunkett) orphans 1809 (?)

Hall, John–Will Bk. A, p. 159, 413–Widow Jane

Holland, Anthony–Will Bk. A, p. 63–Son Ephriam land bought of Geo. Christy, dau. Ruth Plummer, land bought of Moses Bledsoe, son, Geo. W. Holland, dau. Anna Holland under age, dau. Margaret Penn, dau. Elizabeth Mosby, son Henry Holland, son William, my three sons Exrs. 3/20/1799–Wts: Samuel Shepard, Philip Rootes, Alexander Craigmyles, June 1799 (Note: Above Margaret Penn was wife of Shadrach Penn, Sr.)

Henderson, John–Will Bk. A, p. 72–called Henderson in body of instrument and Herndon in index–Will 8/4/1799–To sister-in-law Agnes Smith to support my family, power invested in friend Alex. Smith and John H. Miller, each of ch. to share according to law. Dec. 1799 –Wts: Peter Kerne, Alex. Hamilton

Henton, Jas. Will Bk. A, p. 190–Estate

Head, John Alfred–Will–Bk. A, p. 199–Wife, (Elizabeth) son Wm, dau. Anna Ransdale, Elipah and Elizabeth Kendall, son Benjamin, dau. Sarah Head, son John Alfred, dau. Fanny Head, land Lincoln Co. between wife and 7 ch. equally–Exrs. Wife Elizabeth, Wm. Head and Martin Nall 8/12/18–June 18–.

Hart, Hugh–Will Bk. A, p 209–decd–sett. B. p 17

Hawkins, John–Will–Bk A, p 316–Wife Sarah, ch. —— Jameson, Philemon, Peggy Cave, Sally Smith, Thomas, Nancy Cason, John, Fanny Thomas, Betsy Faulkner, William, Caty Hawkins and Lucinda Hawkins–Exrs., Wife Exrs., Philemon. Thomas, Jameson and John Hawkins, Georgetown and John Payne. 10/30/1804–9/13/1806.

Harris, Thos. H.–Hrs.–Will Bk. A, p 366–Thos., Taliza, Betsy, Polly and Rebecca Harris, ch. of Thos. and under age. 9/28/1807

Henderson, Fanny–Will Bk. B, p. 18–gdn. bond.

Henderson, Thos. Will Bk. B, p. 419–gdn. bond; sett. p. 434.

Hunter, John–Will Bk. C, p. 406–Admr. bond.

Hayden, Turner–Will Bk. B, p. 92–Sale bill.

Heath, Chas. Andrew–Will Bk. B, p. 117–Inv.

Hendricks, Daniel, Will Bk. B, p. 217–Sett.

Hayden, Nancy, Will Bk. B, p. 254–Gdn. bond.

Houston, Harrison–Will Bk. B, p 204–Gdn. bond.

Hawkins, Sally (Widow of John Hawkins and dau. of Peter Johnston of Culpeper Co. Va.) Will Bk. C, p. 37–To Wm. Wilson, to hrs. hereafter designated: Jamison Hawkins, William Hawkins, Peggy Cave, Sally Smith, Thomas, Nancy Cason, Fanny Thomas, Betsy Faulkner, Lucinda Davis, Wts. Alex Steele and Elizabeth Johnson–Codicil–dau. Lucy Davis and ch. equal part of estate of John Hawkins decd. which I hold. 6/17/1817–10/3/1819 Wts. Elijah Hawkins—Hawkins

Harkness, Robt.–Will Bk. C, p. 46–Sett.

Hagan (Hogan?) Jas.–Will Bk. C, p. 79–Inv.

Herndon, John H.–Will Bk. C, p. 155–Sett. with gdn.

Hutcheson, Jas.–Will Bk. C, p 185–Inv.

Head, Jesse–Will Bk. C. p. 201–Admr. bond

Hutchison, Jas. G.–Will Bk. C, p 204–Sale bill

Hufford, Daniel–Will Bk. C, p. 225–Sale bill

Henry. Jesse–Will Bk. C, p. 243–Inv.

Hall, John–Will Bk. C, p. 247–Children: Warren, John, Emily, Boswell (gd. dau. Judith S. Richardson), Wm., Chas, Malinda Darniby, Broadston (or Braxton) P., Thos. G., Bartlett, wife not named but mentioned. Exrs: John Washington, (and), son, Thos. Hall. 3/1817– Wts: Alfred J. Hall, Geo. P. Kelley, D. Flournoy–Note: Descendant stated wife was Isabella, possibly Graves.

Hufford, Wm.–Will Bk. C, p. 256–Gdn. bond

Herndon, Scott–Will Bk. C, p. 264–Estate app.

Hufford, David–Will Bk C, p. 270–Gdn. bond

Herndon, Thos.–Will Bk. C, p. 343–Estate app. Note: Died at advanced age, Nov. 1821, in Rev. War. see Lexington Ky. Gazette.

Henry Jno. T.–Will Bk. C, p. 385–Estate app.

Hunter. John–Will Bk. C. p. 406–Admr. bond

Ingram, Jacob–Will Bk. A, p. 122–decd. hrs. shown in Order Bk. A.

Innis, Nathl.–Will Bk. B, p. 232–Admr. bond

Jones, John–Will Bk. A, p. 3–Estate

Johnson, Benj.–Will Bk. A, p. 6–p. 279 Admr. bond.

Jones, Jno. M.–Will Bk. A, p. 143–Estate

Johnson, Henry Ashton—Will Bk. A, p. 295—Money due from Virginia, wife Nancy and ch., friend and kinsman, Wm. G. Johnson and wife Exrs. 1/9/1806—March 1806 (see Order Books for inf. hrs.)

Johnson, Henry—Will Bk. B. p 47—Sett. with admr.

Johnson, Adam—Will Bk. B, p. 100—Gdn. bond

Johnson, William—Will Bk. B, pp 101, 233—Inv. and Sales

Johnson, Jacob—Will Bk. B, p. 144—To sons, Wm. Isaac, James, wife Sarah, dau. Eleanor Trusil, Sarah ——, Jane Cummins, Kitty Williamson; g. ch. Jacob Johnson Dever, Nancy Dever, Hedgman, Sarah W. —— and Elizabeth Dever. Wts: Alex. Curran. Hugh Sharon, Sam'l. Sharon—prob. Jan. 1815 (no date).

Jones, Benj.—Will Bk. B, p 167—Inv.

Jackson, Colby—Will Bk. B, p. 178—Com'r. bond

Jones, Wm. H.—Will Bk. B, p. 224—Gdn. bond

Johnson, Richard—Will Bk. B, p. 227—Com'r. bond

Johnson, Wm. H. Will Bk. B, p. 281—Gdn. bond

Johnson, Robt.—Will Bk. B, p. 315—Estate app.

Johnson, Wm. A.—Will Bk. B, p. 327—Inv.

James, Ann—Will Bk. C, p. 471—To Teresa Twyman (her present marriage), son Wm. James, gd. dau. Ann Summers or Simms(?), son Joseph James. 1/26/1811—May 1811

Johnson, Betsy—Will Bk. C, p. 71—Dower allotted

Johnson, Madison—Will Bk. C, p. 314—Gdn. bond

James, James—Will Bk. C, p. 391—Gdn. bond

Johnson, Adam—Will Bk. C, p. 433—Sett. with gdn.

Johnson, Wm. H.—Will Bk. C, p. 313—Gdn. bond

James, Jas. decd.—Will Bk. C, p. 391—8/5/1822—Peter Ault gdn. to Scott, Henry, W., John and Kitty James inf. hrs. of Jas. James decd.—bond.

Kirtley, Elizabeth—Will Bk. A, p. 5—Decd.

Kirtley, Elijah—Will Bk. A, p. 8—Decd. see hereafter.

Keene, Jno. Y.—Will Bk. A, p 31—Decd.

Kay. John—Will Bk. A, p. 114—Decd.

Keene, Wm.—Will Bk. A, p. 126—Will—To Capt. John Hunter and wife, my dau., son, Richard property "that I left him possessed of in Maryland," to gd. dau. Margaret Keene, gd. dau. —— gd. son, Greenup Keene—Exrs. Dr. Samuel Keene and Capt. John Hunter. Wts: Hopewell Keene, Jas. H. Price, W. Warren Jr.

Kirtley, Elijah—Hrs. Will Bk. A, p. 183—2/15/1804—Sett. with Francis, Admr. and Simon Kirtley, gdns. to Elijah Larkin Kirtley, Wm. Kirtley, Matilda Kirtley, Ann Kirtley, Jas. Kirtley and Susan Kirtley orphans of Elijah Kirtley, decd.—all to be schooled but Elijah and Larkin, sett. with gdn. Bk. B, p. 164

Keene, Thos. B.—Will Bk. A, p. 191—Will—To wife, Mary, son(s?) Vachel and Richard Keene, div. between all ch. except Vachel for whom provided. 10/9/1802—Mar. 1804—Wts: Robt. Hunter, Chas. Keene, Wm. Warren. (Thos. Keene was an orphan)

Keene, Sam'l.—Will Bk. A, p. 291—Benj. Keene, Admr. Mar. 1806—To Hillary Keene, widow of Sam'l. L. Keene—dower. Aug. 1807

Keene, Sam'l. Y.—Will Bk. B, p. 143—Inv. Gdn. bond in Bk. C, p. 315

Keene, Richard—Will Bk. B, p. 179—Allottment to widow

Keene, Wm.—Will Bk. B, p. 244—Sett. with gnd.

Keene, Sam'l. Y.—Will Bk. C, p. 315—Gdn. bond

Kercheville, John—Will Bk. C, p. 437—Wife ——, four ch. two sons and two daus., sons under age. to daus. grown, one named Louisa. Oct. 19 —— wts: —— Payne, John Lackland, Geo. and Wm. Kercherville admrs. 11/4/1822

Keene, Richard H.—Will Bk. C, p. 417—Wife Dealey, sons John C. Richard L, Benedict C. Keene, daus. Nancy R. Keene, Mary H. Keene, Rebecca E. Keene, Exrs: Joshua Crumwell, Vachel Keene—5/19/1822—Wts: Jas. D. Offutt. Jas. Masterson, Daniel Ford—Oct. 1822

Layton, Rebecca—Will Bk. A, p. 83—Will—My 5 ch: Daniel, Leah, Thos. Rebecca and Peggy Layton, Jesse Griffith should have care of son Daniel and dau. Leah Layton, Spencer Layton to have care of son Thos. and dau. Rebecca, David Layton to have care of Peggy Layton ——. Spencer Layton Exr. 1/17/1798—Wts: Robt. Griffith, Alex. Stinson, Robt. Tortman (?)—Apr. 1798

Long, Daniel—Will Bk. A, p. 132—decd.

Lindsay, Wm.—Will Bk. A, p. 10—Sett. with Exrs. July 1796. Henry and Wm. C. Lindsay— p. 93—later-son of Henry to get estate of his mother etc.

Lambert, Daniel—Will Bk. A, p. 207—Will—Wife Ruth, sons: Benj. and John, daus, Mary Baldwin and Phoeby Thomson—land on Swanee Run, Fayette Co. and part in Woodford adjoining Thos. McClanahan, Exrs: John and Benj. Lambert—6/18/1804—Wts: Rodes Smith, John Brock, Robt. Lemmon, Hugh Dickey. Aug. 1804.

Lewis, John—Will Bk. A, p 218—Hrs.: Patsey Lewis, Buford Lewis and Henry Lewis, orphans under age. Nov. 1804.

Lambert, Jno.—Will Bk. A, p 222, 228, 340—Benj. Lambert Admr., Benj. Glass, Moses Baldwin, Commrs. Nov. 1804—Widow's dower, Polly Lambert, Hannah Lambert, Nancy Lambert and John Lambert, orphans—Sett. Widow, Barbary Lambert. 12/12/1807.

Lowery, Stephen—Will Bk. A, p. 228—Decd.—Stephen Lowery orphan—12/27/1804—p. 274, Catherine and Wm. Lowery orphans under age, 1805.

Lowery, Alex. Scott—Will Bk. A, p. 242—decd. From Chester Co. Pa. See K.C.O.R.v.I (Bible)

Lindsay, John V. Will Bk. A, p. 287—Will—Wife Ann land bought of Wm. Buckner, unm. daus. as come of age equal to what I give m. daus., sons John and Robt., all my female ch. 9/29/1805—Wts: Joseph Eve, Betty Gless, John Eve, J. Bennett—Jan. 1806

Lightburn, John—Will Bk. A—Estate—p. 360, 362, 372, 434—Richard Lightburn Admr. 6/22/ 1809

Layton, Thos.—Will Bk. A, p. 386—Orphans Rebecca Layton —— Jan. 1808

Lewis, Polly, Will Bk. B, p. 46—Gdn. bond

Land, John—Will Bk. B, p. 68—gdn. bond

Logan, Samuel—Will Bk. B, p. 85—Inv.

Logan, Alex. Will Bk. B, p. 125—Gdn. bond

Landrum, Jas.—Will Bk. B, p. 198—Admr. bond

Linchard, Thos.—Will Bk. B, p. 221—Gdn. bond

Louderback, ——? Will Bk. B, p. 222, gdn. bond

Lowery, Abram—Will Bk. B, p. 351—Wife Betsy B. ch. not named, wife Exrx. (Note: Most of this will missing—he was son of Stephen Lowery and Catherine Lewis Lowery, she dau. of Arch. Hutcheson—see Lowery—Hutcheson Bible K.C.O.R.v.I.)

Lowery, Sm'l.—Will Bk. B, p. 407—Gdn. bond

Lewis, Tolman—Will Bk. C, p. 14—Admr. bond

Logan, Wm. B.—Will Bk. C, p. 82—Wife Catherine C. Logan, son, Robt (bro. Alex. Logan), lots in Dayton, Ohio, to son, also Geo. Logan, Cousin Mary Logan, nephew Wm. Smith. bro-in-law Jno. B. Smith, bros. Geo. and Alex. Logan, wife Catherine Exrs. 11/16/1819— Wts; Louis Marshall, Philemon Price. Jas. McConnell. 4/3/1820

Lightburn, Richard—Will Bk. C, p. 85—Wife Temperance, son Alvin W., other ch. 2/15/1820—
Wts: Jno. Whitney, Joel Crenshaw, Thos. C. Sutton, Wife Exrx. Apr. 1820—Note: Richard
Lightburn was son of Col. Richard—see Scott Co. orders E, p 360—wife was wid. of John
Sutton (see will) she d. 10/31/1851 aged 73, dau. of John and Mollie Sutton, Scott Co.
Other ch.: Richard P. Jno. S. Thos. C. Wm. Martha C., Henry and Polly Ann Lightburn.

Lewis, Nathan—Will Bk. C, p. 92—

Lee, Jas. Will Bk. C, p. 150—

Leach, Wm.—Will Bk. C, p. 387—Wife Mary, sons, ——? Reuben, Henry and Benton Leach,
daus. Betsey Peak, Rebecca Leach, Nancy ——, Susannah Fields, Ruthy Peak, Polly
Brown, Harriet Holden —— other sons, Walter and Wm. B. Exrs, Wm. B. and Henry
Leach. 4/22/1813—Wts: F. Bradford, Younger Pitts, Jas. West. 8/5/1822

Lemon, John—Will Bk. C, p. 393—(Almost all missing)—Ch. and step-ch.—Jno. Lemon Jr.,
Jas. Lemon, Geo. Lemon, Marie McCail, Jane Mulberry, Ann Lemon. Exrs: John Lemon
—— Lemon. 5/30/1820—Wts: John Mulberry. Chas. Patterson, Aug. 1822

Moody, Jno. Will Bk. A, p. 17—Wm. Moody Admr. Dec. 27, 1796

Moody, James, decd. Hrs. Will Bk. A, p. 18—Oct. 27, 1796—Wm. Moody Exr.—Elizabeth, Sarah
and James Moody orphans under age.

Morris, Elizabeth—Will Bk. A, p. 17—Will—Dau. Suckey Oldham, all; son-in-law Geo. Oldham
Exr. 8/9/1796—1/23/1797

Monteith, David—Will Bk. A, p. 29—Will—Well beloved wife ——, three ch.: Wm., David and
Esther. 8/4/1797—Wts: Wm. Ward, Edward ——, Sept. 1797

Moony (Moody?), Jas. Hrs. Will Bk. A, p 43—see heretofore

Mulberry, Jno. Will Bk. A.—decd.

McClain, Allen—Will Bk. A, p. 60—Inv. 12/24/1798

McCormick, Hugh—Will Bk. A, p. 69—Wife Katherine, dau. Elizabeth, dau. Mary, sons, Geo.
and Wm. John and Wm. McClure mentioned, money in Pa. due from Elias Harning
(Haming?) and others in 1800, dau. Martha Chamberlin, sons, exrs. 6/17/1799—Wts: Jas.
Rugless, Jas. Officer, Jas. Stephenson—Oct. 1799

Montague, Wm.—Will Bk. A, p. 78—Abram and Elizabeth Dupee, Cave and John Montague
of Boone Co. Ky. appt. Wm. Montague of same place atty. to recover for us that owing us
by Robt. Bradley Admr. of estate of Wm. Montague decd. 1/27/1801

McArthur, (McCarter?) Peter—Will Bk. A, p 90—Inv. 4/27/1801

Masterson, Drury—Will Bk. A, p. 119—Inv. also pps. 195,273—Orphans: John, Zach., Tamer
Masterson, 1805

Mudd (Meed, Mead?) John—Will Bk. A, p 120—Will—Son John Mead and he be educated as
rest of ch., dau. Nancy Mead, dau. Sally Meed, under 21, "all my ch.", dau. Sally be sent
to Mr. Ludlow Branham to raise and educate her, Bartlett Collins to have care of John
Meed. 12/25/1801—Wts: Wm. G. Johnson, Jas. Wood, John Thompson and Sam'l.
Shepherd. Jan. 1802

Milford, David—Will Bk. A, p. 130-205—Inv. May 24, 1802—Robt. Thompson Admr.

Merry, Prettyman—Will Bk. A, p. 144—Ann Mary (Merry)—widow (?)—10/8/1802.

Martin, Thos.—Will Bk. A, p. 163—To Margaret Martin—farm, furniture etc. (evidently wife),
two sons, James and Thos., rest between all ch. except son Robt. now in Pa. and dau.
Margaret in Fayette Co. Ky. to whom I bequeath 10 pounds each of 52 that is due for a
part price for my land in Pa., "My wife aforesaid, dau. Mary Martin, sons, Thos, John,
James, Samuel, Benj. and Alexander Martin—2/2/1800—Wts: Daniel Sinclair, Early Scott,
John Vanzant—Sept. 1803

Monteith, Wm.—Will Bk. A, p. 177—Orphan of David Monteith

Miller, Polly—Will Bk. A, p. 212—Orphan of Wm. Miller.

McCrackin, Wm.—Will Bk. A, p. 411—Hrs.—div. no hrs. named, 6/23/1806

Milam, Archd.—Will Bk. A, p. 312—Will—Wife, two ch. Exrs: David Thomson, Wm. Massie of Scott, Jno. M. Scott of Franklin Co. 4/12/1806—Wts: John Stites, Jan Milain, Richard Steele, June 1806

McClure, Mary—Will Bk. A, pp. 365, 396—Will—To Hanner Worsley and Holbert McClure, to Nathaniel McClure, dau. Rebecca Anderson, to Thos. Anderson, son Moses McClure —— 1804—Wts: Lewis Nuckols, Jno. Kennedy, Jno. McClure

McCullough, Joseph—Will Bk. A, p. 371—Sally McCullough and Wm. and Alex. Tilford and Alex. Tilford Jr. Admrs. (Wm. McCullough was an orphan)

Morris, Robt.—Will Bk. A, p. 372—Martha and David Morris Admrs. Nov. 23, 1807

Merryman, Eleanor—Will Bk. A, p. 435—Hrs: Jas. Combs bound to deliver to his inf. ch., Elizabeth and Susannah Combs, legatees of Eleanor Merryman. (Note: Vital Statistics show Abegail Lynn d. 9/19/1858—aged 64, b. in Conn. and dau. of E. Meryman.

McCullough, Joseph—Will Bk. B, p. 10—Sett.

McFaul (McFael) Iohn—Will Bk. B. p. 19—Wife Elizabeth, adopted son Chard (or Charles), all of New York City, N. Y. 11/29/1806—Wts: Sam'l. Crowder, P. H. Vendover (or Vandown) and Richard Chalk, Aug. 1809

McHatton, Jas. Will Bk. B, p. 149—Inv.

McCoy, Hugh—Will Bk. B, p. 203—Inv.

McKinley, Dabid—Will Bk. B, p. 384—Sett.

McCombs, Martha—Will Bk. B, p. 217—Will—Jas. Parks Exr., nephew Hugh Parks, to Jas. Price a note on Henry Hart and David his son, now in hands of Stephen R. Price, Martha P. Boyles, dau. to Jas. Boyles, bro. Jas. Parks, 5/31/1815—Wts: James———Jeremiah Adams—11/6/1815

McCledys, John H.—Will Bk. B, p. 28—Gdn. bond

McMurtry, Wm.—Will Bk. B, p. 290—Will—Ch: Betsy, Robert, Pinknay, Polly, James, William. Exrs: David McMurtry, Sam'l. Finley—Feb. 20, 1816—Wts: Geo. Short and Addison McPheeters—Mar. 1816

McCoy, Alex.—Will Bk. B, p. 387—Will—Wife Mary, son Alex., dau. Mary Dare, sons, Joseph, Thos. John; my ch: Alex. Johnson, Charlotte Johnson, Jas. and Wm. Johnson, Quintin, Margaret and Elizabeth Dick and Jane, Isaiah, Betsy, Lucinda and———Vinzant (probably meant grandch?) Exrs. Son Alex and son-in-law Thos. Shaw. Nov. 1807—Wts: Jas. Shepherd, Wm. Brown, Will Story—Feb. 1817.

Miner, Jeremiah—Will Bk. B, p. 11—Admr. bond.

Miner, Wm.—Will Bk. B, p. 15—Estate app.

Martin, Thos.—Will Bk. B, p. 64—Sett. with Admr.

Miller, Adam—Will Bk. B, p. 132—Estate app.

Miller, Geo. W.—Will Bk. B, p. 283—Admrs. bond.

Martin, Jas.—Will B, p. 297—Estate app.

Monroe, Jno.—Will Bk. B, p. 180—Sett.

Morris, Martha, Will Bk. B, p. 318—Gdn. bond.

Manliffe, Jas. Will Bk. B, p. 267—Admr. bond.

Miller, Wm.—Will Bk. B, p. 411—Sett. with Admr.

Montgomery, Thos.—Will Bk. B, p. 278—Will—Grandson Montgomery Deremple, other gr. ch: David and Caty Deremple—Jan. 1815—Wts. Jas. Patterson, Jesse Hanna (Jas. Montgomery Deeemple was b. on the 15th of April 1809 and Caty Deremple was b. Jan. 11, 1811—Exr: Nathl. Shannon, Feb. 1816.

Mahan, John—Will Bk. B, p. 424—Sett. with Exr.

Monroe, Andrew—Will Bk. B, p. 434—Admr. bond.

McClure, Wm.–Will Bk. C, p. 12–Adm. bond.

McClure, Thos.–Will Bk. C, p. 43–Estate app.

McMurtry, Wm.–Will Bk. C, p. 53–Sale bill.

McCoy, Z.–Will Bk. C, p. 80.

McCroskey, Saml.–Will Bk. C, p. 174–Admr. bond.

McCroskey, Wm.–Will Bk. C, p. 169–Gdn. bond.

McMillen, Robt.–Will Bk. C, p. 324–Estate app.

Mallory, Chas.–Will Bk. C, p. 15–Admr. bond.

Moore, Robt. Will Bk. C, p. 16–Admr. bond.

Mosley, John–Will Bk. C, p. 32–Estate app.

Marteman(?), Daniel–Will Bk. C, p. 67–Gdn. bond.

Mahoney, Jas. H.–Will Bk. C, p. 69–gdn, of.

Marcy, John–Will Bk. C, p. 70–Admr. bond.

Mefford, David–Will Bk. C, p. 46–Gdn. bond.

Mosby, Jas.–Will Bk. C, p. 90–gdn. bond.

Masterson, Aaron–Will Bk. C, p. 91–

Morely, Jacob–Will Bk. C, p. 98–Ch: Margaret and Susan, others not named, 11/21/1819–
Wts: Francis Atwell, Benj. James–Feb. 1820.

Monne, Andrew–Will Bk. C, p. 193–Estate app.

Martin, Jas.–Will Bk. C, p. 268.

Moseley (Mosly), John–Will Bk. C, p. Wife Elizabeth, ch: Wm.. John Jr.. Sarah Chew
Mosley–2/18/1817–Exrs., Chas Smith, Wm. –––––, Wts: John D. Craig, Sam'l. Keene.
Dec. 1817

Merryman, Amos–Will Bk. C, p. 371–Wife Abigail, Ch: Reuben, Lyman, Pally, Seely
Nobly? Lyon. Sally Berry and––––Lynn (Lann?)–date missing–wts: Christopher––––
and Jas. Harwood, Exrs: Reuben and Layman Merryman–7/1/1822 date of probate.
Note: Vital Statistics–Abigail Lynn d. 9/19/1858 aged 64 b. Conn. dau. of A. and E(?)
Meryman, Scott Co.

Mulberry. Jacob–Will Bk. C, p. 374–Ch: James, Polly Neale, Betsy Mallory, John, Nancy
Pigg–6/29/1820 Exrs: Garret Wall, John Mulberry–Wts: G. Wall, Benj. Pack–7-1-
1822–Note: Vital Statistics Wm. Mulberry Sr. d. 5-11-1852 aged 67, son of Jacob and
M. Mulberry, Scott Co.

Murphy, John–Will Bk. C, p. 411–Admr. bond.

Moore, Geo.–Will Bk. C, p. 440–Admr. bond.

Newenham, Nath'l.–Will Bk. A, p. 56, also pps. 42, 33–Sept. 25, 1797–Joshua Newingham
and Lazarus Cox Admrs.

Neale, Spencer–Will Bk. A, p. 72, also p. 82–Dec. 23, 1799–Daniel Neal admr. Orphans:
Minor (Mina) Neal, Elizabeth Neal, Daniel Neal under age. 12/27/1800–

Neale, Daniel–Will Bk. A, p. 216, p. 280–Will–Wife Jemima, 10 ch: Daniel, Wm., Presley,
John, Thadius, Rhodham, Nancy Kelley, Jemima Leach, Penelope Neale and Susannah
Neale, Exrs: Jas, Kelley, Rhodham Neale and Daniel Neale–"my four orphan ch. 'till of
age–5/10/1802–Wts: Christopher Neale, Joseph Wilson, John Hawkins–Sept. 1804.
(Note: Daniel Neale (p. 280) was gdn. for orphan ch. of Spencer Neale decd. Daniel
Neale was born in Fairfax Co. Va. 1735–see MacKinzies Colonial Families in the U.S.
vol. IV)

Nall, Polly–Will Bk. A, p. 333–Lewis Nall and Martin Nall gdns. to Milley Nall orphan of
Martin Nall decd. 12/22/1806–also Chas. Nall orphan, Jas. Nall orphan and Polly Nall
aforesaid, p. 352, 334

Neale, Wm.–Will Bk. A, p. 364–Mary and Dan'l. Neale Admirs.

Neale, Spencer H.–Will Bk. B, p. 13–sett. with gdn.

Neale, Wm.–Will Bk. B, p. 13–Sett. with Exr.

Nash, John–Will Bk. B, p. 16–Sett. with Admr.

Neale, Daniel–Will Bk. B, p. 346–Will–Wife Sally, sons, Lewis, Daniel, Wm., Simeon, Asa, Presley–10/7/1816–Wts: Jas. Kelly. Thadeus D. Neale, Sarah Neale–Nov. 1816

Neale, Wm.–Will Bk. C, p. 305–Sett. with gdn.

Nutter, David–Will Bk. C, p. 381–Estate app.

Nall, Wm.–Will Bk. C, p. 384–Odmr. bond.

Osborne, Thos.–Will Bk. A, p. 159–Estate app. by Fielding Bradford. Sam'l. Dehaven, Rhoda Coppage, 6/20/1803.

Osborne, John–Bk. B, p. 397, Admrs. bond.

Offutt, Nathaniel–Will Bk. C, p. 197–Wife Deborah, ch: Zedac, Jesse, Anna, Debba(?), Patsy–6-4-1818–Wts: Jno. McHatten. Sam'l. McHatten, Moses A. Ferris–Exrs: Wm. Holden–Apr. 1819.

Owen, Owens–Will Bk. C, p. 319–Admr. bond.

Pawling, Wm.–Will Bk. A, p. 112–see K.C.O.R.v.I.

John Peak–Will Bk. A, p. 289–see K.C.O.R.v.I.

Patton, Philip–Will Bk. A, p.–Will–Negroes to be free, note on Wm. Ham of Madison Co. to be divd. equally between negro Grace and her three ch. 5/22/1808–Wts: John Crackwell, Rhoda Thomason.

Pew, Joseph–Will Bk. A, p.–Admr's. bond, Jan. 1809–Bk. B, p. 14–Joseph Pugh Estate app.

Peak, John–Will Bk. A, p. 289–see K.C.O.R.v.I.

Pettit, Sam'l.–Will Bk. B, p. 76–Estate app.

Patterson, John–Will Bk. B, p. 309–Admr's. bond.

Pierce. Adam–Will Bk. B. p.–Will–Wife Nancy, daus. Mary Pebler, Elizabeth Shaver, Katy Utterback, two younger ch. Wm. and Mary (or May) Pierce, son Adam, son George, son John. (Note: Youngest child according to the way this will is recopied in book is either Mae, May, Mary or Naomia as it is spelled all three ways). Wts. Wm. B. Leach. Wm. Johnson, Rodham Neale, Exrs. son George Pierce, Henry Leach, 9/2/1814–June 1816.

Power, Richard–Will Bk. B, p. 380–Will–Wife Mary, daus. Nancy and Anna ,son Thos. and Ivan E. Power. other ch: Joseph, Sarah––––Robert, Elizabeth McAtee?, John, Susannah Campbell, and Mary Simpson. Exrs. wife and son John Power. 8/20/18– Wts: Wm. Cox–8/5/1816(?).

Payne, Asa–Will Bk. B, p. 353–Gdn. bond.

Peak, Hezekiah–Will Bk. B, p. 365–Admr's. bond.

Porter, Eben–Will Bk. B, p. 371–Admr's. bond.

Pence, Adam–Will Bk. B, p. 378–Admr's. bond.

Pegman, Samuel–Will Bk. B, p. 392–Bond.

Polk, John–Will Bk. B, p. 422–Sett.

Pewitt, V.–Will Bk. C, p. 8 Exr. of.

Peak, Spence, Will Bk. C, p. 59–Slaves Jenny, Hannah etc. to be free at his death. Son, Presley, nephew John Scott–10-1-1817–Exrs: Presley Peak and B. S. Chambers–Jan. 1820. Note: Said John Scott was son of Jno. Scott of Jessamine Co.

Pigman, John B.–Will Bk. C, p. 4–Estate app.

Patterson, Wm.–Will Bk. C, p. 241–Gdn. bond.

Pence, Naomi–Will Bk. C, p. 265–Gdn. bond.

Pettit, Keturah–Will Bk. C, p. 33–Keturah Ann McDowell (relationship missing), sister-in-law, Elizabeth Pettit, Bradford ——–(Miss McDowell lives in Ohio)–1/27/1823–Wts: Eleanor McDaniel, Dorothy Kerr, Exr. David Kerr.

Plummer, Caroline–Will Bk. C, p. 416–Gdn. bond.

Quin, James–Will Bk. C, pps. 281, 337–Estate app. etc.

Ross, Wm.–"Late of Sussex Co. Delaware, now of Scott"–See K.C.O.R.v.I.

Risk, John–Will–See K.C.O.K.vol.I.

Richardson, Wm. H.–Will Bk. B, p. 21Admr's. bond.

Rhodes, Waller–Will Bk. B, p. 22–Sett.

Rainey, Robt.–Will Bk. B, p. 33–Admr's. bond.

Reddish, Jas. H.–Will Bk. B, p. 196–Gdn.

Rossell, Stephen–Will Bk. B, p. 196–Gdn.

Richardson, Jesse–Will Bk. B, p. 250–Estate app.

Redding, Joseph–Will Bk. B, p. 276–Wife Martha Ann, Lettie Osborne's hrs., Sarah Fugget, Susannah Piatt, Eliz. Osborne, Anna Adair, Elijah V—— his dau. Pamelia, Lettie Osborne, dau. of Joseph and Martha Ann Redding, son, Elijah and gr. dau. Pamelia, wife Exrx.–(much missing) Joseph Redding died 1815.

Risk, John H.–Will Bk. B, p. 255–Gdn. bond.

Redding, Martha Ann–Will Bk. B, p. 343–Gdn. bond.

Risk——–Will Bk. B, p. 436–Note–So much missing that only a few names are shown–daus. Jane Bareter, Pegy Bailey, Anna–Exr.–Alex Curray–7/14/1817

Redding, Sally–Will Bk. B, p. 396–Gdn's. bond

Rodes, Clifton–Will Bk. C, p. 40-41–Son-in-law Jas. Burch, son-in-law James Rogers, dau. Agnes Rodes, 9-25-1816–Wts: Caroline Gorham, Elizabeth Prewitt, Exrs. Jas. Burch. V. Prewitt. Oct. 1819 Note: Clifton Rodes m. Sarah Waller, Spotsylvania Co. Va.–see Albemarle Co. Va., Va. Magazine, etc.

Risk, James–Will Bk. C, pp. 286, 409 etc.–Sake bill, admr. bond etc.

Smith, Thos.–Will Bk. A, p. 96–Will–see K.C.O.R.v.I

Shirley, Wm.–Will Bk. A, p.–see K.C.O.R.v.I.

Sanders, Robt.–Will Bk. A, p.–Son Toliver, son Valentine, son Benj., sons Thos. and Walker (or Waller), all sons equally, dau. Nancy T. Sanders, Peter Gatewood Jr. to move to my house with my ch. until Walker is of age, Cato Haskins to be paid. Exrs. David Flournoy, John Thomason, Peter Gatewood. 5/11/1805–Son Valentine Saunders–Wts: Henry Herndon, Jas. Barton, Benj. Wharton–5/27/1805.

Senar, Fredk.–Will Bk. B, p. 41–Estate app.

Sutton, John–Will Bk. B, p. 72–Will–Wife Temperance; ch: John, Wm., David and Polly Swetnam (husband Geo. Swetnam) and Robert and Carolin his wife. Exrs: Rhodes Thomason, Bartlet Collins, Temperance Sutton. 2/14/1790–Wts: Wm. Montague, Benj. Wharton–Aug. 1810.

Sutphin, Stuart–Will Bk. B, p. 90–Estate app.

Sharp, ——– Will Bk. B, p. 94–Admr's. bond.

Shortridge, Wm.–Will Bk. B, p. 99–Will–sons Wm. and John, dau. Sally Neale, other ch. (not named), wife (not named)–Sons Exrs. 6/26/1810–Wts: David Thomson, James Gaines, Roger Thompson–9/5/1814

Stiles, John–Will Bk. B, p. 111–Sale bill.

Smith, Joseph—Will Bk. B, p. 137—Will—Wife Leonna, dau. Sarah Winscot, son—John, Thomas, Moses and Pricilla Cobb, Lucy Roberts and Anna Smith (daus.), Lewis Smith (another son—name missing) Exrs: Lewis and Moses Smith—1/23/1810—Wts: Jas. Bell, Wm. Glass, Id(?) Coppage, Morehead Clear. Dec. 1814.

Sinclair, Daniel—Will Bk. B, p. 152—Admr's. bond.

Shelton, David—Will Bk. B, p. 154—Admr's bond.

Sinclair, Robt.—Will Bk. B, p. 199—Will Wife Sarah, sons, Chas., Morehead, Armstead, Wm., daus. Susanna Scott, Eliza Triplett, sons, Robt, James, Asa. dau. Lucy Sinclair, seven sons, three daus. Sarah Sinclair Exrx. Wm. and Armistead Exrs. 5/31/1815—Wts: Mareen Duval, John Coppage, Thos. Coppage, Aug. 1815.

Swan, John—Will Bk. B, p. 219 and 296—Admr's. bond.

Smith, C. P.—Will Bk. B, p. 229—Admr's. bond.

Sutphin, Richard—Will Bk. B, p. 231—Gdn's. bond.

Snell, Jos.—Will Bk. B, p. 233—Admr's. bond.

Scott, John—Will Bk. B, p.—Will—Wife Hannah, son Joel, dau Nelly Bra———, Sally, son, Ezekiel, dau. Polly Brooking, grandson Sam'l. Brooking ——— Early and Thos. Scott— Exrs: Rhodes Smith, Joel and Ezekiel Scott—11/19/1815—Wts: R. McCalla, Toliver Craig, Joseph Minor, Adm. Herring—12/6/1815

Shirley, Wm.—Will Bk. B, p. 255—Sett.

Smith, Sally—Will Bk. B, p. 281—Gdn. bond.

Scott, Abram—Will Bk. B, p. 349—Gdn. bond.

Smith, Agnes—Will Bk. B, p. 386—"of county of Miami, State of Ohio", Nancy McClung, my niece, Alex. T. Henderson———Henderson and Jno. G. Henderson my nephews. Exr. David McClung—Wts: Alex. (?) Tilford, also of Miami Co. Ohio—pro. Scott Co. 1817.

Short, Eli—Will Bk. B, p. 402—Will—Wife Jessie, ch: Obed, Purnell, son-in-law Talmon Truitt, of Sussex Co. Del., Eli Jr.—Exrs. Eli Jr. and another son—11th day of——1817—Wts: Jas. Howard, Thos. Montgomery—5/5/1817—(parts missing)

Shannon, Nath'l.—Will Bk. B—p. 405.

Stucker, Jacob—Will Bk. C, p. 1—Estate app.

Sinclair, Wm. P.—Will Bk. C, p. 1—Admr. bond.

Shibling, Benj.—Will Bk. C, p. 42—Sett.

Smith, C. R.—Will Bk. C, p. 75—Sett. with gdn.

Sutton, Wm.—Will Bk. C, p. 78—Admr. bond.

Saunders, Robt.—Will Bk. C, p. 139—Sett. with Exr.

Stucker, John and Greenup—Will Bk. C, p. 148—Gdn. bond.

Stucker, David and Polly—Will Bk. C, p. 151—Gdn. bond.

Snell, John—Will Bk. C, p. 151—Ch: Wm. Joseph, John, Cumberland and Robt. Snell, Willis and Landon Snell, Frances Wells and Anne Owens, ch. of (Elijah Snell?). Jack, Gulbert. Tom. Joseph, dau. Eliz. West, other gd. ch., ch. of Joseph Snell, Elizabeth Ann. Lucinda and Susannah Snell. Exrs: Landon and Cumberland Snell. 5-4-1820—Wts: John Thompson, Wm. Haydon and ——— Davis. July 1820—Codicil, 5-4-1820.

Sharpe, Thos.—Will Bk. C, p. 165—Wife Jane, ch: James, Wm., Lunsford, and Benj. Sharp, Sally Green, Lucy Jacobs, Polly Wolf, Eliza, Robt. and Thos. Exrs: Jas. Sharpe and Bob McHatton—8-21-1820—Wts: Coonrad, David and Wm. Wolf. 10-2-1820.

Smith, Wm.—Will Bk. C, p. 198—Admr. bond.

Saunders, Benj. W.—Will Bk. C, p. 199—Admr. bond.

Sproule, Alex.—Will Bk. C, p. 232—Gdn. bond.

Smith, Jane—Will Bk. C, p. 257—Gdn. bond.

Smith, Fanny—Will Bk. C, p. 267—gdn. bond.

Sutton, Jorn—Will Bk. C, p. 279—Exrs. bond.

Sutton, Jas.—Will Bk. C, p. 309—Admr. bond.

Stevenson, Reuben—Will Bk. C, p. 328 (4-18-1823), Admrs. Cassandra Stevenson and Job. Stevenson.

Smith, Robt.—Will Bk. C, p. 335—Ch: Nancy Berryman, Sally Campbell—Ch. of Col. Chas. Smith decd. viz: Elizabeth, Elly Frances, Bradford, Benj. Smith (Murray Mary Burbridges, Louisa, Elly—relationship not shown), son, Geo. W. Smith, son, Benj. Smith, son-in-law Henry Elly and Rodes Smith Exrs.—Wts: John Herndon, 1-12-1822—Apr, 1823.

Stevenson, Ruben—Will Bk. C, p. 340—Admr. bond.

Sutphin (Sulphin?), Lou—Will Bk. C, p. 389—Admr. bond.

Sterritt, Sally—Will Bk. C, p. 393—Gdn. bond.

Snell, Joseph—Will Bk. C, p. 395—sett. with gdn.

Sinclair, Robt.—Will Bk. C, p. 431—Sett.

Sulphin (Sutphin?), Timothy—Will Bk. C, p. 423—Inv.

Trotter, Wm.—Will Bk. A, p. 38—Will—see K.C.O.R.v.I.

Thompson, Ann—Will Bk. A, p. 134—Will—see K.C.O.R.v.I

Thomason, Richard—Will Bk. A, p. 137—Will—Wife Sarah, ch. Frances (only one named)—others attended to). Exrs: Henry Jenkins, Nelson Thomason, David Shelton, Henry Dehoney, Nancy Thomason—6/12/1802—9/27/1802.

Thomason, Nelson—Will Bk. A, p. 470—Will—see K.C.O.R.v.I

Thorp (Allenthorp) Benj. Allen—Will Bk. A, p. 293—Will—William Thorp, bro., sister Martha Thorp. bro. George Thorp, father John Allen Thorp Exr. 1/3/1806—3/24/1806—Wts: John B. Tallbott, Sam'l. Young, David Mitchell.

Tilford, David—Will Bk. B, p. 31—Will (almost entirely missing)—1809—Wts: Geo. Oldham, Jos. Green, Michael Goddard—codicil names son Alex. 9/21/1809—Nov. 1809—Other sons and Exrs. include Wm. Mobley, Alex. Tilford.

Turner, Benj. Will Bk. B, p. 172—Sett.

True, Fred'k.—Will Bk. B, p. 312—Sett.

Tyre, Wm.—Will Bk. B, p. 423—Sett.

True, Frederick—Will Bk. C, p. 301—Estate app.

Trymen, (wyman) Jas.—Will Bk. C, p. 390—Gdn. bond.

Thompson, Sarah—Will Bk. C, p. 322—Religion Roman Catholic, mother Exrx.—most missing —only name that of negro slave Angus.

Utter, Wm.—Will Bk. A, p. 32—Will—see K.C.O.R.v.I.

Viley, Geo.—Will Bk. B, p. 147—Admr's. bond.

Vandeback, John—Will Bk. B, p. 190—6/5/1814—Wts: J. McHatton, L. McHatton—Admr., J. Minor Glenn (rest missing)

Viley, Geo.—Will Bk. C, p. 6—Sett. same p. 212—Div. of land.

Walker, Joseph—Will Bk. A, p. 322—Will—see K.C.O.R.v.I.

Whorton, Valentine—Will Bk. A, p. 66—see K.C.O.R.v.I.

Ward, Sam'l.—Will Bk. A, p. 167—Will—see K.C.O.R.v.I.

Woolen, Edward—Will Bk. A, p.—Will—see K.C.O.R.v.I.

Williams, John—Will Bk. B, pps. 4, 42—Gdn. bond.

Wilson, John—Will Bk. B, p. 93—Sale bill.

Withers, Jas.—Will Bk. B, p. 169—Gdn. bond.

Wollum, Jno.–Will Bk. B, p. 181–Will–wife Elizabeth———Elizabeth Stevenson and Polly Stevenson; ch. mentioned but not named–2/24/1815–Exrs: Jno. Guill(?). Richard (?)ennett Jr. Wts: Jno. Guell–May 1815.

Williamson, Tho.–Will Bk. B, p. 271–Will–wife Hannah, sons, James and Thos. date of writing missing–John McHotton(?)———Mrs. Hutchins–Exrs. Feb. 1816.

Wilson. Richard–Will Bk. B, p. 343–Sett.

Ward, Wm.–Will Bk. B, p. 403–Gdn. bond.

Wilson, Thos.–Will Bk. B, p. 421–Admr's. bond.

Ward. Medley–Will Bk. C, p. 7–Estate app.

Webb, Wm.–Will Bk. C, p. 17–Estate app.

Williams, Jeremiah–Will Bk. C, p. 64–Wife Jane, son Robt. (slave named Washington), Son, James, sons, Samuel, Owen, Wesley and Simeon Williams, dau. Nanna Gunnell, dau. Eliz. Brown, dau. Sucky Harris; Cynthia Williams dau. of son John, decd.; Suckey Harris and her two daus. Lucinda and Polly Harris. Exrs. Robt. and Jas. Williams and Alex. Ewing. 4-16-1819–Wts: John T. Johnson and Sam'l. Theobald–Codicil (p. 65)–Slave to dau. Elizabeth Browning during her life then to her dau. Jane Browning. Wts: Alex. Curry, Joseph Cox, Feb. 1820 (pps. 66-67).

Withers, Jas.–Will Bk. C, pp. 68, 177–Hrs. gdn. bond.

Wolfe, David–Will Bk. C, pp. 60, 800 Gdn. bond.

Webb, Wm. S.–Will Bk. C, p. 71–Sale bill.

Wolfe, Jacob–Will Bk. C, p. 76–Admr. bond.

White. Lewis–Will Bk. C, p. 78–Admr. bond; p. 98–will–To wife Nancy, house and lot in Georgetown rented until oldest child is 21 yrs. ch: George, Lewis Jr., Teresa, Jemima, Richard Johnson White and Edwin White; bros Edmund White and David B. White and Jas. H. Mahoney Exrs. and wife Exrx. 5-9-1819–Wts: Sam'l. Shepard, Jno. Spiers, Thos. Elliott. Feb. 1820.

West, Ann–Will Bk. C, p. 175–Admr. bond.

Williamson, Thos.–Will Bk. C, p. 382.

Wash, James–Will Bk. C, p. 323–Wife Manda(?). ch. referred to but not named–most of will missing–names slaves John, Berry and Winston etc.

Ward, Mitchell–Will Bk. C, p. 341–Adm. bond.

Wilmot, Robt.–Will Bk. C, p. 347 etc.–Sale bill etc.

Wallace, John–Will Bk. C, p. 395–Sale bill.

Winter, Jacob–Will Bk. C, p. 405–Wife B————?, son Geo. dau. Mary Crumbaugh, dau. Betsy Topas (land in Shelby Co.), bond on Alex. Willis $528.00–land in Jefferson Co. Patented and surveyed in name of Michael Waggoner, to Joshua——— Geo. Winter, Exr. 8-20-1822–Wts: Jas Kelly, Chas. W. Hall Oct. 1822.

Wallace, Augustine–Will Bk. C, p. 407–Gdn. bond.

Wilson, John–Will Bk. C, p. 407–Gdn. bond.

Wilson, Mary–Will Bk. C, p. 408–Adm. bond.

Wilson, Mary–Will Bk. C, p. 414–Gd. dau. Mary Gilmon, dau. Sally, sons, Thos., Samuel, Mathews, John, dau. Jane. 9-16-1822–Wts: John White. Jas. Fauls, Jas. Harris. Admr. Wm. McClure–Oct. 1822.

Wallace, John–Will Bk. C, p. 441–Gdn. bond.

Yates, Joseph–Will Bk. B, pps. 109, 159–Sale bill.

Young, Nathan–Will Bk. C, p. 182–Admr. bond.

SCOTT COUNTY ORPHANS COURT

ALPHABETIZED NAMES NOT IN GENERAL INDEX

These items of guardians were taken from the first order "A" book of Scott county in attempt to get all in the book. No doubt many were overlooked in the index. The court house burned there in 1837 and all marriages were entirely destroyed, and the wills were all mostly destroyed. The fragments of wills and deeds have been recopied but are so incomplete that these items taken from the order books which were not so badly damaged are of great value in naming the heirs. Scott county was formed in 1792. All over 14 chose their own guardians. The court appointed guardians for those under 14 years of age.

Adams, Lavender, chose his guardian, April 1801, p. 167.

Burdett, Polly, orphan of Frederick Burdett, chose guardian, Feb. 22, 1798. p. 105.

Berryman, Winifred, under 21, inf. orphan of John Berryman, decd. of Va. chose gdn. Sept. 28, 1801. p. 174. (Much of his will is intact and he is of Spottsylvania Co.) He names Winnifred B. as his niece, orphan of John, decd.

Bailey, Platt, orphan of Benj. Bailey, decd.. July 18, 1793.

Collins, Lewis, orphan of Thos. Collins, decd. chose Bartlett Collins, gdn. Jan. 22, 1793. p. 10.

Campbell, William, Lindsey Campbell, Eliz., Jane, Sarah, James and Molly Campbell, orphans of John Campbell, decd., gdns. Oct. 3, 1793. p. 25.

Campbell, Allen, son of John C., decd. chose gdn. Mar. 26, 1804, 237.

Campbell, Elijah, orphan, Mar. 26, 1804. p. 50.

Campbell, Jane & James Campbell, orphans of John C., chose gdn. Mar. 26, 1804. p. 240.

Dorland, Isaac, inf. orphan of John Dorland, decd. bound out. July 1793. p. 18.

Dadinger, Anna, orphan of John D., decd. bound out, Aug. 1795. p. 50.

Dougherty, Dennis, orphan of John Dougherty, gdn. Sept. 28, 1801, 174.

Dougherty, Matthew, orphan of John Dougherty, decd. was 14 Dec. 25 last, chose gdn. Jan. 25, 1802. p. 181.

Elliott, Thos., orphan of Thos. Elliott, decd. June 14, 1790? (This must have been meant for "95" as county was not formed in 1790.)

Edwards, Wm., Edward, Rebecca and Henry H. Edwards were given by the court Rev. Jos. Redding as gdn. June 26, 1797. p. 85.

Ficklin, Thos., proved he was father of Benj. Ficklin, decd. 1801. p. 271.

Green, John & Eliz., children of Chas. Green, decd. gdn. Mar. 1794. p. 26.

Grant, Israel orphans, James and Wm. Grant, chose Wm. Grant, Jr. as gdn. Feb. 24, 1800. p. 148.

Grant, Rebecca, Wm. and Israel Grant chose gdn. p. 148. Feb. 24, 1800.

Grant, Susanna, wid. and relict of Israel Grant, decd. given her dower, Feb. 24, 1800. p. 148.

Grant, Jesse———— child called "Jesse" in will of his father Israel Grant is now to be called "Israel Grant," by order of court, Feb. 24, 1800. (A-148)

Grant, James, inf. orphan of Israel G., chose Wm. Grant, Jr. as his gdn. A-148. Feb. 2, 1800.

Grimsby, Peggy and Wm. Grimsby, orphans of Nimrod Grimsby, decd. chose gdn. Aug. 1805. p. 268.

Grimsby, Lucy, Thos. and Catherine Grimsby given gdn. 1806. p. 292.

Graham, Fergus, aged 6 years, and Wm. Graham, aged 12 years, bound out. Aug. 1805. p. 269.

Hinch, Wm., orphan of John Hinch, bound to his gdn. June 1790? 1795? p. 44.

Holland, Ann, chose Shadrach Penn as her gdn. Oct. 28, 1799. 141.

Herndon, John J., orphan of Lewis Herndon, bound out till 21. He was aged 6 years Nov. last. Jan. 27, 1800. p. 145.

Hampton, Wm., Henry Hampton, Anthony Hampton, Richard Hampton and Nelly Hampton were given gdns. by court. Feb. 23, 1801, 164.

Hawkins, Jas. W., Margaret Hawkins chose gdns. Left estate by their gd. father. Gabriel S. Hawkins is mentioned. 320. 1807?

Ingram, Samuel, chose his gdn., and Joseph Ingram, Josiah Ingram, Sally & Seth Ingram, all inf. orphans of Jacob Ingram, decd. were given gdn. by court. Jan. 8, 1802. p. 182.

Johnson, Joseph, orp. of Wm. Johnson, decd. May 24, 1796. p. 61.

Kennedy, Sophia, Rebecca, Nathan Kennedy, orphans of Joseph (Jas.?) Kennedy, decd. gdn. Sept. 179_____. p. 187

Kirtley, Elijah, Larkin Kirtley, Wm. Kirtley, orphans of Elijah K., decd. chose Frances Kirtley, gdn. and court appointed gdn. to Matilda, Nancy, James and Sarah Kirtley, orphans of Elijah K., decd. Oct. 27, 1800. p. 159.

Keene, Sally & Richard Keene, orphans of Thos. B. Keene, chose Mary Keene, widow and relict, their gdn., and court appointed her gdn. of Betsy and Polly Keene, orphans of said Thos. Keene. Nov. 26, 1804. (251.)

Lard, James, bound out. p. 141.   1800?

Lindsey, Wm. C. was given gdn. in person of Henry Lindsey, Sept. 22, 1801. p. 157.

Lowery, Stephen, orphan of Stephen Lowery, decd. chose Bartlett Collins, gdn. Dec. 24, 1804. p. 255.

Moony, Eliz. & Jas. Moony, orphans of Jas. Moony, decd. gdn. Dec. 25, 1797, p. 103. (This is Murry in index).

Moore, Jas., orphan of Samuel M., chose gdn. Mar. 26, 1793. p. 11.

Morgan, Jas & Wm., children of Fanny Morgan, bound, May 27, 1794.

Morgan, James, orphan of Jas. Morgan, bound, Nov. 26, 1794. p. 36.

Mefford, Sally, Thos. Mefford and David Mefford, orphans of David M., decd. June 1805. p. 266.

Masterson, James, orphan of Zacharia M., decd. gdn. Nov. 25, 1805. p. 278.

Neale, Minor, Eliz. and Daniel Neale, orphans of Spence Neale, Jan. 27, 1800. p. 145.

Neale, Spencer P. decd. Daniel Neale, Admr., Dec. 23, 1799. 142.

Neale, Daniel appointed gdn. to Minor Neale, Eliz. Neale, and Daniel Neale, orphans of Spencer Neale, decd. Jan. 29, 1800. A-145, and B-229.

Neale, Daniel, dec'd, Sept. 24, 1804. A-248.

Neale, Wm., decd. Louisa and Mandy Neale, infant orphans, Jan. 7, 1811. (B-202, Order).

Nealy, John, orphan of Thos. Nealy, bound, Feb. 25, 1805. p. 258.

Orr, Daniel, orphan of Wm. Orr, 16 years old 16th of May last, bound, Sept. 28, 1801. p. 174.

Pitts, Phebe, orphan of Younger Pitts, chose gdn. Mar. 24, 1795.

Redding, Wm. and Jas. Redding, chose Reuben Redding, gdn. May 1796. p. 61.

Rossell, Matilda, child of Dr. Nehemiah Rossell, June 1797, chose gdn. p. 84. 242.

Rossell, Shadrach, orphan of Nehemiah Rossell, p. 257.

Shipp, Richard ——— Shipp, orphan of Rich. W. Shipp, chose gdn. Court also appointed gdn, for Sally Shipp, Wm. Shipp, Turner Shipp, and ——— Shipp, under 14 years of age, Nov. 26, 1793. p. 21 (Much of Shipp data in this book)

Sterrett, James, heirs. John Sterrett Jas. Sterrett, Sarah S. and Joseph Sterrett, Jan. 1797, gdns. p. 79.

Shipp, Sarah & Wm. Shipp, orphans of Rich. Shipp, chose Dudley Shipp as their gdn. Dec. 23, 1799. p. 224.

Sterrett, Joseph appointed gdn. to Joseph P. Sterrett, orphan of James Sterrett, decd. and John Sterrett, James F. Sterrett, orphans of said Jas. S., chose said Joseph Sterrett as their gdn. April 1801. p. 193.

Thomason, Nelson, orphan of Samuel Thomason, chose Ann Thomason as his gdn. Mar. 26, 1793. p. 11. Nelson Thomason was apptd. Deputy Surveyor, Sept. 1797, p. 101.

Troxall, Frederick, inf. orphan of John Troxall, decd, chose gdn. Dec. 1803. p. 223.

Tompkins, Sally & Polly Tompkins, orphans of Wm. Thompkins, decd. gdn. June 1805. p. 266.

White, Benj. W., Francis N. White, and Jas. White, orphans of Jeremiah White, decd. . . . court appointed Henry White, gdn. Nov. 24, 1795, page 54.

Ward, John, orphan of Stephen Ward, bound to David L. Ward, Oct. 26, 1796. p. 68.

Wallace, David, 6 years old, bound Oct. 22, 1798. He orphan of David Wallace, decd. p. 120.

WOODFORD COUNTY INDEX TO EARLY ESTATES

NOT IN GENERAL INDEX

*Left wills, others inventories and settlements, etc.

BOOK A—1789-1796

Allison, Jno.*
Allison, Chas.
Baily, Samuel
Bell, Thos.*
Beasley, Benj.*
Crimes, Peter
Curry, Jno.
Cook Hose
Cook and Mastin
Cox, Sam'l.
Cox, Agnes—dower
Cavender, Dozier
Davidson, Robt.
Driskill, Timothy
Egbert, Lawrence
Elam, Jno.*
Edwards, Uriah
Fulton, Wm.
Grant, Samuel*
Grenstead, Wm.
Harrison, Harris*
Holeman, Henry*
Hutton, Robt.
Hadden, Wm.
Haynes, Elijah
Jameson, Jas.*
January, Peter*
Jack, Frances*
Johnson, Jos. (or Jno?)
Johnson, Jas.
Johnson, Thos.*
Jackson, Wm.*
McNeal, Thos.*
McBride, Jas.*
McCumpsey, Rob
McNeal, Thos.
Mastin, Lewis
McBride, Jno.
McHarg, Robt.
Moss, Elizabeth
Morris, Binkley
Majour, Wm.*
McCraken, Cyrus*
Martin, Wm.
Nash, John

Proctor, John*
Pemberton, Chas.*
Roberts, Wm.
Rice, Geo.*
Richards, Phin.*
Searcy, Bartlett
Sample, Jno.
Smith, Thos.
Samuel, Jesse
Snead, Fielding*
Sullinger, Thos.*
Todd, Robt.*
Thompson, Anty.*
Tucker, Robt.
Wooldridge, Edmd.*
Weste, Edwd*

BOOK B—1796-1807

Black, Joseph*
Brumley, Daniel
Beasly, Benj. Apprs.
Beavis, Wm.
Cavender, Daniel
Clay, Porter, gdn.
Clay, Henry
Craig, Toliver*
Dupey, Bartholomew*
Duerson, Wm.*
Dale, Elizabeth, dower
Davidson, Jos. gdn.
Dale, Alice*
Doran, Jas.
Edwards, Jas.
Elliott, Robt.
Fields, Henry WS*
Fox, Richard, as gdn.
Groom, Zachary
Hobblet, Michael
Harbison, David
Hollingsworth, Jno.
Hiter, Jas*
Howard, Jno.*
Harber, Amos
Hamilton, Samuel*
Johnson, Jos.
Jack, Patrick, gdn.

Kirtley, Wm.
Lee Jno.*
Long, Jas.
Long, Jno.*
Mason, Thos.
Moore, Jno.
McDugles, Chas.
McClary, Jno.
McClanahan, Thos.
Mitchell, Rosanna*
Pryor, Luke*
Ratliffs, Thos.*
Reeves, Thos.
Ruddle, Stephen*
Redding, Isaac
Rowland, David
Sharpe, Thos.
Sample, Jno.
Samuel, Jno.
Strange, Jno. A.*
Sullenger, Thos.
Smith, Elijah*
Scrogan, Robt.
Stevenson, Jno.*
Snelling, Eli
Shaw, Wm.
Stone, Sebastin
Tull, Henry
Thompson, Elizabeth, d(
Thompson, Sarah*
Taylor, Jno.
Trimble, Jas.
Sullenger, Thos. orp. gdr
Geo. Turpin
Whiteker, Jno.
Walker, Jas.
Woolridge, Edmund
Williams, Jno.
Wade, Jno.

BOOK C—1805-181

Adair, Samuel*
Blanton, Jno.
Bowdry, Jas.
Blackford, Isaiah

Bridgeford, Wm.*
Beasley, Benj.
Bowdry gdn.
Burbridge, Benj.*
Binns, Chas.* of Loudoun
  Co. Va.
Blanton, Benj. orphan
Cox, Agnes
Cook, Charlotte
Cook, Jesse
Carpenter, Francis
Cavender, Geo. gdn.
Clark, Mildred*
Cook, Hosa
Cavender, Saml. gdn.
Cox, Thos.
Crittenden Jno. J.—his
  portion in estate of
  Jno. Lee
Combs, Asa
Carr, Eleanor
Dales, Catesby
Dickey, Jas.*
David, Jas. Jones
Elliston, Robt.*
Francesco, Geo.*
Fox, Arthur, div.
Field, Henry, WS
Francesco, Andrew
Gay, Robt.
Gaines, Jas. P.
Grunby, Elizabeth*
Gum, Jno.*
Glenn, Tyre*
Garnett, Jas.*
Griffin, Wm.*
Gatewood, Chas.*
Garral, Mary*
Green, Jas.*
Garnett, Thos.
Harper, Jacob
Hicks, Harris*
Harpers, Margaret, dower
Howard, Thos.
Hammond, Jas. orphan
  Jermey?
Jarrel, Jenney*
Jones, Chas.
Kirtley, Wm.
Kelly, Samuel*

Kirtley, Elliott
Kelly, Hannah, dower
Liggert, Jas.*
Lee, Henry*
Leland, Leonard R.*
Lockridge, Robt.
Lee, Willis, portion of
  Lee's Estate
Mitchell, Rosanna
Minter, Joseph
Minter, Jane, dower
McCuddy, Williams
Moss, Jno.*
Mitchell, Robt.*
Meek, Chas.
Morton, Jno.*
Marshall, Jno.*
McClary, Elizabeth
Muter (Minter) Geo.*
Minter, Jane
Price, portion of Lee's
  estate
Poor, Thos.*
Redd, Mordicai*
Richards, Phillemon
Rankin, Thos.*
Rucker, Jno.*
Rowland, Richd.
Rogers, Turner
Read, Hanherson
Sullengers, Thos. div.
Samuel, Jno.
Smith, Jno. F.
Shouse, Adam
Scott, Frances, hus. Gen.
  Chas. Scott
Samuels' Widow's dower
Sutor, Andrew*
Stones, Sabastin, div.
Stevenson, Wm*
Strother Wm.*
Stevenson, Jas.*
Smith, Jno. T.
Scott, Wm.
Smith, Elijah, div.
Sellers, Jno.*
Scott, Wm.
Samuel, Jno. orphan
Tillery Fortinatus
Violett, Thos.*

Williams, Wm.*
Watkins, Jno.*
Williams, Jno.*
Webb, Aron
Wooldridge, Isaac
Wake, Jno.—widow
  "now Mrs. Shrieves"
Williams, Jno.
Warsham, Robt.*
  "of Washington Co. Va."
Young, Jno. R.*

BOOK D, 1812-1815

Atwood, Robt.
Atwood, Wm.
Ancell, Wm.
Brook, Jas.
Bowdry, gdn.
Beazley, Wilson*
Bridgford, Wm.
Boone, Josiah
Beachamp, Edwd.
Blanton, Jas.
Berry, Samuel
Bell, Thos.
Crittenden, Jno.
Cooper, Thomas
Carrell, Wm.
Claggett, Thos.
Crosier, Jno.
Cole, Richd.
Cole, Emsy, dower
Campbell, Geo.*
Deadman, Nathan
Davis, Jno.*
Dale, Fortunatus
Dearinger, Michael*
Edwards, Thos.
Elgen, Hezekeah
Edwards, Benj.*
Edwards, Jno.*
Egbert, Delency
Furr, Stephen
Garnett, Jas. div.
Griffin, Wm.
Gaines, Wm.
Gatewood, Chas.
Green, Jno.
Gill, Spencer
Griffin, Peggy, dower

Garnett, Thos.
Gregory, Abraham*
Green, Jno.
Hicks, Wm.
Hiatte, Lewis
Hiatte, Alcey, dower
Hunter, Samuel
Holeman, Isaac
Hudson, Roadham
Hudson, Jno.*
Hunter, Sarah, dower
Jenkins, Ezekel*
Jones, Chas. W.
Kenneday, Wm.
Kidd, Catherine
Lamkin, Jas.*
McKee, Robt.*
Minter, Jane, hrs.
Moss, Wm. and Jno. div.
McCracken, Virgil*
Mitchell, Nathaniel
McCracken, Cyrus, div.
McCracken, Martha, renum.
McClary, Geo. W.
Moss, Jno. div.
Moore, Chas.
McKee, Polly and Peggy--
  land allotted
Mitchell, Nathl.
McKee, Robt.
McIlvain, Wm.
McDowell, Joseph, gdn.
McCuddy, Wm.
Nall, Wm.*
O'Bannon, Jno.
Pew, Jas.
Peart, Francis*
Payne, Moses
Peters, Nimrod
Rennick, Jas.*
Redd, Thos.*
Rice, Richard
Reardin, Nancy, late Searcy,
  widow of Bartlett Searcy
Reed, Hankerson
Ratleff, Thos.
Redd
Ross, Andrew
Redman, Joseph
Railey, Isham

Rice, Wm.
Renick, Robt.*
Sublett, Jno. T.*
Shouse, Adam
Stucker, Geo.
Summers, Thos. C.
Samuel, Anthony*
Stansbury, Thos.*
Sellers, Jno.
Scott, Wm.
Sallee, Elizabeth
Turnham, Thos.
Trabue, Edward*
Trabue, Jane, dower
Todd, Wm.*

BOOK E, 1816-1818

Ancell, Henry
Adams, Wm.*
Beachamp, Edwd.
Burbridge------
Brooking, Sarah*
Bell, Thos.
Buck, Jno.*
Bastin, Richard
Barnett, Jno.
Beasley, Edmund
Bell, Thos.
Blackburn, Geo.*
Brooks, Wm.
Barnett, Jno.
Campbell, Arthur*
Crosier, Jno.
Cash, Wm.
Carrell, Wm.
Cave, Richard
Cash, Wm.
Christian, Jonas
Darnell, Aaron
Dale, Naters
Davis, Jno.
Egbert, Delency
Elliott, Wm.
Edwards, Thos.
Elliott, Jas.
Edwards. Ben
Edwards. Jno.
Elgin, Hezekiah
Furr, Stephen
Forston, Chas.

Gaithers, Procilla
Glenn, Tyre
Gill, Spencer
Hudson, Jno.
Hale, Smith*
Harris, Nathl.
Hopkins, Wm.
Hammonds, Lucy and
  Eliza, gdn.
Hunt, Eleanor*
Hamilton, Jno.*
Hawkins, Moses
Jackson, Jno.
Latta, Matthew
Lee, Jno. div.
Loughery, Alexander
McKee, Robert
McCrakin, Virgil
McIlvain, Moses* Moris?
Moore, Chas.
McDowell, Margaret*
McCraken, Cyrus*
McKee, Robert
Minter, Joseph and Jane
Mitchell, Robert
McCuddy, Wm.
Pleasants, Matthew
Railey, Isham
Redd, Thos. div.
Railey, Susanna dower
Rennick, Robt.
Railey, Thos.*
Ratcliff, Thos.
Searcy, Bartlet*
Scott, Fanny*
Steele, Jno.
Sullivan, Obediah
Smith, Frances
Shouse, Jas.
Snelling, Elizabeth
Sallee, Elizabeth
Shouse, Jas.
Todd, Wm.
Torbett, Jno. A.
Vance, Sarah
Wilhite, Elijah
Wake, Jno.
Williams, Wm.
Walker, Wm.
Young, Richard

Young, Mary, dower

BOOK F—1818-1822

Adams, Wm.
Ashley, Jas.
Arnold, Jno.*
Alexander, Wm.
Arnett, Jas.*
Adair, Samuel
Andrew, Alex.
Ayres, Mary
Bell, Thos.
Bohannon, Elliott*
Brooking, Samuel
Berry, Samuel
Bell, Thos.
Buntin, Margaret*
Beazley——
Brooking, Harriott,
  portion of estate
Booth, Sydnor*
Brocks, Wm.
Berry, Mary
Beazley, Edmd.
Blunt, Sarah*
Brooking, Mary
Brown, Jno.*
Combs, Andrew, gdn.
Coppage, Jas.*
Christian, Jonas
Cunningham, Hughs*
Clayton, Joshua
Cunningham, Eleanor
Conovers, Peter as gdn. to
  Uriah Jones hrs.
Caldwell, Jas.*
Caldwell, Henry
Dedman, Nathan hrs.
Davis, Jno.
Duitt? Elisha
Dickey, Jno.
Dale, Naten
Duvall, Jno.
Darnell, Aaron
Dale, Wm.*
Elgin, Hezekiah
Ellis, Jesse*
Ellis, Jno.*
Elgin, Fredk.

Eaton, Silas
Elliott, Jas.
Ellis, Jesse
Eaton, Silas
Elliott, Wm.
Forston, Chas.
Finn, Jno.*
Froman, Jacob
Furr, Stephen
Foster, Hesekiah
Guinn, Robert* (Guynn)
Gatewood, Jas.*
Goodloe, Vivian
Gaines, Wm. Sr.*
Green, Jno.
Gregory, Mildred*
Gill, Spencer
Garrett, Wm.*
Garner, Sarah Ann*
Goode, Wm.
Hudson, Jno.
Harris, Nathaniel
Howard, Jas.*
Holeman, Edward*
Holeman, Isaac
Howard, Jas.
Hamilton, Jno.
Hawkins, Moses
Hufford, Jno.
Hopkins, Wm.
Hammond, Jno.
Hamilton, Andrew*
Hudson, Jno.
Hazard, Jno.*
Jesse, Saml. gdn. Geo.
  McCracken
Jackson, Jno.
Johnston, David
Jones, Uriah
Kean, Moses
Kinkead, Jno.*
Kinkead, Wm.*
Kinkead, Jos.
Lee, Jno. div.
Loughery, Alex.
Lee, Hancock
Litle, Thos.*
Lauderback ——
Long, Jno. hrs.

McIlvain, Wm.
McCracken, Polly
  acct. with gdn.
  Andrew Muldrow
McClary, Jno.
McKinney, Wm.*
McCrackin, Virgil
Mosby, Nicholas*
Mosby, Jno.
Mosby, Susannah
Meek, Chas.
McCuddy, Wm.*
McCracken V. hrs.
  Martha McCracken gdn. acct.
McCracken, Cyrus gdn. sett.
McCracken, Virgil
McCracken, Geo.
Nicholson, Benj.
Nall, Chas.
Offutt, Milforde*
Peart?
Pearl, Elizabeth wid.
  of Francis
Paul, Jno.*
Porter, Jno. gdn. sett.
Perry, Roderick*
Price, Phillemon
Paxton, Hugh
Quarles, Tunstall*
Railey, Thos.
Railey, Wm.
Railey, Judith, dower
Redmon, Jas.*
Redmon, Jesse K.
Redd, Mordicai
Shouse, Jas.
Stamper, Samuel
Stevenson, Isaac*
Shouse, Henry, hrs. gdn. acct.
Steele, Jno.
Shouse, Thos.
Sthrishley, Susan, her gdn. acct.
Stevenson, Isaac
Spaulding, Wm.*
Silvers, Jane*
Sellers, Jno.
Steele, Jno.*
Scroggin, Robt.
Stone, Wm.

Sterrett, Jno.
Trabue, Jas.
Turner, Bartlett
Torbitt, Jno.
Turner, Alexander*
Taylor, Richard*
Trabue, Edwd.
Vance, Sarah*
Vaughan, Jno.
Wake, Jno.
Williams, Jno.
Wooldridge, Green*
Watson, Jno.
Wilhoit, Elijah
Wilson, Elizabeth
Williams, Winnefred
Wilson, Jos.
Yancey, Robt.
Young, Lewis
Young, Nancy
Guynn, Jane
Gill, Geo.

Will Bk. G—1822-1826

Ayres, Mary
Alison, Jno.
Ashford, Thos.
Arnet, Margaret, gdn. acct.
Ashford, Jno.
Brown, Jno.
Brooking, Mary
Brooking, Saml.
Bell, Thos.
Black, Sally, dower
Bryson, Joseph W.*
Bowdry, Lewis*
Bain, Geo.*
Bowdry (Bowdy) Lucy, dower
Bohannon, Elliott*
Baker, Peter
Barnes, Geo., gdn. sett.
Barnes, Eliza, gdn. sett.
Berryman, Waring
Brown, Jno.
Beasley, Benj.
Cotton, Geo.*
Cole, Wm. Y.
Clark, William*

Coleman, Jas.*
Claggett, Thos.
Campbell, Wm.*
Dale, Fort's div.
Cave, Richd.
Dawson, Wm.
Davis, Henry
Davis, Milly, dower
Davis, Joseph*
Dickey, Michael*
Dickey, Jno.
Eaton, Silas
Elliott, Jas.
Edwards, Thos., gdn. acct.
Edwards, Jno., gdn. acct.
Edwards, F. and B., gdn. acct.
Edwards, Ben., gdn. acct.
Edwards, Jno., gdn. acct.
Edwards, Nancy, gdn. acct.
Green, Jno. hrs.
Gill, Geo.
Guyn, Robt.
Guyn, Jane
Gibbons, Marion, gdn. acct.
Coode, Cordelia, gdn.
Gaines, Wm.
Graves, Jno.
Gilmore, Wm.
Gibson, Wm.*
Gill, Geo.
Gregory, Abrm.
Gray, Jonathan*
Haggard, Jno.
Hawkins, G. L., gdn.
Harris, Wm, gdn. acct.
Hale, Smith
Howe, Edw.*
Hopkins, Wm.
Hawkins, Jas.
Hunter, James*
Hopkins, B. and E., gdn. acct.
Hudson, Jno. hrs.
Holeman, Isaac
Hawkins, Jas.
Hunter, Mary, wid. of Jno.
Hamilton, A. B.
Hawkins, Jas.
Hathaway, Jona.
Hudson, Jno.

Hancock, Wm.*
Hathaway, Mrs. Thomson
   dower
Hamilton, Jno.
Jackson, Jno.
Jackson, A. M., gdn. acct.
Jackson, Wm. S., gdn. acct.
Jackson, E. F.
Jelf, Thos.
Jeffries, Isaac*
Johnson, Isaac*
Kinkead, Jno.
Kinkead, Eleanor*
Long, Armistead, gdn. acct.
Lowderback, Abraham
Lindsay, Joseph
Laforce, W. B.
Mitchell, Edmd.
McCrackin, Geo., gdn. sett.
McCrackin, Cyrus, gdn. sett.
Moore, Wm.
Mosby, Robt. est. div. and
   dower
Martin, Saml. D.
Mitchum, Jas.
Moore, Wm.*
McCrackin, Virgil
Mosby, Nicholas
McKnight, A.
Mitchum, Polly, dower
Meeke, Jas.*
Moore, Chas. gdn.
Martin, Saml.*
Mitchell, Geo.
Mitchell, Lucy, dower
Morton, Wm.*
Morton, Sarah*
Nichols, Thos.
Nall, Chas. L.
Nall, Elen and Geo. gdn. acct.
Owen, E. C.
Offutt, G. H.*
Perry, Roderick
Paxton, H. F.
Peters, Nathl.
Price, Philemon
Price, W. H.*
Price, Samuel*
Rowland, Rich.*

HARROD SUIT—CIRCUIT COURT, MERCER COUNTY

The index revised by the Federal workers show that a number of suits of Harrod vs. Harrod were recorded, but the papers are missing. That must mean that someone interested in the Harrod history took them from the court house, perhaps many years ago.

The following papers were filed according to references given below.

In Box H-45, is the suit of Thos. Harrod's Heirs vs. James Harrod's Heirs, filed Dec. 25, 1815.

Orators John Harrod, James Harrod, Levi Harrod, Samuel Harrod, Isaiah Harrod, Lucinda Harrod, Rachel Harrod, Susannah Harrod, Jane Grooms and Wm. Grooms her husband, Betsy Fauch and John Fauch her husband, Leah McCollister and Wm. McCollister her husband, heirs of Thos. Harrod, deceased, say that said Thos. Harrod their ancestor on the 28th day of October 1779 obtained from Court Commissioners for the District of Kentucky, following certificates (to wit): Thos. Harrod by James Harrod claimed preemption to tract of land lying on Sinking Spring . . .etc. and on 11th day of Dec. entered his settlement. 400 acres, and shortly after Thos. Harrod had occasion to leave this country for the State of North Carolina, and appointed his brother James Harrod as his agent to attend to the survey, etc., and said Thos. Harrod returned to North Carolina where his family then lived, and in a few years departed this life—said James Harrod who undertook to conduct said business on June 7, 1786, had said settlement surveyed in name of said Thos. Harrod, and said Thomas never returned to Kentucky. Said James to defraud said Thomas or his heirs fabricated on June 7th 1786 and forged an assignment to himself. . . . and without the knowledge of said Thomas Harrod, and took possession himself and but for the death of said Thomas, and infancy of your orators (then infants), and remoteness as they still lived in North Carolina after their father's death, for the youngest had only arrived at full age within the last few months past, and danger of travelling from North Carolina to Kentucky, and they knew of the fraud only a few years ago; said James died leaving a will, etc., and left this land to his daughter and only child, Margaret Harrod who afterward married one John Fauntleroy and both are to be made defendants in this suit . . . and about ―― 1812 defendant sold this land to Daniel McIlvoy and John Cochran and both are made defendants ―― said Thos. Harrod not in Kentucky at the time of transfer.

The Transcript of McIlvoy vs. Ford, "to be filed in the Harrod suit" contains about 68 pages, and this is suit over the title of this same land, it appears, but no Harrod genealogy. Daniel McIlvoy's wife was Sally Ford, dau. of Wm. Ford of Lincoln Co.

John Brown of Frankfort, an attorney, gives his deposition on June 13, 1821, in this suit. He says he was counsel for Col. James Harrod in 3 suits of Col. James Harrod vs. Thos. Harrod to recover land near Danville—said James had a power of Attorney from Thos. Harrod to Stephen Langford and to dispose of said land of reference to said bills, Dec. 28, 1784— Brown said he was attorney in the Supreme Court in Frankfort, in 1786.

James Rennick, Sr. at the house of James Murrell, Lincoln Co., May 16, 1820, gives deposition, wherein John Harrod and other heirs of Thos. Harrod, deceased, are complainants, and John Fauntleroy and wife Margaret heirs of James Harrod, deceased, are defendants —and James Rennick states he came to Kentucky in 1782, and returned to South Carolina about 1785 and met Thos. Harrod who was related to him by marriage with his (deponent's) wife's sister—this deponent says he importuned Thos. Harrod (then living in Rutherford

County, North Carolina) to come to Kentucky, but he said he had no interest in Kentucky, but he (Thos. Harrod) said he had sold his land in Kentucky to Stephen Langford—he said he was well acquainted with James Harrod, brother of Thos., and Thos. Harrod died since the death of his brother James. (signed by James Rennick, May 16, 1820)

June 9, 1817, a paper stating lieve had been given to take the deposition of Wm. Harrod of the state of Indiana. This paper had also date of Feb. 16, 1826, thereon. Could not find this deposition in any of the papers.

Jacob Kelley gives deposition, April 29, 1819, and states that Thos. Harrod was in Kentucky in 1775, 6 or 7, and that he lived in North Carolina—that he (Jacob Kelley) lived on James Harrod's land 1779 and was there for 7 or 8 years or more—said he had seen Thos. Harrod in Maryland frequently but never after he moved to North Carolina. Jacob Kelley was a resident of Henry county, Ky. when he gave this deposition. On June 6, 1820, Jacob Kelley gave another deposition worded much as before, but stated he never saw Thos. Harrod in Kentucky, only saw him in Maryland before the fall of 1770—when I was a boy I was well acquainted with the said Thos. Harrod and would not have forgotten it had I ever seen him in Kentucky.

Cochran vs. Crow's heirs contain many papers that are filed in this same suit of Harrod's heirs H-45. This is over the clear title to the land of the Harrods.

Filed in the bundle is a copy of the plat, survey, etc. where Thos. Harrod assigned this 400 acres to James Harrod, 6-7-1786. Jacob Kelley and Peter Vardeman are wts., but Jacob Kelley says he does not recall signing same.

Wm. Crow in his deposition at the house of Richard Davenport, 8-25-1817, says he knew Thos. Harrod was in Kentucky in 1776 and says "I left myself in that year and did not return till spring of 1780 and have been near Danville ever since, and understand Thos. Harrod left Kentucky then and never returned. James Harrod is a brother or half-brother of Thos. Harrod, I understand.

James Brown in a deposition says, "I knew Thos. Harrod in fall of 1775 and I went out of the country July or August 1776 and returned with my family about middle of January, 1780.

James Knox, in Knox County, Tenn. gives deposition, as does Philip Singleton, Sept. 25, 1825, who says Hannah Harrod is the reputed wife of Thos. Harrod, deceased, and that John Harrod James Harrod Levi Harrod, Samuel Harrod, Josiah Harrod, Lucinda Harrod, Rachel Harrod, Susannah Harrod, Hannah Harrod, Polly Montgomery, Jane Grooms, Betsy Fouck (Fouch?), and Leah McAllister are legal heirs of Thos. Harrod, deceased.

Daniel McIlvoy says that Dec. 1784 when Thos. Harrod was on his way from Kentucky to North Carolina he fell in company with Stephen Langford to whom he sold his land. etc. . . . he does not admit that any of the complainants are heirs of Thos. Harrod.

(This Daniel McIlvoy bought this land and he wants to keep it).

John Cochran says that Thos. Harrod left here 1784 for N. C.

Maj. John Fauntletory and wife Margaret are given notice that the deposition of Wm. Harrod will be taken at the house of Evan Shelby in Charleston, Indiana, (Sept. 9, 1819.) to be taken May 15th.

Wm. Harrod's deposition, taken May 12, 1819, at the house of Evan Shelby in Charleston, Indiana— Wm. Harrod says that John Harrod, James Harrod, Levi Harrod, Samuel Harrod (and others as named above) have always been reputed to be the children of Thos. Harrod (uncle of this deponent), and that some of them have visited their relatives in Mercer county, and esteemed as such by them. On being questioned he said he lived at the house of his uncle James Harrod in 1785 and 6 but never heard of his uncle Thos. Harrod being in Kentucky at that time unless in the lower part of Kentucky or Tennesee where he died. (Clark County, Indiana, May 12, 1819.)

In Knox County, Tenn. deposition of James Harrod, heir of Thos. Harrod, deceased. (This is listed as being taken but could not find the deposition).

Reference is given to suit of James Harrod vs. Crow's heirs, Aug. 1808. Court of Appeals May 20, 1808.

Thos. Walker says in his deposition: Thos. Harrod moved into County of Knox, now Roane county, this state (Knox Co., Tenn). He says June 1, 1821 that he is about 47 years of age, and says Thos. Harrod settled in Roane Co., Tenn. about 7 or 8 miles above Kingston in the year of 1801, and says he did not attend the wedding but his bro. John m. Drucilla Harrod, dau. of Thos. Harrod. (signed "Thos. Walker")

In "Harrod's heirs vs. Crow's heirs Orators: John Crow, etc., say that a certain Thos. Harrod on —— day of ——— 1779 got Certificate for 400 acres of land in Kentucky, said Thos. having departed to some Atlantic state where at that time he resided--(Box C-28) (suit of this 400 acres)

In Box D-1—Aaron Day sues Col. James Harrod, May 10, 1787 for bill run at Green River, Nelson county, Jan. 11, 1787. The bill includes 7 and 5/8 gallons of whiskey at different times for himself and his Company.

DEEDS

William Herad (but signed Harrod) of Bracken County, by deed dated 1792, grants to James Harrod, late of Mercer county, 1,000 acres, "Ill. Grant" . . . appoints Isaac Meranda of Bracken Co., attorney to recover for James Herad's heirs, 1,000 acres on Green River on condition that James Harrod convey 1000 acres on Green river. Dated Oct. 10, 1797. (Deed 3, page 346, Mercer Co.)

———※※———

In Hardin county, Ky. Vital Statistics: James Herrod, aged 96, married, born in Virginia, d. in Hardin county, 1857.

Rebecca Herrod, aged 73 years, married, born in Pa., dau. of Phil. and E. Rogers, d. Mar. 10, 1857.

James Harwood was wts. to will of John Mulberry in Scott Co., Ky., July 1829.

James Harrod paid taxes in Bourbon Co., 1790.

Levi Harrod was exr. of will of John Curl in Green Co., Pa., May 25, 1805, and this will was probated in Bourbon Co., Ky., 1814.

ROGERS HEIRS

Original papers, Woodford Co. Ky. Circuit Court of Common Pleas, May 29, 1878 (Bundles numbered 930 and 931).

Note: Geo. Rogers died in Woodford Co. Ky. leaving will (Bk. W, p. 180) recorded Dec. 13, 1877. Those named: Wife, Jane, ch. of decd. bro. Joseph Rogers, he having rec'd. greater part of his father's estate, ch. of decd. bro. Wm. Rogers, ch. of decd. sister Sally Kemper, ch. of decd. sister Elizabeth Stucker, except her son James Stucker, ch. of decd. sister Mildred Coppage except her son John W. Acuff and her son Rhodin Coppage. Exr: Neighbor A. L. Wright of Woodford Co. No settlement of this estate is shown but on Feb. 14, 1878, in accordance with the will of Geo. Rogers, A. L. Wright sold to D. J. Williams, Jr. the farm of Geo. Rogers located on the Frankfort-Lexington pike, three mi. from Versailles Ky. Jane Rogers, wife of Geo. Rogers died a few months before her husband and numerous suits were brought by the heirs of Geo. Rogers for settlement of his estate. These papers show heirs to the fourth generation scattered all over the country at that date (1878); it will prove of great value to thousand of descendants in this year of 1953. Geo. Rogers was the son of Wm. Rogers and wife Ann Johnson Rogers.

On May 29, 1878 in Mt. Sterling, Ky. depositions were taken:

John Green, aged 73, deposes: "He had known Edward Kemper all his life, not related, knew the old gentleman Geo. Rogers, before he came up here to live, he saw Geo. Rogers in June 1877, he was a constant care of Edw. Kemper and his wife." Edward Kemper's mother was Sallie Rogers Kemper, sister of Geo. Rogers, she is dead and left: Simeon Kemper of Mo., Thompson Kemper in Montana Territory, Valentine Kemper in Jackson Co. Mo., Edw. Kemper in Montgomery Co. Ky., Mildred Kemper who m. Daniel Priest of Montgomery Co. Ky., Lucy Ann Kemper now widow of Wm. Chinn, decd. and Sallie, widow of F. Coppage who resides in Marion Co. Ky.

Mrs. Emma Stofer, aged 36, sister of Mrs. Edw. Kemper and wife of Richard Stofer of Montgomery Co. knew Geo. Rogers at the Kempers. Mrs. Fannie Stofer, aged 40, wife of Wm. Stofer, Pres. of Mt. Sterling National Bank, sister of Mrs. Kemper, knew Geo. Rogers for 25 or 26 years. Joe Johnson, aged 52, says: "My first wife was a niece of Mr. Edw. Kemper, and dau. of Daniel Priest." Mrs. Mildred Priest, aged 73, says: On May 30, 1877 that she is wife of Daniel Priest, aged 83 yrs. a farmer and sister of Mr. Kemper; "Geo. Rogers of Woodford Co. was my uncle, and I am one of the devisees—was at Mr. Kemper's the day Mr. Rogers came, and also the day he died." Mrs. Sarah Hearne, aged 48 yrs. dau. of Mrs. Mildred Priest, have known Edw. Kemper all my life. Wm. S. Gay, aged 28 years, son-in-law of Edw. Kemper. Mrs. Martia Gay, aged 24, wife of Wm. Gay, and dau. of Edw. Kemper. Geo. Rogers came to Kempers' to live Apr. 7, 1877 and died Oct. 3, 1877.

A. L. Wright, Exr.

Vs.

Simeon Kemper, G. W. Maxfield, Richard Maxfield, M. E. Jennings and her husband D. H. Jennings, Mary E. Powers and her husband R. H. Powers, W. T. Bryan, H. A. Bryan, J. R. Bryan, J. F. Bryan, last named infs. under 21 yrs., J. W. Coppage, and Milly A. McIntyre and husband, ———— McIntyre, J. W. Johnson, Larkin Stucker, Elijah Stucker, G. L. Stucker, Emily Hemphill and husband, ———— Hemphill, and unknown heirs of Timothy L. Stucker, defts. A. L. Wright says: Since filing of petiton he has learned that Eliz. Maxfield is dead, and she left heirs and ch. G. W. Maxfield, Richard Maxfield, and Margaret E. Maxfield who is m. to D. H. Jennings; and also that Sarah Coppage is dead and left Susan E. who m. —————— Bryan and afterward- died leaving as heir an only ch., defendants Mary E. Powers (m. R. H. Powers) W. T. Bryan, H. A. Bryan, J. R. Bryan, and J. F. Bryan, last of whom is an inf. under 21—the defendant Milly A. her dau. who m. defendant —————— McIntyre, defendant J. M. Coppage and J. W. Johnson. Also learned the heirs of David Stucker who were made party ——————? as unknown heirs and they are as follows, viz: (deft.) Larkin Stucker, Elijah Stucker, G. L. Stucker and Emeline Hemphill, wife of deft. —————— Hemphill; and heirs of Timothy T. Stucker, unknown to the plaintiff (heirs of Timothy Stucker who was a son of David Stucker, decd.) June 18, 1878, says: the Maxfields, Jennings, Powers, Bryans, J. W. Coppage, Milly McIntyre and her husband, J. W. Johnson, Larkin Stucker, etc., Emeline Hemphill are not in Kentucky; Maxfields and Jennings are in Missouri (Shell City, Mt. Vernon Co.) Richard Maxfield in Bowling Green, Pike Co. Mo.; Powers, Bryans, in Paris, Monroe Co. Mo.; Coppage, in Hannibal, Mo.; Milly McIntyre and her husband in Prentice, Ill.; Larkin Stucker, Saline, Kans.; Elijah Stucker in Lomax, P.O. (Taylor or Ringold Co.) Iowa; Emeline Hemphill and husband G. L. Stucker in Washington Co. Iowa; J. W. Johnson in Texas. That heirs of Timothy J. Stucker who was a son of David Stucker who was son of Elizabeth Stucker, decd., who was a sister of testator and a defendant, and his heirs unknown to the plaintiff, A. L. Wright.

Thos. W. Conner, aged 30 yrs., deposition at Versailles, July 27, 1878, 'Lived with Geo. Rogers in 1877 and expects to be in Monroe Co. Ky. Jan. 1879 (term of court) Rogers lived with me Mar. 1, 1877 to middle of April 1877, died Oct. 1877. George Rogers' wife died April 1877, his wife was about 75 yrs. old, active for age; I rented Rogers' farm, they lived with me 'till Mrs. Rogers died, then Mr. Rogers went to Mr. Kempers to live. Mr. Rogers was about 83 yrs. of age."

Richard Maxfield, Pike Co. Mo. deposition, questioned about Geo. Rogers who died Oct. 3, 1877.

Geo. W. Acuff, of Salt Lake Co. Utah Territory, Power of Atty. to Silas Threlkeld. Joseph H. Acuff, of same to same, May 22, 1879.

Joseph H. Bryan, gdn. of Wm. S. Bryan, Daniel Bryan, James, Harriet E. and Annie L. Bryan, minor ch. of said Joseph H. Bryan, Wm. T. Bryan, Sr. gdn. of Joseph L. Bryan, minor child of said Wm. T. Bryan, Wm. T. Bryan, Jr. Henry A. Bryan, John R. Bryan, and Mary E. Powers, adult ch. of said W. T. Bryan, Sr., Sarah Eliz. Acuff, Cornelia Jane Acuff, Wm. M. Acuff, and Mildred Threlkeld, child of Green P. Acuff, decd., and Richard Powers husband of said Mary E. Powers, all of Monroe Co. Mo.; appoint Silas Threlkeld Atty. to get portions of estate of George Rogers, decd., late of Woodford Co. Ky. (Signed by all of above, May 26, 1879).

Silas Threlkeld, deposition, June 17, 1879 (ans. to questions by agent for heirs of Greenville P. Acuff and Sarah Coppage), aged 46 yrs. residing in Monroe Co. Mo. (Granville, Mo.) known heirs of Greenville P. Acuff who was a child of a sister of Geo. Rogers, decd., said Acuff is dead and left the following 9 children: "Mary M. Threlkeld who is my wife; C. Sylvester Bryan; Daniel M. Bryan; H. Eliz. Bryan *neik?* named Bessie and Anna L. Bryan; Elizabeth Acuff; Cornelia Acuff; Geo. W. Acuff; Joseph Acuff; Wm. and Claiborne Acuff." (Note: some lines erased). Known heirs of Sarah Coppage who are: M. A. McIntyre, J. W. Coppage, Mary E. Powers, W. Thos. Bryan, Henry A. Bryan, John Richard Bryan, Joseph F. Bryan. "I am guardian of Claiborne Acuff." Silas Threlkeld.

Joseph H. Bryan, deposition, May 15, 1879, am father and natural guardian of Wm. S. Bryan, Daniel M. Bryan, James, Harriet E. and Annie L. Bryan, my children, and minors . . . Monroe Co. Mo."

Wm. T. Bryan, father and gdn. of son Wm. T. Bryan, gives bond, Monroe Co. Mo.

Claiborne F. Acuff, minor, over 14, Monroe Co. Mo. chose Silas Threlkeld as gdn. June 9, 1879.

Mrs. Minerva White. of Burlington, Boone Co. Ky. aged 65 yrs. deposes Nov. 14, 1878, "Geo. Rogers was my‾ uncle, and his bros. and sisters were: Joseph Rogers, Mildred Acuff who m. ————— Coppage after Acuff's death, Eliz. Stucker, Sally Kemper, and Wm. Rogers, I think none are living; I am the dau. of Wm. Rogers, B. F. Rogers is still living, Lucinda Ash and myself are the only children of Wm. Rogers living—there were 11 children of Wm. Rogers; those of children of Wm. Rogers that are dead are: Elizabeth Maxfield (may be dead, have not heard from her for two years); John Rogers, Mahala Cave, Wm. Rogers, Barnett Rogers, Elijah Rogers, Elmyra Carpenter, Johnson Rogers, all dead; Elizabeth Maxfield had a dau. Sarah who m. ————— Baggerly, I believe dau. Margaret m.————— Jennings, a son named Richard, and if had others I do not know—they lived in Missouri; Margaret Jennings wrote me I believe from Shelby City, Mo." "Think Lucinda Ash lives in Iowa, bro. Ben lives in Macoupin Co. Ill. near Chesterfield. Brother John left one child who m. a man by name of Lucas who is dead; she lives at New Frankfort, Mo." Question: Tell about family of your sister Mahala Cave? Ans. "I knew Wm. Cave, Mary S. Hutchings (she lives in Kans.) also knew Cyrus Cave who is dead, I think; never knew any other children of Mahala." "Mary L. Hutchings wrote me her brother Richard was dead, and she and her brother Wm. were all that were living—wrote from Allen County, Kans., I think."

Question: Give names of children, etc., of bro. Wm.?
Ans.: "There were two, Thos. and Oscar Rogers. Oscar died leaving no ch. Thos. lives in Clinton Co. Ind. Manson, P.O.

Question: Name children, etc. of your bro. Barnett Rogers, decd?
Ans.: "There are three now living: Owen Rogers, Emily Campbell, and Matilda Pickens. Emily m. John O. Campbell, Matilda m. James Pickens; Owen and Emily live in Boone Co. Ky.; Matilda Pickens lives near Cloverdale, Ind. John Rogers one of the 6 children of Barnett Rogers is dead leaving 6 ch. to wit: Elizabeth m. Legrand Gaines; Mary m. J. W. Gaines; Boone F. Rogers; Frances m. Garrett Tyle, both dead leaving 3 ch. Josephine, Mary and Lucy Tyle; James Rogers, and Robert Rogers who is about 20 yrs. of age. Warren Rogers, one of 6 ch. of Barnett Rogers is also dead and left 4 ch. to wit: Elizabeth m. a man by name of ————— Brashear, Martha m. Wm. Moody, Daniel Rogers, and Llewllyn Rogers, the last two infants and represented by their mother Elizabeth Rogers, their Gdn.; they all live in Boone Co. Ky. Olivia Allen, dau. of Barnett Rogers, is dead, leaving 4 ch. to wit: Mary m. James Barnett, Geo. R. Allen; John Allen and Elizabeth Allen (an infant) all of Boone Co. Ky."

Question: Names of ch., etc., of your sister Elmira Carpenter, decd?
Ans: "Parthenia, m. Sim Baldwin; Susan m. Geo. Bush (Busby); Almedia m. Samuel Finch (dead); Nathaniel Carpenter; Wm. Carpenter; Nicholas Carpenter; Cornelius Carpenter and Lucy Carpenter who m. Wm. Shotwell, she is dead and left 4 ch. Aga; Almedia; Anna and Luella, all infants. Parthenia, Nicholas and Cornelius all live in Boone Co. Ky. Nathaniel, Almedia, Wm. and Lucy Shotwell's children live in Gallatin Co. Ky. Susan Busby lives in Ill."

Question: Tell of children, etc., of your bro. Elijah Rogers, decd?

Ans. "Commodore Rogers, dead, and left ch. somewhere in Ill. but do not know how many—I knew Wm. Rogers, Moses, Jameson, Nancy m. Allen Sparks, Manerva m. Joab? Witinger, who is dead, Owen Rogers, Ellender who m. —— Wright, who is dead, John Rogers, Jesse Rogers, Sarah Lovett, Barnett Rogers, Henry Rogers, Washington Rogers (dead) leaving two children whose names I do not know. Wm., Jameson, Manerva, Ellender, and Nancy live in Clinton Co. Ind. do not know P.O. or rest of children's residences."

Question: Give names of ch. of your decd. bro. Johnson Rogers?

Ans. "He had 10 children to wit: Thomas, Barnett, John W. Johnson L. Laborn, Sarah M. m. Thos. Knox, Mollie E. m. John Sam Bond, Talitha m. Robt. Tanner (dead), Madaline m. James Ray, (both dead), left 2 ch., boy and girl: Lavenia m. —— Bledsoe (she is dead, leaving 1 child, name not known) the above named ch. live in Gallatin and Carroll Co. Ky."

Question: Can you give the names of the ch. of your uncle and aunts Joseph Rogers, Elizabeth Stucker, Sally Kemper, Mildred Coppage?

Ans. "No, I do not know anything about them, only from hearsay.

(End of deposition of Mrs. Minerva White).

T. W. Campbell, deposition 32 yrs. old, asked if knew Olivia Allen.

Ans: "Dau. of Barnett Rogers, a son of Wm. Rogers, she had 5 ch.: Mary Barnett, Geo. Allen, John Allen, Owen Allen, and Eliz. Allen, Owen and Eliz. infants, in Boone Co. near Grant—says he lives in Burlington, Boone Co. and is 32 yrs. of age, is son of Emily Campbell, a dau. of Barnett Rogers who was a son of Wm. Rogers who was a bro. of Geo. Rogers." Nov. 1878.

Copy of will of Oscar M. Rogers, Clinton Co., Ind. leaves wife Eliz. A. Rogers all, except $200.00 to Ames Hayden; Jameson Rogers, exr. Dated June 22, 1876, Prob. Jan. 22, 1878.

Mrs. Eliz. A. Moore, and her husband W. E. Moore state she was the widow of Oscar Rogers, son of Wm. Rogers, a devisee of Geo. Rogers, said Wm. being a son of Wm. Rogers, a bro. to Geo. Rogers, decd. said Oscar died childless, 1878. She claims that Oscar was living when will made, and she entitled to his share.

James Stucker of Fountain Co. Ind. appts. Greenup Stucker, atty. (he of Scott Co. Ky.) to receive his part of estate due him of est. of Geo. Rogers, decd. Mar. 12, 1878. W. R. Stucker, son of Eliz. Stucker, decd. who was a sister of Geo. Rogers, decd., gives receipt for $877.00 plus 1/27 of $12,748 and 1/2 of $10,139. M. O. Austin says he has known W. R. Stucker for 50 years and he was a son of Elizabeth Stucker. Apr. 7, 1879.

Edward Kemper's claim for $2000, for board and nursing Geo. Rogers, is filed. Jane Rogers died Apr. 2, 1877, he then took his uncle Geo. Rogers home with him, together with a boy servant, and Geo. Rogers died Oct. 3, 1877. Edward Kemper son of Sally Kemper a sister of Geo. Rogers. (Note: One paper shows 8 p. of heirs).

The following are brief extracts from letters written Mr. Barbour, the atty. in reply to his circular letter to all the heirs. Most of them are dated in Feb. 1878, some few Mar. 1878, so dates are omitted:

Wm. Cave, aged 53, Mason City, Ill. (53 last June) is married, not certain whether decd. Geo. Rogers was his uncle or not; my mother was Mahala Rogers, of Boone Co. Ky. formerly; received letter from the decd. five yrs. ago inquiring of relatives here and elsewhere. I answered that my bro. Richard Cave now dead left 3 minor children: Alice Cave, Julia Cave and Emma Cave.

Oscar Rogers, aged 51 yrs. Hanson, Clinton Co. Ind. "My father Wm. Rogers, decd. was son of Wm. Rogers, named in the will. I have been married 30 yrs."

Elizabeth M. Tyner, Tipton, Tipton Co. Indiana: "Said Elizabeth Stucker is my grandmother, Frances Wolf is my mother, she is Elizabeth Stucker's oldest child—Geo. Rogers was my mother's uncle. I am mother's second child, I was born Dec. 14, 1812, I am 65 yrs. old; I was married June 7, 1832 to Stephen Tyner and we are still living together.

Thos. J. Rogers, aged 38, m. Manson, Ind. "Geo. Rogers was my father's uncle."

Lewis R. (and Caroline) Thomas, Connersville, Ind. "My wife's mother is a niece of Geo. Rogers, and her mother was a sister of Geo. Rogers, my wife's mother was Frances Stucker, she m. David Wolf, and I married her dau. Caroline." "I am 42 and my wife 43, and the youngest child of David Wolf, we have 3 children living and one dead."

Benjamin Taylor Rogers, Chesterfield, Ill. "I am m. am 68 yrs. old, 24th day of last Aug." (dated Feb. 22, 1878)". "Geo. Rogers, decd., was my uncle; my father was Wm. Rogers" (Macoupin Co. Ill.) (Note: A printed circular sent out by W. R. Barbour, inclosed here).

Catherine A. Magill (and John T. Magill) Connersville, Ind. "My father was a son of David Wolf and Frances Stucker (a dau. of Elizabeth Stucker, she was sister of Geo. Rogers). My father and mother are both dead, and I only one living of our family, my name is Catherine A. Magill, aged 33 yrs. have 1 child. Send our next letters to Portland Mills, Putnam Co. Ind.

Lewis D. Webb and Nancy E. Webb, Connersville, Ind. "My mother was niece of Geo. Rogers; her mother was a sister of Geo. Rogers; she married Mr. Stucker, Mother's name was Frances Stucker, she m. David Wolf. I am dau. of David and Frances Wolf; I m. Lewis D. Webb, and grand niece of Geo. Rogers; we have 3 ch. living; I am 59 yrs. old, my sister's children did not receive notice; they are Wm. E. Bradburn (of age) and Geo. Bradburn, inf. ch. of Samuel Bradburn, Franklin Co. Brookville, Ind.

David S. Wolf, Connersville, Ind. aged 54 yrs. have wife and one child, "I am son of Frances Stucker, a niece of Geo. Rogers."

Mary F. Dehaven, Connersville, Ind. "My gd. mother was Eliz. Stucker, sister of Geo. Rogers, I am dau. of Frances Stucker; I am married and 45 yrs. old."

Sally Ann Hackleman, Connersville, Ind. "My gd. mother was Eliz. Stucker, sister of Geo. Rogers, and she was a dau. of Frances Stucker, and I m. Hawkins Hackleman. I am 58 yrs. old."

Wm. Wolfe, Connersville, Ind. "My mother was dau. of Eliz. Stucker, sister of Geo. Rogers. My mother was Frances Stucker before marriage. I am 57 yrs. old."

Geo. W. Wolfe, Connersville, Ind. "Mother was Frances Stucker, dau. of Eliz. Stucker, sister of Geo. Rogers. I am married, 49 yrs. old, my nephews W. Edgar Bradburn and Geo. Bradburn are sons of my sister Emeline Bradburn, decd., one is 23 yrs. and other 17 yrs. old."

Mary Jane Duke, Erie, Neosho Co. Kansas. "I was born Mary Jane Rogers, m. M. L. Duke, dau. of Commodore Rogers, son of Elige Rogers of Clinton Co. Ind. who came from Kentucky. (Note: This is all mixed, written in 1st person and signed by M. L. Duke and also Paris M. Duke. Not sure which one m. Mary Jane, for it says: "I was born Mary Jane Rogers", and "I married Mary Jane Rogers, and signed by two Dukes.")

Jacob Dehaven Connersville, Ind. m., age 60 yrs. "My gd. mother was Eliz. Stucker, sister of Geo. Rogers, my mother was Nancy Stucker."

James Isaac Dehaven, same address, brother of above, m., aged 56 yrs.

Nancy J. Wooters, and her husband Wm. Wooters, Kokomo, Indiana. Nancy Wooters, dau. of Nancy Dehaven, a sister of James Stucker; Nancy Wooters dau. of Wm. Stockdale and wife Sarah Ann Stockdale. Her father and mother are both dead, a brother living with Nancy J. Wooters, gdn. for wife's bro. about 41 yrs. old." (Note: The first statement conflicts with the last part of this which seems to be correct). It appears that Nancy Wooters has two bros. but her husband does not know their ages, both married. (Note: The first must mean gd. daughter of Nancy Dehaven).

Moses Rogers of Frankfort, Ind. "My uncle Geo. Rogers, our father was a son of Wm. Rogers, and uncle Wm. and one Benjamin, was 40 yrs. old Nov. 16, 1877 and m." Moses ried".

Wm. Rogers, Mason, Ind. "I am son of Elijah Rogers, a son of Wm. Rogers, a bro. of Geo. Rogers, and am 60 yrs. old and m."

Jesse Rogers says: "I am nephew of Geo. Rogers, 43 yrs. old and m.–no P.O. address shown.

Moses Rogers of Frankfort, Ind. "My uncle Geo. Rogers, our father was a son of Wm. Rogers, bro. to Geo. Rogers, decd. am 56 yrs. old, and m." Jameson Rogers, 54 and married.

Wm. Rogers, Mason, Ind. "I am son of Elijah Rogers, a son of Wm. Rogers, a bro. of Geo. Rogers, and am 60 yrs. old and m."

Jesse Rogers says: "I am nephew of Geo. Rogers, 43 yrs. old and m." No P.O. address shown.

Moses Rogers says in 2nd letter. "I know very little of my kin, but my father was Elijah Rogers, and uncle Wm. and one Benjamin was 40 yrs. old Nov. 16, 1877 and m." Moses Rogers, Frankfort, Ind. Barnett Rogers was wts.

Julia A. George, Liberty, Mo. "I am single, my husband died Jan. 1860, I am 72 yrs. old. I am dau. of Joseph Rogers, a bro. of Geo. Rogers decd."

Alice Cave, Chapin, Ill. "I was 17 last Oct. (1877), single, said Geo. Rogers was uncle of my father; father being Mr. Rogers' sister's child. I have 2 sisters." Morgan Co. Ill. Feb. 27, 1878.

Columbus H. Acuff, aged 37, m., Joseph C. Acuff, aged 44 and m., Martha Callis, widow, aged 47, sign same letter. Mexico, Mo. Feb. 23, 1878. We are the only children of Christopher C. Acuff, decd. who was son of Mildred Coppage, sister of Geo. Rogers, decd. by her 1st marriage with our gd. father Acuff–our mother who is dead was dau. of Joseph Rogers, a bro. to Geo. Rogers, decd.

Elizabeth R. Mason, of Philadelphia, Mo. (letter written for her by her son J. R. Baldridge) says: "Geo. Rogers was my father's youngest bro., my father was own bro. to those children getting a full share of Uncle George's property. I am a widow, my husband died Feb. 2, 1870, I was born Jan. 9, 1809, making me 69 last Jan. 9, 1878."

George Busy(?), Ripley, Ill., says: "My wife Susan Busby is gd. dau. of Wm. Rogers, bro. to Geo. Rogers, decd., we m. Dec. 27, 1855, I am 46 yrs. old, and my wife is 42."

Mrs. Sallie Lucas, New Frankfort, Saline Co. Mo. "I will be 64 yrs. old in a few months (dated Feb. 27, 1878), widow, husband died about a year ago. Geo. Rogers was bro. to my gd. father Wm. Rogers."

James G. Wolfe, Anderson, Ind. "Elizabeth Stucker was my gd. mother on my mother's side, being Frances Stucker before she m. my father David Wolfe, and her bros. and sister's names were: Nancy Dehaven, formerly Nancy Stucker; Wm. T. Stucker, Valentine Stucker, Greenup Stucker, James Stucker (who is excluded from the will) my mother died leaving 11 children—hence my interest is 1/11 of my mother's part."

Lawyers of Falls City, Nebr. Feb. 25, 1878, write that: Wastman and wife and Lashley and wife in this county just called upon me—their wives are not in town" . . . of Wm. Rogers who was a bro. of Geo. Rogers, decd.—Wm. is dead. Commodore Rogers died at home of James Ashlock, Annapolis, Mo. 1876 or '77, leaving the following children: Amanda Rogers, 15 yrs., Sept. 19, 1877; m. Geo. Henry Eastman; Susan Ellen, 17 yrs., Nov. 2, 1877; m. Wm. J. Ashley; Melvina, m. David Lovett; Jane m. Paris M. Dukes.

George H. Eastman and wife live in Richardson Co. Neb., Flowerdale P.O. Wm. J. Lashley and wife (same) David Lovett and wife in Neb. Dukes and wife in Neosho Co. Kans., Erie P.O. The above named girls are only ch. of Commodore Rogers who died near Annapolis, Mo. 1876-7, left widow Mary Ann who since m. to John Parker and in Richardson Co. Neb. Flowerdale P.O. Commodore Rogers was son of Elijah Rogers and Elijah Rogers was bro. of Wm. Rogers bro. of Geo. (etc. repetition—did they mean "son" and not bro. in line above of Wm. Rogers?)

Lucy Fawkes, Monroe City, Mo. aged 64, m. dau. of Mildred Coppage, and niece of Geo. Rogers, and only one of her mother's children living."

Lucinda Ash, West Union, Fayette Co. Iowa. "I am dau. of Wm. Rogers, and niece of Geo. Rogers, decd. am 77 yrs. old, widow for 30 yrs. m. twice, 1st to Wm. Cave who died, then m. John Ash, live with his son Edwin Ash, my son-in-law (step-son?) I received a letter from Uncle Geo. Rogers written Aug. 9, 1872, and one from Edw. Kemper, Oct. 8, 1877."

W. R. Stucker, Reform, Calloway Co. Mo. "My mother is sister of Geo. Rogers, decd. her name is Elizabeth Stucker, I lost my wife in 1870—have 3 gd. ch. I am 82 yrs. old (.1878). (Note: His father and mother Jacob Stucker and Elizabeth Rogers dau. of Wm. Rogers, m. June 30, 1789, Woodford Co. Ky. before Scott was taken from it, where the Stuckers lived).

Allen H. Vories, a lawyer, St. Joseph, Mo. says: "I studied law with Judge James Pryor of Carrollton, Ky. having for a fellow student the Hon. Wm. S. Pryor, now your appellate Judge, and Mr. Simeon Kemper who resides here is an old and honored citizen of St. Joseph, and now in his old age in reduced circumstances—how much will be coming to the children of Sally Kemper—there are 7 living and 2 dead without issue, they are: Simeon Kemper, Montgomery Co. Ky., Valentine Kemper, Jackson Co. Mo., Mildred Priest of Montgomery Co. Ky., Lucy Ann Chinn, Scott Co. Ky., Sarah Coppage, Marion Co. Ky. Simeon Kemper is m. is 80 yrs. old and oldest son of Sally Kemper sister of Geo. Rogers, decd. (Signed: Allen H. Vories, Atty-at-law).

Nancy Dehaven, Connersville, Ind. says: "My gt. gd. mother was a sister of Geo. Rogers, my gd. mother was Nancy Ann Stucker, and m. Isaac Dehaven, my mother was Elizabeth Dehaven, and I am the only heir. I am 46 yrs. old, and m. Christopher G. Dehaven."

John H. Dehaven of Connersville, Ind. says: "I am m. and 48 yrs. old, I am informed that Geo. Rogers is my gt. uncle."

(Note: One of the printed circulars is signed by John Rogers of Richmond, Iowa, and says that he is m. a nephew of Geo. Rogers, and nothing further).

Silas Threlkeld of Granville, Mo. Mar. 5, 1878, says: "Our father Greenville P. Acuff is son of Mildred Coppage and she was sister of Geo. Rogers. Greenville Acuff is dead and left 8 ch.: Mary M. Threlkeld, wife of Silas Threlkeld, Lucy Katherine Bryant, wife of J. H. Bryant, Mrs. Bryan is now dead and leaves 5 ch. Joseph H. Bryan is their guardian. Sarah E. Acuff, Cornelia Acuff, Geo. W. Acuff, and Joseph H. Acuff (these 4 are over 21 and m.), and Wm. H. M. Acuff, 19 yrs. Claib Acuff, 17 yrs. all of Monroe Co. except Joseph H. Acuff lives in Salt Lake Co. Utah Territory, Alta City. (Signed by Silas Threlkeld).

Valentine R. Kemper of Independence, Mo. says: "Have been on the move, m., 66 yrs. old, son of Sally Kemper."

Minerva Whitinger, says: "I am gd. dau. of Wm. Rogers, a bro. of Geo. Rogers, I am dau. of Elijah Rogers, son of Wm. Rogers, decd. I will be 51 on June 22, 1878 am single, widow (no P.O.)

Richard Hutchens, Mason City, Ill. Mar. 11, 1878, says: "He is 18, unm. gd. son of Mahala Rogers of Ky.

J. K. Rogers, "The letter addressed to Miss Fanny Rogers, was meant for my mother. She is dau. of Joseph Rogers, decd. and has but small interest even if the matter of Mr. Wright's petition should be decided in favor of the heirs." Columbia, Mo. Mar. 11, 1878.

Henry Rogers, Stanton, Neb. says: "Myself and Sarah Lovett are both m. she is past 45, and I am 38 yrs. old. Geo. Rogers is gd. father's bro. Melvina Lovett is our niece, Commodore Rogers' dau. He is dead, she is 37 past and m."

(Note: End of letters).

(Note: Relative to Joseph Rogers' heirs who get $1.00 each:)

John S. Rogers, deposition, Paris, Monroe Co. Mo. Jan. 24, 1879 . . . "Was 63 yrs. old Aug. 20, 1878, nephew of Geo. Rogers, late of Woodford Co., my father Joseph Rogers was his bro. he is dead, he left 11 children: Nancy, m. Jared Fowkes; Valentine; Wm. A. decd; Sally, m. John Waller; Mary, m. Baruch Hall now dead, she died without ch.; Frances m. Wm. Rogers; Julia m. Snyder George; Mildred m. Columbus C. Acuff and she is now dead; Eliz. m. Wm. Baldridge; Joseph, now dead; and John S. Rogers, myself.
Question: About your sister Nancy Fowkes?
Ans. Sister Nancy Fowkes is dead, she had 9 children: 1. Sallie Ann, oldest dau. died before her mother, leaving one child Jas. E. Bridgeford, living in Oregon, her husband was Wm. L. Bridgeford. 2. Lucy Fowkes m. —— Lauther, she died childless before her mother died. 3. Joseph Fowkes, living in Monroe Co. Mo. 4. Valentine Fowkes. 5. Miranda Fowkes (dead) m. Stephen W. Woodson (dead) one child, Benj. Woodson in Monroe Co. Mo. 6. Mary Jane Fowkes, m. J. H. Mills. 7. Susan, m. Newton Wilson, (dead) leaving one child, Amanda who m. a Mr. May and living near Wentzville, St. Charles Co. Mo. 8. Richard Fowkes, living in Monroe Co. Mo. 9. Jared Fowkes, died with children before his mother died.
Question: Your sister Sally Waller?
Ans: Sally is dead, had 10 children: 1. Nancy Waller m. Jeptha Smith, died before her mother and left 2 ch. John W. Smith in Randolph Co. Mo. and Alpheus Smith in Calif. 2. Wm. Waller; 3. Geo. Waller; 4. John Waller, all living in Monroe Co. Mo. 5. Ursula, m. 1st. ——

Evans, who died and she m. 2nd. Wm. W. Bassett, and he died. She is living in Monroe Co. Mo. 7. Mary A. Waller m. Ambrose Crutcher, Monroe Co. 8. Margaret E. Waller, m. Jeff. Bridgeford, Paris, Mo. 9. Valentine Waller, died childless, and 10. Joseph Waller, died childless, both of whom died before their mother.

Question: About your brother Joseph Rogers' family?

Ans: Bro. Joseph Rogers is dead, and left 5 ch.: 1. John Sanford Rogers, dead, do not know if he left any ch. 2. Elizabeth Rogers, m. Jas. McManana and living in Bates Co. Mo. 3. Eliza Rogers m. Thos. Leach, and living in Sherman, Texas. 4. Alford Rogers living in Bates Co. Mo. 5. Enoch Rogers, living in Monroe Co. Mo.

Question: Tell of your sister Mildred Acuff's family?

Ans: My sister Mildred Acuff is dead, left 3 children: 1. Martha m. John Callis, living in Anderson Co. Mo., he is dead. 2. Joseph, and Columbus Acuff both living in Anderson Co. Mo. (Signed) John S. Rogers.

––––––

Depositions of Jefferson Bridgeford: Questions about Mrs. Nancy Fowkes, Mrs. Sally Waller, etc. He answered as all of above, and said he m. Margaret E. Waller, dau. of Sally Waller, decd. When asked about the descendants of Joseph Rogers, he says: "Valentine Rogers lives in Scott Co. Ky., Fanny Rogers, wife of Wm. Rogers, decd. lives in Boone Co. Mo., Julia, wife of Signor George, decd. lives in Clay Co. Mo., Elizabeth, wife of ––––– Bolderidge, decd. heirs: John W. Coppage; 60 yrs. living Hannibal, Mo.; 2. Millie A. McIntyre, about stated by John S. Rogers.

Mrs. Lucy Fowkes, at Monroe Co. Mo. Jan. 8, 1879, deposes: "Am 64 yrs. of age, and was raised by Geo. Rogers, my guardian; my mother's bro." (repeats lot already stated above)—says Martha E. Callis is about 50, C. H. Acuff is about 40, J. C. Acuff is about 45, and of Audrian Co. Mo. that Greenville Acuff left 8 ch.: Mary H. between 40 and 50 yrs. m. Silas Threlkeld, Lucy K. died about '75? m. Joseph H. Bryan and left 5 ch.: Sylvester, Daniel, James, Bessie and ––––– Eliz. Acuff, 30 yrs. Cornelia Acuff, 25, Geo. Acuff 25-30; Joseph Acuff, 21-23; Wm. 19 and Claiborn 17; Sarah Coppage died leaving 2 living and –– deed. heirs: John W. Coppage; 60 yrs. living Hannibal, Mo.; 2. Millie A. McIntyre, about 50; Susan, m. W. T. Bryan and died about 1870, and left 5 ch., Mary E. m. Henry Powers; Thos. Bryan, about 28; Henry Bryan, 26, John Bryan, 21, and Joseph Bryan, 19. 4. Nancy J. (dau. of Sarah Coppage) m. John Johnson died 20 yrs. ago and left 1 heir, John W. Johnson about 25 yrs. old, Comanche, Texas. 5. Lucy Acuff, this affiant, 1st m. James H. Smith, and now wife of Valentine Fowkes, Nancy who m. Jared Fowkes, died in 1873.

Valentine Rogers, Wm. Rogers (dead) Sally m. Waller, 1st. then Jared Fowkes, died Mar. 1878; Fanny, m. Wm. Rogers; Julia m. about 1870, and m. 2nd Wm. Guthrie; Eliz. m. Wm. Bolderidge then a ––––– Mason; Joseph Rogers died 1851 in Calif. and left 4 heirs, and John Rogers (Note: Question not put down, but evidently about heirs of Joseph Rogers given above. Some of them seem to differ slightly).

(Note: Many more pages of depositions as to the heirs, much of it is repetition as to relationships, and given by different persons).

Daus. of Johnson Rogers, decd, son of Wm. Rogers, who was a bro. of Geo. Rogers, viz.: Talitha C.; Sarah M.; Mary E.; Lavina; Madeline, &c. Talitha C. m. Robt. Tanner, and a widow; Sarah A. m. Thos. A. Knox, and both living; Mary E. m. John S. Bond, and both living; Lavina m. ––––– Bledsoe, and died leaving only 1 heir; Lilly M. Bledsoe, an inf. and John Bledsoe is her gdn.; Madeline m. J. M. Ray and both died leaving Wm. and Mollie Ray.

Elizabeth Stucker had 9 children: 1. James, cut off; 2. & 3. Polly and John died without issue. 4. Nancy m. Isaac Dehaven, both died leaving Jacob Dehaven, James I. Dehaven, John H. Dehaven; 5. Elizabeth m. John Davis; 6. Sally m. Wm. Stockdale. Both Eliz. Davis and husband died leaving one child Nancy A. Davis m. Christopher G. Dehaven. Sally Ann Stockdale and husband both died, leaving 4 ch.: Isaac, John; Wm. E.; and Nancy who m. Wm. Wooters. (Note: This seems incomplete).

Wm. Rogers, bro. of testator had 11 ch.: 1. Elijah Rogers died leaving 14 ch. of whom are Wm. Rogers, Moses Rogers, James, Barnett, and Henry Rogers, Nancy Sparks wife of Allen Sparks, Ellender Wright, widow, Minerva Whitinger wife of ———— W. and Sarah Lovett wife of ———— Lovett. 2. Commodore Rogers died leaving 4 ch.: Mary J. Duke wife of Paris M. Duke. Susan, wife of W. T. Lashley, Melvina m. ———— Lovett, and 4. (Unnamed).
(Note: Much omitted, perhaps because given before).

Geo. Bradburn, aged 18, minor heir of Samuel Bradburn, Fayette Co. Ind.

Olivia Allen is dead and left: Mary, m. Jas. Burnett, Geo. R. Allen, John Allen and Elizabeth Allen (last under 21).

John Rogers a son of Barnett Rogers who was a son of Wm. Rogers, bro. to testator, left another child, Robert Rogers an infant.

Sally Fowkes left following ch. by her 1st. husband Waller, Viz: Wm., Valentine, Richard, John, Harney, Margaret, Polly A., Nannie, Ursula and Geo. Waller. Elizabeth Maxfield also left (besides others named) dau. Sarah m. ———— Baggerly, and died leaving heirs unknown, and that in addition to Mary E. Talbott, Almeda Talbott had ch. who are unknown to plf.
(Note: End of 1st large Bundle No. 930).
Second Bundle No. 931:

Greenup Stucker of Scott Co. Ky. deposition: Aged 72 yrs. a blacksmith and farmer, son of Geo. Rogers' half sister Elizabeth Stucker, said Geo. had six bros. and sisters—Wm., Joseph, Mildred Acuff and Coppage, Sally Kemper, Elizabeth m. first Jacob Stucker, and Lucy mar. Wesley Acuff (all dead) Lucy died without issue.
Question: Tell about Eliz. Stucker's family?
Answer: Wm. Stucker living, myself Greenup Stucker, and John Stucker dead and no ch. James Stucker dead and no ch. Polly Acuff dead and no ch. David Stucker dead and no ch. Frances m. David Wolfe and both dead leaving issue; Nancy m. Isaac Dehaven, both dead without issue; Valentine Stucker died and left one child J. Wesley Stucker. (Note: This seems to be very different from other statements by other heirs). Frances Wolfe had the following ch.: Wm. H. Wolfe, David S. Wolfe, Geo. W. Wolfe, James G. Wolfe, Mary F. Wolfe who m. Jas. T. Dehaven; Sallie Ann m. Hawkins Hackleman; Eliz. M. m. Stephen Tyner; Nancy E. mar. Lewis Webb; Caroline m. Lewis Thomas; Jacob S. Wolfe. All of ch. of Frances Wolfe living except Jacob Wolfe, hear Jacob had ch. but do not know. Nancy Dehaven had the following ch.: Jacob Dehaven, Jas. Isaac Dehaven, John H., Elizabeth m. John Davis, both dead, left one child, Ann who m. Christopher Dehaven; Sallie A. Dehaven who m. ———— Stockdale and both dead leaving four ch. whom I do not know. Jacob, James T. and John H. Dehaven are now living.
Question: Tell of Mildred Coppage's ch.?
Answer: Columbus Acuff dead, leaving issue, one of whom, Joseph Acuff, only I know; Greenville P. Acuff dead, issue, only know three: Joseph, Mildred and George; John W.

Acuff dead and no issue. Rhodin Coppage dead, left two ch. (do not know them); Lucy Fowkes is living; Sarah Coppage I hear m. and died, but do not know; other descendants of Mildred I don't know.

Question: Tell of Joseph Rogers' family, bro. of Geo. R.?

Answer: Valentine Rogers living; John Rogers; Julia m. S. George and a widow; Mildred m. Columbus Acuff and both dead leaving Joseph, all I know; Betsy m. ———— Mason and living; Nancy m. Fowkes and died leaving Joseph, Valentine, Sallie Ann, Mary Jane, Lucy, Miranda and Richard Fowkes; Sallie m. 1st Waller, 2nd Jared Fowkes who died recently and had Wm., Waller, Valentine, Geo., Nancy, etc. (Note: See in foregoing records.)

Valentine Rogers deposition: Live in Scott County, Ky. born May 17, 1788, knew Geo. Rogers, half bro. to my father Joseph Rogers . . . my sister now decd. m. Jared Fowkes and left at her death Joseph, etc. . . . bro. Wm. died leaving Joseph J. Rogers, Walter Scott Rogers, Sarah Rogers who m. ———— Kelly and now a widow; Cyrene m. Albert Marshall, Eliz. m. Wm. Graves, Julia m. John T. Bates, died leaving one child, Eliza, who is a minor. Sister Sallie m. Fowkes m. first, John Waller, and then Jared Fowkes who was also husband of my sister Nancy Fowkes. Sallie died recently. Aug. 15, 1878. Valentine Rogers dep'n. end.

Richard Maxfield deposition: Aged 37 yrs. Pike Co. Mo. My mother was a dau. of Wm. Rogers; Elizabeth m. Chas. W. Maxfield and had issue: Sarah Ann Maxfield m. Jas. Baggerly; Wm., Geo. W., Benj., Richardson, Simeon, Burel, Charles Maxfield, Margaret Elizabeth Maxfield m. David Jennings. Sarah Ann Baggerly and her husband are both dead (Jas. B.) and have two ch.: Thos. J. and Otis Baggerly. Ch. of Elizabeth that are dead and no issue are: Wm., Benj., Richardson and Bird (Note: Is this Burel?) Richard Maxfield lives near Bowling Green, Pike Co. Mo.

Jacob Dehaven deposition: Aged 60 yrs. Fayette Co. Ind. Gd. mother was a sister of Geo. Rogers and m. Jacob Stucker.

Sally A. Wolfe, about 64 yrs. deposes that: David G. Wolfe is 55, Wm. H. Wolfe is 58, Geo. W. is about 50, Mary F. Wolfe is 47, m. Jas. T. Dehaven, Caroline Wolfe is 44, m. L. R. Thomas, Emeline Wolfe m. Samuel Bradburn and died before 1877, left two ch.: Edgar Bradburn 24, and Geo. Bradburn 18, Nancy Wolfe 47, m. Christopher G. Dehaven. Sarah Dehaven m. Wm. Stockdale and had four ch.: Nancy m. Wm. Wooters, etc.

Wm. H. Wolfe deposition: 58 yrs. Elizabeth Wolfe 66, m. Stephen Tynes, Sally A. 64 m. Hawkins Hackleman, Wm. H. Wolfe 58, David G. 55, Geo. W. 50, Mary F. 47, m. James T. Dehaven 51, Nancy E. Wolfe 58, m. Lewis Webb (Note: Some repetition of above). Rhodin Coppage heirs: W. M. Coppage, Jas J. Coppage, Lucretia M. m. S. H. Templin, J. W. Coppage.

J. Wesley Coppage deposition: Aged 38 yrs. Harrison Co. Ky. (?) says he knows none of the heirs of Mildred except Rhodin Coppage, one of her ch. who was my father—she left other heirs unknown to me. Rhodin Coppage dead and left four heirs (before named).

W. M. Coppage, aged 34, Connersville, Harrison Co. Ind. (?) son of Rhodin (son of Mildred), Rhodin decd., left J. Wesley, Harrison Co., James J. (Think he lives in Girard, Crawford Co. Kans.), Lucretia H. Templin, Boone Co. Ind. and myself.

Elender Wright, aged 46, Frankfort, Ind. Dec. 19, 1878, says: Geo. Rogers uncle to my father Elijah Rogers, died Mar. 28, 1872. (Note: lot follows about Caves and Maxfields, already given). My father Elijah Rogers died leaving: Wm. Rogers now 61; Commodore

Rogers, died 1876, widow Mary Ann m. —— Parker and Melvina m. W. D. Lovett, Stantion, (Neb.) Mary J. m. —— Duke (above), Moses Rogers, aged 57, Jameson Rogers, 55, Owen, 47, John Rogers about 45, Jesse Rogers about 43, Barnett about 40, Henry about 38, Washington Rogers died 9 yrs. ago leaving a widow (since m. Robinson) and two ch. Jesse W. and Josephine C. about 7, Nancy Sparks about 53, wife of Allen Sparks; Minerva Whittinger about 51, deponent 46 is dau. of said Elijah, decd. Sarah Lovett (m. N. C. Lovett) about 41.

Wm. Rogers, son of Wm. Rogers and bro. of said Elijah died Mar. 1876, leaving widow Mary L. still living, and two sons Oscar M. Rogers, since died leaving a widow Eliza A. and no ch.; and Thos. J. Rogers about 40, and others not known by me.

Mary L. Rogers, Clinton Co. Ind. deposition: Aged 73 yrs. says on July 25, 1878: In 1830 Geo. Rogers was at the residence of my late husband Wm. Rogers, in Boone Co. Ky. My husband Wm. Rogers died Mar. 24, 1875, leaving me (widow) and two sons: Oscar M. and Thos. J. Rogers, etc.

Susan Rogers, Dec. 20, 1878, Clinton Co. Ind. aged 79 yrs. Sept. 14, 1878: My father-in-law Wm. Rogers, my late husband Elijah Rogers decd. was a son of said Wm. Rogers, bro. of Geo. Rogers decd. My husband Elijah Rogers died Mar. 28, 1872, and left: Wm. 61, Moses, 57, Jameson 55, Owen 47, John 45, Jesse 43, Barnett 39, Henry 38. . . . two sons Commodore died Mar. 1856 and Washington died eight yrs. ago and left widow and 2 ch.; Elijah left the following females: Nancy Sparks, Minerva Whitinger, Elender Wright and Sarah Lovett.

Jesse Rogers, dep'n., aged 43, Clinton Co. Ind.

Moses Rogers 57, deposition: My father Elijah was son of Wm. died Mar. 28, 1872, aged 74 yrs. and 20 days and left widow Susan Rogers.

Mahala Cave, sister of Elijah, and dau. of Wm. (bro. of Geo.) died about 1843 and left four sons and three daus. . . .

Wm. Cave depostion: (Jan. 2, 1879, Mason Co. Ill. aged 54 yrs.) Geo. Rogers bro. to my gd. father Wm. Rogers, knew only my gd. father Wm. Rogers who is dead—ch. of Wm. Rogers: Barnett, Lucinda (Ash), Johnson Rogers, Wm., Mahala (Cave) Eliz. Rogers, (Pickens) Almira (Carpenter) Benjamin, Minerva (White); Barnett left John, Owen, Warren and others I do not know. Elijah was living twenty yrs. ago, and had Wm., Commodore, Moses, etc. Lucinda Ash had: Amanda (decd.) Alonzo, Adaline, Matilda, Edwin, Ellen. Johnson Rogers dead and had: Thomas, Talitha, Madaline, etc. Wm. Rogers living twenty-four yrs. ago, and had: Oscar and Thos. Mahala Cave was my mother, her first husband was Richard Cave and had: Wm., Mary Louisa Hutchins (widow), Cyrus (dead), John (dead), Sarah Hutchins (dead, ch.), Richard dead (ch.), Almeda (dead), mother had no ch. by second husband Robert Moore. Gd. father Wm. Rogers died when I was ten or twelve yrs. old. I lived with his widow Sarah Rogers. (Signed) Wm. Cave.

Answer of Joseph J. Rogers, Scott Rogers, Sarah Frances Kelly, Cyrene Marshall and Albert Marshall her husband, Eliz. Graves and Wm. B. Graves her husband, Eliza Bates by her gd'n. Joseph J. Rogers, only ch. and descendants of Wm. Rogers, decd. of Scott Co. Ky. Their ancestor was a son of Joseph Rogers, a bro. of Testator. Filed Jan. 31, 1878. (Note: Chart on heavy manila paper of descendents of Wm. Rogers a bro. of Geo. also one of Eliz. Stucker—four generations—Mildred Coppage, 3 gens. and Sally Kemper, etc.).

Benjamin T. Rogers, Dec. 6, 1878, Macoupin Co. Ill. 69 yrs. old last Aug., nephew of Geo. Rogers. . . . Wm. Rogers children: Lucinda Rogers m. Wm. Cave and had: Amanda Cave, m. Wesley Goldsberry; Adaline Cave m. ——? Alonza Cave; Edwin Cave; Matilda Cave m. ——— Ash; Ellen Cave m. Joseph Ashby. Lucinda Rogers Cave m. 2nd.

Mahala Rogers m. Richard Cave and had: Wm. Cyrus, (as before listed) and m. 2nd. Moore. . . . Almira Rogers m. Nicholas Carpenter and had Parthenia (m. Simeon Baldwin) Almeda, Nathaniel, Wm. Elizabeth Rogers 67, m. Chas. Maxfield. Minerva Rogers 65, m. ——— White, Boone Co. Ky. (Signed Benj. T. Rogers)

Julia George deposition: Jan. 22, 1879, Liberty, Clay Co. Mo. aged 73 yrs. niece of Geo. Rogers, dau. of Joseph Rogers, bro. of Geo. Rogers. Joseph Rogers dead left: Valentine Rogers, etc. (heretofore listed). Elizabeth Rogers m. Silas Mason and now a widow.

In a petition heirs are set forth as:

Geo. Bradburn and Aggie, Almeda, Anna, and Louella Shotwell, Josephine, Lucy and Mary Ryle, Daniel and Louella Rogers, and Alice, Emma, Julia, Ally M. and Chas. Cave, Jesse and Clarinda Rogers, Eliza Bates, etc. . . .

TESTATOR NOT IN GENERAL INDEX

Adams, Francis, old soldier, produced schedule in court—Mercer Co. Orders 1825, p. 137

Adkins Hrs—(Deed Bk. O, p. 330 Scott Co. burned records. 1832—) Adkins, Jas. Hrs: Henry Boaz and Judy Boaz, Clement Griffith and Nancy Griffith, Jas. Adkins, Jno. Adkins, Jas. Adkins (in body of deed) and wife of Jackson Co. Ind., remainder of Scott who are widow and hrs. of Jas. Adkins decd.

Cir. Ct. Harrison Co. Suit—Wm. Davis' devisees vs. Gdn. Box 174—Allison, Alex, Joel Frazier states Alex. Allison killed in Dudley's defeat, May 5, 1813. Chas. Allison, father of complainant John Allison, died 1787, he thinks, and John abt. 20 yrs. old at his father's death, and his bro. Alex. abt. 10 when father died.

Harrison Co. Cir. Ct. Box 174—filed 9/17/1816—Anderson, Wm. aged abt. 62 states he resided at Ruddles Station 1786 with bros. etc. and John Hinkston is his father-in-law by his 1st wife and Thos. Ravenscroft is his brother-in-law by his 1st wife—dep. taken 12/13/1815

Apperson (Franklin Co. Deeds M, p. 376, 1828—) Apperson, James P.—"Of Chas. City Co. Va.", a son of Edmund Apperson late of New Kent Co. Va. apps. Thos. Winn of Woodford Co., Ky. atty. to get estate left him as legatee of Richard Apperson, decd. of Franklin Co. Ky.

Amos Hrs: (Bourbon Cir. Ct. suit Nicholas Amos' hrs. filed Nov. 1816—) He died Bourbon Co. abt. Aug. 1815 leaving: Mary m. Josiah Barton, Thos., Mordecai, Nancy m. Wm. Connaway, Christina m. Elias Melot, Ben., Abraham, Elijah, Sarah m. Daniel Thomas, Ditto, Pathia m. Jno. Barnett, all living at time of death of Nicholas Amos; and Elizabeth m. Parker then decd. had Cassandra m. Mahlon Hall, Clemency m. Michael Hornback, Mary m. Joseph Brown, Christiana m. Geo. Hughes, Henry. Wm. and Levi Parker and Ruth m. Michael Hornback Jr. then decd. had Elizabeth and Barbara infants; and William Amos then decd. had Christiana and Kitty with Geo. Barkett (Barnett?) Gdn.

Arrowsmith Hrs: (Petition for Sett. of Estate, Bourbon Cir. Ct. Box 694, May 1828—) Arrowsmith, Richard decd. left: James, then under 21 yrs. with Henry Fisk gdn. apptd. by Montgomery Co. Court—widow Cassendra (Casender) who m. 2nd Henry Fisk, John, Alex., Wm., Mary m. David Longnecker, Cynthiana, m. Greenberry Howard, Rebecca m. Wm. Garrott (Garriott), Elizabeth m. Ambrose McMahill, Margaret m. Jas. Welch (Welsh) Lavinia m. Jno. Forgy, Alvin (Jas. Mitchell apptd. his gdn.) Sally m. Wm. Earle (Earyl)

Armstrong Hrs: (Mercer Co. Bk. 21, p. 193, 7/12/1837)—Armstrong, Wm. hrs.—James, Joseph, Wm. Adams and wife Priscilla, late Armstrong, Edward Slaughter and wife Susanna, late Armstrong, John L. Lillard and wife Nancy, late Armstrong, hrs. of Wm. Armstrong decd. Note: Refers to suit and deeds, James, Alex. Abel, Wm., Benj. and John Armstrong in agreement—Deeds 10, p. 15—Mercer Co. June 1816.

Madison Hrs: (Fayette Co. Deed Bk. D, p. 306, 11/14/1808)—Francis Allen and wife Eliza. L., late Madison, dau. of Gabriel Madison, decd. and her ch. by sd. Francis Richard Allen, Jr. 2nd part and Richard Allen and Price Curd 3rd part—whereas Francis is possessed of slaves obtained by m. to sd. Elizabeth, and being entitled to div. of estate of Gabriel Madison and to provide for his widow and ch. Francis Allen conveys slaves in trust to Richard Allen and Price Curd.

Arnold Hrs.—(Mercer Co. Orders, Oct. 4, 1824, p. 100)—Arnold, Jersitia and Robert Arnold, inf. ch. of Terry Arnold, made choice of Blake Arnold as their gdn.

Arnold Hrs—(Order b. Bourbon Co. Oct. 1797)—Arnold, Isaac— John and Thomas Arnold inf. orphans of Isaac Arnold made choice of Elijah Thompson as gdn. and same apptd. gdn. of Polly, Frances and Elijah Arnold, infs. of Isaac.

Allison, John—1801—Bourbon Cir. Ct. dep. in suit Harrison vs. Veitch, Jones, others—in Nicholas Co. states his father's claim was part of the land held by claim of Daniel Calahan 1785. His father Chas. Allison bought of Thos. Johnson, etc.

Alexander, James—(Bourbon Cir. Ct. in suit Hamilton's hrs. Box 846)—Isabella (Ibby) Hamilton, Sarah Ann Hamilton, Theriza (Thezy) Hamilton and Caroline Hamilton by James M. Cogswell gdn—many yrs. ago their grandfather James Alexander died intestate in Bourbon—left seven ch. of whom Hamilton was one, that their mother—Hamilton departed life—they received no part. Sarah Alexander was the widow of said James— their land bound by Darnell, Commrs: Darnell & Wm. Rogers.

Briscoe, John, Jr. (see Hawkins vs. Humphrey Marshall, No. 425, Franklin Dist. Ct.—Briscoe, Hez. vs. Wm. Stewart's devisees, Box 17-30, Franklin Dist. Ct.) claim, 1780, Big Bone Lick in Logan Co., later. Hez. Briscoe, devisee of John Briscoe, Sr., John B., Sr. died, son John Briscoe, Jr., also had many acres of land in Nov. 10, 1796. George Briscoe, dep. says John Briscoe, his bro. died, always meant to move to Ky. and occupy lands. John Briscoe, Jr., dep. says his father had owned lands since 1770 and he started to Ky. fall 1779 (Nov. 10, 1796) Hez. Briscoe says that in 1779 his father John Briscoe, Sr. had cert. for 1400 acres of land. John, Sr. died, will, Monongalla Co., Va.

Barrett, Peter (will bk. E, P. 439, Harrison Co., Ky.) property to be sold—money divided among ch.—that portion of estate coming to ch. of Enoch M. Tilton and ch. of Thos. Philips—until ch. are 21—dau. Margaret Barrett—gd. daus. Nancy Tilton and Nancy Heddleson, son Lucas Barrett—exrs. sons Lucas and Wesley—May 7, 1842—Jan. 11, 1847—wts: Andrew Moore—Stephen Harber.

Baseman, John, hrs. (Bourbon Cir. Ct. box 125) Wm. Tilley and wife Rachael, John Smith and wife, Ruth, Elijah Hopper and wife Catherine, Joshua Hall and wife Nancy and John Baseman under 21 by gdn. John Baseman decd. in 1789 was possessed of 500 acres in Bourbon, etc.

Barger, John (Bourbon Cir. Ct. Abraham Bowman vs. Melton box 328) was at Ruddles Fort 1779-1780 until Indians took it.

Branham, John, hrs. (Scott Co. hrs. deeds M. p. 165, 1833, July 6) Henry Branham and w. Mary, Sanford Branham and w. Matilda, Beverly Branham and w. Polly of Scott and —— Branham and w. Nancy, Elias Staffs and—— and Milton Staffs and—— of Indiana, hrs. of John Branham senior, late of Scott 1st pt. and John Branham of Scott ——heirs signed: Elias Staffs, Susan Staffs, Milton Staffs, Robert Branham, Nancy Branham, Henry Branham, Polly Branham, Sandford Branham, Matilda Branham, Beverly Branham, Martha Branham in Jefferson Co., Ind. came Elias Staffs, Robt. Branham, Milton Staffs, Susan Staffs, Nancy Branham, Eliz. Staffs.

Barton, David (Bourbon Cir. Ct. box 206) and wife Charlotte—she dau. Thos. Marsh—Rachel Corbin, wife of Abraham (late of Md.) decd. she of Nicholas Co., Ky.—states she gave slaves to her son, Thos. and by him transferred to Capt. John Neal of Bourbon—she had also a son Abraham, etc. Suit Barton vs. Neal.

Bishop, Isaac (Bourbon Cir. Ct. Box 844, 1837 vs. Andrew Bishop) hrs: widow Nancy and Andrew, Benj., Louisa, Sally, Angelina, Thos., Mary and Jno.—some infants under 21 yrs.

Barlow, Thompkins (suit 403, Bourbon Cir. Ct. 1807-1817) died intestate. Hrs: Thomas Barlow, Alvin Barlow, James Barlow, Henry Barlow, William, Patsy, Nancy and John Barlow.

Brough, Richard (order B. p. 337, Mercer Co.) of Cumberland, and Valentin Brothers of Maryland—wts. for Stephen Hannah, dep. ordered to be taken Mar. 29, 1792.

Broughton, Chas., hrs. (FF—498, Jefferson Co., Ky. deeds) Dec. 13, 1831. Henry Hart, Evans Moore and wife Susan, Robt. Samuels and wife Elizabeth, Catherine Miles, Chas., John Squire and Mary Eliza Hart, Polly Simmons, Abner Collings and wife Harriet, Wm. Vanvacter and wife Maria, Joseph Harned and wife Eliza., Hez. B. Waters and wife Sally, Owen Crigler and wife Polly, Dennis Purcell and wife Jane, Nancy Duvall, Cynthia Lutes, Chas. H. Duvall, Abel Shain and wife Lydia, parties of 1st part and portion of his heirs and descendants of his heirs, to Wm. Reed, lot Louisville., Wm. Reed claims as his own, etc. Bullitt Co., Cath. Hart, Collings, Vanvacters, and rest, also.

Campbell, Lewis, hrs. (Bourbon Ct. deeds 1857) Elizabeth Campbell, Edward Byran and wife Elizabeth, Wm. W. Campbell, Jas. L. Campbell.

Crawford, Jno (deed Scott Co., M. 400) hrs: Elizabeth C., widow of Jno S. Crawford, decd. and hrs: Jas. B. Crawford, Thos. B. Crawford, Elizabeth S. Crawford, Nath'l. Crawford, Patsy, wife of Isaac Skillman, Lethe, wife of Jacob Jacoby. wts: Tyson Bell, Wm. M. Crawford—Apr. 9, 1834.

Coil, Jacob (Bourbon deeds, 32 p. 466, June 1834) hrs: John Coil, Noah Coil, Soloman Coil, Eliph Coil, Geo. Coil, Polly m. Admiram Allen, Margaret Coil, Elizabeth Hill—she late Eliz. Kiplinger.

Case, Joseph—(sett. of estates A. p. 467) died Bourbon, intestate leaving some inf. hrs. and others—wife was Deliliah Case—she died here also intestate—Jos. Case div. 9 parts—Samuel Case's hrs: Mary J. Hughes (she m. George Hughes); Moore Case; Theophelus Case; Deborah Keith (m. Gabriel Keith); Sally Lasky (m. Jos. Lasky); Jno. Case (prob. m. Nancy Tucker); Geo. Case—Dec. 31, 1823—above Mary J. Hughes may have m. 1st Wm. Paslay. Delilah Case died 1834—order bk. K, p. 353—Theophelus Case admr. March 3, 1834.

Joseph Case (eeds S. p. 124—1925—see also suit Sam'l. Case hrs. box 764—Bourbon Cir. Ct.) Delila—widow—George—Theopelus and wife, Polly, Deborah m. Gabl. Keith, Polly J. m. Hughes, Sally m. Joseph Lasky, Joseph Case and wife, Nancy and Joseph gdn. of Samuel Case's hrs: Jno. Case and Julia Moore Case and Polly late of Bourbon County.

Chambers, Silas (Box 628 Bourbon Cir. Ct.)—Hrs. vs. Thos. Young filed May 16, 1820) dep. of Alex Breckenridge would show Chambers departed life 1818 intestate hrs: Abigal, Polly, Hazle, Wm.?, Jno., Phoebe, Betsy, Daniel, John, Rachel, Lilly—wife previously departed life—principal part of land had come by her—two eldest ch. (not named) are 21 yrs. and have sold their interest to Thos. Young. Alex. Breckenridge was apptd. gdn. of other ch.

Banta, Abram (Gen. Court, K.–269, Franklin Co.–deeds others named) heirs, Jas. B. Stephens and wife Leah Banta, Rush Co., Ind., decd. Oct. 21, 1825.

Bradford, Enoch (Scott Co., Ky. deeds M. p. 96, Feb. 20, 1833) Wm. T. Bradford, Bealey E. Bradford, deed land on which their father Enoch Bradford died. Deed to Daniel Bradford–signed Wm. T. B., B. E. Bradford and Narcissa Bradford.

Bushby, James—(Bourbon Orders N. Dec. 1842 and Bourbon Orders, L. p. Feb. 7, 1843) pension application—Elizabeth Bushby files claim—she being widow.—Elizabeth Bushy formerly Elizabeth Shackelford produced a certified copy of her marriage bond executed by Jas. Bushy with Roger Shackelford security, for m. of sd. Bushy and sd. Elizabeth in Albemarle Co. Va. Mar. 4, 1790 sd. Bushy d. July 18, 1838–85 yrs. Robt. Bushy stated he is bro. of sd. Jas.

Brewer, Daniel (Mercer Co. Orders May 1, 1826, p. 230) heirs to wit: Isaac Brocaw and wife Mary (late Brewer), Stephen V. Brewer, Jacob Whallon and wife Margaret (late B.) John Brewer, John Williamson and wife Christiana (late B.) Abraham, Peter, Daniel and Sarah M. Brewer (last two being infants)—bond of D. Brewer to Abraham Ripperdan, Mar. 1813.

Breathitt, John (Deeds F, Logan Co., Ky. Dec. 17, 1817)—To sisters Eliza and Susan B., and bro. George B., for love and affec'tn. to Cardwell Breathitt all I get at decease of my father in estate of said father, to be held in trust by Cardwell B. (Note: Geo. Breathitt, bro. of Gov. John, death notice in Commonwealth, June 4, 1833. John, the Gov. death in Feb. 25, 1834. Mrs. Eliz., mother of Gov. B., Apr. 15, 1834)

Bowles, Jane (C-372, Woodford Co. deed June 12, 1802) Isaac Pierce and wife Sarah, Edward Holland and wife Eliz., James Renney and wife Eliz., land allotted to Jane Bowles as heir to James McBride, issue of Isaac McBride.

Blue, Uriah (Deed bk. 1793-1803 p. 605, Logan Co. Oct. 21, 1800) Uriah Blue and wife Susannah, Oct. 10, 1800, of Hampshire Co., Va. deed lands in Logan Co., to Benj. Neale, "Va. Mil. Land" on Muddy R. Salt Peter Carr cr., patented in Ky., Mar. 24, 1796.

Bledsoe, Wm. M. (p. 55, complete records E. Franklin Cir. Ct. Dec. 1814) Wm. M. Bledsoe's heirs: Joseph, Moses O., Wm., Betsey M., Willis, Burelle, A. Bledsoe, Media, Vestina Scott and Margaret A. Bledsoe, ch. and heirs of Wm. M. Bledsoe, decd. Patience and Moses O. Bledsoe, exrs.

Bacon—"widow" (see John Jones, will in suit of John C. Bacon and wife vs. Bacon's extrs. box 180, Franklin Cir. Ct. 1816) Much Bacon data—She was widow Bacon with three ch.: Benedict, Nath'l., and Eliz. Bacon and m. John Jones, then she m. Stanley P. Gower. Edmund Bacon says def't. went to Va. and bro't. here his sister Elizabeth, one of the compts.

Baker, Joseph (Garrard Co., affidavit order 1819-1821, p. 91) Rev. soldier, aged abt. 60, says Aug. 20, 1820, in Rev. war, enlisted 1780, in Capt. John Wilson's 10th N.C. Reg't; Col. Zach Dozier, 12 mos., again 6 mos., farmer, wife aged 50 yrs.—10 ch. 2 boys and 1 girl with him, boys 13 and 15, girl 7 plus.

Barbee, Ezekiel (Mercer orders p. 25, 1823-1827) inf. heirs: Harriet and Bryan Barbee chose Robt. Barbee, gdn. Court appointed him gdn. of Maria Barbee, inf. Joshua Barbee, admr. of Ezekiel Barbee. On motion of Polly Deer, late Polly Barbee, her dower allotted, thirds, Sept. 1, 1823.

Barnett, James (Woodford Co. deeds, D-49) Deed bet. James Barnett, agt. for Ambrose Barnett of Va. of 1st part and Marquis Calmes of Woodford Co., of 2nd part for $1.00 Barnett sells to Calmes a tr. in Madison Co., Ky. on middle fork of Ky. river, 7 mi. in a straight line from the mouth, 500 a., Feb. 26, 1806. I, Ambrose Barnett of Fauquier Co., Va. apt. Jas. Barnett, of Madison Co., Va. to recover property, etc. Dec. 3, 1805 (D-49 Woodford). Note: Many such deeds of Barnetts in Woodford. Ambrose Barnett m. in Fauquier Co., Va. Judith Neavil, July 18, 1766. Ambrose Barnett, pensioner in Nicholas Co., Ky. Capt. Jas. Barnett m. Milly Neville and had son Ambrose who m. Margaret Helm & to So. Va. Jas. & Amb. bros.

Burch, John (Jessamine Co. deeds B-647-E-258-F-7-G-357-H-118-K-281-K-334) John Burch buys land Dec. 12, 1810, in Nich'ville. John Burch deeds to Henry Burch for keeping two ch. of said John, Mar. 6, 1818. Wm. & John Burch, 1818–Mary Burch, Jas. Burch, Geo. I. Burch, and Wm. Burch, and Stephen Richardson of Garrard Co. of 1st part, hrs. of John Burch, decd. to Moses Spencer of Jessamine Co. Jan. 18, 1823–Johnson J. Burch also signed the deed. Wm. Burch of Garrard Co., to Jas. Burch, land near Nich'ville. Nov. 1824. Jas. Burch of Garrard, Sept. 19, 1833. Ezekiel Burch of Jessamine buys 1833. Jas. J. (I?) Burch Aug. 1, 1836, wife Mary of Jessamine, deed, etc.

Barbour, James (Jefferson Co. deed 8, p. 8) heirs: Thos. Barbour, Jr. and wife Mary, Richard Barbour and wife Mary, Philip Barbour, John Harrison and wife Sarah of Garrard Co., David Walker and wife Mary of Logan Co., John G. Bailer and wife Lucy, of same Co., all of Ky. heirs of Jas. Barbour, decd. deed Ohio Co. lands 5,408 acres, Sept. 17, 1806.

Beadles, Wm. (Lincoln Co. will bk. 195, p. 189, p. 202) Inv. July 1825, Rice, Anderson, John and Eliza. Beadles, etc. bt. at sale; Rice Beadles, decd. inv. 1-787-195, 8-30-1826, widow Sarah Beadles, Anderson, Joel, John, Sarah, Rice Beadles, Jr., Arch Brown, etc. at sale, also Elijah Richardson, and Sarah Beadles, Jr., Eliz. Beadles widow, July 1827; Lewis Beadles, (L.W.B) aged 13, Aug. 25, next, orphan of Lewis B., decd. John Dood, his gdn. (orders 8, p. 202) June 1823; Sarah Beadles, widow of Rice B. relinq. admn. to John B., Aug. 1826 (orders 9, p. 60), Rice Beadles vs. Lewis Beadles, admr. Sept. 1825. Lewis Willis Beadles, orph. of Lewis B., decd. over 14, chose Eliz. Beadles gdn. Mar. 1825. (orders 9, p. 46)

Beauchamp, John (Order bk. L, p. 115, Franklin Co. Jan. 17, 1842) John Beauchamp m. Narcissa Butler, dau. of Geo. Butler (so says George B.) Jan. 19, 1817 and he left Hardin Co. where he lived 8 or 9 years, and went to Tex., and died and left his widow Narcissa Beauchamp and children: Zarilda Brown, wife of Granville Brown, Martha Bassett, wife of Henry Bassett, Stephen Beauchamp, John R. Beauchamp, Matilda and George Beauchamp.

Bell, Margaret Steele and Clement Bell her husband (deed Fayette Co. Z-311) heirs of Andrew Steele, decd. Maria, Eliz., Jane, Ann, Clementina, Margaret, and Ezekiel Bell, ch. and heirs of Margaret Bell, decd. late M. S. and Clement Bell, her husband, all named in heirs of Andrew S.

Bell, Samuel, (box 319 Franklin Cir. Ct.) Thos. B. Monroe, admr., Lucy P. Bell, Thos. and Susan Bell, heirs of said Sam'l., land in Mason and Fleming, deed in Mercer Co. to Thos. Bell, July 18, 1821.

Branham, Richard T. (suit of Johnson vs. Juliet Branham, Feb. 1, 1850, Scott Co. Cir. Ct., Box 239) R. T. Branham died intestate, and left widow Juliet and ch.: May C. Branham, Gertrude, Cleon, Fanicius, John, Chas., and Marg't. Branham—all ch. infants.

Blackwell, Robert (Garrard Co. orders 1819-1821, p. 77) Affidavit, Rev. soldier, July 17, 1820, aged 59 years last Dec. 28th, in Rev. 2 yrs. in Co. of Capt. John Roberts in Reg't. com'd. by Francis Taylor, Va. line, guarding prisoners, at Albemarle Co., to Winchester, Va., wife and 2 ch. (Note: See Franklin Co. for marriages of ch. of Robt. Blackwell.)

Blaine, Ephraim (will, copy in deed F., Dist. Ct. Franklin Co., F-302) of Middlesex Co., of Cumberland, St. of Penna. Feb. 19, 1800—to wife Sarah Eliz. my est. in Middlesex—support and education of my son Ephraim till 21, but if he marry 1,000 pds. to my gd. son Ephraim Blaine, son of James Blaine, mills and water works, 251 acres to gd. son Ephraim Blaine, son of my son Robert Blaine, to my son Eph., 500 pds., at int. till he is 21—my sons James and Robert.—David Watts, exr. H. Miller and James Armstrong, wts. Mar. 19, 1804—copy from will G. Vol 1, p. 27? Aug. 1815, see p. 305 for further deeds. (Note: James Blaine, of Fayette—Pa. of Att'y.—many Blaine deeds in Franklin Co.)

Betsy James (Ct. Orders 51 Mercer Co.) late Betsy Lillard, widow of John Lillard, Jr., dower Jan. 5, 1824.

Layson, John hrs. vs. Isaac Layson hrs. (Box 777, 1830, Bourbon County, Ky.)—Jno. Layson owned 300 acres 1 mi. from Paris—left 150 to son Isaac— John Layson left following ch. and gr. ch.: John, Sally m. David W. Pond, Nancy m. Stephen Owens, sold their part to Raine, Margaret m. Oliver Forsythe, sold their part to Chas. D. Lennox, Robert who was a non-resident— Isaac Layson who was decd. had: Wm., Zedekiah, Margaret Ann, Robt. Martin, America Layson.

Nathan Lipscomb of Madison Co., Ky. deed July 1823, (Order bk. E, p. 283 Madison Co.)—Lipscomb hrs.—Wm. Wood and wife Nancy of Union Dist., S. C., Agnes R. Lipscomb, widow of Thos. Lipscomb, decd. John Lipscomb on behalf inf. hrs. of said Thos. Lipscomb of Spartansburg, etc.—David Lipscomb, Jr. and wife Sally—Wm. Littlejohn and wife Eliz. of Spartansburg—and John Lipscomb of Spartansburg Dist., to Nathan Lipscomb.

Lyttle, Wm. hrs. (Scott Co. deed No. 1, 1807-1814, p. 11) Mentions "Fayette Co. fire"—Mary Blanchu is dead, leaving ch. unknown, Eliz. Lyttle m. Robt. Bradley, Jane Lyttle m. Robt. Todd and she died leaving Robt. Todd and Wm. Todd her ch. only heirs, Sarah Beattie since m. ——— Brooks, John Rowan and wife Nancy, Robt. Bradley and wife Eliz., Robt. and Wm. Todd, def'ts. April 1829.

Lyne, Edmund, legatees—(Box 34-69, Franklin Dist. Ct.)—Wm. Lyne, John, Henry, Edmund Howe and wife Ann—Wm. Starling and wife Susannah, 1795 etc.—Wm. Starling, att'y. for hrs. of Edm. Lyne, Aug. 1798.

Lightfoot, Edward, decd.—(Division of Estates—Jefferson Co. p. 123)—on motion of Wm. E. Lightfoot, division to Martha Lightfoot, widow and to Mary Hasbrook, wife of Abram, Francis and Goodrich Lightfoot, ch. of Edw. L., decd. Dec. 1823.—(Mezzanine floor of estates)

Logan, Hugh, decd. Jefferson Co., (p. 220 of "division of estates" on mezzanine floor shelf) into 6 parts—to Hugh Logan, John Logan, Vandora Logan, James Logan, Eliz. A. Prince (husband Lawrence R. Prince), and children of Phebe Logan Shively, decd. formerly Phebe Logan, namely Philip L. Shively, Wm. V. Shively, Eliza Shively— Mar. 16, 1835.

Lapsley, Eliz. Rowe (Mercer Co. p. 14, 1823-1827 court orders) Rowe Lapsley, dau. of James F. Lapsley, had Charlotte Lapsley appointed gdn. Aug. 4, 1823; also to Sarah Jane Lapsley, John and James Thomas Lapsley. p. 14. Charlotte Lapsley, widow of James F. Lapsley, dower, p. 15.

Lee, Wm. and wife Sarah, of Nelson Co., (July 20, 1796, Hardin Co. Deeds) sell land in Hardin Co. 100 acres on Knob Cr., Rolling Fork, (Jno. Paul, Chas. Morgan, Jno. Farmer). Wm. Lee and wife Sarah (C-102) late widow of John Morgan, decd. and Jane Morgan one of the hrs. of Chas. Morgan, decd. of Nelson Co. Jno. Archibald and Sus. his wife, Nicholas West and Eliz. his wife, hrs. and reps. of Chas. Morgan, decd. of Hardin Co.—July 2, 1805.

Lee, Hancock, hrs.—(J-200, Woodford Co. deeds) Pamela Lee, Mary W. Lee, Fanny, Elizabeth, Ann G. and John A. Lee of Fauquier Co., Va. ch. and heirs of Hancock Lee, appoint bro. Thos. L. Lee of Woodford Co., Ky, atty. Feb. 2, 1822, 1500 acres of land. Hancock Lee of Fauquier Co., Va., appoints bro. Thos. L. Lee of Woodford Co. atty. land in Woodford and Scott—June 24, 1822. (J320—Woodford Co. deed)

Lee hrs.—(Woodford deeds G-315)—Sam'l. Wallace 1817—Sally O. wife of Jno. J. Crittenden, Elizabeth, wife of Lyddall Wilkenson, Mary W. Price, wife of And. F. Price, Jno H. Lee, Lucinda Lee of Fayette, Logan and Woodford Cos., Ky.

Elliott, Thomas—Hrs. vs. Jas. Garrard (Bourbon Cir. Ct. box 382, filed March 1798)— Thomas Elliott (decd.) in the year 1780 made entry with surveyor of Kentucky County on a military warrant—2000 acres on So. fork of Licking—Rev. James Elliott made deposition in Woodford Co. Ky. Aug. 30, 1816—that the ch. of Thomas Elliott decd. were Temple, Thomas, Catherine, William, Benjamin and Agnes and that the four last were at the time of death of their father, who d. in King William Co. Va. where he was b. and resided until his death in 1792 or 3, under the age of twenty-one the youngest about six or eight and balance gradually older, that Agnes Elliott intermarried with Wm. Hunton and that both are now decd., that Mary Catherine Hunton and John Carter Hunton are hrs. of Agnes Hunton, that he, deponant, is a kinsman.

Note: There were others of the name Elliott in Bourbon and Harrison Cos. at early date. One William Elliott b. 5-12-1752 Cumberland Co. Pa. moved to Bedford Co. Pa. enlisted in Rev. as Ensign, came later to Ky. where he lived twelve years and where he consented to mar. of dau. Anne to Robt. Patterson in Bourbon Co. 8-19-1802 and where his sons John, Samuel and William lived. William Elliott Sr. then moved to Jennings Co. Ind. where he applied for pension and where he d. 1838, his wife having d. earlier. According to an old letter written by his granddau. Mary Ann Patterson, b. 10-29-1810, to "Cousin Mary Ann Elliott, Paris, Ky." (copy at Ky. Historical Society) her grandfather William Elliott had eight ch.: Ann b. 11-6-1781 (wife of Robert Patterson), John, Robt., Sam'l., David, Joseph and "two others"—one of these was evidently William, known brother of John of Bourbon.

Griffith, Amos—Hrs. (Bourbon Co. Deeds S, pps. 44, 80—1825) Joel Griffith and wife Peggy, Moses Grooms and wife Ruth, Urial Griffith and wife Sally, John Griffith and wife

Ann, Amos Griffith and wife Addellaid, Noah Griffith of Pyle Co. Mo.—power-of-atty. to John Griffith. Note: Amos Griffith died intestate Bourbon Co. (Inv. B. 252, 8-3-1804) —pps. 536, 537—Mary Griffith apptd. gdn. of Ruth, Uriah, John, Edith, Amos, Jane and Noah Griffith infant hrs. of Amos Griffith decd. and Mary and Esther Griffith chose Mary their gdn.

Griffith, Abel—Hrs. (Bourbon Deeds X, p. 348–5-18-1830) Enoch Haydon of Marion Co. Mo. and Hester late Griffith widow of Abel, Samuel Griffith, Benj. Haydon and wife Martha. Dan'l. Bradley and wife Polly, John Griffith, Abel Griffith, Sarah and Jane Griffith.

Ledgerwood, Sam'l.—Hrs. (Bourbon Cir. Ct. box 378, suit filed 1809) Ledgerwood in lifetime (1780) made entry with surveyor for 1000 acres, and sd. Ledgerwood d. intestate leaving Sam'l., Molly m. Jno. Alexander, Peggy m. Jas. McClanahan, Rebecca m. Wm. Hill, Isabella m. Robt. Grill, and one Wm. Mitchell purchased part of land, etc.

Nesbitt, Samuel—Hrs. (Bourbon Cir. Ct. box 682—suit Wm. Nesbitt hrs. vs. Owings, filed 1827) Hrs: Wid. Elizabeth, since m. to Jas. Robinson; John, d. intestate without ch.; Wm. m. Patsy had ch. Elizabeth E. and Sam'l.; Elizabeth m. Sam'l. McConnell and Rachel.

Neal, Daniel—Hrs. (Bourbon Co. Cir. Ct. box 595—Suit Elijah Amos vs. Abram Hite, 1824)— Among hrs: Ditto Amos and Patsy and Wm. Ashcraft both Patsy and Wm. under 21, ch. of Sally Ashcraft decd. late Neal, Jas. Neal, Thos. Neal, Jas. Ellis and wife Letty late Neal, Rozy Neal and Nancy Neal.

Overton, Martha (Fayette Co. estates—3-16-1815) Div. of Estate of Waller and Martha Overton: To legal representatives of Thos. Overton (slaves) and paying to Mrs. Elizabeth Smith $4,500; to Archibald Overton (slaves) and $50.00 to Jno. Overton; to James Overton, to Sam'l. (slaves) and money for Lucy and Jno. W. Barry; to Lucy L. and Jno. Barry hrs. of Lucy Overton, late Barry; to Jno. Overton; to Mrs. Elizabeth Smith; to Mrs. Martha Overton; to Mrs. Sarah Ann Whitley; to Dabney Overton. Note: Waller Overton came from Louisa Co. Va., was b. 1750—d. 1827—Martha (Ratcliffe) Overton his wife b. 1757—d. 1814. Note: Record of Ratcliffe hrs. filed in Nicholas Co. Ky.

Protzman, Lawrence. (Bourbon deeds, 11-195, Nov. 20, 1805)—Indenture bet. him of Rockingham Co., Va., by Thos. Jones, Sr. his atty. land to Troutman, where John T. and his family lived 1789, and part of which Hugh Brent now lives on.

Proctor, John vs. Jer'h. O. Gullion, Frankfort (Box 28., Franklin Cir. Ct.)—Westmoreland Co., Pa., debt to Proctor, Feb. 1, 15, 1800—suit, Apr. 1786, N. 130, Westmoreland Co., Pa. vs. Jer'h. O. Gullion. Aug. 26, 1796.

Powers, Lewis—aged 66 (July 1820 Ct., Shelby Co. Orders, p. 308) "from Franklin Co." in Rev. July 1776, 2½ yrs., etc. under Col. Lewis Jones and Capt. Bland of Va., discharged at Winchester, Va. 1778—wife very old—dau. 17 living with him, others all m. and gone.

Powell, Richard (Garrard Co. Orders 1819-1821, p. 89) aged 62 yrs. (says Aug. 21, 1820) in Rev. war under Capt. John Spottswood 1777, Capt. Green's 10th Va. Reg't. 3 yrs. His wife is 63, he has five children doing for themselves.

Pope, Robert—(July 1819 p. 12, Garrard Co. orders 1819-1821) in war 1812, July 1, 1812 was at Mt. Vernon, Rockcastle Co., under Lt. King, 17th Reg't. for 8 mos., said Pope died on Car—? river Jan. 27, 1813 in service, he m. Eleanor Vance—his widow.

Phillips, Philip hrs.—(Gen'l. Ct. Franklin Co. deeds, G-435 July 1818, between May's hrs. etc.) Eliz. H. Purdy, formerly Phillips, wife of Robt. Purdy; Eleanor Nally (form. P.) wife of James Nally; Mary Williams (form. P.) wife of Elisha Williams, Joseph Phillips, Nancy A. Phillips, ch. of Philip P.

Pettitt, Thos. (p. 307 Shelby Co. Orders Nov. 1810-1820 July) aged 56 yrs. (July 1820 Court) in Rev. under Capt. Lyn, and Col. Roxburg, in Md., discharged at Fredericktown, Md., in many battles (named), one child living that he knows of, married, one son in U. S. Army, and does not know if he is alive.

Perry, David, decd.—(Dist. Ct. Deeds "B", p. 405, Fayette Co.)—Hrs: Joseph, Samuel, Betsy and Sally Perry, his hrs. John Hamilton and wife Sally, late Sally Perry and Betsy Perry of Woodford Co., deed to Edw. Payne of Fayette land in Fayette (Co. ct. D. p. 149)

Penn, Benj. (Order bk. M, p. 363, Sept. 20, 1852 Franklin Co.) proved that he was in Rev. army, died May 10, 1827, and left Reb. Penn his widow, who d. Jan. 10, 1840 and left Axey Marshall, Ephraim Penn, Chas. Penn, Betsy O'Nan, and Reb. Shadwick who are her only living children—Wm. Penn, decd. will prob. June 19, 1854, wife Susan admr. He was son of Chas. Penn.

Parrish, John & Patsy, late Patsy Gilespie (B— Cir. Ct. 403, Fayette Co.) marriage contract May 20, 1803, agreement, July 8, 1805.

Parker, Winslow, (Sr), decd.—(Lewis Co., Ky. notes) will B-129, 11 131, etc. Nov. 1824. Motion of Rowland Thomas Parker admr. sale—buyers Winslow Parker, Jr. R. T. Parker, etc.—Henry Parker died intestate, July 1824, B-132— Joanna Parker wid's. dower, 133 acres divided, p. 139— 8 ch.: Charles, John T., Robert, Harry, Harriet, Malinda, Patsy, and Nancy, signed by Chas. Parker, John T. Parker, Robert Parker, Harry Parker, Nancy Parker, John Kendrick for himself and Malinda his wife (Parker) David Thomas for self and wife Patsy (Parker), and said D. Thomas agt. for James Winter and Harriet (Parker) ch. and reps. of Harry a long and beautiful tribute to their mother, to p. 153, agreement. Nov. 18, 1824. John Kendrick m. Malinda Parker, dau. Harry, Dec. 24, 1808 —Alex. Parker of Spotts. Co., Va., apts. Thos. Parker of Ky., att'y. to demand negro who eloped from "my son Wm. Parker of Ky." and since been in poss'n. of Wash. Stubblefield of Natchez, Oct. 16, 1812. Murdock and Eliz. Cooper, wts.—Harry Parker of Lewis Co., to Thos. Parker and John Thurston Parker—I, having property and being "old" and infirm, land on Salt Lick. Apr. 12, 1817 (C-120)—Harry Parker to dau. Harriet Winter and her husband James Winter, m. 1817 (C150) Rowland T. Parker and wife Eleanor Mar. 2, 1818 (C-21) Winslow Parker for love and affec. to dau. Ophelia Daniel wife of Jas. Daniel of Montgomery Co., Ky. and to Wm. P. Parker (Barker?) of Lewis and Wm. Stubblefield.

Pemberton, Mary (Order K, p. 17 Franklin Co.) widow of Bennett P., decd. Jan. 19, 1835— she decd. Apr. 20, 1835—same p. 34—Margaret Mitchell entitled to share of her decd. bro. estate, John Pemberton.

Patten, James, decd. (Jefferson Co. deeds, RR-344—Jan. 16, 1836) Geo. W. Marshall of New Albany, Ind., at present at Mobile, Ala. of 1st part, Polly Gracy, John W. Marshall, of other part, on Dec. 9, 1834 execution was issued from Jefferson Cir. Ct., name of Lewis Harmon vs. est. of Jas. Patten which descended or devised by him to Wm. Marshall and wife Phoebe who was Phoebe Patten, exrx. of will of Jas. Patten, and Geo. Gracy and wife Polly who was Polly Patten, and devise of Jas. P., and said Geo. Gracy and Polly, John M. Talbott and wife Sally, Edw. Tracy and wife—, Jas. Nelson and wife Mary David Nelson hrs. of Geo. Patten who was son of James Patten, decd. etc.

Pearson, Meshack—(1830 Order, p. 65 Franklin Co.) Dec. 4, 1830 aged 76, in 1775 in Va. in Co. commanded by Capt. Geo. Slaughter, in Reg't. by Col. Muhlenberg at Valley Forge, etc.

Pickett, Martin—hrs. (Box 497 Bourbon Co. Ct. Ct.—1818) Lucy Marshall late Pickett, Anne Brooke late Pickett—Anne D. Clarkson, Henry Clarkson, Caroline Clarkson, May Clarkson, Mildred Clarkson ch. of Mildred Clarkson late Pickett decd.—Chas. Johnson, Lucy Johnson, Edward Johnson ch. of Letitia Johnson late Pickett decd.—Arthur Slaughter, Augustine Slaughter, Henry Slaughter, Martin Slaughter, Diana Slaughter, Anne Slaughter, ch. of Judith Slaughter late Pickett decd., John Scott and wife Elizabeth B. Scott, late Elizabeth Pickett, all hrs. of Martin Pickett decd.

Patterson, Wm. hrs. (10-486) Oct. 13, 1832—Wm. Swift, complainant, and Sam'l. Taul, admr., and Johnson Patterson, Zarelda P., and Mary Armilda P., hrs. of Wm. P. decd. land bt. of Jas. S. Johnson, 1816.—Chas. Patterson of Claiborn Co., Miss., April 8, 1818 appoints Chas. P. Bacon (of Port Gibson, Miss.) of Frankfort, atty. for estate of Chas. and Eliz. Patterson, decd. (G-458) Dec. 20, 1817—(H-286 Frankfort) Martha Patterson, Chas. Patterson, Mary Worley, Margaret Patterson, Henry Patterson, Wm. Letcher and wife Jane, Wm. F. Gray and wife Frances, Chas. P. Bacon, Chas. McReynolds and Mary B. McR., hrs. and co-hrs. of Chas. Patterson, decd. to Chas. Mills, (Wm. F. Gray, gdn. of Chas. P. and Mary B. McReynolds)—Dec. 18, 1818. Christian Co., Frances Gray)

Reading, Isaac, decd. (Woodford Co. G-243, Jan. 1825) Receipts: cash paid Abijah Reading, H. Roberts, John Forster, Jas. Tinders, Ely Reading, Isaac Mason, Felix Reading, Eliz. Reading.

Robertson, John, aged 59 years, dep. Apr. 27, 1807—Abram Buford vs. Sam'l. Shannon, (Box 180, Franklin Cir. Ct.) See also suit of Robertson's admr. and Kennedy's hrs. No. 539.

Mercer Ct. Orders, p. 53. Ransdall, John, decd. court appointed Nimrod Cornwell gdn. to William, James, Shelton, Sandford, Jane Ann and Arletha Ransdell, orphans of John R., decd. Jan. 1, 1824.

Ramsey, Thos.—Garrard Co. orders 1819-1821, p. 86—says, Aug. 21, 1820, in Rev. war, enlisted in Essex Co., Va., Feb. 15, 1776, under Lt. Jas. Upshaw, 2 yrs., Capt. Sam'l. Haus? (Hans?) Reg't. com'd. by Alex. Spottswood 2 yrs. at Valley Forge, Pa., Feb. 15, 1778, in Battles of Brandywine, and Lennantown (Sennentown?) etc.—age about 63 or 64 yrs., infirm, wife 64, 2 dau., one 23 on Jan. 10, next, one 18 Apr. 4, last; 5 sons married and left.

Davis (Wm.) devisees vs. gdns. of Allison and others—dep. 1815, (Harrison Co., Ky. in suit Box 174)—Ravenscroft, Thos.—filed suit Sept. 17, 1816—he says he was aged about 59, was at Harrison Sta. in 1786, and had lived in same neighborhood ever since. He says: My bro.-in-law m. Benj. Harrison's dau.—Joseph Davis the father of Wm. Davis, the ancestor _____? he (Thos. Ravenscroft) m. 1786, dau. of Col. Hinkston—bro.-in-law of Wm. Anderson. (see Anderson, and Davis) all dep. dated Dec. 13, 1815.

Reading, Wm. hrs. (U-68, Logan Co., deeds)—Joel C. Rice and wife Rebecca Ann (Reading) Eliz. H. Nantz late Eliz. Reading, sole hrs. of Wm. Reading decd. to Henry Smith, Sr. Dec. 24, 1835. In 1820 it says Joel C. Rice and Reb. A., and Thos. Nantz and Betsy (Reading), 1818. (U-200, etc.)

J. Froman vs. McMurtry's hrs. Woods hrs.—(Box F-6, Mercer Co. Cir. Ct.)—Robertson, Alex. hrs.—Eliz. Robertson m. James George, Peggy Robertson m. Benj. Letcher (10/22/1793), Jenny Robertson m. John Hann, and James, Alex., Martha, George and Charlotte Robertson children and hrs. of Alex. Robertson, decd. last 3 infants. (June 1805 decree)

Rice, George—hrs., (p. 37 Complete Rec. Franklin Cir. Ct.)—hrs: Ruth Roach, Eliz. McCormick, Polly Wilson, Geo. Rice, Rebecca Keger, and John McCormick, Jan. 18, 1816.

Orear vs. Tanner (Fayette Cir. Ct. Jan. 29, 1806 Box 110) Tanner, Edward, of age, states about 6 or 7 years ago his father John Tanner lived in Woodford Co., and about 4 years ago he took charge of his fathers business in consequence of his age and infirmity, and his intention to remove to the Green river country.

Taylor, Samuel, Sr., decd. (Deed 10, p. 211, Harrison Co., Ky.) Dec. 12, 1826. John Taylor, George and Wm. Taylor, Samuel Taylor, Coleburn Brown and wife Jane (Taylor); John Wallace and wife Nancy (Taylor), Ale. Galbreath and wife Marg't. (Taylor), James Micks and wife Sarah (Taylor), heirs of Samuel Taylor, Sr., decd. deed to John Cook. Samuel Taylor, Sr. died intestate. Deed dated Jan. 13, 1827.

Tyler, Robt. (Franklin Cir. Ct. Box 182—). He states at Isaac Watkins Tavern in Shelby Co., Oct. 13, 1807, that in spring of 1780 he went from Falls of the Ohio (Louisville) to Boones Sta., Harrodstown.

Theobald, Samuel of Lex., Ky., deeds to Joel Herndon in trust for the benefit of his mother Mary Theobald, Nov. 13, 1823, (E-339, Scott Co.), signed by Samuel, Wm. and Mary Theobald.

Tucker, Enoch, decd. sett. of his estate made by Harry Innis, 1786-1787, etc. In his sett. book at Hist. Soc. the hrs. named are: Rachel Tucker, widow, John Patterson and wife Letitia (Tucker), Rebecca Owens (John Owens), Edward Tucker, Nancy Tucker, (husband Joseph Turner) 1/9 to each; Hannah Tucker, Philip Tucker, Sally Tucker, and Henry Tucker heirs.

Inv. H-136, Madison Co., Nov. 1842, Thurman, Henderson, decd. widow Thurman. James and Nancy Thurman bought at sale p. 140, Thurman, Patsy, decd. Inv. J-38, Feb. 10, 1848.

Wm. Tebbs hrs. vs. Benj. G. Orr filed Aug. 20, 1817 (1818) Charlotte Tebbs, Daniel and James Tebbs, Walker Reid and wife Ann Tebbs, hrs. of Wm. Tebbs, say that on Mar. 27, 1795 at Westmoreland Co., Va., the Orrs were bound to said Wm. Tebbs, bond for Ky. lands (see 1818 records, 6th shelf from bottom, 1st closet on left). Tebbs, John, hrs. (Franklin Co., 1-174) Jas. Taylor of Campbell Co. att'y. for hrs. of Willoughby Tebbs, who was hr. of John Tebbs, decd. John Spence, Mary F. Spence, Thos. Triplett, Marg't. C. Triplett, Ann F. Tebbs, Betsy Tebbs gdn. hrs. Tebbs hrs. birthdates Q-7. Ct. of Appeals.

Taylor, Richard, Jr. says Jan. 10, 1822 (old Frankfort paper wrapped around some papers in Cir. Ct. box No. 193) that he intends to move to the lower end of the state, and wishes to sell his farm on Big Benson, Ky. river, good brick bldg., separated from Frankfort by Benson cr. 320 acres, etc.

See Ogden & Masterson, vs. McClelland—(suit in Shelby Co. Cir. Ct.) Talbott, Nath'l. said in dep. that he came to Shelby Co. 1798, then moved away after living there 10 years (one acc. of Dan'l. Talbott)

Tadlock, Ann, dep. 1803 (Box 180 Franklin Cir. Ct.)—James Harrod's hrs. etc. Ann Tadlock, gdn. of James Harrod's dau. says in 1775 Patrick McDonalds came with Samuel Coburn, etc.

Utterback, Harmon—(will, E-478, Nicholas Co.)—Dau. Eleanor all pers. property, and rest bet. dau. E. and all of my ch. son Benjamin U., Mar. 10, 1848, Jan. 1855.—(F-144) Reuben C. U. admr. May 27, 1856.—Harmon Utterback bt. of Fleming Co. May 4, 1817, (E-98, Nicholas Co.)—Benj. Utterback of Bath Co. (Q-294) Feb. 20, 1855 exr. of Harmon U., decd. and Reuben U. of Bourbon Co., also admr. land in Nicholas Co. to be sold.

Vance, Joseph—Revolutionary claim (old index burnt records, Scott Co. Cir. Ct. office) p. 446, June 3, 1823—aged 68; 2 yrs. Aug. 9, 1776, Va. Cont. Line under Capt. Michael Boyer, reg't. of ——— Wood, served till ——— 13th, 1778, wife aged 70, Peter Burns aged 15, Sally Burns aged 8, son and dau. of John Burns (in household?).

Vance, John (D-132, Mason Co.) of Franklin Co., Pa., apts. John Brownson of Mason, Att'y. to represent me in Mason Co., land on Mill Cr,. by Jane Vance, Sr., decd. Nov. 26, 1795, Jan. 1796. Vance—indenture, between David Masterson of Mason Co., Dorcus Iordan. David Vance and wife Rachel of Brown Co., Ohio, John Masterson of Mason, land inherited from their father John Masterson, decd. (deed 42-143. Oct. 31, 1835, Mason Co.)

Vincent, Susan—(Mercer Co. Cir. Ct. Order B, 322)—aged about 10 yrs., Thomas, abt. 7 yrs. Jeremiah about 5, orphans of John V., decd. bound out to George Smith, Eliz. Gibb and John Thomas, Mar. 27, 1792.

Zumwalt, Adam buys of Isaac Ruddell and Eliz. (6-20-1786, Deeds A—p. 1, Bourbon Co.) 100 acres whereon Adam lives, below Christopher Zumwalt.

Zumwalt, Andrew—(Deed A, p. 3, Bourbon Co.) buys from same, June 2, 1786.

Zumwalt, Christopher—(A-5 Bourbon deeds)—buys of same, 6-20-1786, Cor. to Adam Z.

Zumwalt, Jacob—(A-69, 153, Bourbon Co.)—buys of same, Mar. 20, 1787.

MISCELLANEOUS COURT RECORDS

TESTATOR NOT IN GENERAL INDEX

Bland, John (see will in Nelson Co.; suit in Box 70-83, Franklin Dist. Ct., B. Blands heirs vs. Combs, Bardstown, Sept. 6, 1797) Stephen Kincheloe's dep'n. he was in Ky. 1780-81, Lewis Kincheloe, there in 1781. Osborn Bland, oldest son, says Mar. 12, 1800, that he was at the station in 1780 fall, and Daniel Bland says he was there 1780 and made a contract. John Bland, Jr. dep'n. in May 10, 1794 says he is of age and was with his father when he was living in Prince, Wm. Co., Va. 1781.

Byrd, Otway (Complete Records, E. p. 85, Franklin Co.) heirs, Ann Byrd, widow, and admx. and Wm., Maria, Beverly, Eliza, Evelyn, Anna and Abby Byrd, heirs and devisees, Jan. 4, 1816, Byrd's Hrs. vs. Wm. Fleming.

Butler, John decd. (Apr. 14, 1830 Franklin Cir. Ct., Box 537) and George Butler issued by Morris Fox. Mrs. Lucy Butler admx. of John Butler. John Casey in a dep'n. says that "John Butler married my sister" (Hardensville rent). Dep'n. of Wm. S. Pemberton says his mother paid 100 pds. year 1819 for Butler's Tavern (brick house) then built a tav. on opp. side of road—1820-1821. Wm. Phillips, son of John P. says that Mrs. Butler then appeared childish, 1830, and not in right mind. Eleanor Philips said Lucy Butler came to her house, ill; Milly Philips, named; Stafford Pemberton refers to his mother, Mrs. Wilcox. (much data)

Burdett, Margaret, decd. (Ct. Orders, Mercer Co., Feb. 6, 1826, p. 214 and p. 226)—her ch: Jeptha, James, Minerva, Penelope, Ruth Ann, Lucy, Joseph, Andrew, John, Francis, Enoch and Susannah Burdett, inf. ch. Thornton K. Thompson apt'd. their gdn's. as inf. heirs of James Thompson decd. (tr. of land, etc.)

Bullock, Edward (Mercer Co. 1825- Orders, p. 155), appointed by the court gdn. for his son John W. Bullock to divide lands in Barren Co. with Wm. Bullock, Ranley Bullock, 6-6-1825.

Burwell, Nathaniel (Deeds F, (will) p. 238, Franklin Co. Dist. Ct.) "Of King Wm. Co., Va.", whereas sometime ago I sold to Jas. B. Crosbie of King and Queen Co., Va., land on Herring Cr. in King Wm., gave him title—apt. Edw. Carrington, John Hickshan?, and Lewis Burwell of Richmond, Exrs. of this my last will for benefit of my wife and ch. as ch. come of age, or marry—to be eq. wife Martha B., Tues. Mar. 30, 1802. Wts: Wm. Baynham, and Claudius S. Levert, Apr. 26, 1802. Claudius and Lewis Burwell, exrs. Isaac Quarles, Justice.

Bryant, Ann (see Garrard for R. Arnold-Lincoln deeds B-280) m. Bartlett Brown, 3-10-1789, consent of Reuben Arnold, gdn. Lincoln Co. Bryant, Jas. "of Powhatan Co., Va.", deeds to John Bryant of Lincoln Co., land in Lincoln, 260 A., Nov. 4, 1793.

Brunner, Geo. Hrs.—(Jessamine Co. deed E-288 Mar. 24, 1818), Henry Brunner, George Brunner, Caty Howser, David and Samuel Brunner, Eliz., Benjamine Brunner, John and Jonathan Brunner, heirs of George Brunner, decd. of Jessamine Co., whereas James Hawkins in his lifetime, etc. Ulrige Brunner, father of said George Brunner, Sr., etc.

Brown, Wm. (Bk. C, deeds, p. 228, Woodford Co., Ky.) "of Bourbon" deeds to Wilson Brown of Woodford Co., all rt. of land in Worchester Co., Md. which John Coleburn, decd. willed to Andrew Brown and wife Grace at their decease to Coleburn Brown, the father of said Wm. Brown, Wilson Brown, att'y. Sept. 3, 1800.

Bowman (June 23, 1849, Box 264, Scott Co. Cir. Ct.–Coil vs. Bowman) Deft. Samuel–Jacob Bowman admits his father Jacob Bowman, decd. poss'd. land in Scott Co., Jacob Bowman had two wives, and children as follows: Samuel, Jacob, Eliz. Fisher, Wm. B., James, and Nancy Bowman, (Jan. 14, 1852) land sold to his bros. and sisters, Joseph, Thos., Sarah and Nancy, Thos. Bowman died unmarried, Sarah died unmar. and childless; Joseph died unmar. and without issue.

Bell, Clement (box 541, Franklin Cir. Ct. Oct. 4, 1828), etc. vs. Macey's reps. Andrew Steele's heirs, Margaret Bell, wife of Clement Bell, Ann Steele, wife of John Steele, Abraham Vandergriff and wife Jane, John Steele formerly of Lou. and afterwards of Fayette, Wm. Steele, Priscilla Francisco, (orators Clement Bell and John Steele) other heirs appointed them attorneys–said Margaret Bell, decd. and Clement Bell entitled to her int. Alex. Macey's heirs named–Priscilla Francisco afterward married Verpile Payne–Leander Long of Henry Co. (Alex. Macey's heir), Alex. R. Macey of Warren and Logan Cos., others of Woodford, Franklin and Fayette. Heirs named again of Andrew Steele and Jeremiah and Samuel Luckett, Alex. V., Jane, John, Wm., and Ann Steele, Priscilla Payne, Eliza Ann Chinn, Morgan B. Chinn, and Harry J. Anderson.

Barbour, James (Hardin Co. deeds, July 15, 1814, F-9), decd. heirs: Ambrose Barbour, Mordecai Barbour, Thos., Rich., Gabriel, and Philip Barbour, Sally Harrison, wife of John H., Fanny Moore, wife of John M., Lucy Baylor, wife of G. W. Baylor, David Walker, late husband of Mary (formerly Barbour) a tenant and by courtesy in trust for his children, by the said Mary, heirs of James Barbour. Richard Barbour, of Orange Co., Va., will: To Elisha Freeman, son of Thos. F., my sister Mary Harrison, Cave Instone, land to myself and Merry Walker, & Thos. Barbour. bro. Ambrose Barbour, Bro. James, Thos., Ambrose B– bro-in-law Benj. Instone. Aug. 18, 1790-Oct 27, 1794. Orange Co., Va. (F-13)

Ballew, Charles–Hrs. (Madison Co. Deeds H, p. 308–Sept. 13, 1811)–Deed for land located on Tates Cr., Madison Co., consideration seventy pounds–Polly Ballew, wid., Leonard Heatherly and w. Elizabeth, David Massey and w. Jane, Geo. Hubbard and w. Polly Hutson Hollis and w. Suckey, Thos. Ballew, Jno. Hubbard and w. Anna "all of Madison Co. Ky. except David Massey and w. Jane, they being of Territory of Louisiana" deed Edward and Sarah Brown. Note: One Chas. Ballew served in Rev. from Cumberland Co. Va. and one Chas. Ballew left will in that county 1767.

Brady, Chas. Anderson (Mercer Co. p. 359, Orders 1) and Peter Butler, Edward Hammond, John Partee, Richard Peter, because of great age and infirmity are exempt from taxes, July 28, 1789; Wm. Murray and Thos. Davis admitted to practice of law, Mercer Co., July 28, 1789, p. 359; Joseph Scott to erect a water grist mill, Scotts cr., Aug. 15, 1789, p. 360, Mercer; Samuel Givens, John Lawrence, Wm. Lawrence Rich. Ballenger, Henry Yocum, Peter Tardiveau, jury July 28, 1789, Mercer, p. 360: The following subject to work on road, July 28, 1789: Thos. Barbee, Christopher Greenup, Harry Innis, James Spilman, Benj. Beall, Wm. Hughes, Samuel Irvine, Abraham Yimberlin, Yeiser? and Berry, Peter Tardiveau, Robt. Coughram, John Coughram, Robt. Corbin, Wm. McDaniel, Peter Widner and others.

Catlett, Maj. Thos., survey 66 acres of King's land in the Parish of St. Mary's in county of Caroline (Va.) (*Surveys of Caroline Co., Va. in Campbell county, Ky. court house.*)

Crow, John, decd. heirs (Box 94-114, Franklin Dist. Ct., Frankfort Cir. Ct. files) Joel Crow, John Cochran and wife Jane, John Thompson and wife Nancy, John, Benj., and Elijah Crow, heirs of John Crow, decd. Jan. 1801, Dist. Ct. of Danville. James Thompson, employed by John Crow in 1780, Mercer Co.

Ann Tadlock's dep'n. (James Harrod's heirs)—Coburn, Samuel (1803 Franklin Cr. Ct., Box 180) came to Ky. 1775, and Patrick McDonald came with him. Patrick McDonald died at home of James Coburn in N. C. 1776, and was a single man, etc.

Coleman. James. Sr. (Dist. Ct. B, p. 51 Franklin Co.) Jan. 17, 1801—and wife Eliz. of Harrison Co. deed to Jas. Coleman, Jr. of Franklin Co., (land for officers and soldiers of the Cont'l. line) on fk. of Tradewater, 200A.

Clark, James (Mercer Co., Ky. Cir. Ct. Box C-44) aged 62, residing in Mercer Co., Mar. 13, 1821, appears in court, says he served in the Rev. War as follows: 3 yrs. enlisted in Orange Co., Va., in Co. commanded by Capt. Burleigh, under Col. Francis Taylor, Va. Cont'l. line, Certificate No. 12929, July 21, 1819, shoemaker, dropsy, unable to work, wife Eleanor nearly 60 years old, very fat and inactive; he has 5 children, all married and settled, but poor.

Clarke, Wm. heirs (N-56, Mason Co. deeds) Peter Clark, John, David, William, James, Felix Hover and wife Sarah (Clarke), James Gunsaulus and wife Margaret (Clarke), John Curtis in behalf of his late wife Nelly (Clarke) decd. deed to John Whaley, Dec. 16, 1809.

Chaplin, Abraham (deed, etc. May 4, 1824, Mercer Co. Orders, p. 57) and Willis, William Harrison, son of Wm. Harrison and Ellin Chaplin, who with Isaac Chaplin, and Jacob Chaplin, all heirs of decedent Abraham Chaplin.

Childress, Goldsberry (Garrard Co. orders 1819-1821, p. 98)—says Aug. 22, 1820, he is 64 yrs. old; in Rev. War in fall of 1775, under Capt. Wm. McKee, 12th Va. Reg't. under Col. Jas. Woodard? for 2 years—wife is 56, 2 ch. at home, dau. 19, and son 14 years.

Cave, Wm. Strother (Mercer Co. deeds, A-436, Oct. 15, 1792) and wife Ann of Woodford Co.—John Cave and Wm. Cave of Scott Co., apt. bro. Richard Cave attorney for our bro. David Cave, decd. of Culpepper Co. Va.

Caldwell, George, decd. (Inv. B-237, Fayette Co. sett. C-380, etc.) Susannah Caldwell, exrx., A. Dunlap, Jr. exr. May 30, 1811, Wm. Caldwell, Eliza Caldwell, orphans of John Caldwell, decd. boarding Wm. Caldwell, 2 yrs. James McDowell and Samuel Caldwell, gdn. of Wm., Sally and Eliza C., infs. of John C., Mar. 9, 1814, (p. 382, C, p. 106 D.) —div'n. to Sally Thornton, Wm. and Eliza. C. Aug. 1816. George Caldwell, div'n: Gideon Maus, only one named—(Apr. 12, 1817, D-185); George Caldwell buys of Andrew Steele, 9-10-1793 (A-203) Fayette.—George Caldwell, heirs, Dec. 29, 1817 (Cir. Ct. (248 Fayette) and heirs of Richard James, decd.—Patsy Caldwell, Kitty C., Betsy and Pauline Caldwell, Alex. Dunlap and wife Polly, heirs of George Caldwell.

James, Richard heirs (Cir. Ct. A-248 Fayette Co.) Mary James, Fred'k. William James, Wm. James, Kitty James, George Gilliam and wife Mary Jefferson, heirs of Rich. James, decd. of Cumberland Co., Va. to George Caldwell.

Caldwell, George Heirs—(deed Z-311 Fayette 7-7-1825) Alex. Dunlap and wife Polly, Joshua Worley and wife Milly, Patsy Caldwell, Betsy and Paulina C., inf. by Alex D., special gd'n. for Patsy, Betsy, Milly and Paulina.

Carter, Abraham's heirs (Box 367, Franklin Cir. Ct.) Carter's heirs vs. Carter's Admrs. Orators:
David Osborn McCracken and Ann Mommia Carter his wife, Wm Carter and wife Emily
(Carter) said Abraham Carter their father died intestate and Ann M., and Emily (mr.
McCracken and Carter) died intestate and also Madison, Emerine, Wm. H. Harrison,
Granville and Abraham Carter, his heirs, and reps. and left much estate. Ann Carter,
admx. and widow, and Madison, Wm. H. H., Emerine, Granville, and Abraham are in-
fants, March 1824, suit. 7 heirs; Ann M. Carter m. D. A. McCracken, Wm. Carter m.
Emily E. Carter,—Acct. 1818, clothed Mommia 1 1/2 years, Emily 4 yrs, Emerine 5 yrs.
Harrison 5 yrs., Granville, 5 yrs., Abraham J. P., 5 yrs. One time Sarah was named after
Madison. Note to Mrs. Ann Carter says, "Dear Sister", and signed "your bro. James
Tarleton", Abraham Carter's est. appraised Apr. 1818 (Box 367)

Caldwell, Jas., decd. (Woodford Co. bk. M) John G. Anderson and Adaline Anderson, of
Davidson Co., Tenn., town of Nashville, reposing confidence in our bro. Henry N. Caldwell of Woodford Co., Ky., apt. him att'y. to convey titles to land, etc. tract whereon Jane
Caldwell, widow of Jas.. C. now resides, the portion devised to Adaline as one of the
ch. of said Jas. C. Jan. 12, 1830.

Collins, Jos. (1-16, Franklin Co. Dist. Ct.) in dep'n. says that in 1784 or 5, Arthur Fox, decd.
told him etc. Mar. 16, 1797 (suit of Holeman vs. Craig)—David Darst said that in 1784
he was employed by Edw. Holeman to carry chain in Fayette Mar. 16, 1797. Joel Collins
in Woodford Co. June 16, 1798 says his sister m. Robt. Bowmar.

Cook, Coleman—heirs; (G-169 Scott Co. deeds) Joseph Cook and wife Ruth; John Cook and
wife Mary, Wm. Cook, Aaron Cook, Geo. Cook, Benj. Cook, Lucy Cook (since m. Ira
Balding), Harriet Cook (signed by Lucinda Balding) Nov. 19, 1825.

Curd, Merryman B. (H-34, Jessamine Co.) deeds to all his ch. all of his property, slaves, etc.
being part of John Curd's 826 acre tract; said children and their guardians: Robert Kay,
Wm. A. Leavy, Rich. A. Curd of Fayette, and John Green, and Willis Curd, Samuel H.
Woodson of Jessamine and to pay all debts of their father, M. B. Curd, etc. 7-12-1823,
Jessamine Co. (deeds, H-27)—M. B. Curd and wife Polly K. Curd, deed, Mar. 2, 1824.

Curd, George R.—(Mercer Co. Orders 1824, p. 119)—came into court and qualified as exr.
of G. Belcher, decd. Benj., Joseph and Stephen Curd, sect'ys. Oct. Dec. 6, 1824. (Mercer
orders 8-118)—Property be divided between Polly Jenkins and Lucy Curd as said will
directed. Geo. Belsher names g. dau. Lucy Ragsdale Curd, Sus. Curd, Geo. Ragsdale
Curd, Apr. 6, 1824.

Crump, Goodrich (will, Gen'l. Ct. Deed E, Franklin Co.,) of Powhatan Co., Va., wife—son
John, dau. Eliz., dau. Judith Anderson Crump, 5 sons: John, George, James Ottoway,
Richard and Henry Crump, daus. under age and unm. Wm. Hickman, and Rich. Crump,
gdn's. of all my ch. July 3, 1795—wts. Vincent Markham, Jacob Williamson, N. Patterson,
W. M. Lewis, Powhatan Co., Dec. 17, 1795.

Crump, Turner of Frankfort (Box 180, Franklin Dist. Ct. in Bacon's suit of heirs) says Oct. 8,
1814, that he was the son of Benedict Crump of New Kent Co., Va.

Crane— (p. 176 Mercer Co. orders, 9-5-1825) on motion of Nath'l. Crane, ordered that sum-
moned be issued against Polly Broyles, late Polly Crane to show why Nancy Crane, John
Jackson Crane, Sally Glover Crane, and Morris Crane, her ch. may not be bound out as
law directs.

Cox, Wm. heirs (G-147, Scott Co. deed) Jan. 1, 1824—Jasmine Cox, Daniel and James Cox, Jas. Glenn and wife Nancy (formerly Cox) Wm. Cox., Benj. Menifee and wife Betsy (Cox), Wm. Causey and wife Julia (Cox) John Cox, Nath'l. Cox, Patsy Cox, Hannah Miller (Cox), heirs of Wm. Cox, decd. to John Estill, of Scott—deed signed by Janus (James?) Cox, and Ann Cox, Wm., Nancy, B. Pel . . . , Eliz. Menifee, etc. Wm. Bailey and Julianna, James H.: Nancy Glenn, Hannah Miller, Nov. 15, 1825.

Cornet, Nicholas (P. A., Deed C, 427, Mason Co.) of Mercer Co. appoints father-in-law Wm. Been of Mason Co., att'y. to get estate of his decd. bro. Wm. Cornet, of Mason Co., Sept. 27, 1796.

Curry, John (Mercer Orders, 1823, p. 31)—Cornelius Demaree appointed gdn. to Phebe Curry; Abraham Comingore apt'd. gdn. to Nancy Curry; infant orphans of John Curry, Nov. 1823; Mary Ann Curry, infant, of John C., John Smock apt'd. gdn., May 4, 1824, ref. same, p. 67.

Curtis, Peter (declaration—Garrard Co. Orders, 1820, p. 88) Aug. 1820 Thos. Walker and Rachel Finney say they knew him in N. C. they were in same neighborhood. He was a Rev. soldier in the continental army; in battles of Guilford, Eutaw Springs; he and his family were good soldiers.

Currins, James (Orders 312, 1826, Mercer Co.) apt'd. gdn. of his ch. Eliz. and Harrison, est. of their gd. father, John McCoun—decd., Feb. Apr. 1826.

Collett, John (Box 180, Franklin Cir. Ct.) aged 49 (b. 1756) deposition Franklin Cir. Ct. Apr. 27, 1807, set out from near Danville, fall 1783, with Sq. Boone, Wm. Hansborough, Thos. Threlkeld, Mr. Gaines, etc. (where Maj. Thos. Lillard now lives)

Collett, John (Franklin Co. Order bk. "1-1830" p. 137) decd. (Rev. Soldier) heirs: Nancy Collett, Harriet, Eliz., John, Alsey, Matilda, Cath., Mary, Joshua and Benj. Utterback and his wife Mary, late Mary Collett, sole heirs and children of John Collett, Rev. soldier, decd. Apr. 16, 1832.

Collett, John (July 1820, orders of Shelby Co., 1818, Nov. to July 1821) near 63, etc. wife and 10 ch. 3 sons, 7 daus. oldest over 21, next son 10 years, other 4, daus. 25, 23, 18, 16, 12, 8, etc.

Darneall, Jno. (Complete Rec. Bourbon Co. 1803 p. 557, Feb. 11) heirs: Corneleus, Wm., Henry, Thos., Reuben, Jno., Amos, George, Zenas.

Davis, Nath'l. (suit Box 803, dated 1820, Bourbon Co. Cir. Ct.) Richard Davis, Thos., Igo and w. Polly, Thos. McClair and Dan'l., Elizabeth, Nath'l. Davis, Solomon Davis, Levy Davis, Fielding Loucer and w. Peggy.

Denny, David (suit in Clark Co. Cir. Ct. Marcus Calmes vs. Thos. Goff, others, 1824, see West. Cit. Jan. 15, 1825) and w. Hannah, and Samuel Denny and w. Polly.

Dunn, Thos. (Bourbon order F. p. 519, Sept. 2, 1822) entitled to bounty warrant for Rev. service. Had dau. Elizabeth m. Frederick Reed—proof by Jno. G. Martin.

Dooley, Jno. (Bourbon Cir. Ct. 1848, suit 1156—Levi Ashbrook vs. Allen, etc.) dep'd.—left Clark Co. abt. 1844, left children: Thos., Jno., Betsy m. Drury Edes, Sarah m. Asa Allen, Polly m. Simon Davis.

Dougherty (Franklin Co., Orders I-137, Apr. 16, 1832) proved that Rachel Dougherty, Kitty D., Arthur C. D., and Nancy D. are the sole heirs and children of Dennis D., decd. a Rev. soldier, who died and his wife is also dead.

Drake, James P. (G-94, Scott Co., Ky.) and wife Catherine of Fontaine Co., Ind., John Brockman and wife Frances (Franky) Rich. W. Polk and wife Polly (Pack?) George Chishom and wife Winney, Henry B. Drake and wife Barsheba, legal heirs of Thos. Drake, decd. Nov. 21, 1831.

Drake, Thos., decd. (Scott Co. D-342, May 18, 1818) division of negroes, belonging to heirs of Jas. Drake, decd. Franky Brockman, late F. Drake, Polly Drake, Jane Drake, Winney Drake, Henry B. D., and all heirs of Thos. Drake, decd. and Lewis . . . late Betsy Drake and Isaac Foster and . . . were pd. to John ―――― heirs of Thos. Drake, decd. ―― Foster ―――― to Lewis Valandingham.

Dorland, Garret Ward (Mercer orders, 1823-1826, p. 60) orphan of Garret Dorland, decd. chose Lanty Armstrong, gd'n., Mar. 1, 1824.

Dunn, James, decd. heirs. (Mercer orders p. 290, Nov. 7, 1826) gd'n. to Samuel D. Davis Williamson Dunn, Sophia Irvine Dunn, inf. hrs. of James D., and Jane H. Alexander, late Jane H. Dunn, wife of Robt. Alexander, division of land.

Davidson, Wm. decd. heirs (Deed C. p. 278, Logan Co., Ky.) George McLean and wife Pamela McL. (formerly Davidson), Finis Ewing and wife Margaret E., (formerly David-son) all of (Logan?) County aforesaid, and Ephrim Brevard Davidson of Stewart Co., Tenn., appt. our bro. George Lee Davidson of Iredell Co., N. C., attorney to sell 300 A. of 640 a. granted by State of N. C. to Gen'l. Wm. Davidson, decd. in Buncombe Co., N. C. on Willises Cr., and waters of Fr. Broad River by George and Pamela McLean, etc., July 23, 1811.

Deringer, John, legatees (Woodford Co. deeds, C. No. 2, p. 187) Michael Deringer, Andrew D., Henry Hendricks, Joseph and Martin Deringer, legatees of John D. of Woodford Co. give their parts to the widow. June 8, 1798.

Eades (Edes), Jonathan (Scott Co. 1828-30 Bk. G, p. -- Nov. 22). Heirs: Chas. W. Eades, Clanock Edes, Elizabeth Edes, Mary, wife of Job. Stevenson, Louisa Edes, Jno Adair Edes, Cary Ann Edes, Margaret Milvina Edes, Pamelia Edes.

Ellis, Wm. (Harrison Co. deeds Bourbon L. p. 34—1814) Sally, Eliza, Ellina, Joel, Kitty, Nancy, Lucy—hrs. of Wm. Ellis decd. late of Harrison 1814.

Eastland, Wm. (Mercer Co. deeds 12-223, Nov. 18, 1820) heirs: Thos. Eastland and w. Mary, of Nashville, Tenn. John Moss and w. Sarah, John A. Eastland and w. Nancy, Ashbury P. F. C. Eastland and w. Mariah, Joseph Akin for himself and att'y. in fact for Eliz. Eastland and gdn. for John A. Rice, Wm. E. Akin, Caroline E. M. Akin, Julia Ann Akin, Joseph E. Akin, and Thos. Akin, infants, all of Co. of Green, Ky., all heirs of Wm. East-land, decd.

Eastland, Thos. (dep'n. Aug. 10, 1802, suit Crows heirs, Box 94-114, Franklin Dist. Ct.) of Greensburg, at his home, deposed, he was a Lieut. in 4th Reg. USA, and enlisted Thos. Dunn, now of Woodford Co. in USA in 1791, and was recruiting in Danville, Ky. 1800.

Edgar, Henry (see Bourbon suit Scrogin vs. Jno Allen Box 731) from Sussex Co., Del. to Ky. he m. Betsy Coper who m. 2nd Jno. Allen.

Edmiston, David of Ross Co. O (suit Bourbon 431-434, 1804) gdn. of Elizabeth Edmiston, infant orphan of Robert Edmiston. In Bourbon Co., Ky. marriage bonds: David Edmiston to Margaret Foster, 1790. Edmistons of S. W., Va. at Kings Mt. (N. C.) battle.

Edmiston, Robert–Robt. and Elizabeth orphans (Bourbon orders 1798.)

Estill, Jas. Hrs. (with ages in suit Morrow vs. Clay 652, Bourbon, 1824) Benj. "now 51", Wallace 49, Jas. 47, Jonathan who if living would be 45, Sarah, w. of Robt. Miller, 42 or 43–only ch. of Jas. Estill who was killed by Indians 1782, said Sally m. Miller in her 17th year.

Elliott's Hrs. (Scott Co. Deeds M. p 293–Sept. 1, 1834)–Louis Pullen and w. Ruth, Theodore Elliott and w. Polly Ann, Rebecca Elliott, Burton L. Elliott, hrs.-at-law of Thos. Elliott decd. of Floyd Co. Ind. deed Lodowick Davis land that descended to them at death of sd. Thos. Elliott decd.

Eulape, Jacob Hrs. (Scott Co. Deeds M p 87–Oct. 4, 1833)–Joseph Coulter and w. Polly of Scott to Thos. Goddard, George Harlen, George ——, Jacob Eulap, Polly Martin, David Nutter and James Eulap of various counties of Ky. and Ohio, did convey (1831) to Joseph Coulter land in Scott and whereas Chri—— Patton was also one of hrs. of sd. Jacob Eupal and was living at death of sd. Jacob but since decd. leaving 9 hrs.–5 by her 1st husband and 4 by her 2nd husband, her first was Colvin Ball and 2nd was Wm. Paton and whereas sd. Wm. Paton has conveyed his right to parties of 2nd pt., his life estate, in one eighth part etc.–Oct. 1833.

Evans, John (Mar. 26, 1814-June 26 1817–Box 238 Franklin Co. Cir. Ct.) Will, in Phila. Pa.– Prop. in Frankfort, Ky. wife Barbara dau. Rachel Redmon, wife of John Redmon of Salem, N. J. My kinswomen Reb. Potter, Sarah Day, Hannah Alexander, 1000 acres, their bro. Thos. Redman, Jr., my cousin Mary Shepherd and her son John E. S., relatives, Rebecca Lawrence, Mary Redman, and their bro. Dr. Thos. Redman, kinsman, Alex. Elmslie? to Nath'l. Holland, John Simmons, Joseph Price, my apprentices. —— late partner in trade John Elmslie of Cape of Good Hope, and to John Shephard, to Thos. Young and wife Sarah (shopkeeper) Dr. Joseph Redmon of Bordentown, N. J. many pp.

Ellis, Daniel (Mercer Co. Orders 1824, p. 69) Revolutionary soldier, d. Mar. 2, 1824, certified, May 4, 1824.

Edwards, Haden (Franklin Co., Oct. 12, 1795, Quar. Ct. deeds) of Prince Wm. Parish, Dist. of Buford, So. Car., late of Franklin Co., District of Beaufort, July 19, 1805, p. 327 quarterly court deeds, Franklin Co. deeds. Haden Edwards and wife Sus. Jan. 8, 1802, Franklin Co., Uriah and Eliz. of Franklin Co.–Benj. Edwards of Nicholas Co.–May 27, 1830.

Floyd, Col. John–Devisees: (Bibb Vol. IV. Ky. Reports) John Floyd made entry 8-8-1781, will for benefit of wife and ch. Wm. Pope and Jenny Floyd, exrs. After death of Floyd wife made entry Oct. 23, 1783. Jenny Floyd assignee of Benj. Netherland. She subsequently m. Alex. Breckinridge. Fall term 1816.

Ford, Elisha (Orders 1833 Shelby Co., p. 153) late pensioner, Shelby Co. (widow living) d. Sept. 29, 1833.

Fox, Arthur, heirs (Mason Co. N-97 deeds) Oct. 17, 1812—Wm. Wood, of Ohio, by Comrs. Lawson Dobyns and wife Mary (Fox), Andrew Wood and wife Matilda (Fox), Arthur Fox by his gd'n., John Graham, Richd. Brent Graham, infs. under 21 by Richd. Graham, late of Lewis Co., but now of U. S. Army, said John and Richard Graham being heirs of Eliz. G. who was heiress of said Arthur Fox, decd. to Thos. Morton, Geo. B. Morton, John Morton, Lucy Morton, Nancy Morton, Mary Morton and Frances Morton, heirs of Robt. B. Morton, decd. late of Mason Co. (suit in Chancery bet. Morton's heirs and Fox's heirs.) (Arthur Fox d. 1794, buried in Wash. Cem. his widow Mary Fox m. Gen. Henry Lee H. Scott) Richd. Graham gd'n. for Arthur Fox, Jr.

Franklin, Rosanna (Orders Mercer Co., 1825, p. 186) widow of Edmund Franklin, late soldier in Capt. Edw. Berry's Co., Col. Gab'l. Slaughter's Reg. proved that she is widow of decd. Nov. 7, 1825.

Froman, Jacob (Mercer Co. Orders, 1, p. 382) Aug. 26, 1789. The persons appointed to examine the court house built by Jacob Froman and John Mosby reported as follows, to wit: July 29, 1789 . . . etc. find it 38 ft. 9 in. long in the clear, 30 ft. 9 in. wide, the foundation we cannot examine being under ground, the walls from the foundation twenty one ft. 10 inches high, two side windows to the court room 24 lights each, two opposite to the Justices seat 18 lights each arranged by bond as they were directed, two windows opposite the gallery in the sides of the house instead of the end 18 lights each; one window to each of the jury rooks, 18 each, etc. the gallery 28 ft. 8 in. by 12 ft. 6 in.

Fleming, James, (p. 184, State of Ky. Acts—1834-1835)—late of Lex. d. intestate, widow Susan F., ch.: Wm. W. F., Mary Vaughan, Priscilla, wife of Chas. Robinson, Jane, wife of John Keiser, Isabella F., and Augustus Fleming, the last two infants.

Fleming, John (will, M-508, Montgomery Co. Ky.)Directors to sell farm in 3 years, to buy land in neighborhood and adjoining land in Lewis Co. on Cabin Cr.—wife Elizabeth, 2 ch. Elizabeth Mary Jane and John G. Burnsides Fleming. If possession be obtained of land in Lewis Co. my wife move there with her ch., etc. Wm. G. Bullock, exr. Apr. 11, 1843—May 1843.

Flournoy's Hrs.—(Mercer Co. Orders, 1824, p 52)—James Rogers gdn. to Richard, Emily and Patsy Flournoy Jan. 5, 1824. Note: James Rogers m. the widow Flournoy.

Gist. Christopher—(Bourbon Co. Feb. 1, 1793 (A-615 Order bk) wife Sarah Howard, certificate from Buckingham Co., Va., saying Nath'l. Gist was eldest son of Christopher and Sarah, and that Thos. Gist was his younger bro. (Thos., decd.)

Gayle (Scott County, Ky. data—Deed B, p. 338, 1816) Judith Gayle, widow of Matthew Gayle, relinquished any claim on M. Gayle, Sr. estate. —— Gayle and Kitty, his wife heirs of Wm. Gayle, Sr. decd. (Deeds C-530) Mar. 22, 1821, most missing. Gayle's heirs—Temple C. Gayle, and —— Gayle decd. Wm. Gayle, decd. (suit), Mar. 7, 1822 Wm. Gayle, Josiah, Temple E., Robert W. Gayle, and Wm. Gayle, devisees. (F 208, deeds). R. Gayle, W. Gayle, Fanny Gayle, and Mary Gayle, Aug. 30, 1823—Gen'l. Phillip Thomas and Fanny Thomas, —— ayle and Wm. Gayle, the husbands of the said —— Mary all of Parish of East Baton Rough of —— (La.) apt. Benj. Thomas of Mason Co., Ky., att'y. —— whereas John and Sarah Hawkins of Scott County, have departed this life, who were father and mother of our late mother Fanny, leaving estate, and we being legal heirs of said John and Sarah Hawkins —— at end it says John Gayle and

Wm. Gayle and [Fanny Gayle and Mary Gayle) (deeds H. p. 151 Scott Co.) (H. p. 153)–] John Gayle and wife Fanny, and Wm. Gayle and wife Mary. Dec. 15, 1823 of La., etc. Thos. Gayle, decd. (order B, p. 82) Job Stevens gd'n. of heirs–1817-1821 —— Jos. Rossell m. Margt. Gayle, Va. Vaughan m. M. Gayle heirs of Thos. Gayle, Jan. 3, 1822–Kitty Gayle, decd. admn. 1818-1826, Nov. 1825 p. 246–Thos. Gayle, decd. gd'n. apt'd. for Peggy and Polly Gayle, over 14, and Walker Gayle, infants of Thos. under 14 (p. 291, B-1818-1826) Peggy and Polly chose Job Stevenson, gdn. 7-7-1817. Mary Gayle, dower.

Grettin, Wm. Hrs.: (p. 293, 1827–Orders, Mercer Co.) Rebecca, Hamilton, Hogland Grettin, chose Aaron Grettin, gd'n., and court apt'd. him gd'n. of Ferman, Mary, Marg't. Wm., and Jane Grettin. Jan. 1, 1827.

Gregory, Mrs. Margaret–dep'n., Louisville, Ky. June 21, 1849, (Suit of Samuel Nock vs. Smith Gregory and John Stodgill, Box 418, bundle 9, Shelby Cir. Ct.) she says her son Smith Gregory was b. Mar. 10, 1817 and her oldest dau. Eliza Hungate of Shelby Co. has the Bible. Tilford Gregory gives dep'n. that he is 5 years older than Smith.

Greenlee, John (Lincoln Co., E. p. 102 deeds Nov. 19, 1808) of Rockbridge Co., Va. appointed son John Greenlee of Ky. att'y. to sell 500 acres bt. of Wm. Montgomery, dec'd. on Green River.

Grayson, Wm. Hrs: (Box 34-69, Franklin Dist. Ct.) George Wash. Grayson, Robt. Har. Grayson, Heabert Smallwood Carter and wife (Grayson), Robt. Carter and wife (Grayson), Alfred Grayson, Andrew Ramsey and wife Catherine (Grayson) Rich. Graham, dec'd. John, George, and Rich., heirs, May 1802–Geo. W. Grayson, Alfred Grayson, Richard Graham are residents of Mason Co., the rest are not of this commonwealth.

Graham, Eliz. (Mercer Co. Orders. Dec. 5, 1823, p. 43) came into court and chose Chas. Craig, gdn. Nov. 5, 1823–Peyton R. Graham, decd. admn. gtd. to James Spillman and Ann Graham, widow (same, Dec. 1, 1823, p. 47)

Garnett, James (Woodford Co., Cir. Ct., Box 37) heirs–before Justices of Cir. Ct. of Caroline Co., Va., May 15, 1794. On Oct. 7, 1788 Henry Gatewood and his wife Delphia, James Garnett, Jr., who is an infant, by his next fr. Henry Gatewood sued, etc. James Garnett, Jr. exr. of James Garnett, decd.–Chas. Pemberton and Thos. Garnett say that about 1770 Larkin Garnett, son of James Garnett about to pay his addresses to your oratrix Delphia, dau. of Chas. Pemberton of Spotts. Co. and to encourage and induce said Larkin to marry said Delphia, he said Pemberton promised slave to sd. dau. in case of marriage, and James Garnett to induce sd. Delphia to marry said Larkin, etc. said James did promise to give sd. son Larkin a slave, etc. said Larkin Garnett d. about 1772 leaving an only child, son James Garnett, an infant about 1776 sd. James Garnett the eldest died leaving will, apt'd. wife Sarah and sons Thos. and James Garnett exrs. Caroline Co. court; sd. James Garnett qualified, and to James Garnett son of Larkin G. a slave. Larkin to Orange Co. and back to Caroline; "old Mrs. Sarah Pemberton" answers Aug. 15, 1789 by Thos. Garnett. At court Aug. 14, 1793, suit abated by death of Chas. Pemberton. James Garnett (will copy of Caroline Co., Va.); wife Sarah G., son Thos. (500 a. in Orange Co.) near Adam Lindsey, son James G. gd. son James G. son of Larkin G., decd. dau. Eliz. Lindsey, land in Orange Co., dau. Sally Noell, Tabitha Shipp–1776, probated in Caroline Co., dated Sept. 1775. Reported in

1788 that inf. pltf. (James) was to be m. to a dau. of Robt. Foster Bowling etc. Wm. Tinsley, bro. of Isaac, at home of Bennett Pemberton, Woodford Co. said in 1791 he was at house of Henry Gatewood; also dept'ns. of Wm. Tureman and Eliz. Edwards of the Va. actions, 1790 etc.

Galloway Hrs: (H-77, Scott Co. deeds). Ruth Lambert, Margaret Galloway, John G., James and Samuel G., Mary G., and Nancy G., Anny G., Rebecca and Eliz. Galloway, deed to Sidney Burbridge, Aug. 22, 1823.

Gaines, Wm. F. (Scott Co. deeds T-104) of Randolph Co., Mo. appts. John J. Gaines of same, att'y. to receive all property etc., in Scott Co., as heir at law of my father, Thos. Gaines and Frances Gaines, my mother who before marriage with my father was Frances Branham, due me as heir at law of my mother Frances Gaines, decd. proceeding from est. of Eliz. Branham my grandmother, and George Branham, my uncle, etc. May 10, 1845 (Macon Co., Mo., May 10, 1845). Beverly Branham and wife Patsy deed to Wm. C. Duvall, Oct. 25, 1844 (T-13, Scott Co.,) (see deed of John and Eliz. Branham in Franklin Court deeds.) Wm. Gaines, decd. heirs: Wm. Gaines, Thos G., Jas. & Geo. Gaines, Richard Barnet G., of Franklin Co., heirs of Wm. Gaines decd. from Thos. Withers, Mar. 18, 1828 (L-312, Woodford Co.)

Givens, Samuel (p. 134, Mercer Court orders)—furnished horse for use of the expedition to the Blue Licks against the Indians in August 1782, says Major Hugh McGary in a certificate. Aug. 30, 1787, produced in court, and horse lost, appraised at 30 lbs. certified on order of Samuel Givens.

Gillison, John (deed bk. M. p. 286, Franklin Co.) decd. soldier of the Rev. War, officer, in Fauquier Co., Va., heirs named in deed book (many heirs named Beale).

Glass, Robert, exr. of Joseph Glass, decd. (Shelby Co., Ky. Order bk. 1810-1814 p. 70) deeds land in Frederick Co., Va., to Joseph Glass, acknowledged in court July 1812.

Gibson, W. d. Bardstown, Nov. 1, 1852, (B'town. Herald, Nov. 4, 1852) aged 79 yr. b. Berkeley Co., Va., 1774, to Ky., 1790, B'town. in 1801, War 1812, Hopkins campaign, family etc.

Gibbs, John (Garrard Co., Orders 1819-1821, p. 79)—affidavit says July 17, 1820, he was 65 years last Dec., in Rev. 9 mos. under Capt. John Farrow, to Savannah River under Capt. Mills, Reg. com'd. Col. Arch. Lyttle, N. C. line, 1776-1777 at Charleston, S. C., at taking of Ft. Stono from British—no family given.

Gibbs, Julius Hrs: (Scott Co. deeds M-274) and N-139)—wife Cath. Gibbs, James Guthrie, Barnett Sisk, James and John Gibbs, Benj. Roberts, Robt. F. Gibbs, C. J. Gibbs, Sam'l. C. Gibbs, and Jas. Roberts. Agreement with Julius Gibbs, Dec. 5, 1835. Samuel C. Gibbs of Calloway Co., Mo., apts. Robt. F. Gibbs of Boone Co., Mo. att'y. to get his est. as heir of Julius Gibbs, Oct. 7, 1834 (0-67, Scott Co. deeds) Julius Gibbs in Rev. war, declaration (Orders C p. 374). He was pensioner, d. July 25, 1834. (p. 111. C).

Hawkins, Samuel Overton (Albemarle Co., Mar. 1812, G-107, Fayette Co.) of Franklin Co. to John T. Hawkins of Fayette, int. in Mrs. Eliz. Hawkins estate, heir to Thompson. Hawkins, John T. of Fayette, for love and affec, to his dau. Eliz. Thompson Hawkins, slaves, etc. Dec. 1, 1812, Mary Hawkins, wts. (G-303, Fayette.) Wm. Cochran and wife Mildred, John T. Mason and wife Eliza B., John T. Hawkins, and Littleberry Hawkins, deed., Joseph H. Hawkins and wife, Geo. Ann, Thos. W. Hawkins, 1816. Edm. Hawkins decd. heirs, Joseph H. Hawkins and wife Geo. Ann, Littleberry H. and wife Mary, Hudson Martin and wife Mary Ann (P-402 (462?), Feb. 28, 1817, Fayette.

Hynes—(p. 435, G. Franklin Gen. Court) heirs Sarah Churchill, decd. heirs, Abner Hynes, Mary Hynes, Nancy Duvall (formerly Hynes, wife of Wm. D.); Andrew Churchill, Armstead Churchill, Eliz. Churchill, only ch. of Sarah Churchill, decd. who was Sarah Haynes, wife of Armstead Churchill, Senr., deceased and heirs of Eliz. Harrison decd. who was wife of Burr H., and formerly Eliz. Hynes, all of lost representatives by Hynes are legal reps. and heirs of Andrew Hynes, decd.

Huston, Eli, hrs. (K-57, Franklin Cir. Ct. orders) Nov. 16, 1835, John Morris, gdn. to Eliz., Felix and Sarah F. E. Huston, inf. hrs. of Eli. Huston, formerly of State of Miss.

Hunter, John (E. complete recs. P. 163, Franklin Co., Cir. Ct.) heirs—John Hunter, Ichabod Hunter, Mary Wallace and Jean Caldwell, devisees, Jan. 13, 1816.

Hazelrigg, Hannah (Shelby Co. deed, E2-58) heir of John Morgan, decd. and widow of Graham Hazelrigg, decd. appoints Daniel Boone of Clark Co. att'y.—Mar. 5, 1830—wts. Elijah Tinsley and Jas. H. Hazelrigg.

Hynes, Andrew (Nelson Co.) decd. heirs. Whereas Wm. R. Hynes, Dr. Burr Harrison and his ch.; Laura Ann Harrison, Eliz. H., Mary L. H. heirs of Eliz. Harrison, decd. late Eliz. Hynes, Wm. P. Duvall and Nancy his wife Mary Hynes, Abner Hynes and Alfred W. Hynes, heirs of Andrew Hynes, etc.

Hopkins, Josiah (K-50-66, 96, etc. deeds, Nicholas Co. Apr. 17, 1833) decd. heirs: Wm. Stevenson and wife Ruth, John Stephenson and wife Grizzilla of Nicholas Co., Albert Hopkins, Milton, Wm., Nancy Rhoda, James, Mary, and Jane Hopkins, ch. etc. of Josiah Hopkins, decd.

Houston, James (deed 21 p. 66, Nelson Co.) heirs: July 17, 1815—Isaac Collins and wife Jenny, to Eliza Caroline Huston, Madeline Clermont Huston, Mary Jane Huston, Louisa Ann Huston, and Wm. Harrison Huston.

Holt, Wm. (Box 1-16, Dist. Ct. Franklin Co. Cir. Ct.) (will) wife, Peachy, lot in Williamsburg, son Daniel, dau. Eliz. Coleman, sons, Wm., and David, land in Monongalia, son John, son Samuel (land in Charles City) son Henry (all est. in Surry) their sisters, Jane and Mary, Sarah, and Frances Jerdone (not to have any estate) sons Samuel and Henry (residuary legatees) wife Peachy, Wm. Russell and Robt. Greenhow, Wm. Coleman exrs. dated Jan. 11, 1791—probated court of Hustings Williamsburg, Va., June 6, 1791. Elias Wills and Peachy his wife late Peachie Holt, and formerly Peachie Purdie, suit July 25, 1796. Mrs. Peachie Purdie Wills, vs. Holts Devisees, June 3, 1790, entered 1,000 acres, Mar. 16, 1781 in Jefferson Co., Mar. 6, 1793.

Hite, Abram. (Box 17-53, Franklin Cir. Ct.) decd. heirs—Abram, Rebecca, Isaac, Joseph—his entry in Mercer, 1780, Oct. 30—he d. Jan. 1, 1790, will recorded in Jefferson Co., suit in 1793.

Herdman, George (Logan Co., I-J deeds, 313) decd. heirs—Aug. 13, 1821, of Warren Co., Ky. James Herdman, Jane E. Herdman, Lavinia and Augustus Herdman, John, Mary Eliza and George Ann Herdman, infant heirs, from Alpheus Wickware.

Henderson, Wm. hrs.—Bourbon to Wm. Ford (Deeds Y p. 163, Bourbon Co.) March 11, 1831—
400 acres. Wm. H. Davis, Thomas Davis and Eliza Davis ch. of Owen Davis, husband
of Jane decd. late Henderson, dau. of Wm. decd. Nancy I. Henderson, Jane Henderson,
Wm. C. Henderson and Martha W. Henderson chn. of James Henderson, son of Wm.
decd. and Martha Wilson, late Martha Henderson, dau. of Wm. decd. by Jno. B.
Raine commr.

Hardin, Wm. (Order bk. 9, Lincoln Co.) James and Martin Hardin, over 14, orphans of
James Hardin, decd. chose gdn's. Aug. 1826; also gdn. to John Timothy, Mark and
Samuel Hardin, infants of James H., decd. p. 96.

Hardin, Benjamin d. Sept. 30, 1852 (obit. in Bardstown Herald), d. Sept. 24, 1852, b. Feb.
29, 1784 in Monongahela Co., Pa. (Va.) with his father to Ky. 1788, Washington Co.,
tribute in Feb. 17, 1853, Herald . . . b. Pa., his gt. gd. father a Huguenot, helped to
colonize S.C. His gd. father mover from S.C. to Va. and his father sett. on a farm in Pa.,
then to Ky., Washington Co., m. Mar. 31, 1806, Eliz. P. Barbour, then to Elizabethtown,
and to Bardstown—thrown from a horse when entering gate of son-in-law, Dr. Palmer
of Washington Co., ill, etc. wife d. suddenly Aug. 1, dau.—Palmer d. and 2 sons d.
(son James) returning from grave drew his 3 daus. to him, Mrs. Gov. Helm, Mrs. Riley
of Lou., Mrs. Dixon of Memphis, etc. his wife Mrs. Eliz. P. Hardin, dau. of Maj. Ambrose
Barbour who came to Ky. when she was 9 yrs. old, m at age of 20—d. Aug. 4.

Harris, Joshua (p. 306, Nov. 1818, July 1821, Orders Shelby Co.) aged 61 yrs. appeared
in Court, asked for pension, was in Rev. war, fall, 1779, 18 mos., under Capt. Stripling,
Col. Campbell, in Battles of Guilford Ct. House, Camden, Siege of 96, got pension
Cert. 16739, 1819, wife and 4 ch. living with him, wife very old, he a crippled, 2 sons,
oldest about 19, other 12, oldest dau. 16, other abt. 8, declared July 1820.

Harris, Nathaniel (deed, H-180, Woodford Co., Ky.)4 decd. heirs, John Harris and wife
Nancy (Mary?), Jas. Phillips and wife Nancy, Susan Harris, Richard Harris and Frances,
his wife, Robert Ramsey and wife Martha, Benj. Wood and wife Eliz., John Cave and
wife Martha, Lewis Harris and William Harris, heirs of Nath'l. Harris, decd.

Harlan, George (Complete Records, No. 9, Lincoln Co. Cir. Ct.) and Silas, Wm., Elijah,
John and Matthew Harlan, heirs of Elijah Harlan, decd. p. 1, Feb. 1806.

Hampton, Wm. heirs (Box 563, Franklin Co. Cir Ct.) ch.: Hannah, Preston, Theodore, John
Hampton, Wm. Hampton, widow Dorcus H., m. Isaac Calvert, unhappy and separated—
sett. and agreement—Sept. 19, 1836.

Hall, Leonard, Sr. (Scott Co. deeds 1, p. 28) decd. of Barren Co., Ky. Aug. 26, 1822. Anderson Harlow and wife Naomi (dau. of Leonard Hall), deed to Micajah Harlow,
Scott Co., land grant from Patrick Henry, Mar. 26, 1816 (grant Jan. 28, 1783).

Hawkins, John Hrs. (Dist. Ct. C, 415, Fayette Co.) decd. (of Hanover Co., Va.), Heirs:
Thos. Irvin, Martin Hawkins, in his own right and as admr. of est. of Edmund Hawkins, decd. John Hawkins, Percival Butler, John P. Thomas, and Robt. Stewart of Ky.,
legatees of John Hawkins of Hanover Co., Va., decd. money due to the est. of said
John Hawkins. Mary Hawkins, exrx. of will of said John Hawkins, apt. James Hawkins.
att'y. Jan. 6, 1801.

Hawkins, John T. of Albemarle Co., Va. buys of Mary Hawkins title she has in lands of late Eliz. Hawkins, decd. who was heir of of John Thompson, decd. land in Albemarle Co., Va., 1165 acres sold by John Williamson to Thompson and by him devised to Eliz. Hawkins, decd. May 5, 1804. J. Hawkins, Jr. Wts. (Cir. Ct. A. p. 363, Fayette Co.)

Henry, Wm. (Box 266-298, Frankfort Cir. Ct., Dist. Ct.) and Daniel and John Henry and Jeanett Irvine, a dau. and heir at law of Sally Irvine, formerly Sally Henry, which said Wm., Daniel, John, and Sally were heirs at law of Robert Henry, decd. all of Ky., and John Middleton, formerly of Charlotte, Va., etc. (Sept. 19, 1788) dated Dec. 11, 1809.

Helm, Joseph, Sr. and wife Susanna of Lincoln Co., Thos. Helm of Stanford, June 8, 1816, deed in Shelby Co. (S-64). Thos. Helm and wife Mary of Lincoln, June 14, 1821, deed (S-66, Shelby Co.) Thos. Helm d. in Shelby, Inv. July 1832, comrs. met at Samuel Helms, admr. of Thos. Helm, Aug. 24, 1834. (will 10, p. 314) application of Samuel Helm, gdn. of Wm., John and Thos. Helm heirs of Thos. Helm decd. Apr. 16, 1852. (will 21, p. 98, Shelby Co.) John Helm, Sr., Inv. Sept. 6, 1843, (15-199, Shelby Co. wills) Joanna Helm, dower, June 1844 (16-21) Leonard Helm will, "infirm wife", and youngest dau. Nancy under age, have given each of other ch. (will 18, p. 71, Shelby Co.), Joanna Helm, decd. Oct. 29, 1847, Nov. 1847, Leonard Helm's will, eq. to all. Joanna Helm, decd. Inv. July 1837 Shelby Co.

Harrison, Valentine–(Franklin Co. D-199) Hrs: Harriet P. Surghnor and Jas. Surghnor of Frederick Co., Va., Seldon Harrison of Loudon Co., Va., Addison Harrison of Fauquier Co., all heirs and reps. of Valentine Harrison decd. of Loudon Co. and Ann Harrison (wid?–named first)

First court held at Harrodsburg, Aug. 1, 1786 present: John Cowan, Hugh McGary, Gabriel Madison, *Alexander Robertson, Samuel Lapsley, Samuel Scott, Samuel McAfee, John Irvin, and Samuel McDowell, Gent, a Commission of the Peace, directed to William Christian, John Cowan, Hugh McGary, Gabriel Madison, (as above except Joseph Gray added) constituting and appointing them Justices of the Peace and Oyer and Terminer, John Cowan, Gent. administered the oath of fidelity, etc. Samuel McDowell first sheriff (p. 2) Thos. Allin, clerk; Gabriel Madison, county lieut., John Thomas, county surveyor; following Capts: Samuel Scott. James Ray, John Irvine, Jas. Harlan, James Kinkead, Stephen Arnold, James Coburn, Andrew Beall, Lewis Roberts, John Harrison. Lieuts: George Scott, John McMurtry, Wm. Caldwell, Jeremiah Briscoe, Henry Wilson. Robt. Armstrong, Isaac Pritchard, Joshua Barbee, John Smith, Benj. Cooper. Ensigns: John Wilson. Isham Talbott, Jas. Brumfield, Samuel Ewing, Thos. McClure, John Arnold, Lucas Vorhis, David Lawrence, John Curd, Henry Wilson. Jr., Hugh McGary, Lt. Col. of militia (6) 9-5-1786; Anthony Crockett, Major of mil., (6) (Jan 12, 1786, 9-5-1786); James Overton and Thos. Hall, licensed att'ys. at law, Nov. 7, 1786, (p. 10) Rev'd. John Samuel Moore licensed to perform marriage rites. Nov. 27, 1787, Orders. 1, p. 146.

Hinton–(Box 166-192 (or 176) Franklin Dist. Ct.) Thos. Hinton, Sr., vs. Thos. Hinton heirs at law of Joseph Hinton, decd. In 1775, Jos. Hinton moved to his father-in-laws in Va. and bro't. with him his wife and son Thos., then about 2 years old, and in fall of 1775, deponent (Robt. McKay) said Joseph Hinton started for Ky., and arrived in 1776-1779. Jos. Hinton and fam. with said son Thos. started for Ky. and at Richland creek, no food, and stopped etc.

Helm, Thos. (Gen'l. Ct. deed H, p. 483, Franklin Co.) heirs, John Helm, Benj. Helm, George Helm, Chas. Helm, Sally Crutcher, Evelyn Boyce, Thos. Boyce, Chas. Boyce, Sarah Jane Boyce, Mary Ann Boyce heirs of Polly Boyce, decd. late Polly Helm; Polly Hobbs, George Hobbs, Joshua Hobbs, Jane, Maria, Samuel and Eliz. Hobbs, heirs of Celia Hobbs, late Helm—heirs of Thos. Helm decd. July 19, 1820—deed to heirs of John Crow, decd. (heirs named) Grayson Co. land, etc.

Knox, Jas. (Franklin County Dist. Ct., Feb. 3, 1798—Gibson Taylor vs: Gabriel Jones, Box 1-16) (dep'n.) came to Ky. 1774 with John Floyd, Hancock Taylor, Isaac Hite, Jas. Douglas, etc.

Jenkins, Thos. hrs. (Scott Co. deed N. 512-1834) Robt. Manning and Eleanora, Austin Jenkins, Jas. H. Gough and Cordelia C. Gough. Jenkins and others to Offutt (deed M 390 Scott Co.) signed R. B. Rose and Margaret Rose, Eliz. Jenkins, Wm. Jenkins, E. C. Offutt—1834.

Jones, Thomas (deeds S. p. 29, 1824, Bourbon) heirs: Thomas Jones and Polly, Jas. Jones and Elizabeth, Garrard Jones and Ann, Joseph Berry, Jane C. Jones, following pg., Elizabeth Irvin, Sally Jones, daus. of Thomas, 1825. See deed p. 69— one Thos. Jones and wife, Polly deed of gift to dau. Elizabeth, wife of Henry Warren, dau. Elizabeth Smith Warren, 1825.

Jones, Gabriel, decd. (see Franklin Co. Dist. Ct. papers, Cir. Ct. office, Box 1-16) heirs: Robt. Jones, Gabriel Jones, Francis Slaughter Jones, Mary Jones (now wife of Rich. Young Wiggington) heirs and children and legatees of Gabriel Jones, decd. of Dunmore Co., Va.

January, Thos. (Fayette, Bk. 10-367 deeds) heirs: Eliz. Rector (late January) Peter W. January, Thos. J., Derrick J., Chas. J., Matilda J., and Sidney January, children and heirs at law. Peter January, Jr. and son Thos. January, partners, merchants, Nov. 1797— Peter J. and wife Marg't.

Jones, John (will in box 180, Franklin Cir. Ct.) John C. Bacon, etc. vs. Bacon's exrs. 1816. John Jones of New Kent County, Va. St. Peters Parish, names wife Lucy Jones (she was widow of. . . . Bacon, then married Stanley P. Gower—see Owen Co., Warren Co.? for S. P. Gower—then he names wife's three ch: Benedict Bacon, Nathaniel Bacon, and Eliz. Bacon, and wife Lucy, exr. dated Nov. 20, 1796 prob. Apr. 13, 1797 (much Bacon data).

Kirtley, Richard, heirs (Bourbon Co. Ct., bk. 36, p. 36, 1838) Davenport R. Gillock pty. 1st pt. to, Paschal Fretwell, Elijah Kirtley, Wm. Kirtley, America Hearn (late Kirtley) Mary Kirtley, Simeon Kirtley, surviving hrs. of Richard K. decd. Nov. 1826

Keith, Adam (Harrison Co. Orders D. 504) d. intestate admrs: Lewis Keith and Mary Keith. Henry Keith, Lewis Keith, Ellis Ashcraft, Wm. Ashcraft named in sett. of estate.

Kelly, Sam'l. hrs. (Woodford Co., Ky., deed K. p. 51, Aug. 13, 1823—there are several other deeds from hrs.) Jno. Kelly and Martha (Patsy), Patrick Welsh and Eleanor, Margaret Robb, Jno. Downey and Sally of Clark Co., Ind. appt. Wm. Kelly atty. to dispose of tract in Woodford claimed by "ourselves and others as hrs. of Sam'l. Kelly decd. late of Woodford."

Kincheloe, Stephen (dep'n. Dec. 17, 1798, Bland's heirs, vs. Combs, 1797, Box 70-83, Dist. Ct. Franklin Cir. Ct. files) says in dep'n. he was here in 1780 and 81. Lewis Kincheloe, here also in 1781. Wm. Kincheloe, of Pr. Wm. Co., Va., dep'n.

Kilgore (Box 18, Fayette Cir. Ct.) Cumberland Co., Pa., Wm. McClure, and Wm. Clark of the county, vs. Chas. Kilgore, etc   Chas. Kilgore, father of said Chas. Kilgore, owned land, etc. His will, Jan. 5, 1778–filed Cumberland Co., Pa., signed by many. Suit dated 1799.

Keller, Isaac, decd. (K-21, orders, Franklin Co.)   Mary Keller, widow, ch. and heirs: John O'Nan and wife Margaret, Thos. Smith and ·wife Sally, Edward Dougherty and wife Catherine, Nancy Gates, Reb. Keller, John, Isaac and Acenith Keller, Elizabeth Keller, Isaac, Acenith and Eliz. by gdn. Mary Keller, Jan. 19, 1835.

Kennedy, Ezekiel (John C. Bacon and wife vs. Bacon's exrs. Box 180 Franklin Cir. Ct.) age about 60 years, gives dep'n. Apr. 27,1807, was on Benson in 1781. Note: see also Box 539, suit of Robertson's admr. and Kennedy's heirs)

Keller, Abraham (box 827, Bourbon Co. dated 1833) he d. intestate–. Heirs: Jacob, John, Edwards and w. Elizabeth, John Snell and w. Rebecca, Wm. Kiser and w. Menerva, Abraham, John Edwards, Jr. and Margaret, and Jno. Jos., Nancy, Isaac and Noah last five under 21.

Lee, Hancock of Fauquier Co., Va. (Franklin deed D, p. 365) to Willis A. Lee of Franklin Co., for affection, house and land where Willis Lee lives, N. side of river, Leestown. 6-27-1814

Morrow–(Clark Co., Ky., records deeds, 11 p. 130 Nov. 13, 1814) Robert Morrow of Bath Co., Ky., to Thomas F. Morrow and Thos. Jones of Clark–whereas Jas. Morrow, late of Clark Co., Ky. did by mortgage July 21, 1800 convey to Robt. Morrow, whereas Jas. Morrow, late of Clark Co., deptd. life without a will, etc.–Thos. F. Morrow and wife Margaret of Montgomery Co., Ky. deed Clark Co. land Dec. 29, 1817.

Morrow, James (Bk. 10 deeds Clark Co. p. 227 Mar. 10, 1814) hrs: Wm. Morrow and Nancy w. of Bullitt; Robt. Morrow and Peggy w. of Montgomery Co., Ky. David Gibson and Polly w. of Gallatin–James Browning and Jane· w. of Clark, James Morrow and Anny w. of Clark–Jas. Morrow, Sr. hrs. all daus. are given as "late Morrow."–Thomas F. Morrow and Peggy of Clark, Jno. Morrow of Clark, Christopher Morrow of Clark deed Thos. Jones–land granted by Va. Jan. 1785 to Jas. Morrow in Clark.

Madison, Gabriel, heirs (G-468 Gen. Ct. Franklin Co. deeds), June 17, 1818–Eliz. Allen, wife of Francis A., decd. (form. E. Madison), Wm. Madison, Lucy M. Gabriella Hawkins wife of J. H. Strother (late G. Madison), George Madison and Martha M., heirs of Gabriel Madison.

Madison, Thos. heirs (Gen. Court, Commissioners bk. p. 115, Jan. 8, 1827, Franklin Co.) Henry Bowyer and wife Agatha, Sylvester Johnson and wife Peggy, Patrick H. Madison, Chas. Hart and wife Peggy, Thos. Madison, George and Betsy Roland, Wm., John and Susan Madison, last 9 being heirs of John M. decd. all heirs of Thos. Madison decd. deed, Robt. Baker's heirs. Ambrose Madison gd. fa. of President, d. 1742, Orange Co., Va.–Jan. 1925, Va. Mag. VI, 434, etc.

Marshall, Wm. (C No. 1, 224, Woodford Co. deeds) and wife Alice of Henrico Co., Va. deed to John Brown of same, 586 acres pat'd. to Marshall, 1785, in Fayette on Ky. r. June 3, 1800.

Martin, Arch., (deed 2, p. 129, Mercer Co., 1793) of No. Car., in Revolutionary War, in Capt. John Hunter's Co., Thos. Evans' Reg't.

Mav. Iohn (Ct. of Ap. P–489, much data of them in deeds and court records in Cir. Ct. Frankfort) heirs: John L. May, Daniel Epes and wife Polly, are only ch. and heirs of Ann Lewis, decd. late wife of Thos. Lewis and formerly wife of said John May, decd. which Ann was sole exr. of will of John May, etc.

Matthews, Gen. Geo.–(Gen. Ct. Deed B, Frankfort, Aug. 15, 1797) of State of Ga., of first part to Isaac Telfair and Jane his wife, (of Mercer Co.), dau. of Gen. Matthews for love and affec. to his dau. Jane, part of mil. wt. No. 1934, issued Nov. 2, 1780 by Va. to said Geo. Matthews, 1,500 set apart for a survey May 18, 1785 in Dist. soldiers of Rev. war, etc. Mar. 1804

Mav. George, dep'n. (Box 17-33, Franklin Co. Dist. Ct.) at his home in Dinwiddie Co., Va. July 15, 1795.

May, Jemima (Orders Mercer Co. p. 186) appt'd. gdn. to her chn. Harriet, Emily, Thomas ana Horatio May, Nov. 7, 1825.

May, Henry, adm'n. granted, Nov. 7, 1825, p. 186.

McAfee, Jas., decd. (Order A, 38 Scott Co.) on motion of Jas. Craig, admn. is gt'd. him on the estate of Jas. McAfee, decd. who thereupon took oath and entered into and acknowledged bond with sec'y. as law directs, Dec. 23, 1794.

McClure, (Thos.) Hrs. (C–20–Scott Co. 1818) Jenet McClure, relict of ––––– decd., John McClure, ––McClure, Caty McC., Nancy, –––––––, Robt. McFerson and wife Jenny, Alex. Stephenson and wife Nancy, heirs of aforesaid Thos. McClure, decd.

Meek, Jas. (K-26 Woodford Co.) of Woodford Co., Oct. 2, 1823, for love and affec. to Geo. Caplinger of Fayette for many acts of friendship, 118 acres I reside on–James Meek, 9-22-1825 to Samuel Wallace,, land on Lees br. of So. Elk., part of tract of Jas. Meek, Sr., d. poss'd. of and in div'n. of est. allotted to Jas. Meek of Greenup Co.–divided as lot no. 4. (K-416, Woodford Co.) Joseph Meek of Tenn. 9-26-1826, to Christian Wallace, whereas said Meek by last will of his uncle Jas. Meek did make Joseph Meek his nep. one of his heirs (L-199, Woodford Co.)–John Meek of Clay Co., Mo–8-6-1830 to Sam'l. L. Wallace (M-311, Woodford Co.)

McCoun, James, Jr. (deed 7, p. 356, Mercer Có.) legatees, Aug. 28, 1809–Lawrence McGuire and wife Margaret, Eliz. McCoun, Polly McCoun, (land in Franklin Co.) John H. Gibson and wife Anna A. Gibson, (wits. Robt. McAfee, and Samuel McCoun).

James McCoun, decd. legatees, Dec. 27, 1802. John McCoun, John McGee and wife Polly, Samuel Adams and wife Jane (5-12 deeds, Mercer Co.)

McGee, John–Hrs.–(deed 11, p. 355, Nelson Co.) Eliz. McGee, widow of John, decd. and those about 21: Thos. McGee, and wife Eliz., John B. F. McGee, James McGee, Isaac Cox and wife Jane, Jonathan Cox and wife Polly, and others for heirs under 21, July 18, 1811.

McGinnis, Agness (Mercer Co. Orders–1823-1827 p. 19) wife of Jesse McGinnis, is dau. of Mrs. Sarah Hix, (late Sarah Lee) whose husband was James Hix, now decd. Proof ordered to be certified Aug. 5, 1823–proved by Benj. Durham, Samuel Daviess, etc.

McIntyre, Joseph (Nuncp., Fleming Co., wills A–365) (May 1, 1815)–names dau. Betsy, lame and to have a slave–rest of his ch., his bro. Aaron to manage–Mary Richthie and Rachel Chapman, wts. he died Feb. 8, 1815.

Joseph McIntyre, (F-81) will dated May 24, 1837–Michael Hedrick, exr. widow Mary and heirs–Aug. 28, 1837, Fleming Co.

Elizabeth Elliott, late widow of John McIntyre, dower, and 4 divisions (heirs not named) Jan. 23, 1837–(F-1, Fleming Co. wills)

McKnight, Andrew (Box 70-83, Franklin Co. Dist. Ct., Cir. Ct. files) deposes that he came to Ky. in 1795.

McLaughlin, James dep'n. (in case of Jack vs Russell Willson, Box 472, Fayette Cir. Ct.) says he came to Fayette from Maryland about 33 yrs. ago, and lived a mile from Jacob Carsner, and Mrs. Carsner his mother lived with Jacob. John McLaughlin said his father came from Md. about 1784 when he was 7 years of age, filed 7-12-1817.

McPherson, John heirs (Logan Co., Ky. deeds F p. 352)–May 6, 1817, Evan McPherson, Murdock McP., and Wm. McP. heirs, of Logan Co. to Thos. Towsend.

McQuiddy, Thos. (Franklin Co. Orders K-271) heirs proven–Oct. 15, 1838–Mary Newman, wife of Thos. V? Newman hath departed this life, leaving Thos., Ann, John, Jane, Eveline, and Sarah Newman her only ch. and heirs; and that Sarah Pate has d. leaving Mary, Poindexter, Will and Thos. Pate, her only heirs.

Montgomery, James (Franklin Co. Order bk. 1, p. 12) proven soldier of Rev. He was a Lieut. and d. Jan. 1787, intestate and without issue. His elder bro. Wm. Montgomery of Franklin Co. Feb. 15, 1830.

Moore, Jonathan (Order E. p. 46, Bath County, Ky.) Wm. Moore came into court, Jan. 1852, 12th, and says he is a bro. to Jonathan Moore who d. in the spg. of 1827 or 8–he was m. to Susan Smith, and had 4 ch. when he d.; and his wife shortly after had another–the names of the ch. are Elizabeth, Polly, Sarah, Isaac and Catherine–Eliz. m. John S. Richards, Polly m. Jas. Richards, and she d., then James Richards m. Sarah; sometime after the death of Jonathan Moore his widow, Susan, m. Jas. C. Stancliff, and at the division Aug. 1841, Stancliff and wife moved to Missouri.

Marshall, Robert, decd. (Mason Co. Estates B, p. 104, May 1800); Admr. of estate granted Robert Marshall Jr. (Orders D, p. 118, Apr. 1801); Div. of estate of Robert Marshall (C, p. 191) Robert Marshall decd.–to M. Marshall for motion, to T. Marshall, clerk (this for recording); to Md. from Downing; to boarding Hannah and the children, five, from Aug. 17 to Sept. 24; to 2 qts. of whiskey for burial; to M. Marshall 1/3 personal property; to Ro. Marshall 1/3 of ditto; to legatees per account rendered 1801 to 1810; Henry Marshall's dept'n. ordered recorded (not found) (D, p. 192); To Robert Marshall $250.00 making his allottment equal with James Curtis, Simon R. Baker, Alex. Edwards and Robert Marshall assignee of John Hurst--their divisions added together. Note: Robert Marshall Jr. was a Revolutionary soldier, born in Md. and resided at time of enlistment seven miles from Hagerstown, he was in Boone and Campbell Cos. Ky. after leaving Mason Co., the other child of Robert Marshall Sr. was Elizabeth m. Jacob Edwards, 1779, he born 1753 and they had Sarah Emily b. 1780 m. 1796 James Curtis, Milly m.

John Hurst, Mary m. Simon R. Baker and Alexander Curtis. Jacob Edwards d. Mason Co. 1791 and Richard Marshall was exr. The will of John Hurst. Fairfax Co. Va. mentions gr. dau. Elizabeth Marshall (Will March 10, 1787–Dec. 21–1789); Robert Marshall Sr. moved to Fairfax Co. Va. from Maryland. See Fairfax Census; see wills of Richard Marshall and wife Mary Marshall, Charles Co. Md. 1750 and 1782 respectively.

Morris, Daniel (Fayette Co. deeds, B. p. 330) whereas I, Daniel Morris, did leave money and lawsuits in Delaware to be carried on by my sons Curtis and John Morris and when gained to be divided between Curtis and John Morris, Zebulon Hopkins, John Hopkins and Ephraim Polk, and if they agreed to have paid their parts of the lawsuit, etc. and they did not–I disclaim all right and title they have and give it to Curtis and John Morris, Nov. 8, 1806.

Morrison, Robt. (p. 33, Complete Record E. Franklin Cir. Ct.) heirs, Dec. 1814, Joseph, David, Robert, John and Wm. Morrison, Alex. Henderson and wife Elizabeth.

Morton, Thos. Evans (Gen. Court deeds A, p. 3-?–John Adams S. Carolina, wts.–Franklin County, Ky.) and Mary Ann Morton of Edgefield Dist., S. Car., apt. David Clarkson of Albemarle Co., att'y. to us as gdns of, Wm. Ragland Morton, Thos. Walker Morton and John Rhodes Morton of Ky. Nov. 1801.

Muldrow, Rachel (M-552, Woodford Co. deeds) widow of Col. Andrew M., decd. recently departed this life, will, etc. in favor of Margaret P. Thomson wife of Sam'l. T., said Samuel being desirous etc. she being niece of said Rachel Muldrow, sell to Caleb Worley of Lex., June 23, 1832.

Macey, Alex (heirs names in suit in Box 541, Franklin Cir. Ct.) with Clement Bell, etc. heirs of Andrew Steele. Charles Macey d., will, wife Polly heirs: Eliza. Ann Macey, Wm, Alex. Macey, Reuben Thomas Macey, Silas N. Macey, ch.–Eliza. Ann after death of her father m. Morgan B. Chinn, Sally Bryan d. leaving husband Jas. Bryan and only one child, Robt. Alex. Bryan.

McConnell, Alex. (Box 188-89, Franklin Dist. Ct.) in Scott Co., Mar. 19, 1806, deposes that he settled in Lex. in spring of 1779, coming to Ky. in 1778.

Mackey vs. Watkins–(Box 70-83, Dist. Ct. Franklin Cir. Ct.)–Mr. Thos. Mackey, c/o of Ebenezer Stott, Petersburg, Va., a letter from Isaac Coles, from Phil, Dec. 30, 1795 (Mem. Congress) Silcock, a soldier in Amer. Army, decd. Col. Isaac Coles of Halifax Co., Va. Mem. Congress.

Martin. James (Woodford Co., Ky. Order bk. F. p. 207, Jan. 1833) decd. was a revolutionary soldier, and William, James and Anthony Martin his heirs, says, Jeptha Dudley, he was a Corporal, James Martin now lives in Mo.

Moss, Francis (deed N. 362 Franklin Co.–see will) heirs–Benj. Cox and wife Eliz., James Church, James Moss, Wm. Stephen Moss, Daniel Berry Moss, and Polly, Samuel Moss, Jesse Moss, John Moss, and Nancy Moss, heirs of Francis Moss, their int. in land of late Francis Moss at death of Polly Moss and still undivided, Oct. 18, 1830.

Patty Withers suit box 585–Bourbon Co., Ky. vs Wm. McClelland) Contains will of Thomas Massie, Fanquier Co., Va. as follows: wife Dolly, son John, dau. Nancy Triplett, ch.: Asa, Thos. Saml. Josias, Benj. Moreland and Jno. Massie. Mentions negros made over to his ch. by John Moreland; ch., Robert, Dolly and Nimrod; "my ten children", land he claims in Kentucky; wife and Joseph Chilton exrs. Oct. 20, 1801–wts: Jos. Chilton, Edward Shacklett, John Cooke and Jon. Smith, Dec. 28, 1801. Deposition of William Latham was acquainted with John Suddeth for yrs., and with his ch.: William, James, Margaret (Peggy) who. m. John Hood, John, Mary (Polly) and Millard (Milly), had understood another dau., Susannah had m. Reuben Clark and was still in Virginia, another son, Lewis, was lost at the Battle of River Raisin. Deposition of George Pinkard of Millersburg 1817– was formerly acquainted with Thomas Spillman of King George Co., Va. and his family– he was m. and had children, among whom William, his eldest, Wm. Spillman, also was m. and had children to wit: Nancy, Jane, James, Susan who survived their father; said Thomas Spillman d. 1782 or 3 leaving William who moved about 1801 or 2 and year after he moved to his neighborhood, William d.–Nancy was 20 or upwards at father's death, Jane 18, James 15, Susan not less than nine; that the names of the children of Thomas Spillman are: William, Rebecca, Thomas, Lettice and Margaret by his first wife and John, Sarah, and Samuel by his second wife and Samuel was two or three years old at his father's death.

Meyers, Jacob (Ct. of Appeals, p. 547, Jan. 21, 1814–Jacob Meyers will in Lincoln Co.) decd. Michael Myers and wife, Jacob Meyers and wife Barbara, David Meyers and wife Docia, Abraham Bosler and wife Rebecca, Benj. Meyers and wife of Lincoln Co., Lewis Myers and wife Betsy of Garrard Co., Jacob Bearn and wife Mary of Washington Co., Ky. deed to John Meyers of Bullitt Co., children of Jost Meyers, decd. bro. of Jacob Meyers decd. devised to them by Jacob Meyers, decd. John Meyers of Bullit Co., son of Jost Meyers, decd. and wife Hannah (P-544)

Mount (Shelby County, Ky. Cir. Ct. records) Mount's heirs vs. Mount–Thos Mount said his father, Thos. Mount d. (will, Oct. 30, 1815), left Ezekiel, Mathers?, Amos, John, Eliz. Mount, Mary Barnett and husband John B., Rhoda Besly? and her husb. James B., Hannah Mattox, Letitia Swindler, James and Thos. Mount, Eliz. and Mary Mount, Wm. & Sally Mount and an infant of Fanny Mount, unknown, who are heirs of Wm. Mount, decd. and Thos. Mount and Eliza Mount who has intermarried with Wm. C – – – ? and Wm. Mount, Mathias, Maria, Mary, James and Joseph Mount heirs of Joseph Mount, decd. heirs and legal reps. (Jonathan Swindler named) Ans. of John, Alfred and Wm. Mount, Joseph Williams and wife Polly (Mount), Samuel H. Mitchell, and wife Lena (Mount), Boston Holly and wife Harriet (Mount), heirs of Thos. Mount, decd. by Thos. Mount son of decd.–say they are heirs of Elijah Mount, Decd. one of the hrs. of Thos. Mount, decd.; most of them are nonresidents, Ezekiel, Mathias, Amos, Mary Barnett, Hannah Maddox, James, Thos., Eliz. Mary Williams, Sally, John, unknown heirs of Fanny Mount, Betsy, Thos., Eliz. Coghill and Wm. C., Wm Mount, Nancy, Mathias, Maria, Mary, James, Jasper, Etc. (suit June 3, 1824)

Montgomery, Wm. (Lincoln Co. Order bk. 1795-1798) decd. heirs–guardian appointed to James, Alex., Polly, Wm., John, Smith, Robt., and Nancy, Montgomery, heirs of Wm. M., decd. and Thos. Montgomery one of the heirs on his own part–Feb. 1795.

Montgomery, Thos. (G-366 Franklin Co. Dist. deeds) of Lincoln Co., and Alex M., bro. to said Thos., M. deed land, 1/2 of 5000 acres in Breckinridge and Daviess Cos.

Moffett, George (C1-532 Woodford deeds) and wife Sally of Augusta Co., Va., to Jas. Moffett of Rockingham Co., Va., 827 1/2 A Woodford Co., Ky. part of said George Moffett's Military Survey, July 1, 1775, Glenn's Cr.–George Moffett of Augusta Co., Va., apts.

son James Moffett of Rockingham Co., Va., atty. to execute deeds of lands to following to wit: "my bro. Robert Moffett of Woodford County and his 2 sons George Moffett and John Moffett, 350 acres land, etc. Sept. 28, 1803–(C-596) George Moffett of Augusta Co., Va. "for love and affec. toward my son George Moffett and because he is my son, I give him land on Elkhorn in ye state of Ky., on which he now lives for which I obtained a grant being for military service, 1000 acres, from Gov. of Va., June 14, 1780., also 50 acres to my dau. Margaret relict. of Gen Joseph McDowell, decd. Sept. 29, 1808–(D-428) George Moffett and wife Rebecca of Fayette Co., Ky. to Edward B. Wood, June 2, 1810, tract of land in Woodford Co., part of military land which King of Gt. Britain gave to George Moffett, Sr. for his military services, 1000 acres (E-101)

Morgan (Sept. 1834 16-336, Fayette Co. deeds) whereas, Mary Morgan, Wm. Morgan and Carolyn Morgan, heirs of James Morgan; Wm. and Daniel Morgan heirs of Daniel Morgan, and Joseph and Wm. Morgan, Sarah Withers and John and Wm. Bruce, recovered vs. Mary W. Crittenden and R. B. Parker, heirs of Alex. Parker etc.

Morehead, Chas. (will, Logan Co. Ky. D-173) my son, Charles Morehead, dau. Elvira Piper, gd. dau. Mary Murrel (under 21), gd. ch.: Margaret Wintersmith, Richard Wintersmith, and Eliza Wintersmith, my wife Margaret, my dau. Margaret Warder, dau. Harriet Briggs, dau. Eliza Curd–Oct. 2, 1828, Mar. 2, 1829.

Massie, Silvanis and Thos. (Madison Co. deeds H. p 308–Sept. 1, 1795) Both "of Madison Co. Ky." appt. Thos. Shearer atty. to dispose of lands in Virginia in Co. of Campbell.

Massie, Harris (Madison Co. deeds D, p. 400–Feb-Mar. 7, 1798) Harris Massie deeds David Massie personal property.

Morgan, Chas. (Bk. A. p. 160–deed–Hardin Co. June 1798) Styled himself "of Alleghaney Co. Pa." Morgan, Chas. (Deed "C" Hardin Co. p. 102) Wm. Lee and wife Sarah, late widow of John Morgan decd. and Jane Morgan, one of the heirs of Chas. Morgan, decd. of Nelson Co., John Archibald, and Susannah his wife, Nicholas West and Eliz. his wife, Heirs and reps. of Chas. Morgan, decd., of Hardin Co. July 2, 1805

Mav, John (will in Franklin Co. Ct. Ct. Box 357) My mother Agnes May, my wife Ann May, children (also see Owen Co. Cir. Ct. A-17 box) John and Polly May (under 21) my bros. Stephen and David May–sisters, Agnes and Lucy, my bros. George, Wm. May, and wife Ann, exs. Mar. 5, 1790–Chesterfield Co., Va., Feb. 10, 1791–wts: Chas. Johnson, John Craig–David Ross, admr.–Ann May, widow, died 1811, married Thos. Lewis, before July 3, 1797. Polly May married Daniel Epes before Feb. 21, 1815. "Mrs. Mary P. Epes, widow of Daniel Epes, decd. formerly of Va., d. in Frankfort, July 5, 1852, aged 64 (Petersburg, Va. papers-copy)

McKee, Wm., Sr. (Garrard Co., Ky. bk. D) (will) son James, 700 acres; on Sulphur Park of Russell's Creek; son David L. McKee, land in Canawa, and Cable counties, Va. gd. son Darius (under 21) son Samuel (all I have claim to as one of the heirs of John McKee late of Kers Creek, Rockbridge Co.) (decd.) sons and daus. to be equal. son Wm., land I conveyed to him in Mason Co., 500 acres in Ohio; to legal reps. of John Garrent of Goochland County, Va., 500 acres in Ohio for friendship I had for Gen'l. Garrent; 2 gd. sons Wm. and George McKee sons of Samuel McKee; to gd. dau. Mariam McKee, and gd. son, Alex. R. McKee, eldest dau. and son of David L. McKee, son Hugh W. McKee (son Hugh, exr.) May 18, 1816–Oct. 1816. Samuel McKee deeds to John Lapsley, Apr. 4,

1809 (C-392) Samuel McKee and wife Patsy, deed, Feb. 16, 1818, (F-39) Samuel McKee (will)—wife Patsy, all- her bro. Geo. Robertson, exr. Oct. 6, 1826, Dec. 11, 1826 (F-289) Mary McKee (Jas.) dau. Mary Lapsley, (will G-159) Wm. McKee (will K-249) bro. Hugh- other relations have already received—Oct. 9, 1839—Nov. 1840 (K-249)—all Garrard Co., Ky.

Smith, John and others (H. Marshall vs. Jas. Hawkins, heirs, Box 425, Franklin Cir. Ct.) came down Ohio 1773, and again 1774 with 32 men, and again 1775, etc. May 10, 1810. Flournoy, John J., of age dep'n. Jan. 19, 1818, frequently at house of Wm. Willis, who lives in Boone, built large commodious brick house, etc. his son-in-law (Willis?) lives on farm there. Sodowsky, Jacob, dep'n. at Versailles, June 5, 1818, said he was at Big Bone Lick 1774 and 5. He was with Jas. Douglas, John Floyd, Hancock Taylor, Isaac Hite, and his bro. James Sodowsky, etc. and in 1775 with Col. Abraham Hite, Peter Casey, Nath'l. Randolph, Robt. Shanklin, Peter Higgins, etc. between 1791 and 3 went to Big B. Lick, and in spg. of 1797 moved his family and settled there for 2 yrs. and 9 mos., managing Salt works; in 1784 moved his family to Ky. on Pleasant Run at Sta. called Sandusky (Sodowsky?) now Washington Co., and there a season and to where I now live in Jessamine Co., to Ky. 1774 and 1775 till Sept. 1777, returned and back fall of 1779, and here till Sept. 1780. Sodowsky, James, dep'n., about same. Edward Williams with him 1779. In 1773 was with Col. Thos. Bullitt, Jas. Harrod, Abrm. Haptonstall, Jacob Drennon, etc. In 1774 with John Cowan, David Williams, Mordecai Batson, Col. Jas. Knox, etc. 1775 with David and Edw. Williams, Wm. Stewart, Ovid McCrakin, etc. 1779 with John Scott, Chas. Cleaver, Anthony Sodowsky, Geo. Hart. Patterson, Robt., at house of John Grimes, Dayton, Ohio, Aug. 4, 1809, said in May 1778 with Gen'l. Roger Clarke's Exped. from Wheeling, ordered from Lex. Aug. 1782, with 40 militia, etc. Montgomery Co., Ohio, Benj. Vancleave, clerk (This sent to Hawkins at Port William, Ky.—Gallatin.) Hall, David, dep'n. Sept. 1, 1810, in Frankfort, said he lived in N. C. about 40 yrs. ago, man named John Finley came to that country and told him, this deponent, Daniel Boone and several others had been a prisoner among the Indians, and that he, Daniel Boone, Squire Boone, Ezekiel Smith, and 10 others came to Ky. two years or more before Boonesboro was settled etc. Hawkins, Joseph, dep'n. Boone Co., Mar. 5, 1810. Johnson, Samuel, dep'n. at home of Benj. Netherland, Jessamine Co., Apr. 28, 1810 known big Bone Lick since 1782 or spg. 1783. Smith, John (Woodford County) dep'n. at Big Bone Lick in 1773. Dickerson, Archer, aged 55 gives dep'n. at Bone Lick, Aug. 8, 1810 (born 1755) in a letter addressed to Willis Lee, Esq. dep'n. taken at home of Wm. Smith Boone Co. Ryle, Jas., Boone Co., dep'n. Mar. 5, 1810, lived there 10 or 11 yrs. Robinson, Jeremiah, aged 47, says 20 years ago he was with Robt. Connelly, etc. on Ohio river, with Capt. Thos. West, Thos. McMillian, etc. lived in Ky. since 1784, one mile from Cynthiana, July 10, 1805. Corn, Capt. George, May 27, 1805, about 43 years, at Big Bone Lick 1780, taken by Jameson Hawkins, Boone Co., 1805. Connelly, Arthur, Boone Co., Mar. 5, 1810, dep'n. says he was at Big Bone Lick, Oct. 1783. Brady, Capt. Wm., Dep'n. Boone Co. Mar. 5, 1810.

Stamper, Joshua (Mason Co. Cir. Ct., Bruce's heirs vs. Barbour's heirs, 1818—3rd shelf from top, left closet), aged 64, to Ky. fall 1779, and sett. at Strode's Sta., etc. given in dep'n. Dec. 9, 1817, Bourbon Co. Wm. Steele, (Mason Co. Cir. Ct. 1818) aged 77 years, of Bourbon Co., says he came to Ky. in 1775. John Stephenson, at home in Christian Co., "of age", May 5, 1818, says he was with Boone, etc. in 1780, and helped to bury Edward Boone, on Grassy Lick. John Smith, of Woodford County, says Oct. 29, 1818, he is 65 years of age, and that he came with John Harrod from Harrodsburg to Cabbin Cr.,

Lower Blue Licks, in 1775. James Rowland, age 47, says he sett. on Cabin Cr. 1793, and here since, is son of the widow Rowland, in Ky. in 1793, dep'n. Nov. 18, 1818. Wm. Dyal, says he came to Ky. in 1781 via the Ohio River and that Wm. Brooks is an old resident (Nov. 1819). Daniel Boone, age 84, gives dep'n. at St. Charles Ty. (Mo.) on Sept. 17, 1817, that the indians killed his brother Edward Boone, Oct. 15, 1780, etc. George Bryan, age 66 years, says in dep'n. 1818, he to Ky. in 1776 and back same year, to Ky. again in spg. of 1779 and resided at Bryan's station, part of that year and 1780, signed: "Bryan". Flanders, Calloway, age 63, at house of John B. Calloway, St. Charles Ty. Mo., Sept. 22, 1817, says he settled at Boonesborough in 1775. Robert Patterson, dep'n. says in 1817, that he knew Stone Lick in 1775 that he came from Ft. Pitt with David Perry in Nov. 1775, with Wm. McConnell, and Steven Lowry, etc. "Perry had been to Ky. before and piloted us to Leestown on the Ky. River." John McIntire, age 57, says in dep'n. of 1817— came to Ky. in 1779 by Crab Orchard, stopped at Boonesborough, and to Strode's Sta. fall of 1780 or 1781, with Col Daniel Boone, Chas. Gatliff, James Estill, James Ray, Wm. McConnell and others, 60 or 70 people, to bury, Edward Boone, bro. of Daniel Boone, and to pursue the Indians who killed him, and stopped at the Upper Blue Licks, passed Plum Lick Cr. and buried said Boone on that Creek —— many pp. taken at home of Henry Timberlake, Paris, Ky. Nov. 1-13, 1817. John Martin, at his home in Lincoln Co. Mar. 28, 1818, says he was on Cabin Cr. 1775, with John Haggin, etc. Simon Kenton, age 60, at home of Baldwin B. Stith, Aug. 16, 1814, says James Shackelford and George Farrow knew No. Fork before 1780. Wm. Stewart was killed at Blue Licks, etc. Thos. Kennedy, age 74, says on Dec. 9, 1817, in Paris, Ky., that he came to Ky. in 1776 by the Old Wilderness Rd., returned to Va. and back to Ky. in spring of 1779, and sett. at Boonesborough, then back to Va. and back to Ky. with my family and settled at Strode's Sta. till fall of 1779 and there till 1785, then where I now live, near Paris (Probably the same Thos. Kennedy who died in Campbell Co.)

Steele, Catherine Thompson (D-370, Woodford Co. deeds) late C. Steele, of Rockbridge Co., Va. apts. Peter Alexander, att'y. to sell 1000 acres located in the names of Catherine, Molly, Jinny, and Sally Steele (1/4 already laid off for Nat'l. Wilson, heir of above named Sally Steele, Jan. 14, 1808). Jas. Steele, (Woodford Co., deeds D-113,)—"of Rockbridge Co., Va." deeds to Wm. Steele of Woodford Co., Dec. 8, 1806, land in Franklin Co. pat'd. in names of David Steele, Samuel, Robt., and Jas. Steele, beg. at 3 beeches, cor. to Dennis Howley. David Steele "of Jessamine Co.",—(D-349, deeds Woodford Co.) 8-8-1808.

Stephens, Jas. B. (K. Gen. Ct., 269, Franklin Co.) and wife Leah, (formerly Banta) of Rush Co., Ind., Oct. 21, 1825, etc. heirs of Abraham Banta, now dec'd. of Rush Co., Ind., assignee of Squire Boone, (Henry & Shelby Co. lands)

Sneed, Wm. (Box 94-114, Franklin Dist. Cir. Ct. files), dep'n. Aug. 15, 1801. Last of March 1783, Mr. Thos. Ayres of Eessex Co., Va. widower m. Mary Sneed of Caroline County, late wife of Benj. Sneed, Sr., decd. (he d. 1781) of said Co. Mr. Ayres came to live on the plant. Benj. Sneed, Jr., and infant son.

Stout, (Franklin Co., Ky. Ct. records) Daniel Stout and Eliz. deed to John Payne of Mercer Co., 45 1/2 acres where Daniel Stout lives, Oct. 19, 1810. Same sells Mar. 8, 1813, 100 acres—Hammonds Cr. (D-207) Amos Stout sells lot 112, Frankfort, May 21, 1821 (I-164) Rich. Stott of Jenings Co., Ind. to Thos. Stott, (I-198) David Stout buys 83 a. on Benson, 9-20-1833 (P-11) John B. & Anna Stout, of Floyd Co., Ind. Apr. 12, 1859 (O-451)

Louisa H. Stout and Sarah N. Stout, inf. ophans of Rich. K. Stout, decd., above 14, chose Jane Stout, their gdn.–(Order Bk. M., 76, Jan. 1850). Jane Stout appt'd. gdn. to John S. Stout, inf. orph. of Rich. K. Stout, under 14, Jan. 21, 1850 (M-76 order) David Stout of Port William, Nov. 17, 1795, buys 2 lots of Cave Johnson, (A-51). Jonathan Stout, Mar. 25, 1808, from Sam'l. Hutton, 37 1/2 a. on Hammonds Cr., Franklin Co. Daniel Stout and John Arbuckle, wts. (B-308). Daniel Stout buys (1808, Jan. 20)–100 a. Hez. Stout and Jonathan Hutton, wts. (B-310). Jonathan Stout and wife Agnes, Mar. 1, 1809 of Franklin Co. to Jos. Everett 37 1/2 a. on Hammonds Cr. Daniel Stout, Sr. and Jr. wts. (C-133)

Smith, Obediah (F-Gen'l. Ct. Franklin Co., Ky. deeds) Wm. Watts of Orange Co., Va., Peter F. Smith and Jordan Smith both of Chesterfield, Co., Va., 3 co-heirs of Obediah Smith, decd. of Chesterfield Co., Va. appoint John H. Smith, who is himself remaining heir of said Obediah Smith, decd. attorney to sell and convey patent of 62,781 acres in Ky. to which said Wm. Watts and the three Smiths are entitled as heirs, July 30, 1815.

Searcy, Bartlett (Box 21, Woodford Co. Ct. Ct.), d. 17–left widow Ann S., now Ann Reardon, and John, Elijah and Sarah Searcy, infants, Apr. 10, 1794.

Scott, John A. (Franklin Co. Order M. p. 70) heirs: Wm. L. Scott, Lewis W. Scott, Levi Scott, and James Scott, only brothers, and Nancy Harrod, sister of John A. Scott decd., who was private in Co. C, in 1st Reg't. Ky. Vol Cavalry, never married, no wife and children, Nov. 12, 1849.

Scott, Matthew (L-416, deeds, Garrard) heirs–June 15, 1835, Esther Scott, widow and Cynthia, Becky, Sally, James, Jincy, Susan, Betty (Billy?) Nathan, Mary Ann, Henry and Nancy.

Scott, Nathaniel heirs (deed, Garrard Co., L-438, 1835) Hannah Scott, widow, Malissa Scott, Milton Tracey and wife Manaley, David Scott and wife Juretta, of Shelby Co., and Elijah Scott, lately of Garrard Co., to Joshua Dunn.

Scott, James, decd. (deed C. p. 219, Feb. 20, 1813, Adair Co. deeds), heirs: John Scott, Elijah, Stephen and Phebe Scott of Adair, Thos. Scott of Lincoln, Jane Ewing and her husband Robert Ewing–(she m. said Ewing of Cumberland Co., Ky.)

Shipp, Rich. W. (D-30, old Franklin Co. deeds–P-119, order A. p. 3, Scott Co.) Aug. 20, 1786, Va. patented to R. W. Shipp and Coleby Shipp 3603 A. (same not divided) Rich. W. Shipp d. leaving Polly Shipp, Wm. Shipp, Dudley S., and Sally Shipp (Martin Hawkins having m. Polly) deed Oct. 3, 1810, bet. sd. Martin Hawkins and Polly. Colby Shipp and Wife Sally, (Laban, Margaret A. and Meune? Shipp, wts.) (May 1, 1811 Franklin Deeds P, p. 119). Rich. Shipps heirs, gd'n. Wm. and Sarah, gd'n. 1798, div'n. to Martin Hawkins a child's part, Joab Shipp, Wm. Shipp, Turner Shipp, Dudley Shipp (each a child's part (Scott Co. Orders A. p. 31). Jan. 27, 1800, Heirs of Wyatt Shipp, deceased: Polly, Sally, Turner and Dudley, 1798, Eliz. Kay, dower (Scott Co. Orders A p. 83).

Silva, Samuel, (K-348, Orders, Franklin Co.) late pensioner, d. Sept. 18, 1839, cert. 1569, Franklin Co., Feb. 27, 1835–Susan Silva, widow, living Dec. 16, 1839.

Simmons, Johnson (Q-433, Madison Co. deeds) and wife Peggy, Oct. 3, 1825, deed to John Simmons their part in property of John Simmons, decd. left to his 2 sons Johnson and John Simmons.

Sisk, Pluright (Woodford Co. deed, E-26, 1809) and wife Ruth. Sisk, Ellen (Q-532, Wood-ford Co., deeds) "of Rappahanock Co., Va." apts. John Jett, att'y. to receive from T. W. Sellers, exr. of my father Geo. Shelton, late of Woodford Co., Ky., int. I have in his est.

Slaughter, Jesse, decd. (Mercer Co. Orders, p. 121, Dec. 1, 1824) Motion of Edmund Burris and wife Polly, Jesse Slaughter, Gabriel Slaughter, Jr. (by Gabriel, Sr. his gdn.) Wm. B. Slaughter, Francis T. Slaughter, Daniel (David?) S. Slaughter, Thos. Slaughter, Lewis Slaughter, and Sally, his wife and Susanna H. Slaughter who are the only heirs of said decd. etc.—division of lands, etc.

Smith, Obediah, heirs (deed F. p. 288, Franklin Co.) Wm. Watts of Orange Co., Va., Peter F. Smith of Chesterfield, Co., Va., Jordan Smith of same, three of co-heirs of Obediah Smith, decd. of Chesterfield, appoint John H. Smith (remaining heir of said Obediah) of Woodford Co., Ky. att'y. Jan. 30, 1815, 62,781 Acres.

Smith, Ezekiel (Franklin Co. deeds), "of Windsor, Co. of Middlesex, N. J." from Levi Coven-hoven, of Ky., (Woodford Co.) Sept. 26, 1793 Joseph Covenhoven, wts. Smith, Ezekiel of Windsor, in Co. of Middlesex, N. J. to Levi Covenhoven, of Ky., tract 16299, etc. to E Smith, 9000 acres, May 4, 1784, from Va., part of another tract in Nelson Co., bet. Salt River and Chaplin Fork (Wm. and Martin Hogland, Jr., wts.)

Sollars, Isaac, (order A. p. 48, Will A. p. 27) Inv., Feb. 23, 1790, Mason Co., Ky. Eliz. Sollars, admx. Jan. 1790 A-343, suit: Eleanor Sollars by her att'y. vs. John Lewis and wife Ann Lewis, Mary Sollars, inf. orphan of Isaac S., over 14 chose Eliz. S. her gdn. Aug. 1793, and she apt'd. gdn. to Ruth, Eleanor, Samuel, Isaac and Eliz. S.

Stephens, Rich. (see 1-16, Box, Franklin Dist. Ct., Boone vs. Boone, Vancleave) heir to Joseph S., decd. entry Big Bone Lick, Apr. 29, 1780; also Nicholas Smith said he 1st came to Boones Old Sta., 1785, there 3 yrs. dep'n. taken Shelby Co., Sept. 5, 1795.

Winchester, Stephen (Ct. of Appeals deeds, M-62) of Fredericksburg, Va. to Chester Clark, of Bennington Co., Vt., Jan. 19, 1808.

Webb, Aden (p. 216, Vol 3, Lexington, Ky.)—Isabell Robinson, spinster of Jessamine County, Ky. to bro-in-law Aden Webb of same house carpenter, power of att'y. to recover any-thing coming to her, Isabell, by her grandmother Sarah Leslie, also from John Henry, Rockingham Co., signed at Lexington, Ky. Mar. 21, 1799. Webb, Adin, (p. 216, Vol 3, Chalkley, records of Augusta County, Va.)—of Jessamine Co. in right of his wife Mary, who was Mary Robertson, a devisee of Sarah Lessley and as attorney for Isabell Robert-son above, conveys to Samuel Lessley, etc. John Henry of Rockingham married Jane Robertson.

White, Ambrose (Pensioner)—(see Franklin Co. wills, records, etc. see Court of Appeals, N-133)—First wife was Elizabeth—he was from Bedford County, town of Liberty, Va. as deed shows in 1810.

White Ambrose and wife Elizabeth of Franklin Co., Ky. deed to John D. Helm of Bedford County, Va., lot No. 30 in town of Liberty, Bedford Co., Va., Feb. 7, 1810. (Jas. and Wm. White and Peggy Phillips, wts.)

Wallace, Michael (will, B-173, Garrard Co., Ky.) Feb. 18, 1808, Apr. 1808—wife Anne, (graveyard), son, Williams's orchard—son Michael, youngest son Josiah (the Bible), dau. Hannah Anderson, son John—names in order—William, Hannah, John, Michael, Atten,

Elizabeth, Shannon, Sarah Duff, and Josiah (150 acres in dispute bt. of McBride) son-in-law, Jas. Anderson, to Polly Miles, step dau. of my dau. Mary Giles--son John's son Cantly Wallace. Deed--Shannon Wallace and wife Eliz., Wm. Wallace and wife Lucy, to their mother Sarah Wallace, slave, Sept. 24, 1834, land she lives on willed to her by our father Wm. Wallace, decd.--170 acres (L-325) Garrard Co. Wm. Wallace (Garrard Co. Will Bk. E-436) wife Sarah, oldest son Salem, son Rankin (youngest ch. under age) land in Green Co., Ky. pt. of 30 acre entered in name of Alex. Reed, Michael Wallace, and myself--3rd son Shannon Wallace, 4th son Taylor? W. 9 each of minor ch.--Eliz. R. W., Wm. Wallace, Jason W., Arnon W., and Sarah Ann Wallace--sons Salem and Rankin, exrs. Oct. 1, 1824. (Jas. Wallace)

Ward, Isaac, (Box 182, Franklin Co. Dist. Ct.) about 33 years, (Apr. 27, 1807) gives disposition in Franklin Co., at res. of M. Clark, says he lived 7 years on Benson and was hunting with his uncle James Arnold, in 1786 or 1787, on Benson.

Watkins, Benj. Sr. (E-155, Woodford Co., Ky.)--1810 of Powhattan Co., Va. by Benj. Watkins, Jr. his att'y. of Woodford Co. to Joel Dupuy of Woodford Co., 92 a. part of 1,000 a. survey in name of Benj. Watkins, etc. Joseph Watkins wts.

Walls, Maj. George--heirs (Hardin Co., Ky. deeds, C-461) Samuel Patton and wife Elizabeth, Samuel Duree and wife Anna D. (late Walls), Christopher Miller and wife Mary (late Walls), and Samuel Walls, legatees and heirs of Maj. George Walls, decd. appoint our bro. George Walls of Bourbon Co., Ky., att'y. to sell lands except 400 acres in Woodford Co., in name of Thos. Walls which we get by heirship from our late father George Walls, and our late bro. Thos. Walls. Jan. 20, 1808.

Wallace, Robert (C-349, Mason Deeds) and wife Sarah, of Fayette Co., 8-22-1794 deed to Robt. Campbell, 300 acres in Mason, part of 3000 acres preemption made to Robt. Wallace on Johnston's Fork of Licking. R. W. assignee of Wm. Hays. Walace, Robt. (Deed E--Mason Co.) of Warren Co., Dec. 4, 1798, deeds to Andrew Linn, land in Mason. Wallace, Robt. of Warren, 6-18-1821, to Wm. & Johnston, 200 a. in Mason, pat'd. to Wallace 1792, claim proved inferior to claim of Thos. Bodley, patent for 16000 a., Apr. 21, 1798. Wallace bt. of Bodley (X-224, Mason deeds) Wallace, Robt. of Barren Co. June 1821. Mason Co.

Warnock, Michael (Franklin Dist. Ct., Box. 188-189), in a dep'n. at Georgetown, Scott Co., Mar. 1806, says he came to Lex., Ky. in fall preceding the winter of 1780, and in Lex. 3 yrs.

Whitehead, Rich, heirs (Dec. 23, 1814, p. 36 Complete Records "E", Franklin Cir. Ct., p. 41) John Whitehead apt. gdn. to Rich. and Geo. Whitehead. Wyatt Jones and wife Lucy, John Davis and wife Sally, Harry Rainey and wife Martha, Nat'l. Hare and wife Polly, John Whitehead, Geo., and Wm., and Richard Whitehead, heirs of Rich. decd. 1814.

Wilmore, Jane (Jessamine Co. deeds, E-417), widow of John W., decd. late of Pa. and Co. of Summerset and Jas. Wilmore, Jacob Wilmore, Hannah W., Thos. Hawkins and wife Ann, (late A. W.), John W., Jane Wilmore heirs and reps. of John Wilmore, decd. apt. Geo. Walker of Jessamine Co., to get lands, etc. in Pa., Jan. 21, 1819.

Wood, Daniel (Feb. 20, 1835, p. 193, Acts of Ky., 1834-1835) of Mason Co., d. intestate, leaving Elizabeth, Maria, David, Benjamine, Thos., Alfred, and Samuel Wood, all minors under 21.

Woods, Samuel, Sr. (p. 217, Orders, Mercer Co.) proof that he was a Rev. soldier, that he d. Feb. 3, 1826.

Woods, John (Order B. p. 322, Mercer Co. Ct.) orphan of David Woods, decd.—Hugh Logan, by an order of the Botetourt Co. Ct. is appointed his gd'n.

Wright, Wm. heirs (complete records, Land Cases, Lincoln Co. Cir. Ct. not paged or indexed) "in chancery", Aug. 3, 1805, bill, James Wright, Samuel Wright, Polly W., Hannah W., Sally and Wm. Wright, infants under 21, by Samuel Wright, next best friend, and also Cornelius Welding, husband of Jenny Welding late J. Wright, his reps., their father bt. land, etc.

West, Chas. (will, Scott Co. F-58) of Lexington, Jan. 14, 1833—nieces, children of my decd. bro. Ignatius West, 2 daus. of decd. bro. Thos. West, "I forget their names, but they are unmarried"—nephew Henry West, son of Ignatius West—to Frances and Rebecca West, daus. of Samuel West of Scott Co. and his son Albert West, exrs. Jan. 14, 1833—Aug. 1833.

West, Wm. P., 48, m., b. Va., son of John and Athey West, d. Nov. 27, 1852 (Owen Co. statistics—Ky. Historical Society)

Withers, James (Woodford Co., deeds, K-326) decd., heirs—Fauquier Co., Va., Mar. 21, 1825 —Thos. Withers of Woodford Co., Ky., Eliz. Withers, Wm. Campbell and Dickerson Wood and wife Hannah, Lucy Davis, John Wilson and wife Cynthia, John Cain Withers, Wm. Withers, Enoch Withers, John Withers, Presley Payne and wife Cynthia, Francis Payne and wife Patsy, ——? Redwell and his wife Sally, legatees and reps. of Jas. Withers, decd

ALPHABETICALIZED NAMES NOT IN GENERAL INDEX

Atchison, James, Sr., 67th year, d. at residence in Scott Co. (Com., Apr. 24, 1868).

Alexander, Mrs. Harriet W., 57, wife of G. Alexander, wife, mother, etc. d. Mar. 29, 1867 (Apr. 2, 1867 Com.).

Arnold, Mrs. Sophia, 64, d. at home of son-in-law, Henry Birchfield, left a widow with three inf. daus. early; a Bap. (Sept. 25, 1855 Com.).

Ashurts, Mrs. Rebecca, 84, d. Sept. 24, 1855 (Oct. 15, 1855 Com.).

Alston Col. Wm. of the Rev., aged 83, d. June 26, in Charleston, S. C. (July 16, 1839 Com.)

Adams, Henry

Alston, Col. Wm of the Rev., aged 83, d. June 26, in˙Charleston, S. C. (July 16, 1839 Com)

Adair, Gen. John—of Astoria, Ore. Ty.—his dau. Ellen Adair m. at Astoria, Ore., Oct. 8, 1858, Lieut. Geo. ˙H. Wendell, U.S.A., Gen. Adair, formerly of Ky. (Dec. 20, 1858 Com.)

Adams, Mrs. Catherine Elizabeth—At res. of Mrs. Innis, Mrs. Adams d. in this Co., dau. of late Judge Innis of Ky., and relict of Samuel G. Adams of Richmond, Va. . . . in her 56th year. (Nov. 23, 1836 Com.)

Alexander, Miss Mary Ann . . . , formerly of Ohio, m. Tuesday. May 23, 1843, in Jacksonville, Ill., Dr. Wm. M. Long, formerly of Ky. (June 6, 1843 Com.)

Anderson, Mrs. M., relict of Worsham A., d. in Mason Co. aged 70 yrs. (Apr. 1, 1834 Com.)

Anderson, O. H. P. has house for sale, property of Reuben Anderson, decd. between Bagging Factory and Penitentiary. (Sept. 14, 1838. Com.)

Anderson, Reuben, d. last Mon., aged 72 yrs. (Wed. Apr. 13, 1837, Com.)

Andrews, John—formerly of Fleming Co., d. Brenham, Washington Co, Tex., Sept. 20, 1853, aged 61 yrs. (Oct. 25, 1853 Com.)

Atchison, Wm., Sr. . . . late of Fayette Co., b. Carlisle, Pa., Feb. 2, 1780, d. at res. of son in Clay Co., Mo., Jan. 20th, (Feb. 21, 1854 Com.)

Atkinson, Maj. . . . home in Russellville, death in list of Cholera victims, (1835, Aug. 1 Com.).

Ayres, Mrs. Agnes, wife of Walter Ayres, d. aged 57, Woodford Co., Sept. 22, 1837. (Wed. Oct. 4, 1837 Com.)

Ayres, Walter, 60, d. Woodford Co., (5-21-1838. Com.)

Alexander, John D., Senator in Legis. 1843, Marrowbone, Cumberland Co., Ky. b. in Ky. 1805 (Com.)

Abell, Jesse, Rep. in State Legis, 1843, Lebanon, Ky. b. in Md. 1780. (Com.)

Baker, Obediah, in Gen'l. King's Brigade in last war, d. in Cumberland Co., the 19th (Tues. May 28, 1839 Com.)

Bass, Emily E.—see Rich. Gillespie.

Beall, Samuel m. at Bardstown, Oct. 22, 1833, Eliz. Ann Duvall, dau. of Gov. Wm. P. Duvall, of Fla. (Oct. 22, 1833 Com.)

Belt, Osborn m. Mrs. Frances McCrackin, Jan. 12, (Jan. 19, 1841 Com.)

Berry, George, aged 78, d. in Scott Co., May 10, 1839 (Com. May 28, 1839)

Berryman, Thos. A., see Mrs. Nancy Wells.

Bingham, Col.—see Wiggington.

Blackburn, Jonathan, d. in 58th year Feb. 11, 1834 (Com. Mar. 11, 1834)

Blackburn, Geo., eldest son of Thos. Blackburn, d. at res. of his father on last Sat. eve, in Scott Co., youth, consumption, lived in Frankfort for several years. (Com. Apr. 10, 1839)

Blackburn, Thos., aged 82, d. 22nd at 4 A.M., in Scott Co. (Fri. Nov. 29, 1867 Com.)

Blythe, Jas. E., of Hanover, Ind., m. Mary C., dau. of late Joseph Venable, in Shelby Co., 14th ult. (Nov. 10, 1840)

Boyd, Mrs. Nancy, wife of Wm. Boyd, aged 63 years, native of Bedford Co., Va., came to Ky. soon after her marriage in about 1797, member of Presby. Church since 1801, left orphans, aged and afflicted partner, d. Mon. 3rd. (Aug. 11, 1840, Com.)

Branham, Mrs. Sarah, 78th year, d. Scott Co., May 11. (June 4, 1839 Com.)

Brasfield, Maj. W. R., aged 74, d. in Clark Co. (Com. June 3, 1839)

Brown, Miss Marietta B., see W. R. Finley.

Bryant, John, b. in Powhatan Co., Va., Jan. 1760, d. July 4 in Garrard Co., a Rev. soldier. (Com. July 16, 1833.)

Buckley, Capt. Wm., 83rd year, early pioneer of Ohio Valley, soldier of the Rev. under Geo. R. Clark, d. last Sun. (Maysville Eagle Sept. 2, 1840) (Com. Sept. 8, 1840.)

Bullock, Mrs. Caroline Breckinridge, dau. of late Joseph Cabell Breckinridge, d. Nov. 4, 1867 in Baltimore, Md.—large family. (Fri. Nov. 29, 1867, Com.)

Blackburn, Thos., aged 82, d. 22nd at 4 A.M., in Scott Co. (Fri. Nov. 29, 1867—Com.)

Berkley, Mrs., wife of Daniel Berkley, of Clark Co., burned to death in Clark Co. (Com. Apr. 30, 1867)

Blackburn, Mrs. Ann E., aged 73, d. June 1, 1867 (July 7, 1867, Com.)

Brown, Col. Orlando, aged 66, d. July 26, 1867, born in Frankfort, kind father and husband. (Com. July 30, 1867)

Butler, Mrs. Eliza S., 68 years, widow of Pierce B., d. in Maysville at res. of Thos. M. Green, July 28, 1867, dau. of distinguished John Allen of Shelby Co., 3 ch.: Mrs. Thos. M.

Green of Maysville, Col. Russell Butler of Frankfort, Capt. Wm. Butler of Carrollton; buried at Carrollton, (Com. Aug. 9, 1867).

Buckner, Aylett H., of Clark Co. bar. (Memoriam of, Com. Sept. 20, 1867)

Bristow, Samuel, formerly of Franklin, d. at Whitley's Point, Moultrie Co., Ill. on May 18th. (Com. June 5, 1868)

Banta, Mrs. Nancy G., aged about 66 years, d. Dec. 10, at home of her son H. G. Banta— Meth. Church (Com. Dec. 11, 1868)

Bacon, Mrs. Sarah Jane, 56 years, d. at Ft. Clark, Tex., Feb. 27, 1869, of this place. (Com. Mar. 26, 1869)

Brown, Preston, aged 66 years, 4 mos., and 7 days, d. at Lexington, McLean Co., Ill., Mon. July 19, 1869, son of Jesse and Eliz. Brown, b. Mar. 13, 1803, on South Elkhorn, 6 mi. from Frankfort, 7th son of 11 children; to Ill. in 1834, next year m. Millie, eldest dau. of John Scroggin of Franklin Co., 4 children, all dead, leaves widow. (long obit.) (Com. Mon. July 19, 1869)

Bush, Izzard Bacon, d. on 20th in Anderson Co., aged 63 (Com. Nov. 26, 1869.)

Butler, Mrs. Catherine, 76, widow of Tobias B., of Jeff. Co. (Com. Mon, Feb. 26, 1855.)

Belt, Osborn, of this County, d. in Fleming Co. the 7th, late merchant of Frankfort. (Apr. 16, 1855 Com.)

Blackburn, Mrs. Prudence, d. in St. Louis at res. of son E. C. Blackburn, May 21, 1855, in 72nd year. (Com. 1855.)

Bartley, Robt., d. in Scott Co., in 76th year, Oct. 15, (Com. Nov. 13, 1855)

Bush, Samuel S. of Gallatin Co., Tenn, m. Miss Mary Ann Cornelia, dau. of Judge Z. Wheat and granddau. of Hon. Ben Monroe, Tues. eve. (Com. Mon, Oct. 15, 1855.)

Blunt, Mrs. Clarinda, wife of Jas. F. Blunt, b. in Morgan Co., Ky., Sept. 6, 1829. m. Feb. 22, 1853, d. Aug. 22, 1865, etc. at Beattyville, Ky. (Com. Nov. 10, 1865.)

Blackburn, Capt. E. M., aged 81 years, d. 18th at Spring Sta., (Com. Mar. 22, 1867.)

Brown, Mrs. C. W., aged 65, widow of Geo. L. Brown, of Nicholasville d. Oct. 2, 1867. (Com. Oct. 11, 1867)

Conway, Mrs. Susan, wife of Jesse P. C., d. June 15, 1867. (Com. June 21, 1867.)

Churchill, Mary B., dau. of Col. Samuel B. Churchill of Frankfort, m. Dr. R. O. Cowling of Louisville, Sept. 24, 1867, at Episc. Ch.

Cowling, Dr. R. O.—see Churchill.

Corbin, John R., 83 years, m. in Scott Co., Oct. 21, 1867, Mrs. Sarah Simpson, aged 73, at res. of Wm. Chinn. (Com. Nov. 1, 1867)

Cook, Nat., aged 55, d. in Frankfort. (Com. Jan. 17, 1868)

Crouch, Mrs. Hannah V., aged 65, widow of late Rev. B. T. Crouch, Sr. of Ky. Meth. Confer- ence, d. at Lebanon, Sun. 4th. (Com. Oct. 2, 1868)

Cook, Wm. L., d. at res. in Rockcastle Co., on 31st, ult., b. May 30, 1819 in same house, kind father, husband, etc. (Com. Feb. 12, 1869)

Cammack, Christopher, d. July 15, at Natchez, in his 28th year, (Com. Aug. 6, 1833.)

Campbell, Harvey Wolf, 23rd year, late of Union Town, Pa., d. Thurs. 12th at the Mansion House, (Com. Sept. 17, 1839)

Calk, Wm., aged 20, son of Thos. Calk, d. Apr. 7, 1839, in Montgomery Co. (Mon. May 14, 1839 Com.)

Chinn, Mrs. Eliz., wife of Morgan Chinn (M. B. Chinn), d. last Sun. in Frankfort. (Com. Sept. 17, 1839)

Clark, Matthew, of Natchez, Miss., d. at res. of Wm. Woods, in Maysville, June 3. (Com. June 18, 1839)

Clark, John W., son of John W. Clark of Lexington, d. the 1st. (Com. June 9, 1839)

Clarkson, David, in 44th year, and his son in 19th year, d. in Charleston, Ind., near home of his bro. C. S. Clarkson. (Com. June 18, 1833.)

Cole, Richard, d. Mon. July 8, at his home in Woodford County at an advanced age; well on Monday, found dead in bed. Tues. (Com. July 16, 1839)

Cook, Norborn B., of Mercer Co., m. Henrietta, dau. of Lewis Singleton, in Jess. Co., the 18th ult. (Com. July 9, 1839)

Conover, Miss Amaryllis Andrew Anna (see John Prewitt, Pruitt.)

Collins, Robt., of Bardstown? d. Oct. 12, 1833, in 90th year, soldier.

Corlis, John, Sr., aged 72, of Boone Co., d. Fri. 21st, ult. (Com. 7-9-1839)

Craddock, J. W. of Hart Co. m. Miss Harriet W. Theobald, (Jan. 19, 1841 Com.)

Crutcher, Rev. Isaac, father of Lucinda V. Crutcher, aged 14, d. on 7th inst. (Apr. 10, 1839)

Davidson, J. W. of Logan County, m. M. C. Keene, dau. of Greenup Keene, Jan. 14, 1841 (Com. Jan. 19, 1841)

Dorsey, Hon. Caleb, and Priscilla Dorsey—see Robt. Wilmott.

Duvall, Gov. Wm. P.—see Samuel Beall.

Duvall, Geo.—see Cosby Price.

Duvall, Mrs. Mary W., wife of B. F. Duvall of Versailles, d. in Fayette Co., on 21st. (Com. May 28, 1839)

Depau, Peter, 81st year, d. at his res. in Lincoln Co. last Friday. (Wed. Apr. 10, 1867) (Central Ky. Gazette–Danville)

Dudley, Mrs. Jeptha, widow of Jeptha D., d. at res. of her dau. Mrs. John Speed Smith, Madison Co., Ky., July 6, 1867, aged about 90 years; twice married–1st husband Gen. Green Clay (ch. were Gen. Cassius Clay, minister to Russia; Hon. Brutus Clay, Mrs. J. Speed Smith, Mrs. Wm. Rhodes, mother of wife of John Watson of Frankfort–no Dudley ch. (Com. July 12, 1867)

Dale, Mr. E., aged 50, d. Oct. 4, 1867 (Com. Oct. 11, 1867)

Delph, Mrs. Mary A., 47, d. Oct. 23, 1867, widow of Col. Jeremiah Delph of Fayette Co. (Com. Nov. 1, 1867)

DeMoss, J. H. W., aged 35, b. in Bracken Co., d. Mar. 13, 1868, wife and 4 ch. (Com. Apr. 10, 1868)

Dougherty, Mrs. Mary Ann, 69, d. 24th at her res. in Millville, Woodford county. (Com. Mar. 26, 1869)

Dudley, Gen. Peter, 83, d. Thurs. June 17, 1869 (Com. June 18, 1869)

Davis, Col. John F., of Shelby Co., m. Mrs. Mary P. Gray, of Woodford Co., at res. of bride's father Judge W. J. Steele, in Versailles, 17th (Com. June 25, 1869)

Divine, Mrs. Jane, 82, widow of Roger Divine of this Co., d. Fri. Apr. 6, 1855. (Apr. 16, 1855–Com.)

Evans, Mrs. Mary, 76, d. 14th. (Com. Mar. 18, 1870)

Edwards, Eliz. West, aged 49, consort of Fielding Edwards, d. Sept. 11, 1867 at Normans Landing, Red river. (Com. Sept. 20, 1867)

Edwards, Hon. Ninian, d. at Belleville, Ill. of cholera, (Aug. 6, 1833 Com.)

Edwards, Mrs. Susanna, 86, d. in Bourbon county, (Oct. 15, 1833. Com.)

Elliott, Miss Mary T., aged 73, sister of Rev. Jas. Elliott, d. in Woodford county the 9th inst. (Com. Oct. 20, 1840)

Espy, Lavinia–see Jas. Turner Morehead.

Espy, Jas. M.–see Jas. Turner Morehead.

Finley, W. R. of Shelbyville, m. Miss Marietta B. Brown, of Bloomfield, Apr. 2nd. (Com. Apr. 16, 1839)

Fisher, Henry, 63, d. Sept. 3, 1867, in Lexington, Mo., native of Woodford Co. (Com. Sept. 20, 1867)

Farrar, Asa, aged 96, d. Fri. Sept. 7, 1866, at res. of son in Fayette. (Com. Sept. 11, 1866–see Frankfort Cemetery)

Gaines, Bernard, d. last Sunday A.M. of apoplexy, at an advanced age, Captain in U.S.A. in Indian Wars, (Com. July 2, 1839)

Gillispie, Richard, formerly of Madison Co., m. in South Frankfort, last Thurs. Miss Emily E. Bass, (Com. Tues. Apr. 23, 1839)

Glass, Jr., Samuel—see Mrs. Mary M. Robinson.

Gorin, Mrs. Louisa F., wife of Franklin Gorin of Glasgow, d. on 21st inst. in 39th year. Dau. of Capt. John and Francis M. Underwood, late of Goochland Co., Va., m. in 1818 Franklin Gorin; husband and several ch. (Lexington Int.) (Com. Feb. 2, 1840)

Gower, Stanley P.—see Mrs. Nancy Wells.

Grant, Joshua D., m. May 16, 1839, in Bardstown, Miss Eliz. Howell, dau. of Maj. D. S. Howell, (Com. Tues. May 28, 1839)

Grundy, Hon. Felix, aged 67, d. Sat. 4 o'clock, Sen. in Congress from Tenn., b. in Va., m. in Ky., to Tenn. about 33 or 34 years ago., Congress 1811, Davidson Co., legislature. (Nashville Banner) (Com. Dec. 29, 1840)

Golden, Wm., d. in Madison Co. in 106th year, b. in Albemarle Co., Va. 1760, to Madison Co. in early youth with the Rodes, Harrises, Millers, Gentrys and Maupins, etc. In War of 1812, etc. (Register) (Frankfort Com., Oct. 2, 1866)

Garrard, Col. Daniel, near 90 years, d. in Clay Co., Sept. 20th, father of Col. Jas. H. Garrard and Gen. Theophilus T. G., (Com., Oct. 2, 1866.)

Gibbons, Thos., 75, formerly of Lex., d. in St. Louis, Oct. 21, 1855 (Com. Nov. 5, 1855.)

Garrard, Col. Daniel, 75, of Clay Co., m. Oct. 16, 1855 Mary F. Adkins, of Knox Co., aged 24 years. (Com. Nov. 5, 1855)

Gess, Mrs. Ann, relict of John Gess, decd. aged 73, d. at res. of dau.-in-law in Lexington, Dec. 26th. (Com. Jan. 22, 1856)

Goin, Mrs. Mary Ann, wife of Capt. Sanford Goin, d. the 3rd, (Com. Mar. 4, 1868)

Gray, Mrs. Sarah P., wife of W. H. Gray, d. Sept. 2, 1867, ch. etc. (Com. Sept. 6, 1867)

Goodson, Maj. John A., 74, ex-Sen. of Kenton Co., Mayor of Covington, committed suicide last week in Boone Co. (Apr. 26, 1867 Com.)

Gwin, Mrs. Julia A., 59, wife of G. W. Gwin, d. 28th. (Com. June 5, 1868)

George Bohanan, youngest son of Capt. Wm. George, d. in Woodford Co. last Sun. (Com. Nov. 29, 1867)

Hazelrigg, Ann, dau. of Dillard H., aged 16, d. Mon., Sept. 24th, at Mt. Sterling, (Com. Oct. 6, 1840)

Hazelrigg, John H., 18th year, son of Chas. H., d. on Fri. 11th, in Mt. Sterling, (Oct. 6th, 1840, Com.)

Hinton, Mrs. Rhenariah, upwards of 70 years, d. in Fleming Co., Mon. 14th inst. (Wed. Apr. 10, 1839, Com.)

Holton, Wm. Harrison, son of Capt. John A. Holton, d. Aug. 27 aged 18. (Com. Sept. 3, 1839)

Howell, Maj. D. S.—see Joshua D. Grant.

Hickman, Jas. L., aged 67, d. in Todd Co., Aug. 24, 1855, formerly of Lexington, in War of 1812. (Com. Sept. 3, 1855)

Hann, Mrs. Leonora, wife of Dr. Albert H., dau. of Dr. Allen F. McCurdy, b. in Frankfort, Jan. 24, 1812, d. in Madison Co., Sept. 20, etc. (Com. Oct. 9, 1866)

Hart, Col. Wm. P., 62 yrs., d. 17th. (Com. May 22, 1868, Woodford Co.)

Harlan, Mrs. Eliza S., 64, relict of Hon. Jas. H., d. 10th, at res. of Dr. J. G. Hatchitt, (May 13, 1870, Com.)

Herndon, Joel, aged 65, d. in Owen Co. the 1st (Com. Jan. 22, 1856)

Houston, Mrs., widow of Jas. Houston, 01 years of age, d. in Bourbon Co., 28th of Feb. (Com. Mar. 12, 1855)

Hocker, Samuel, 74, d. in Boyle Co., Mar. 3, (Com. Mar. 12, 1855.)

Head, Capt. Ben T., formerly of Franklin Co., d. in McLean Co., Tues. 11th (10th?), b. in Orange Co., Va., Dec. 13, 1791, to Franklin Co. with his parents; 1808 boatman to New Orleans, in War of 1812, 1844 Buck Run Bap. Church, to Davis Co., 1850. (Com. Apr. 23, 1855.)

Holton, Capt. John A., d. the 11th, (Com. June 18, 1869 (see Frankfort Cem.)

Hall, Mr. T., 78 years, soldier of War of 1812, under Gen. Cass, d. at res. of John Shaw, in Danville, the 23rd. (Com. Nov. 12, 1869)

Harris, Thos., 45 years, d. 6th at res. of S. S. Clay, this county. (Com. May 15, 1868)

Harlan, Wm. L., aged 45, d. Mon. 23, at res. of J. G. Hatchitt. (Com. Mar. 27, 1868)

Helm, Gov. John L., d. near Elizabethtown, Sun. Sept. 8, 1867, b. July 4, 1802, buried Sept. 10th, at E'town. oldest son of George Helm of Hardin Co., parents of Va. His father d. when he was 17, leaving a large family. m. Lucinda B. Hardin oldest dau. of Hon. Ben Hardin, left large family. (Long obit. in Com. of Sept. 13, 1867.)

Hawkins, Col. Strother Jones, aged 77, d. at res. near Henderson, Ky., born in Fayette Co. 1790, in War of 1812. (Long obit. from Henderson News) (Com. Oct. 11, 1867)

Hughes, Mrs. Ellenor, d. Oct. 21, 1867 at Millville, Woodford Co., widow of John E. Hughes of Little Falls, N. Y., sister of J. W. Quin and Mrs. Fannie Lyons—2 sons. (Com. Oct. 25, 1867)

Hise, Hon. Elijah, aged 65 years on July 4, 1866; committed suicide in Russellville, May 8, 1867, wife and relatives—left note dated Apr. 21, 1867 (Com. May 14, 1867)

Holman, Rev. Wm., Meth. Epis. church, d. Aug. 9, 1867, aged 77, at Centreville, Ind. ———
in Kentucky. (Aug. 30, 1867 Com.)

Hunton, Mrs. Ann, 82, d. at res. in Danville, on Sun. 24th. (Wed. Mar. 27, 1867) (Central
Ky. Gazette, Danville, Ky.)

Handy, Maj. John G., one of oldest citizens, d. in Mercer Co. 19th (Mar. 27, 1867 Central
Ky. Gazette, Danville, Ky.)

Hann, Dr. Alex R., 58, d. at Kirksville, Madison Co., Ky., Mon. 12th (Aug. 14, 1867.) (obit.
Aug. 21st.) (Central Ky. Gazette, Danville, Ky.)

Innis, Judge (see Mrs. Cath. Eliz. Adams)

Irwin, Ann Maria, Winchester, aged 32, wife of Col. Jas. W. I., d. in Logan Co., 14th; husband,
4 children and step-son. (Tu. Jan. 30, 1844)

Irwin, J. W., member state Legis, 1843, Logan Co., b. Va. 1804.

Jacobs, Wm. W., (see Mrs. Susannah Duvall)

Jackson, Mrs. Sarah, wife of Wm. J., d. Franklin Co. Oct. 20, (Nov. 1, 1842)

Jackson, Richard G., (see Maria A. Cotton)

James, Mrs. Sarah, relict of Daniel James, d. at res. of her son-in-law, Rev. Geo. Blackburn,
in this county, Apr. 10, 1837—a venerable matron, one of first settlers in this county. (Apr.
19, 1837)

January, Prissie F., dau. John M. J., of Cynthiana; m. Jas. H. Haydon, of Mo., at home of
J. S. Boyd, on 11th. (June 1, 1852)

Jennings, John R., son of Mrs. A. G. Daniel of Danville, aged 21, d. in Galveston, Tex. at res.
of his uncle, Col. Jas. Love, Sept. 13, (Oct. 11, 1853)

Jett, Matthew, aged 75, d. Franklin Co. Mar. 15, (3-28-1854)

Johnson, Cave, Col. of Boone Co., m. Mrs. Margaret Keen, Franklin Co., Thurs. Dec. 1,
(Dec. 21, 1836)

Johnson, Mrs. Eliz., aged 24, husband and ch., dau. Capt. Robt. Collins, d. Hickman Co.
(Sept. 10, 1844) (Capt. Robt. Collins once lived in Franklin Co., his dau. m. Hiram
Egbert)

Jones, Mrs. Sarah, widow of Maj. Dumas Jones, decd. Harrison Co., d. Charleston, Ill. Sept.
13, in 85th yr. (Nov. 1, 1853)

Jones, Maj. H., Jr. (see Joseph Proctor)

Jones, Col. Humphrey, Sr., in 83rd yr., d. at Richmond, Ky. last Sat. (Mon. Jan. 31, 1853)

Jones, Thos. W., (see John R. Scott)

Jones, Miss Sidney J., dau. of Thos. W. Jones, m. John R. Scott, in Frankfort Mon. aft. (Oct. 18, 1837)

Johnson, R. M., Reps. 1843, Scott Co., b. Ky. 1781.

Jonston, Jas., Reps. 1843, Ohio Co., b. Pa. 1774.

Jones, T. M., Reps. 1843, Calloway Co., b. Ky. 1807.

James, Thos., Sen. 1843, Clinton, Hickman Co., b. N. Carolina, 1796.

Jesup, Samuel B., Sen. 1843, Todd Co., b. Va. —— .

Johnson, Benj. B., Sen. 1843, Frankfort, b. Ky. 1793.

Jouett, Lee B., son of Mrs. Sallie Jouett and the late Col. W. R. Jouett, of U.S.A., d. 18th in 23rd year. (Com. Dec. 20, 1867)

Jenkins, Mrs. Eliza, 58, wife of John J., d. at Bridgeport, Tues. June 23—Baptist. (Com. July 3, 1868)

Johnson, Mrs. Eliz., aged nearly 100, d. at res. of son Fant(ley) Johnson, in Woodford Co. Jan. 22, 1869 (Com. Feb. 5, 1869)

Jones, Mrs. Frances, 80, d. in Paris the 14th. (Com. Sept. 24, 1855)

Johnston, Maj. James, 81, d. April 15, 1855, in Ohio Co. (Com. May 7, 1855)

Johnson, Mrs. Eliz., 72 years, d. Fri. 18th at res. of Jas. G. Hearn. (Com. Apr. 1, 1870)

Jackson, Capt. Reuben, aged 95, d. at home of son J. C. Jackson in the county. (Com. June 24, 1870)

Johnson, Mrs. Jane Martin, 53 years about, wife of Francis Johnson, native of Ky., dau. of Col. Richard Young, compatriot of Boone, etc. died on the 8th inst. (Lou. Courier-Journal) (Com. Mar. 17, 1840)

Karsner, John, 65, volunteer under Col. Dudley. 1812, d. Owen Co. (Tu. Nov. 22, 1853) Oct. 29th.

Knight, Eliz., dau. of Jos. W. K. ——, Lou., m. in Louisville, Thurs. 23, Lucien Wingate, formerly of Frankfort. (11-28-1843)

Keene, Oliver, (see Mrs. Sarah Blackburn)

Keene, Mrs. Margaret, m. Col. Cave Johnson (see Johnson)

Kelly, John, aged 98, Rev. Soldier, d. in Muskingum Co., Union Township, Ohio. June 11. (Tu. July 5, 1853)

Kemper, John, Sr., aged 95, d. at res. of son-in-law in Garrard Co. (Oct. 25, 1834)

Kennady, Mrs., wife of Jesse Kennady, of Bourbon Co., d. Sun. Jan. 22, in 49th yr. (Feb. 8, 1837)

Kennedy, Mrs. Mary E., 31, wife of Eli M. Kennedy, d. Mon. Aug. 30, in Bourbon Co. (Sept. 20, 1852)

Kennedy, Matthew, 71 yr, formerly of Lex., d. in Lou. last Wed. (Mon. Apr. 25, 1853)

Kenton, Gen. Simon, aged 82, d. in Logan Co., Ohio, Apr. 29 (May 25, 1836)

Key, Thos., b. 1767, aged 66, also his wife Sara Key, b. 1770, aged 63, d. in Mason Co. (May 21, 1833)

Kidd, George, grandson of the late Rev. John Hargrove, of Baltimore, d. in Galveston, Tex. in Aug. (Oct. 1, 1844)

King, John, 76 yrs., d. last Sat. in Bourbon Co. (7-27-1852)

Kirtley, Mrs. Matilda, wife of John Kirtley and eldest dau. of Capt. John Cave, d. at North Bend, Boone Co. Ky. Mar. 17th, (Capt. John Cave, of Woodford Co.) (Tu. Apr. 2, 1844)

Knight, John, Sr., aged 87, b. Scotland, 1751, in the Revolution, in 9th Va. Reg., Surgeon's Mate . . . with Col. Crawford at Mingo Town, Ohio River, May 1782 . . . m. Miss. Stephenson, niece of Col. Crawford, and then to Ky.; widow and family . . . Dr. Jos. W. Knight of Lou. (Lou. Adv.) died in Shelby Co., Mar. 12, 1838.

Kerr, Mrs. Frances, (matron at D. & D., Danville) 1831 (see Com.)

Kerr, Rev. J. R., Supt. and Teacher.

Key, Marshall, Reps. 1843, Mason Co., b. Va. 1788.

Kitchen, A., Reps. 1843, Carter Co., b. Va., 1791.

Kohlass, T., officer State Legis. 1843, Clark Co. b. Ky. 1814.

Keene, M. C.—see J. W. Davidson.

Keene, Greenup, see J. W. Davidson.

Keene, Col. Rich. R., d. at St. Louis—in Spain for several years; born in Dorchester Co., Md., 1st wife dau. of celebrated Luther Martin of Baltimore; 2nd wife a native of Spain survives.

King, Mrs. Mary Ann, wife of Col. Alfred King, aged 20 yrs., m. Col. King at home of her father Mr. Henry Adams, of Dallas Co., Ala. in winter of 1838, d. at Burkesville. Left 2 ch. (Com. Mar. 30, 1841.)

Kennan, Wm., d. on 16th near Orangeburg, Mason Co., Ky., son of Wm. K., the celebrated Indian fighter who saved the life of Gov. Madison. He was aged 69 yrs. (Com. Mar. 26, 1869)

Kerby, Richard, aged 76, d. in Bourbon Co., Oct. 1, 1855 (Com. Oct. 15, 1855)

Kinkead, John, 71, father of Hon. W. E. and Geo. B. Kinkead, d. Apr. 2, in Woodford Co. (Com. Apr. 16, 1855).

Long, Thos. of Cumberland County d. His father was Capt. in Rev. War. (Com. July 16, 1833.)

Long, Mrs. Bathsheba D., 82, d. last Tues. 22nd, member of Presby. Ch. since 1828, husband d. over 40 years ago; large number of children; one son now consul to Panama. (Com. Fri. Mar. 25, 1870)

Logan, Jas. K., 46, son of Dr. Benj. Logan of Shelby, grandson of Gen'l. Benj. Logan, d. (Com. Oct. 25, 1867)

Lucas, Mrs. Jane, 81, d. at res. of son W. C. Lucas, at Danville, on the 20th. (Com. July 3, 1868)

Lowry, Jas. H., 64, d. Nov. 24, 1866, in Jess. Co. (Com. Dec. 4, 1866)

Luckett, Mrs. Maria, d. Sat. 23rd, 79 years, (Com. July 29, 1870)

Laffoon, James, 90, in Rev. War, Va. Line, Battles of Guilford, Court House, etc. d. in Fayette Co., Dec. 27. (Mon. Jan. 10, 1853 Com.)

Langford, Mrs. Lois, widow of Stephen Langford, (decd. long since); one or first settlers of Rockcastle Co., has been in constant attendance on the sick in the last 20 yrs. d. at Mt. Vernon, Ky. 21st. (Nov. 29, 1831 Com.)

Langhorn, Maj. Maurice, aged 68, d. in Jefferson Co. June 3. (July 6, 1841)

Laughlin, Col. Thos., 82nd yr., of Whitley Co., Pensioner for his services against the Indians in the Rev., commissioned in battalion in War of 1812, under Gov. Shelby, d. May 29, 1844. (June 4, 1844–long obit.)

Lawson, Mrs. Mary 84, widow of Robt. Lawson, Sr., decd. of Shelby Co., d. on 9th. (Tu. June 17, 1853)

Leavy, Mrs. Sarah, widow of Wm. Leavy, of Lex., d. in Lex., Oct. 26 (Nov. 8, 1853) 1853)

Lee, Elder Samuel V., (see Thos. McCauley)

Letcher, Gov. (see Mrs. Mary Samuel)

Lewis, Col. Wm. L., of So. Carolina, m. Miss Letitia Floyd, dau. of late Gov. John Floyd, of Va., Mar. 13, in New Orleans. (Wed. 4-15-1837)

Lewis, Sarah, 85, widow of late Col. Joseph Francis Lewis, one of earliest settlers of Ky., d. at res. of Dr. Joel Owsley, near Burkesville, Ky., Apr. 21, 1837. She was a sister of the late Col. Whitley who fell at the Battle of Thames. (Wed. May 10, 1837)

Lewis, Col. (see Goldberry Childers)

Lewis, Cadwaller, m. Eliz. H. Patterson, dau. of late Alex. Patterson, of Pr. Edward Co. Va., in Franklin Co. Wed. 13th (Wed. 2-20-1839)

Lloyd, Ann Maria Frances, dau. of Dr. Francis Lloyd, m. Geo. Stealey, in Franklin Co., Tu. Oct. 24 (Nov. 7, 1843)

Long, Mrs. Mary, wife of Richard L., dau. of late David and Ann W. McChesney, b. July 25, 1821, m. Dec. 13, 1839, d. at Frankfort (Feb. 7, 1853, Mon.)

Long, Armstead, d. Jan. 18, 1835, in Woodford Co.

Long, Dr. Wm. M., late of Ky. m. Miss Mary Ann Alexander, formerly of Ohio, at Jacksonville, Ill., Tu. May 23. (June 6, 1843)

Logan, Sarah, (Miss) dau. of late Col. John Logan, d. at res. of Mrs. Blaine, in Frankfort, last Fri. (Mar. 13, 1839)

Love, Col. James, (see John R. Jennings)

Lowery, Miss, (see Samuel McKee)

Luckett, Maj. Benjamin, —— at whose res. his grandson, Lewis Luckett Taylor aged 3, d. (Dec. 27, 1853)

Lincoln, A., Esq. . . . (see Mrs. Eliz. Rice)

Loving, Wm. V., Senator, 1843, Bowling Green, b. Va. 1803.

McAfee, Robt. B., Senator, 1843, Mercer Co., b. Ky. 1784.

McBrayer, Robt. C., d. in Anderson Co., Sun. Sept. 10. (Sept. 19, 1843)

McCaulay, Thos., aged 102 yrs., d. at res. of Elder Sam'l. V. Lee, Harrison Co. . . . he was a Rev. soldier. (Mon. June 6, 1853)

McChesney, Ann W., (see Mrs. Mary Long)

McChesney, David, (see Mrs. Mary Long)

McClung, Mrs. Susan, aged 85, relict of Judge Wm. McClung dau. of Col. Thos. Marshall of Rev. fame; born in Fauquier Co., Va.; she had 9 children, outlived all but one—the Rev. John A. McClung, D.D. She died at Maysville on the 2nd. (Nov. 17, 1858)

McClanahan, Jane, consort of Irvine McC., died in Richmond, Sept. 1, dau. Judge Ben Monroe of Frankfort. (Mon. Sept. 13, 1852)

McConnell, Mary Ann, m. Henry S. Boyden, May 27, in Lou. (June 6, 1843)

McConnell, Mary C., dau. of Gen. Jas. McConnell, m. Geo. W. Murch of Scott Co., Oct. 24. (Nov. 14, 1843)

McConnell, James, aged 75, a soldier, d. in Fayette Co., Mar. 21. (Fri. Mar. 25, 1853)

McConnell, Col. John M., aged 44 yrs, d. in Greenup Co. Sat. A.M. last, lawyer. (Maysville Eagle of July 10, 1834)

McCoun, Mrs. Nancy, in 63rd yr. d. Paris, 10th (4-19-1842)

McCoy, Daniel, 75, formerly of Garrard Co., d. in Adams Co., Ill. (May 11, 1836)

McCurdy, Dr. A. F., (see Mrs. Maria Louisa Robertson)

McCrackin, Virgil, mid-shipman, U.S.N., d. in Versailles, Sept. 14th. (Sat. Sept. 20, 1834)

McDonald, Mrs. Elizabeth, wife of Col. Francis McDonald, she aged 64, d. Oct. 7, in Clark Co. (Tu. Nov. 15, 1853)

McDowell, John, Maj. one of first settlers of Fayette Co. d. in Fayette. (Aug. 1, 1835)

McHatton, Gen. Robt., d. in Marion Co., Ind., May 20, some years ago Member of Congress from Ky. (May 30, 1835)

McIlwain, Wm. H., 21st yr, d. at res. of his step-father Jas. Stevenson, Woodford Co. (Apr. 1, 1834.)

McKee, Capt. Wm., father late Samuel McKee.

McKee, Samuel, aged 78, one of youngest of soldiers in the War of Rev., d. in Mt. Sterling, Mon. 6th, b. in Rockbridge Co. Va., July 3, 1764; when 16, a private, 1784-5, to Kentucky, settled at Bear Grass Cr. in Jefferson Co.; m. Miss Lowery after going to Harrodsburg, 1791, then to Clark and Montgomery Cos. (June 28, 1842)

McKinney, Capt. John, aged 82, d. in Versailles, Thurs, Aug. 24, 1837.

McKinney, James G., m. Mrs. Eliza O. Payne, Fayette Co., Oct. 15. (Oct. 24, 1838)

McNeil, Mrs. Sarah, relict of late A. McNeil, d. at res. of Jas. McNeil, Fayette Co., Dec. 27. (Fri. Jan. 14, 1853)

McElroy, Hiram, Senator, 1843, Morganfield, b. Ky. 1800.

McCrackin, Mrs. Frances—see Osborn Belt.

McNary, Mrs. Ann Maria, wife of Col. W. C. McNary, d. in Muhlenberg Co., Dec. 23, 1839 (Com. Jan. 14, 1840)

McBrayer, Andrew, aged 62, early emigrant to the state, d. (Com. May 21, 1839)

McKee, James, aged 76, d. in Attala Co., Miss., Nov. 18, 1866, at res. of son-in-law Allen Dodd—father of Rev. J. L. McKee of Lou. (Com. Feb. 13, 1867) (Central Ky. Gazette, Danville, Ky.)

McEwan, Mrs. Mary, aged 80, formerly of Scotland, d. Sept. 11, 1867, 23 yrs. in Frankfort. (Com. Sept. 13, 1867)

McQueen, Caroline, m. Wm. Cardwell, 1843.

McQueen, Joshua, d. a few days ago in Franklin Co. aged 106 yrs. Soldier of Rev., appointed Sergt. under Gen. Washington, leaves wife, son, dau-in-law, and grandch'n. (Mon. May 2, 1853)

McQuiddy, Mrs. Alice, 82 yr. d. last Sun. in Frankfort. (Aug. 15, 1835)

Massie, Mrs. Susan, widow of late Gen. Nathaniel M., aged 57, d. May 22, in Chillicothe, Ohio. (Com. June 18, 1833.)

Massey, Jas. H. m. May 30, in Mt. Sterling, Miss Ann Raney, dau. of Jas. Raney, all of Miss. (Com. June 4, 1839)

Martin, Luther--see Rich. Keene.

Mason, James, 106 years of age, of Scott County, b. in Waterford in Tipperary, Ireland, Jan. 1, 1727, in King's Service in Ireland, in the Revolutionary war, d. in Scott Co. (Com. July 9, 1833.)

May, John L. (S?) lawyer d. in Frankfort, aged 56 years, his father was a victim of the Indians. (Com. Jan. 21, 1840)

Mayhall, Timothy, 66, volunteer under Wayne, d. Feb. 29th. (Com. Mar. 3, 1840)

Mills, Dr. Chas. d. here aged 59 (57?) (Com. Feb. 25, 1840--Mar. 3rd?) (m. Joyce Patterson, 1807, big family)

Morehead, Jas. Turner of Frankfort, m. at Columbus, Ohio, Lavinia M., dau. of J. M. Espey of Ohio. (Com. Oct. 8, 1839)

Mills, Rev. Thornton A., d. of apoplexy at Hoboken, N. J. (July 18,) 6-25-1867, son of Hon. Ben Mills, decd., of Kentucky Court of Appeals, bro. of our citizen Capt. J. M. Mills, wife and ch. (long obit) (Com. July 18, 1867)

Macklin, Benoni, aged 40, d. Aug. 23, 1867 (Aug. 30, 1867 Com.)

Morton, Dr. David T., 53, d. in Lex. 28th. (Com. Jan. 3, 1868)

Middleton, M. F., dau. J. A. Middleton, aged 6 years, 3 mos., 20 days, d. Feb. 10th at res. of her gd. father Lewis Neal in Shelby Co. (Com. Mar. 6, 1868)

Middleton, M. A. W., wife of J. A. Middleton, aged 32 years, 8 mos. 27 days, d. 13th at same place. (Com. Mar. 6, 1868)

Middleton, Jas. A., 36 years, d. same place the 16th, 4 in the family died in 2 weeks. (Com. Mar. 6, 1868)

Mitchell, Thos. one of our oldest and best citizens, d. at res. of son Thos. P. Mitchell, in Danville, Fri. Apr. 10th (Com. Apr. 24, 1869)

Morris, Sallie P., 76, d. in Hopkins Co. May 15, at home of son-in-law G. G. (S?G.) Slaughter, many years in Frankfort, Presby. church. (Com. June 4, 1869)

Montague, Mrs.   wife of Sim M., aged 40, d. in Frankfort Sun. 19th, puerperal fever, (Com. Sept. 24, 1869)

Macy, Mrs. Sophia Jane, 57, wife of Lee W. Macy, d. 16th at res. of her son-in-law O. S. Walcutt. (Com. Nov. 19, 1869)

Murray, Mrs. Georgiana, widow of John M., 44 years, eldest dau. of Jas. & Rebecca Conover, d. Sun., Apr. 29, 1855, in this city, formerly of Lex.

Macon, Mrs. Sarah, 79, wife of late Thos. Macon of Orange Co., Va., last surviving sister of Jas. Madison. (Oct. 17, 1843)

Maddox, Capt. Wilson, 73, Shelby Co., d. 12th inst. (Tu. June 17, 1853)

Maddox, Nathaniel W., aged 34, formerly of Fauquier Co. Va., d. at home of his mother-in-law Mrs. L. A. Owsley in Shelby Co. on 28th. wife and 3 small daus. (Apr. 8, 1853)

Maddox, Mrs. Sarah, 81, d. at Midway, on 18th (3-23-1858)

Macklin, Eunice T., wife of John Macklin, in her 43rd yr. d. 10th. (Dec. 17, 1844)

Madison, James (see Mrs. Sarah Macon)

Madison, George, son of late Gov. Madison, d. at res. of Mr. Andrew Alexander, in Frankfort, Oct. 8, 1831) (see Commentator)

Major, Benj. P., 26, native of Franklin Co. where he lived till 1835, d. at Warsaw, Mo. Mar. 13, 1844. (Tu. Apr. 2, 1844)

Major, Francis, aged 80 yrs., 6 mos. 9 days, Volunteer in Rev. war, early settler of Ky., while on a visit to his nephew Rev. John S. Major, Franklin Co., d. Oct. 31. (Nov. 21, 1835)

Mallory, Gibson, (see Samuel M. Taylor)

Mansfield, Col. Geo. W., 57, d. Allen Co., Sun. 6th (9-13-1852)

Marks, Capt. Hastings, 73rd yr., joined N. W. Army under Gen. Wayne, served with Harrison also in late war under Wayne., d. Clarke Co. Feb. 27. (Mar. 7, 1843)

Marcee, Rev. Thos., 83 yrs., d. at home of Mount Perciful, in Hardin Co., Thur. 8th. (Tu. Sept. 29, 1853)

Marshall, Hon. M. P., (see Mrs. Lucy Coleman)

Marshall, Thos. (see Mrs. Lucy Coleman)

Marshall, Frances, (see Mrs. Lucy Coleman)

Marshall, Anna R., widow of late John J. Marshall, d. in Lou. at Galt House, aged 66 yrs. (Mar. 4, 1858)

Marshall, Thos., son of Chief Justice John M., d. Fauquier Co. Va., killed by debris from building under which he took refuge from storm. 6 children . . . burial at Oakhill, Fauquier Co. Va. (July 11, 1835)

Marshall, Col. Thos. A., (see Mrs. Susan McClung)

Marston, John, m. Eliza Ann, dau. Cyrus Wingate, Dec. 26, 1833. Owen Co. (Jan. 1, 1834)

Martin, Maj. Wm. M., of Woodford Co. m. Mrs. Sarah True of Scott Co., in Marion Co., Mo., Tu. 6th, (Oct. 19, 1836)

MEMBERS OF STATE LEGISLATURE, 1843.

Morgan, Daniel, Senator, Flemingsburg, Ky. b. Va. 1792.

Morgan, John S., Senator, Carlisle, Ky., b. Ky. 1799.

Mayhall, J., officer in Senate, Frankfort, b. Ky. 1792.

Marshall, Thos., Reps. 1843, Lewis Co., b. Ky. 1793.

Marshall, W. C., Reps. Augusta, Ky., b. Ky. 1807.

Maxey, Radford, Reps. Monroe Co., b. Va. 1786.

McKee, G. R., Reps. Garrard Co., b. Ky. 1810.

Morehead, C. S., Reps., Frankfort, b. Ky. 1802.

Morgan, R. D. S., Reps. Meade Co., b. Ky. 1797.

Murrell, H. P., Reps. Warren Co., b. Va. 1795.

Murrell, Jas., Reps. Barren Co., b. Va. 1799.

Martin, Mrs. Letitia, 77, d. Tu. 6th in Woodford Co., one first settlers in Ky., left native State of Pa. at age 12 yrs. . . 12 ch. all grown, 2 died before her. (July 19, 1853)

Massey, Alfred, of Scott Co. m. Marilda Vinzant, (May 11, 1836)

Massey, John; heirs-advertised taxes on lands, Campbell Co. Ky. (Com. 10-11-36)

Massey, John C. (Massie) 58, d. in Louisiana, Pike Co., Mo. June 28. (Aug. 16, 1853)

Massie, Theodrick M., of Palmyra, Mo. m. in this county, Susan Shannon, dau. of Hugh Shannon, last Sun. (Mar. 22, 1837)

Mason, Nimrod, d. in Frankfort on 30th, at advanced age. (June 30, 1858)

Masterson, Capt. James, 87, Rev. Soldier, d. at Lex. Jan. 16, 1838

Mayhall, J. officer in Legislature 1843, b. Frankfort, 1792.

Mead, Mrs. Sarah, 63, d. Lou., Oct. 3. (Oct. 11, 1853)

Meaux, Maj. John G., d. near Danville, Sun. May 1, at advanced age. (May 10, 1842)

Mendell, Lieut. Geo. H., U.S.A., m. Ellen, dau. Gen. John Adair, at Astoria, Oregon, Oct. 8th. . . formerly of Ky. (Dec. 20, 1858)

Merriwether, Capt. Wm., aged 84, late of Jefferson Co., officer in Revolutionary War, d. in Hickman Co. (Tu. Mar. 8, 1842)

Mercer, Gen. Hugh, Brig. Gen. U. S. A.; native of Scotland, to Fredericksburg, Va. and m., in Wars 1755, etc., Revolution; Mrs. Gordon mother of widow of Mercer. 5 ch. 1 dau., 4 sons, (2 columns obit.) (Aug. 19, 1834)

Metcalfe, Gen. Thos., (see Mrs. Jane Lee Campbell)

Milam, Capt. John, 63, d. in Franklin Co., Mar. 8, (Tu. Mar. 14, 1843)

Milam, Maj. James, (see Mrs. Mildred Noel)

Miller, Aaron, 64, husband and father, mem. Bap. Ch., d. Frankfort. Sun. Jan. 28. (Sat. Feb. 3, 1844)

Miller, Joseph, 65, merchant in Millersbrug, d. last Tues. (Tu. Sept. 20, 1853)

Miller, Col. John, (see Joseph Proctor)

Miller, Col. John, 86, veteran of two wars, (86 yrs. 7 mos. 20 das.) d. on Feb. 3rd, in Scott Co., (Mon. Feb. 14, 1853)

Miller, Harriet R., m. Edw. R. Weir (see Weir)

Millikin, Mrs. Mary, consort of Capt. Samuel Millikin, d. in Paducah the 30th (Jan. 28, 1853)

Mills, (Mrs. Eliz. C. P.,) dau. late Judge Mills, of Frankfort, Obit. poem, 1850 . . . anonymous. (Apr. 27, 1852)

Mills, Mrs. Mary R., 71, widow of Judge Mills, (Ben), b. Apr. 10, 1782, Caroline Co. Va., d. on Fri. July 16th. She third dau. of Col. Anthony Thornton, of Rev. of that County; In 1808 to Bourbon Co., in Paris until 1829; to Frankfort. He died 1831. (July 20, 1852) Obit. July 27, 1852. She married Judge Mills, in 1809, and preceded to grave by husband, 5 bros., 4 sisters, 1 son, 2 daus., 3 dau.-in-law, and 3 gd. ch. etc.

Mills, Judge Ben., 52 yrs. b. Md., to Pa. early, to Ky. 1805, or 6, Bourbon Co., 1817 Judge of Montgomery Co. Court, 1820 Ct. of Appeals, to Frankfort 1828, d. Dec. 6. (Dec. 6th, 1831—Com.)

Mitchell, Jos., Sr. 78th yr., in War of Rev., d. Paris, Apr. 4th. (Apr. 19, 1842.)

Mitchell, Dr. Thos. D., (see Mrs. Susan B. Scott)

Monroe, Judge Ben, (see Jane McClanahan)

Morgan, Kosciusko, m. Caroline M. Cox, of Franklin Co. at res. of Gen. Sidney Sherman, San Jacinto Bay, Tex., Sept. 26, 1843. (Dec. 10, 1843)

Morehead, Chas. D., d. of Yellow fever in New Orleans on 23rd, his wife Emma Morehead d. on 24th, Chas. E. Morhead d. on 19th Emma Morehead d. on the 22nd . . . all of the family wiped out . . . from Bowling Green, Ky. formerly. (Tu. Sept. 20, 1853)

Morrison, M. B., (see Mrs. Ann Taylor)

Moseley, Samuel H., m. Mary Ann Singleton, dau. of Mason S., all of Jessamine Co., Thurs. 25th. (Aug. 6, 1844)

Moore, J. L. (see Mrs. Jane Benton)

Murphy, Mrs. Amanda Frances, wife of John Murphy, of Murphy and Crafts, dau. of Capt. Rice Boulton, formerly of Dover, Bourbon Co., d. Aug. 19th of yellow fever, at New Orleans, aged 24.

Mitchell, Mrs. Margaret, 67th yr., relict of J. A. Mitchell, dau. of late Bennett Pemberton, long in this Co., d. on Mon. 21, at res. of son-in-law Mr. Scarce. Fri. Feb. 24, 1853.

Mitchell, John, aged 75 yr., 7 mos. 14 das., of Woodford Co. soldier of last war, d. Aug. 5, 1841, parents to Ky. in 1779, a soldier in his youth. (Aug. 24, 1841)

Minter, Mrs. Eliz., 77, d. at res. of son-in-law, E. Walton, Mercer Co. Tu. 8th. (Wed. Mar. 23, 1853)

Morgan, Daniel in Ky. Legislature 1843, from Flemingsburg, b. in Va. 1792.

Morgan, John S. in Ky. Legislature 1843, B. Ky. 1799, Carlisle, Ky.

Montgomery, Capt. Jas. (see Mrs. Fitch)

Montgomery, Thos., 74th yr. d. in Mason Co. Jan. 28, (Wed. Feb. 9, 1853.)

Morehead, Mrs. Susan, wife of Hon. Jas. T. Morehead, d. Frankfort. (Wed. Mar. 14, 1838.)

Morris, John (see Mrs. Sarah Huston)

Neal, Geo. aged 62, d. in Jessamine Co. . . . . (Tu. Mar. 18, 1854)

Neel, Stephen, formerly of Fredericksburg, Va. d. in South Frankfort last Wed. (Oct. 3, 1835)

Neet, Jacob, 58th yr. d. in Lexington, Mo. of cholera, July 30, 1852, father of Dr. A. Neet of Franklin Co., formerly of Jessamine Co. (Fri. Aug. 6th, 1852)

Netherland, Mrs. Theodocia, 87 d. in Nicholasville, (Tu. Oct. 20, '53.)

Noel, Mrs. Mildred, 79, d. at the res. of Maj. Jas. Milam, this county, Nov. 11. (Nov. 26, 1844)

Noxon, P. S., civil engineer of Portland, Me., w. in Lex. last Tues., at Phoenix Hotel. (Aug. 2, 1853)

Newell, Hugh, in Legis. Mar. 1843, from Cynthiana, b. Ky. 1793.

Noe, A. T. in Legis. 1843 from Trigg Co., b. Ky. 1804.

Newell, Hugh, Senator, 1843, Cynthiana, b. Ky. 1793.

Orr, Mrs. Mary, widow of Col. Alex. D. Orr, of Mason Co., aged between 65 and 70 years, d. in Paris, Ky. on Thurs. night, (Maysville Eagle) (Com. June 12, 1839)

Owings, Elisha, 72, d. Thurs. 13th in Bath Co. (Com. Aug. 19, 1840)

Owsley, Judge—see Albert Talbott.)

O'Hara, Theodore, formerly of Kentucky, d. in Bourbon county, Ala. Fri. 7th. poet and wit. (Wed. June 6, 1867) (Central Ky. Gazette, Danville, Ky.)

Ogden, Mrs. Nancy, 74, wife of late Rev. Benj. Ogden, d. Princeton, Ky. (Oct. 10, 1838)

Ogden, Dr. S. F. (see John Davis)

Oldham, Hannah, 73, d. Madison Co. (Feb. 7, 1858)

Oliver, Willis, aged 60, d. at res. of his bro. Rice W. Oliver, Oct. 29. (Nov. 21, 1843)

O'Neal, Dr. Chas., 65, d. Harrison Co. July 19. (July 26, 1853)

Owens, Robt. (see Geo. Davidson)

Owings, Col. Thos. Dye, 77, formerly of Owingsville, d. at his res. in Brenham, Tex. (Tu. Nov. 22, 1853)

Orr, Col. Alex. Dalrymple, 71st. yr. d. at home in Paris, Ky. June 21. (July 11, 1835)

Outten, M. (see Thos. Hill)

Owsley, Mrs. L. A. (see Nat'l. Maddox)

Owsley, Dr. Joel (see Sarah Lewis)

Parke, Hon. Benj. 58 yr., d. Sun. 12th, . . . to Ind. 1800 or '01 b. N. J. Sept. 2, 1777, to Lexington while young, studied law, etc. (Indiana Monitor). (Aug. 1, 1835)

Parker, Maj. Thos., 83rd yr. d. Lewis Co., Clarksburg, on 7th. (Fri. Feb. 18, 1853)

Parrish, Dickinson, 67 yrs. 6 mos. 17 days, d. Clark Co. Mon. Sept. 20. (Fri. Oct. 1, 1852)

Parrish, Capt. d. of cholera in Russellville (Aug. 1, 1835)

Paul, Wm. G., formerly of Hardin Co. Ky. d. at New Orleans, Aug. 9th. (Sept. 6, 1853)

Paxton, Rebecca, widow of late Thos. Paxton, d. last Thurs. in Franklin Co., at advanced age. (Dec. 3, 1844)

Pemberton, Bennett (see Mrs. Margaret Mitchell)

Peddicord, John, 89 yrs. 12 days, d. Mason Co. Mar. 28. (Apr. 13, 1836)

Perciful, Mount (see Thos. Mercee)

Pepper, Jesse, formerly high sheriff of Mason, d. (July 11, 1835)

Pepper, Wm. F., son of above d. also.

Peter, Dr. Samuel, 78, d. McCracken Co. (Mar. 5, 1854)

Pettit, Mrs. Eliz., wife of F. D. Pettit, d. Franklin Co. Thurs. Oct. 27 (Nov. 1, 1853)

Page, Cordelia W., wife of Rev. Wm. B. F. J., aged 28, d. at res. of her father, Thos. S. Page, Thurs. 12th, (Com. Nov. 13, 1868)

Price, Mrs. Mary D., 77, d. at res. of son Dr. J. S. Price, Oct. 29, (Com. Nov. 1, 1867)

Perry, Mrs. Eliz., wife of Capt. Robt. Perry of Kenton Co., d. Wed. A.M., in 77th year, (Com. Mon. Sept. 24, 1855)

Pearce, Judith M., 68, wife of Wm. A. Pearce, d. Sept. 5, 1866, in Franklin Co.–mother, Baptist. (Com. Sept. 18, 1866)

Pattie, John, aged 66, d. (Com. July 30, 1833)

Patterson, Jas., Jr., aged 20, d. on 27th day of May, at home of his father, Col. Jas. Patterson, in Scott Co. (Com. June 2, 1840)

Patrick, Mrs. Jane, widow of Dr. A. P., d. in Woodford Co. (Com. May 24, 1839)

Payne, Col. Samuel, aged 55, d. in this county on 12th, (Com. Dec. 29, 1840)

Pruett, John W. m. in Lex. on Tues. A.M. May 28, Miss Amaryllis Andrew Anna Conover, of Lex., (Com. June 4, 1839)

Price, Mr. Cosby of Fayette Co., m. Mary Jane Duvall, dau. of Geo. D. of Woodford Co., Tues. June 11th. (Com. June 18, 1839)

Poe, Virgil, aged 83, soldier of Revolution, wounded, etc. d. in Franklin Co. the 10th. (Com. Oct. 27, 1840) (Va. & Ind. papers copy.)

Pogue, John, eldest son of Gen. Robt Pogue d. late in Aug. Mason Co., also Col. Wm. Pogue and Maj. Thos. Pogue, fever, Mason Co. near Mayslick, Sat. last at home of his bro. Mr. Robt. Pogue, youngest son of late Gen. Robt. Pogue. (Sept. 21, 1836)

Pope, Gov. John (see Mrs. Eliz. Cocke)

Posey, Lucy F., dau. Maj. Fayette Posey, m. Dr. Robt. C. Slaughter of Rumsey, in Henderson Co. (Fri. Jan. 20, 1843)

Powell, Capt. Walker d. Scott Co. Aug. 31 (Sept. 19, 1835)

Price, Mrs. Hannah, 79, res. of Frankfort for more than 50 yrs. d. in Frankfort on Mar. 19, dau. of Col. John Upshaw of Essex Co. Va., at whose house she was m. to Richard Price in 1801 and same year to Frankfort. Her husband the late Capt. Rich. Price was Adj. of 28th Reg. of U. S. Inf. commissioned by Col. Thos. Dye Owings 1812, d. in service during the war, last of large family of bros. and sisters. (much more) (Wed. Mar. 23, 1853)

Price, Willis aged 75 yrs., d. Fayette Co. 9th (Apr. 13, 1852)

Price, Philemon D. of Jacksonville, Ill. formerly of Georgetown, Ky. (Sept. 19, 1835)

Price, John M., son of Maj. Daniel B. Price of Nicholasville, d. in Pensacola, Fla., Dec. 2, 1835. (Jan. 6, 1836)

Pringle, Mrs. Susannah, 80 yrs. d. Thurs. 15th at res. of her son H. Wingate. (Tu. Sept. 20, 1842.)

Preston, Gen. Francis of Va. 70th yr. d. in So. Car. at res. of his son Hon. W. C. Preston. (June 13, 1835)

Prewitt, Willis, 55, d. in Montgomery Co. (May 18, 1852)

"Proctor, Joseph, the last remaining soldier of Estill's Defeat is no more"—d. at Irvine, Estill Co. 2nd inst., 90th yr., b. "Roan" Co. No. Car. removed to Long Islands of Holston in 1777, entered as reg. soldier in Rev. Army for 4 years. In 1778 ordered to Ky. and stationed at Boonesborough and Estill's Station. (Col. John Miller and Maj. H. Jones, Jr., under Capt. Mahone to Irvine to take charge of remains, etc.) lived in Madison Co. (Column of obit . . . Farmers Chronicle, Dec. 14, 1844. (Dec. 31, 1844)

Patterson, Eliz. H. dau. of the late Alex. Patterson of Prince Edward Co. Va. m. in this county Wed. 13th, Cadwaller Lewis. (Wed. 2-20-39)

Payne, Mrs. Eliza A. m. in Fayette Co. Oct. 15, Jas. G. McKinney. (Oct. 24, 1838)

Payne, Theodocia S., dau. of Nathan Payne of Lex. m. in Fayette Co. Oct. 24, Jas. W. Cochran of Lex. (Nov. 7, 1838)

Payne, Theodocia, dau. of John F. and Carrie Payne, d. at res. of her father in Scott Co. on 2nd. (Fri. Aug. 13, 1858)

Payne, Dr. Geo. M., aged 34, d. Thurs. 3rd. inst. (Maysville Eagle, July 10.) (July 15, 1834)

Payne, Mrs. Hannah, widow of Col. Duvall Payne, of Mason Co. d. at Mt. Carmel, Fleming Co. on last Thurs. (Wed. Sept. 27, 1837) d. at advanced age. (Maysville Eagle)

Pendleton, Mrs. Elizabeth, aged 73, d. at res. of Dr. Burr Harrison in Bardstown, (Jan. 5, 1838.)

Penn, Chas., an old and respected citizen of the county, d. at the home of his daughter Mrs. Smither, on Fri. Dec. 24th. (Dec. 27, 1858)

Pettus, John of Christian Co. m. Marie Bergen of Hopkinsville, Sept. 10, 1838.

Pickett, Mrs. Ellen, wife of Col. Jas. C. Pickett, 2nd. dau. of Ex-Gov. Desha, d. in Washington City, Nov. 17th, in 37th yr., native of Mason Co. (Nov. 15, 1837) (Mar. in Mason Co.)

Price, Mrs. America, aged 56, consort of Maj. John G. Price, d. Fri. Aug. 20. (Liberty, Mo. Tribune) (Sept. 16, 1858)

Palmer, Dr. Robt. C., Senator, 1843, Springfield, b. Ky. 1801.

Payne, Thos. Y., Sen. 1843, Maysville, b. Ky. 1801.

Pirtle, Henry, Sen. 1843, Louisville, b. Ky. 1798.

Pope, N. K., Reps. 1843, Allen Co., b. Va. 1795.

Quinn, Rev. B. T. of Scott Co. m. in Madison, Ind., Thurs. 1st, Miss Carella Stapp, dau. of Gen. Milton Stapp of Madison, Ind. (Sept. 13, 1853).

Rankin, Wm., 78 yrs., d. in Mason Co. (Apr. 27, 1836)

Read, Mrs. Eliza Ann, 62, formerly of Georgetown, Ky. d. in Tallahatche Co., Miss., Oct. 20. (Nov. 19, 1852)

Reading, Samuel P., Jr. m. Agatha Ann Hughes, June 10th, in Franklin Co., (July 20, 1836)

Reading, Mrs. Mary, aged 82, relict and widow of John Reading who d. here several years ago, and one of the Revolutionary patriots, d. 18th. (Observer and Reporter). (Mon. Mar. 1, 1847)

Reading, Maj. Samuel, a soldier of the Revolution, d. last Saturday. (Wed. Aug. 29, 1838)

Read, Thos. M. of Calif. m. Eliz. H. Finley, Fleming Co., Oct. 20 . . . (Nov. 8, 1853)

Reed, Jos. B., mayor of Maysville, (Tues. May 23, 1843)

Reed, Mrs. Mary, wife of Gen. Wm. Reed, d. in Mason Co., June 21, in 65th yr. (July 4, 1835)

Reed, James, Revolutionary Soldier, 75 or 80 yrs. of age, d. in Maysville. (July 11, 1835)

Reed, Mrs. Judith, 49, wife of Capt. John M. Reed, d. at Shannon, Mason Co., July 14th. (July 27, 1841)

Reading, John M., veteran of the Revolution, d. (Com. July 2, 1833)

Raney, Miss Anne E.—see Jas. H. Massey.

Renick, Col. A. H., father of Eliza T. Renick who d. at his home Mon. 19th, aged 19. (Com. Oct. 29, 1840)

Robinson, Mrs. Mary M., dau. Samuel Glass, Jr. of Scott Co., d. Sun. night, Feb. 9th. left husband and 3 ch. (Com. Feb. 25, 1840)

Robb, Mrs. Frances, wife of J. Robb, dau. of late Dr. Crockett of Franklin Co., d. in Mercer Co., June 20, 1855, 32 yr. (Com. July 16, 1855)

Richardson, Samuel, of Fayette, d. Aug. 5, 1855. (Com. Aug. 20, 1855)

Rankin, Mrs. Eliz., wife of Jas. Rankin, d. in Louisville, Aug. 29, aged 60 years. (Com. Sept. 3, 1855.)

Read, Mrs. Susan H., aged 48, dau. Evan Shelby, d. in Tampico, Mexico, Oct. 23, 1866 (Com. Dec. 26, 1866) Central Ky. Gazette, Danville, Ky.

Robinson, Rich. M., d. June 17th, in Garrard Co., born Sept. 15, 1817, near Lexington, his father d. when he was 6 years old, husband father, etc. (long obit.) (Com. June 25, 1869)

Reed, Wm., aged 63, d. in Paris, Sept. 4. (Mon. Sept. 13, 1858)

Reeves, Chas. G. of New Lisbon, O. m. Mary W. Davidson, dau. of Col. Jas. D. of Frankfort at Aberdeen, O., Nov. 7th, (Nov. 14, 1843)

Reily, Lieut. John, aged 92 yrs. 11 mos., father-in-law of the editor of Shelby News, d. 10 miles north of Shelbyville, 12 o'clock A.M. on 18th He was Revolutionary Soldier of Frederick Co., Md., to Loudon Co. Va. with parents, then to Berkley Co. (now Jefferson Co.) m. there, came to Shelby Co., 1798 or 1799, and on farm one mile of Shelbyville till 1830. (Jan. 29, 1847)

Rice, Mrs. Eliz., wife of Wm. Rice, Jr., dau. of A. Lincoln, Esq., d. in Clay Co., Mo. Aug. 14, in 28th yr. (Sept. 6, 1853)

Rice, Mrs. Phoebe, 70th yr., wife of Gabriel Rice, d. in Garrard Co. Nov. 29 (27?) (Jan. 2, 1838)

Rice, Rev. N. L., D.D. (see Rev. Jas. K. Burch)

Richardson, John D., 68, d. near Frankfort, Mar. 12. (2-26-1844)

Richardson, Mrs. Eliza, wife of Nathaniel Richardson, d. in Lewis Co., Mo. (July 3, 1837)

Richmond, Mrs. Edmonia, wife of Col. R. F. Richmond, formerly of Frankfort, d. in Hannibal, Mo. Apr. 9th. (Tu. May 3, 1842)

Rizer, Capt. Joshua, listed as ill of cholera at Russellville (Aug. 1, 1835)

Robinson, Geo., 73, d. in Henderson, Sat. Sept. 3, (Tu. 9-20-1853)

Robinson, Maj. Alex., d. Fayette Co., Wed. 12. (Jan. 18, 1842)

Robinson, Mrs. Wm. 54th yr., d. Madison, Ind. Mar. 24, 1834.

Roberts, Capt. Benj., 87, pioneer of the west. Culpeper Co. Va. to Ky. 1773 with Harrod, John Cowan, &c. In Revolution, to Ky. 1780 with his family, sett. near Louisville, and to Shelby Co. where he lived for 50 yrs., d. in Shelby Co., Mar. 16th. (Lou. Apr. 4, 1837)

Robertson, Mrs. Maria Louisa, aged 25, wife of Geo. Alex. R., (bookseller) at home of her father in Frankfort, Dr. A. F. McCurdy. (Oct. 25, 1834)

Rodes, Col. Wm. (see Mrs. Eliz. Slaughter)

Rodman, John of Lagrange, m. in Simpsonville, Shelby Co., Miss Ann Eliza Russell, dau. of G. E. Russell, formerly of Franklin Co. (Tu. May 21, 1844)

Rosson, Wm., 61, d. at Forks of Elkhorn Jan. 9th, one of first settlers in Ky. (Jan. 16, 1844)

Rudd, Gen. John H., formerly of Bracken Co., Ky., d. May 12 at Yazoo, Miss. (July 4, 1835)

Rupe, Mrs. Mary, 80th yr., wife of Nicholas Rupe, d. Franklin Co., Nov. 20. (Dec. 6, 1853)

Russell, Ann Eliza m. John Rodman, (see Rodman)

Rodes, Wm., Senator, 1843, Lexington, b. Ky. 1792.

Rosson, John, aged 90 or 91, d. in Madison, Ind., Mar. 7, 1868, 2 campaigns of War 1812, in Co. of Gen. Peter Dudley, (Com. Mar. 27, 1868)

Sacrey, Mrs. Polly, wife of Robt. Sacrey, d. Jan. 28th, 1847, aged 64 yrs. (Jan. 29, 1847)

Sale, Mrs. Margaret M., relict of late Rev. Anthony Sale, of Warrenton, N. C., d. near Owensboro, Ky., aged 84 yrs. (Oct. 18, 1853)

Samuel, Mrs. Mary, relict of late Reuben Samuel, sister of Gov. Letcher, d. in Franklin Co., 67th yr. Mar. 30. (Tu. Ap. 11, 1843)

Sands, Col. Wm. L., victim of cholera at Russellville, (9-5-1835)

Saufley, Mrs. Jane E., wife of Harold P. Saufley, aged 37 yrs. 10 mos., 22 days, d. in Burkesville, Oct. 11, native of Tazewell Co. Va., m. June 6, 1822. 3 children: Wm. P., Adelia M. C., J. J. C. Saufley. (Oct. 22, 1844)

Saunders, Mrs. Catherine, 87, many years a res. of Lexington, d. Paducah, Ky. Thurs. 22, Apr. (May 4, 1852)

Sawyer, Mrs. M. A., wife of Capt. J. Sawyer, of Lou., d. 3rd., aged 43 yrs. (Apr. 19, 1842)

Scearce, Mr. (see Mrs. Margaret Mitchell)

Scearce, Wm. H. (see Mrs. Amelia Barnes)

Scearce, Henry (see Mrs. Amelia Barnes)

Scott, Dr. Joseph, d. Lex., Tu. June 6th, b. Feb. 19, 1781, 62 yrs., 3 mos., 18 days, long obit. from Protestant Herald. (June 20, 1843)

Scott, John of Gallatin Co. m. Mary A. Whitehead, she was divorced from Samuel H. Waller, church decided she had a right to marry: he their pastor since 1802. Meeting of Sharon Bap. Church, Apr. 3, 1835.

Scott, Thos., 92nd yr., d. Henry Co. Sept. 24, 1834, from Va. to Ky. 1783. (Oct. 11, 1834)

Scott, John R. m. Miss Sidney J. Jones dau. late Thos. W. Jones, in Frankfort. Mon. Aft. (Wed. Oct. 18, 1837)

Scott, Mrs. Susan B., wife of Isaac W. Scott, dau. Dr. Thos. Mitchell of Louisville, d. suddenly the 19th. (July 26, 1853)

Scroggin, Jos., 53, formerly of Franklin Co., d. Morgan Co. Iowa. (Tu. July 6, 1841)

Scroggin, Thos., Revolutionary Pensioner, 80th yr., d. in Franklin Co. (Jan. 25, 1844)

Scott, Isaac W. (see Mrs. Susan B. Scott)

Sebree, Lydia (see Samuel W. Boehne)

Seaton, Nathan Kendall, 65, d. the 11th, at Greenup, Ky. (Mar. 23, 1858)

Selby, Ben (see Mrs. Mary J. Harris)

Semones, Mrs. Jane, aged 115 yrs. d. in Franklin Co. Mar. 29. (Apr. 3, 1839)

Settle, Wm. A. J., only son of Franklin Settle, d. at Rocky Hill, Barren Co., Ky., June 16th, aged 19. (Tu. July 6, 1841)

Shannon, Susan, dau. Hugh Shannon, of this Co. m. last Sunday, Theodrick M. Massey of Palmyra, Mo. (Mar. 22, 1837)

Shannon, James (see Jas. S. Clarke)

Sharp, Mrs. Eliza Jane, wife of John M. Sharp, dau. of late Dr. Jas. Wilson, of Russellville, d. at "Trunk Spring", Warren Co., Sun. Aug. 7, 1853, aged 25 yrs. (Aug. 16, 1853)

Sharp, Mrs. Eliza T., widow and relict of the late Solomon P. Sharp, d. Jan. 4, 1844, in 45th yr. (Jan. 18, 1844)

Shaw, Mrs. Nancy, wife of John R. Shaw, d. in Lex. (Sat. Nov. 29, 1834)

Shelby, Susan, dau. of Gen. Jas. Shelby of Fayette Co. m. at Richland, Tu. May 20. Col. Wm. G. Carter of Carter Co. (June 6, 1843)

Shelby, Evan, son of Gen. Jas. Shelby, d. in Fayette Co. Sunday. (Jan. 28, 1853)

Shipp, Rich. D., Sr., 74th yr., d. Woodford Co., Tu. May 3, to Ky. from Va. when small boy, and to Woodford Co. (Wed. May 11, 1853)

Sherman, Gen. Sidney, (see C. Cox, and K. Morgan.)

Shipp, Dudley, 65 yr. d. in Fayette Co. 13th. (Oct. 18, 1853)

Shortridge, Mrs. Mary, 95 yrs. d. Scott Co. (June 22, 1836)
Shreve, Wm. d. Jessamine Co., Jan. 26, 1837. in the Revolution, battle of Guilford Court House, etc. (Feb. 1, 1837)

Simpson, Benoni, 82nd yr., d. in Harrison Co. July 22. (Tu. Sept. 20, 1853)

Singleton, Mary Ann, dau. of Mason Singleton, m. Samuel H. Moseley, Thurs. 25. all of Jessamine Co. (Aug. 6, 1844)

Slack, Capt. Jacob, 79th yr., d. Mason Co. Mar. 31 (Wed. Apr. 13, 1836)

Slaughter, Mrs. Elizabeth, widow of late Gov. Gabriel Slaughter d. Sept. 23, in her 73rd yr., at res. of her son Col. Wm. Rodes in Lex. (long obit. copied from Baptist Banner) (Nov. 7, 1843)

Slaughter, Dr. Robt. C. of Rumsey m. in Henderson Co. Lucy F. Posey, dau. of Fayette Posey (Major), Jan. 5. (Fri. Jan. 20, 1843)

Slaughter, Thos. S., 60th yr. d. Russellville (Sept. 24, 1838 (Oct. 1, 1838)

Slaughter, G. Clayton, Senator, 1843, Bardstown, b. Ky.

Sterett, Wm., Senator, 1843, Hawesville, b. Ky. 1803.

Sympson, Jas. C., Senator, Greensburg, b. Va. 1792.

Stonestreet, Jas., Clerk, Legislature, 1843, Clark Co. b. Va. 1787.

Shelton, Medley, Reps. 1843, Woodford Co. b. Va. 1792.

Stitt, Jas., Reps. 1843, Carlisle Co., b. Ky. 1795.

Swingle, Maj. George, d. Dec. 15, 1840 at his res. in this county, aged 84, major under Gen'l. Washington in the Rev. war. (Com. Jan. 12, 1841) (buried in Frankfort cemetery)

Short, Miss Jane A.–see Jas. Weirs.

Sanders, Mrs. Mary Jane, wife of Andrew Sanders, d. in Gallatin Co. (Com. Oct. 19, 1838)

Sanders, Mrs. Hannah wife of Wm. Sanders. (Com. Mar. 14, 1839)

Sanders, Andrew J., 25, son of Hugh Sanders of Franklin Co., d. Mar. 10, 1839. (Com. May 7, 1839)

Singleton, Lewis–see Norborn B. Cook.

Smith, Mrs. Judith, 93rd year, widow of Reuben Smith, d. June 13, 1839 in Lincoln Co. where she had lived 54 years. (Com. Tues., July 2, 1839.)

Smith, Rev. Eli, native of New England, graduated at Dartmouth, to Ky. in 1816, to Frankfort, Baptist church, d. Oct. 22, aged 53 years. (Com. Dec. 10, 1839)

Shannon, Mrs. Mary, aged 80, widow of Dr. Samuel S., d. June 22, 1865. (Com., July 18, 1865)

Simpson, Mrs. Mary L., 61, wife of Jas. S., d. in Winchester, Ky. (Com. Sept. 11, 1866)

Stone, Mrs. Nancy, 71, d. in Leavenworth, Kans., Sept. 15, wife of Samuel Stone, formerly of Madison Co. (Com. Oct. 2, 1866)

Scott, Joel T., son of Robt. W. and Eliz. Scott, aged 21, d. Sun. aft. (Aug. 20, 1855).

Samuel, Mrs. Catherine, wife of Larkin S., d. Sat. at advanced age, Oct. 8, 1855, in So. Frankfort. (Com. Oct. 15, 1855)

Stigall, Mrs. Miriam, widow of Thos. S., aged 76, d. at Somerset, Oct. 18th. (Com. Nov. 5, 1855)

Spears, Mrs. Margaret, widow of John S., d. in Boyle Co. the 13, at home of son Geo. C. Spears, aged 78, late of Fayette Co. (Com. Nov. 19, 1855.)

Scrugham, Col. Jos., 76, d. in Lex. Thurs. (Com. Jan. 22, 1856.)

Sneed, Mrs. Eliz. Campbell, wife of Alex. Sneed, 85 years, d. near Danville, Sun. A.M. last (Central Kentucky Gazette, Wed. May 15, 1867)

Smith, Mrs. Mary Logan, 86, d. Oct. 22, 1867 in Shelbyville (Com. Oct. 25, 1867)

Stone, Capt. F. Payne, of Shelby m. Miss Sallie Murphy, of Spencer Co., at the Burnet House, in Cincinnati, Dec. 5th. (Com. Dec. 20, 1867)

Shindlebower, Mrs. Mollie, wife of Rev. G. W. S., aged 29, d. Nov. 12, in Lancaster, Ky. (Com. Jan. 3, 1868)

Shelby, Maj. Thos., 82, d. 14th, in this county, was son of Gov. Isaac Shelby (Lexington Gazette) (Com. Feb. 19, 1869)

Semonis, Milton, 68, d. May 31, 1869 in county. (Com. June 4, 1869)

Shockley, Capt. Flood, d. May 31, at Stockton, Calif., aged about 50 years, buried at San Francisco, aged mother, etc. (Com. June 11, 1869)

Smith, Mrs. Sarah, 67, widow of late Capt. Nelson Smith of Scott Co. d. in Scott Co. (Tu. Apr. 27, 1852)

Smith, Joseph, 62, many years a merchant in Frankfort, and many years in Sangamon Co. Ill., d. at his res. in Richland, Ill. Aug. 2. (Aug. 16, 1853) b. Loudon Co. Va. See Sangamon Co. Ill. records. p. 668.

Smith, Maj. Joseph, 68 yrs. 6 mos., 20 days, d. at res. in Ohio Co., Oct. 11, Volunteer from Nelson Co. in War 1812, under Bob Wilcox. (Nov. 8, 1853)

Smith, John, aged 106 yrs., 5 mos. 14 days, d. at his res. in Hardin Co. Aug. 18th. left children, grand children and gt. gd. children. b. Va. Mar. 4, 1735. (Tu. Sept. 7, 1841)

Smither, Mrs. (see Chas. Penn)

Sneed. Achilles. see Joseph Gray

Snell, Mrs. Mary wife of Robt. Snell, dau. Carter Blanton, decd. d. Franklin Co., aged 42. June 8, 1836.

Southern, Col. Simeon F., 48 yrs., late of Danville, d. in Indianola, Tex. (Oct. 25, 1853)

Sodowsky, Mrs. Hannah, wife of Jacob S., d. Shelby Co., June 29. (July 13, 1841)

Spotswood, Dr. Norbourn B., surgeon of War 1812, d. at Columbia on 1st inst. . . . b. in Orange Co. Va., grand son of Alex. Spottswood, early Gov. of Va., his father also served in the Revolution with distinction. (Sept. 1, 1858)

Stapp, Gen. Milton (see B. T. Quinn)

Stealey, Geo. m. Ann Maria Frances, dau. of Dr. Francis Lloyd, Fri. Oct. 24, in Franklin Co. (Nov. 7, 1843) (Dr. L. lived where K.T.H. now sands.)

Stephens, Artemesia D., dau. of late John Stephens of Franklin Co. m. in Frankfort, Thurs. Dec. 29, Sen. John Wallace, from Boone Co. (Jan. 3, 1842)

Stephens, Gen. Adam (see Mrs. Ann Hunter) Dist. Officer in Rev.

Stephens, John, Sr. (spelled Stevens), 81 yr., d. last March, in Franklin Co. (Tu. May 3, 1842)

Stephenson, Mrs. Mary, aged 25, wife of Maj. Jas. Stephenson of Bourbon, d. at res. of her father, Capt. Wm. Darnaby, in Fayette Co., July 4, left husband and 3 small children. (Aug. 1, 1843)

Stevenson, Mrs. Jane, about 80, d. in Scott Co., June 15. (Sat. June 27, 1835)

Stevenson, Jas. (step-father of Wm. H. McIlwain, Woodford Co. see McIlwain)

Stephenson, Miss (see Dr. John Knight)

Stoughton, Catherine, 67, wife of L. B. S., b. in Schenectady, to Ky. 20 yrs. ago. Episc. Church member for 40 yrs., d. 16th. (3-18-1858)

Stone, Micajah, 67 yrs., d. Woodford Co. Dec. 31. (Mon. Jan. 10, 1853)

Steele, Robt. 76, d. Franklin Co. 21st. (Fri. Feb. 25, 1842)

Sullinger, Capt. John d. in Woodford Co. Thurs. Sept. 30, at advanced age. (Oct. 8, 1858)

Sullivan, Lewis m. Mrs. Sarah Henry, Franklin Co. Thurs. July 22, (July 28, 1852)

Sweeney, Chas. 83, d. in Casey Co. (Nov. 1, 1853)

Sweeney, Sarah A. of Macon Co., Tenn., m. Jas. C. Weir of Logan Co. Nov. 8 (Tu. Nov. 22, 1853)

Swigert, John, aged 72, d. in this Co. last Mon. (May 16, 1835)

Swingle, Mrs. Mary, wife John S., d. in this Co. Aug. 25. (Sept. 5, 1843)

Swingle, Maj. Geo., aged 84, d. at his res. in this Co. Dec. 15, 1840. Maj. under Washington in the Rev. (Jan. 12, 1840)

Talbott, Aquilla, Bourbon Co., d. Sun. 12, aged 74. (3-28-1854)

Talbott, Gen. Richard, late of Madison d. Wed. June 19, at So. Hanover, Ind. (July 4, 1835)

Talbott, Isham (see Mrs. Margaret Dudley)

Talbott, Isham (see Mrs. Martha Featherstone)

Taylor, Samuel M., 68 yr., formerly of Winchester, d. on 17th at home of Gibson Mallory, in Jefferson Co. (July 26, 1853)

Taylor, Capt. Samuel F. announced the death of Lieut. Jas. B. Clark at meeting of Light Inf. Co. at arsenal Sat. Ev. Aug. 16, 1843. (Sept. 5, 1843)

Taylor, James, aged 83, native of Va., early emigrant to Ky. soldier in Revolution, d. Franklin Co. Dec. 27. (Dec. 31, 1844)

Taylor, Joseph M., son of the above Jas. Taylor, d. at res. of his father Dec. 10th, he was late of St. Louis, in 32 yr., leaving wife and 5 children. (Dec. 31, 1844)

Taylor, Wm., Heirs Vs. Morris (Feb. 22, 1837)

Taylor, Mrs. Mary Ann, venerable relict of Col. Richard Taylor of Frankfort, d. at res. of her son-in-law M. B. Morrison, in Lex. last Monday. (July 23, 1852)

Taylor, Richard, 45, d. in this Co. Fri. 23. (Oct. 31, 1835)

Taylor, Capt. Richard, Jr., 56th yr. clerk of Hickman Co. Court, d. Oct. 8, in Hickman Co. (Oct. 24, 1835)

Taylor, Maj. Wm., 68, d. in Shelby Co. 2nd. (Feb. 17, 1836)

Temple, Rev. Benj., Mins. of Meth. Church, d. last Sat. at Russellville. (Adv. Mar. 23, 1838.) (Wed. Apr. 4, 1838)

Thomas, Benjamin Ware of Shelby Co., d. at New Orleans, Aug. the 12th. (Aug. 30, 1853)

Thomas, Gov. (see Capt. Benj. Field)

Thompson, Elias, 70 yr., d. at Harrodsburg, Sun. Sept. 18, (Oct. 4, 1853)

Thompson, Gervis, (Jarvis) 95 yr., early pioneer of Scott Co., Soldier of Revolution, d. in Scott Co., Sat. 17. (Feb. 22, 1853) b. 1758.

Thompson, Chas. R. m. Miss Julia Drake, dau. of late Col. Abram S. Drake, in Lex. (Oct. 15, 1833)

Thompson, Wm. R., Sr., 86, d. at Versailles 8th; a son Dr. Robt. J. Thompson. . . (May 20, 1858)

Thomasson, Lydia, 80, d. in Woodford Co. "good wife", ect. (May 31, 1842)

Thomson, Mrs. Cath., formerly Mrs. Catherine Van Cleave, mother of Benj. and Wm. Van Cleve, d. last Sunday. Came to Dayton Apr. 1796, 1st Husband, John Van Cleve, he killed by Indians in 1791, June 1; second husband, Samuel Thomson, drowned. 20 yrs. ago . . . left 13 ch.; 87 gd. ch., and 90 gt. gd. ch. (Taken from Dayton Ohio Journal) (Com. Aug. 16, 1837)

Thornton, Col. Anthony, of Rev. (see Benj. Mills and Mrs. Mary P. Mills)

Thornton, Mrs. Nancy W., 70, d. in Montgomery Co. Dec. 25th, widow of Dr. Chas. Thornton decd., came from Va. 45 yrs. ago. (1-10-1854)

Thornton, Jas., aged 81 private in Rev. d. in Woodford Co. Sun, 4th. (June 13, 1843)

Thornton, Miss Sara D. m. in Woodford, John P. Cammack, of Frankfort, July 1. (July 4, 1835)

Tibbatts, Jno. W., Reps. 1843, Newport, b. Ky. 1801.

Tilford, Mrs. Mary, 57, consort of Maj. John Tilford, d. in Lex. at 1 o'clock last Sun. (Lex. Observer) (Com. Mon. Jan. 6, 1845)

Tingle, Mrs. Ann C. m. Harry J. Cowan of Mercer Co., in Lou. Oct. 18. (Oct. 24, 1838)

Todd, R. S., Reps. 1843, Lexington, b. Ky. 1792.

Todd, Peter, 68, d. in Madison Co., Jan. 17, 1859 (Feb. 7, 1858)

Trabue, Chasteen H., old citizen of Franklin Co. d. last Thur. (Fri. Sept. 6, 1852)

Trigg, Mrs. Susan, relict of late Maj. Wm. Trigg, d. in Frankfort at advanced age, On Mar. 6, 1844. (Mar 26, 1844)

Triplett, Mrs. Nancy, 73rd yr. d. at res. of Maj. Hedgman Triplett in Franklin Co. Nov. 22, member of Baptist church at Buck Run (Dec. 7, 1836)

True, Mrs. Sara W. of Scott Co. m. in Marion Co., Mo. Tu. 6th, Maj. Wm. H. Martin of Woodford Co. (Oct. 19, 1836)

Tunstall, Mrs. Mildred, d. Oct. 24th, in 84th yr., at res. of A. G. Hodges, in Frankfort. (Oct. 25, 1837)

Turner, Nelson, 77, d. in Lex. last Sat. (Jan. 28, 1858)

Tibbatts, John W., mem. of State Legis. 1843, from Newport, Ky. b. Ky. 1801. (Mar. 1843)

Taylor, Hubbard, Sr., d. in Clark county at advanced age, native of Va., to Ky. early (Com. Dec. 29, 1839)

Tyler, Capt. Chas., 83, in Revolutionary War for 7 years, battle of Monmouth, etc., d. on last Wed. (Com. Sept. 29, 1840) (see will, etc.)

Talbott, Albert, m. Mrs. Eliz. Talbott, dau. of Judge Owsley, Lancaster, Ky., (Com. Wed. Apr. 10, 1839)

Taylor, Maj. Edm. H., 67 year, d. in Bullitt Co. (Com. Apr. 23, 1839)

Theobald, Miss Harriet W.—see J. W. Craddock.

Tibbatts, Thos., d. in Newport, Feb. 24, aged 83 years, native of England, one of earliest emigrants to the Western country, settled in Lex. in 179— and after being there 50 years, to Newport Oct. last. (Com. Mar. 2, 1841)

Thomas, Mrs. Ann, 83 years, d. July 31, dau. of Walter Chiles of Spottsylvania Co., Va., widow of late Edmund Thomas of Frankfort, citizen of Frankfort for 55 or 56 years. (Com. Aug. 6, 1855.) b. 1772

Trabue, Anderson H., d. Aug. 5, 1855. (Aug. 20, 1855—Com.)

Taylor, Robt. B. m. Mary A. Corton, at Episc. Church, the 7th (Com. Nov. 10, 1865.)

Taylor, Rev. James, Sr., b. Currituck county, N. C., Apr. 1, 1790, to Ky. 1810, to Clark Co., Ky., then to Breckinridge Co., d. Mar. 23, 1867. Meth. Minister for 40 years. (Com. Mar. 29, 1867)

Temple, Mrs. Eleanor, aged 85, d. Oct. 27, 1867, at res. in Frankfort of her son John B. Temple. (Nov. 1, 1867—Com.)

Todhunter, Parker E., 70, d. Sept. 20, 1867, in Jessamine Co. (Com. Oct. 11, 1867)

Thayer, Mrs. Marian, dau. late Hon John Bridges, d. 18th (Aug. 29, 1866, Cent. Ky. Gazette, Danville, Ky.)

Underwood, Capt. John and Frances M. U. (see Gorin)

Upshaw, Col. John (see Mrs. Hannah Price)

Utterback, Jacob, 99, Rev. soldier, d. Woodford Co., May 20. (May 31, 1842)

Van Cleve, Mrs. Catherine (see Mrs. Cath. Thomson)

Van Cleve, Benjamin, Wm., John (see Mrs. Cath. Thomson)

Vaughan, John W., Reps. 1843, Fleming Co., b. Ky. 1812.

Venable, Joseph—see Jas. E. Blythe.

Vest, Harriet, widow of John J. Vest, d. Frankfort, Apr. 19, 1852 (Apr. 20, 1852)

Vigo, Col. Francis, b. in Sardinia, d. Knox Co., Ind. Mar. 22. in Rev. War . . . Geo. Rogers
    Clark, (Wabash Courier, long obit.) Apr. 6, 1836

Walker, Jas. V., Senator 1843, Logan Co., b. Ky. 1799

Wallace, John, Senator 1843, Boone Co., b. Ky. 1800.

Wattes, W. R. Reps. 1843, Washington Co., b. Va. 1778.

Waddle, Mrs. Sarah M., of Ohio, dau. late Samuel H. Woodson, d. Sept. 11, at res. of her
    mother in Jessamine Co. (Sat. Sept. 20, 1834)

Walker, Maj. David d. Jan. 21, 1838, Scottsville, Ky.

Wallace, Caleb of So. Carolina m. Ann Buford, dau. Col. W. B. in Woodford Co. (Oct. 15,
    1833)

Wallace, Capt. Wm. B. (see Mrs. Eliza Dedman)

Wallace, Gen. John, Sen. from Boone Co. m. in Frankfort. Thurs. Dec. 29th, Miss Artemesia
    D. Stephens, dau. late John Stephens of Franklin Co. (Jan. 3, 1842)

Waller, Samuel H. (see John Scott)

Walton, E. (see Mrs. Eliz. Minter)

Ward, Mrs. Martha, 67, Bourbon Co., widow of late Jas. Ward, d. last Wed. (Jan. 24, 1854)

Ward, Capt. Chas., 72, d. in Washington, Mason Co. last Wed. night. (Jan. 16, 1838)

Ware, Maj. N. A., 72 yr., d. in Galveston, Tex. Sept. 18, (Oct. 4, 1853.)

Ware, Col. Thompson, 84, d. in Bourbon Co., on the 9th. (Mon. Sept. 20, 1852)

Warren, Miss Maria, 18th yr. d. in Scott Co. (Apr. 1, 1834)

Watson, Mrs. Louisa, wife of Dr. Edm. Watson, dau. late Benj. Hickman, d. last Sat. (May 3,
    1837)

Webb, Elder Chas., 86, Baptist Ch. more than 60 yrs., d. Wed. Apr. 1, in Nicholas Co. (Mon.
    Apr. 11, 1853)

Webb, Benjamin . . . bill for him in State Legislature. (Jan. 1835)

Weir, Edw. R., Reps. 1843, Muhlenberg Co., b. Ky. 1817. (Greenville)

Weir, Edward R. m. Harriet Miller, Sept. 2, 1838, Owensboro, Ky.

Weir, Emily M., dau. Jas. Weir of Greenville, m. Samuel M. Wing, merchant of Owensboro,
    in Greenville, Sept. 2, 1838.

Weir, Jas. C., Logan Co., m. Nov. 8th, Sarah A. Sweeney of Macon Co. Tenn. (Tue. Nov. 22, 1853)

Wells, Sarah, (Mrs.) relict of late Isaac Wells, 79th yr. d. in Lex. of cholera. (Aug. 13, 1833)

Wendover, Mrs. (see Jacob Creath)

Wheeler, John, Reps. 1843, Pendleton Co., b. Ky. 1797.

White, Wm. (see Margaret Hoyt)

White, Elizabeth, dau. of John B. White, m. last Mon. Egbert Wooldridge of Louisville, (Mar. 14, 1835)

Whitehead, Mary A. (see John Scott)

White, D., Reps. 1843, Clay Co., b. Ky. 1812.

Weisiger, Mrs. Mary H., dau. Gen. Jacob Castleman, decd. of Woodford Co., d. at her home in Victoria, Tex. (Sept. 29, 1858)

Whittington, Mrs. Matilda R., aged 40, wife of Isaac W., d. in Versailles, June 27. (July 4, 1843)

White, Jabez, Reps. 1843, Madisonville, Ky. b. N. C. 1793.

Wilcox, Bob (see Maj. Joseph Smith)

Wilkinson, Mrs. Eliz. T., relict of late Dr. Lydall W., d. in Frankfort last Tuesday. (Aug. 8, 1835)

Williams, Zehaniah, recently of Frankfort, patriot of War of 1812, Lex. Light Inf. under Capt. Hart, d. in Dubuque, Iowa, July 21. (Mon. Aug. 1858)

Williams, Mason, Senator 1843, Licking Sta. Morgan Co., b. S. C. 1780.

Williams, Elias M. (see Mrs. Emily Hoover)

Williams, S. L., Senator 1843, Mt. Sterling, b. Va. 1781.

Wilson, Dr. Jas. (see Mrs. Eliza Jane Sharp)

Wilson, Capt. John, 62, d. in Paducah, Jan. 5. (Jan. 21, 1853)

Wilkerson, J. R. E., Reps. 1843, Graves Co., b. Va. 1811.

Wing, Samuel M., merchant of Owensboro, Ky. m. in Greenville, Ky. Sept. 2, 1838, Emily M., dau. of Jas. Weir of Greenville.

Wingate, Eliza Ann, dau. of Cyrus Wingate, of Owen Co. m. John Marston, Dec. 26, 1833 (Jan. 1, 1834)

Wingate, Lucien, formerly of Frankfort m. in Louisville, Eliz., dau. of Dr. Joseph W. Knight, Thurs. 23. (Nov. 28, 1843)

Wingate, H. (see Mrs. Susannah Pringle)

Wingate, Cyrus, aged 54, d. at res. in Owen Co. Aug. 14. Member of State Legis. 1824, etc. (Aug. 17, 1841)

Winlock, Matilda B. m. Wm. Gume, Shelby Co., dau. Gen. Joseph W.

Winlock, Mary Jane m. John Davis, Shelby "both married Dec. 26, 1833," both daus. of Gen. Joseph Winlock. (Jan. 21, 1833) (discrepancy in dates.)

Winlock, John K., d. in Logan Co., at adv. age. Nov. 7. (Tue. Nov. 15, 1853)

Winn, Mrs. Susan, late of Fayette Co., d. Dec. 16, in Jackson Co., Mo. (Fri. Jan. 14, 1853)

Wilkins, J. C., Reps. 1843, Warren Co., b. Ky. 1806.

Winfrey, F. H., Reps. 1843, Burkesville, b. Va. 1798.

Winslow, Maj. Wm., 73, d. at Warsaw Oct. 30 (11-21-1838)

Withers, Letitia J., (Miss), dau. of Mr. J. Withers of Georgetown, m. in Lex. May 2, Jas. H. Garrard of Clay Co. (Wed. May 10, 1837)

Witt, Elisha, Soldier of War of 1812, d. in Estill Co., at his res., aged 66, on Sept. 2. (Mon. Sept. 13, 1858)

Woodson, Tucker, Senator, 1843, Nicholasville, b. Ky. 1804.

Wood, John, 85, d. in Logan Co., Tue. Sept. 15, (Oct. 4, 1853)

Woodard, Miss Sarah, Clark Co., m. Dec. 30, Geo. Gentry of Pike Co., Mo. (Mon. Jan. 10, 1853)

Woodruff, Nodiah, 74th yr. d. in Franklin Co. last Thurs. (Aug. 23, 1837)

Woods, Capt. Joseph, elder bro. of late Col. John Woods of Frankfort, d. in Mercer Co. Sept. 28. (Oct. 24, 1838)

Woods, Martha Ann, dau. of Arch'd. Woods, m. Jas. M. Estill in Madison Co., Sept. 22, (Oct. 4, 1831 Com.)

Woodson, Samuel H. (see Mrs. Sarah M. Wadle)

Woodson, David M. m. 6th, Lucy McDowell, dau. Maj. John McD. of Fayette Co. . . . (David M. W. of Jessamine Co.) Oct. 8, 1831 (Com.)

Wooldridge, Egbert m. Eliz. White, dau. J. B. White, last Mon. (he of Louisville) (Mar. 14, 1835)

Wooley, Maj. (see John Howard)

Woolfolk, George, lawyer, d. Frankfort Tue. 7th, b. in Caroline Co. Va., 1793 . . . to Ky. with parents near Louisville when quite young, began study of law at Shelbyville . . . in Legislature. (Tues. Nov. 21, 1843)

Woolfolk, Mrs. Mary, 88th yr. d. in Woodford Co. June 28th. (July 4, 1835)

Wright, John E., old citizen, d. Nov. 28 in Lincoln Co. (Jan. 31, 1854)

Washington, R. W., 71, d. in Danville, June 23 (Com. July 3, 1868)

Walcutt, Mrs. Sarah P., wife of Oliver H. Walcutt of the county, d. Apr. 3, 1868 (Com. Apr. 17, 1868)

Williams, Wm. Howe m. Miss Nora Brightwell, Feb. 22, 1870, in Cincinnati, both of Frankfort. (Com. Feb. ——— 1870)

Wingate, Mrs. Ester E., widow of Elias W., 78 years, 10 mos., d. Oct. 25, near Danville. (Com. Nov. 5, 1855)

Watson, Mrs. Sarah, 83 years, 10 mos., d. at Merriwether Hotel, Thurs. 14, Aug. 1873, (Lex. Herald, Fri. Aug. 22, 1873, Frankfort News)

Whaley, Col. B., 75, of the Revolution, d. in Bourbon Co., (Sept. 24, 1833, Com.)

Williams, Maj. John, aged 74, Rev. soldier, d. Simpson Co., 10 years in Senate from Warren Co. (Com. —— 1833.)

Woods, Wm.–see Mathew Clark

Webb, Col. John V., d. in Scott Co., May 7. (Com. June 18, 1839)

Walker, Nathan H., 19, son of R. L. Walker of Hartford, d. at Mt. Merino College June 1, (Com. June 18, 1839)

Walker, Jos. L., aged 30, died Feb. 15, in Springfield, (Com. Mar. 2, 1841)

Wilmot, Col. Robt., patriot of Rev. war, d. in Bourbon Co. Aug. 20, 1839, aged 82; when 18 commissioned by Md. legislature, his native state, Lieut. of Artillery, and joined the Rev. army and active till close; when 24, m. Miss Priscilla Dorsey dau. Hon. Caleb Dorsey, of Md. in 1786 he came to Ky., and settled in Bourbon; reared 4 sons and 5 daus., etc. signed R(obt.) W(ilmot) S(cott) (Com. Tues. Sept. 13, 1839.)

Wells, Mrs. Nancy C., late of Smithland, Ky., widow of Wm. K. Wells, decd. and dau. of S(tanley) P. Gower, of latter place, d. May 31, at res. of Thos. A. Berryman of Owenton, Ky. (Com. June 16, 1840)

Weir, George–by his will, land advertised for sale in Woodford and Scott Cos., by James Weir, exr. (Aug. 1840)

Weir, Jas., Esq. of Greenville, Ky., m. on 23rd to Miss Jane A. Short, of Louisville. (Apr. 23, 1839)

Wigginton, Mortimer, Esq., d. on Wed. last at res. of Col. Bingham, came to Texas few months ago, native ot Ky., lawyer, New Orleans his res., Ky. legislature. (Brazos (Tex.) Courier) (Com., Nov. 26, 1839)

Young, Col. Richard–see Mrs. Jane M. Johnson.

Yonce, Mrs. Jane, 79 years, d. Danville, Tues. 11th, (Central Ky. Gazette, Danville, Ky., Wed. June 5, 1867)

Young, Asa, Senator 1843, Barren Co., b. Ky. 1795.

Young, Mrs. Nancy, 74th yr., wife of Maj. Jas. Young, decd. d. on 9th at res. of Wm. T. Hardin, Shelby Co. (Feb. 21, 1854)

Young, Wm., att'y. of Mo., m. in Shelby Co. Miss Martha Ann Boyd, dau. of Col. Wm. G. Boyd of Shelby. Thurs. 11th. (Tue. Aug. 16, 1831). (Com. pub. in Frankfort, Ky.)

Young, Thos. I., Reps. 1843, Bath Co., b. Va. 1797.

INDEX

MRS. HORACE M. DAVIS

212

Index

M

www.ingramcontent.com/pod-product-compliance
Lightning Source LLC
Chambersburg PA
CBHW031120020426
42333CB00012B/159